COMMON GROUND

COMMON GROUND

*A Priest and a Rabbi
Read Scripture Together*

ANDREW M. GREELEY

and

JACOB NEUSNER

The Pilgrim Press
Cleveland, Ohio

The Pilgrim Press, Cleveland, Ohio 44115
©1996 by Andrew M. Greeley Enterprises, Ltd., and Jacob Neusner

Rabbi Neusner's translations are all from *Tanakh: A New Translation of the Holy Scriptures According to the Traditional Hebrew Text* (Philadelphia, New York, Jerusalem: The Jewish Publication Society, 1985), © 1985 by the Jewish Publication Society, and are quoted with permission of Jewish Publication Society.

JN thanks William Scott Green.

Printed in the United States of America on acid-free paper

01 00 99 98 97 96   5 4 3 2 1

Library of Congress Cataloging-in-Publication Data

Greeley, Andrew M., 1928–
    Common ground : a priest and a rabbi read Scripture together /
Andrew M. Greeley and Jacob Neusner.—[Rev. ed.]
        p.   cm.
    Rev. ed. of: The Bible and us. c1990.
    Includes bibliographical references and index.
    ISBN 0-8298-1120-6 (alk. paper)
    1. Bible—Criticism, interpretation, etc.   2. Bible. O.T.—
Criticism, interpretation, etc., Jewish.   I. Neusner, Jacob, 1932–
II. Greeley, Andrew M., 1928– Bible and us. III. Title.
BS538.G65   1996
220.6—dc20   95-52006
                                                         CIP

For Erica Reiner

CONTENTS

FOREWORD

Common Ground brings together two uncommon commentators. The first two chapters identify Jacob Neusner as "a" rabbi and Andrew Greeley as "a" priest, but they are probably *the* rabbi and *the* priest that all others in this country know. *Books in Print* certainly lists more titles by Neusner and by Greeley than by any of their colleagues among scholars of religion.

Such statistics by themselves are not likely to lure readers into this book, which is designed to lure them into reading the Bible. But they do suggest something of the experience these two writers bring to their common task. Whoever is to read about the scriptures in order to read the scriptures is well advised to pick reliable guides. The continent boasts numbers of world-class commentators, women and men schooled in ancient languages, the social worlds of the Bible, and the history and science of interpretation. Many of them, however, deal with the texts molecule-of-ink-and-parchment by molecule, ever deepening their scholarship but often losing their relevance. They often are "trees" people, but most readers need a sense of the forest before they start dealing with this leaf, that bark, those branches and paths. Here is where Neusner and Greeley come in, using a different kind of expertise to help readers find their way.

Some years ago novelist Dan Jacobsen wrote *The Story of the Stories*, a book about how Jews have not had the choice sites for the past three thousand years. All they had was the story. But that was enough. This rabbi and this priest live in daily dialogue with the inherited old story, and both of them are capable of recognizing a good new story now, or telling one, if they have to or get to. The story character of God's dealing with humans and humans humanizing each other is what grips the two authors and what they hope will grip readers.

Twenty-two chapters pass before the distinctively Christian parts of the biblical plots receive direct treatment. Since Christians simply swooped down on the libraries and synagogues and seized the whole Hebrew scriptural canon, henceforth considering it their own, Father Greeley belongs in the dialogue over what Christians call the Old Testament. Does Rabbi Neusner belong, then, when the two turn the page to what gets called the New Testament? He shows that he does, and in doing so teaches something about how different the same texts can look to two people from two communities.

My first publisher used to say about Jews and Christians, their common ground and differing but lasting covenant, their outlooks on life: "Yes, we have much in common. But whenever you look out the window, you say the world has been redeemed. When I look out I say that the world will be redeemed. Those are two very different ways of seeing things, and we have to reckon with that." Awareness of two different ways of seeing things promotes binocular vision and helps us see what we might have over-looked or have previously seen only in limited perspective. Neusner and Greeley introduce readers in non-technical ways to such vision and better perspective.

We all will have our favorite stories and chapters. I like the way Neusner deals with Jacob and Greeley with Hosea, Jeremiah, Ezekiel and the "faith-less bride." As I read such I am reminded of a class of bright undergraduates who were taking a course on biblical interpretation without ever having read the Bible. The instructor sent them home to read it. They gathered three weeks later, full of "What a book!" and "You'd never believe it!" and "No one told me this wasn't boring!" comments. If any young people have to do book reports on the Bible after reading this book, I can picture them reaching for exclamation points for the endings of their sentences. Readers can each make up their own personal versions of such gasps of astonishment at the startling things they will read here and then in the scriptures to which they are guided.

There is some surprise in chapters 37 and 38. The two friends of the scriptures and each other who conspired to produce an earlier version of this book were less ready then than now to speak of common ground. This time, with so many things growing more complex on the interreligious scene, but thanks to some personal experiences, Rabbi Neusner and Father Greeley are more ready to talk and to expect breakthroughs than they were a few years ago. If one needs more argument for the possibility of creative dialogue between Jews and Christians, I have one piece of advice: turn the page and start reading. You will learn of the still remaining great distance between communities and then, in startling ways, of their nearness. If the dialogue comes easier yet in another six years or so, and if more are drawn into it along the way, chalk up some of the progress on that front to common readings of common texts in much of the Bible. And to two commentators who would lure readers into an often closed book that, once opened and entered, can take care of itself—and of those who read it with open hearts and open minds.

Martin E. Marty
Fairfax M. Cone Distinguished Service Professor
The University of Chicago

INTRODUCTION
Reading Scripture Together

Let us introduce ourselves and tell you how we know each other.

The priest is Andrew Greeley, a priest of the Diocese of Chicago, a professor of sociology at the University of Arizona in Tucson, and a research associate at the National Opinion Research Center in Chicago. Ordained in 1954 at St. Mary of the Lake Seminary for the Archdiocese of Chicago, Father Greeley served for ten years as assistant pastor at Christ the King Church in the Beverly Hills district of Chicago and obtained his Ph.D. from the University of Chicago in 1962. A sociologist of religion, Father Greeley is the author not only of works of scholarship in sociology, but also numerous novels.

The rabbi is Jacob Neusner, who was ordained in 1960 as a rabbi by the Jewish Theological Seminary of America, earned a Ph.D. in Religion at Columbia University–Union Theological Seminary, and is now the Graduate Research Professor of Humanities and Religious Studies at the University of South Florida in Tampa. The rabbi is a historian of religion, specializing in Judaism in the age in which it took shape, the first seven centuries C.E., that is, A.D. (Jews call the age beyond the beginning of Christianity the Common Era [C.E.] and Christians the Christian Era [A.D.]). Beyond the titles and the subject area, the man is a believing and practicing Jew.

We are an ordained priest of the Roman Catholic Archdiocese of Chicago and an ordained rabbi in the Conservative movement in Judaism, respectively. We are also a social scientist and a humanist, respectively. So we differ from each other not only in religion, but also in learning. Rabbi Neusner is also Professor Neusner, a professor in the humanities, specifically, a historian of religion. He devotes his life to the study of texts and to the interpretation of those texts in all their distinct and particular qualities. Father Greeley is also Professor Greeley, a professor in the social sciences, specifically, a sociologist. Sociology treats the world today. It tells us about how people are, before they portray how they are in writing and preserve the writing for posterity. The history of religion studies the records of religions, the written account of the experience, not necessarily as it was, but as people want the future to know about it. These are very different kinds of evidence, each requiring its own methods appropriate to the kind of information of which each is meant to make sense. What sociology knows, the history of religion can scarcely imagine: real people doing real things, whom we can see and interrogate. What the history of religion knows sociology does not address: the memory that humanity forms so as to shape the initial experience to instruct a distant tomorrow.

The difference in religion—Roman Catholic, Judaic—scarcely matters so much as the difference in intellectual attitude. The two authors differ in professional training and in perspective. These differences shape the styles with which each of us approaches sacred Scripture.

Here is an example of how the difference in modes of thought takes place. Rabbi Neusner in the history of religions is concerned with the shape of ideas that develop once doctrine is formed and therefore recently wrote: "Religions form social worlds and do so through the power of their rational thought. That is their capacity to explain data in a . . . self-evidently valid way." How does Father Greeley express the difference between history of religion and sociology? He modifies the sentence by inserting the words given in italics: "Religions form social worlds and do so through the power of *the intense religious experiences and vivid religious imagery that are persevered in illuminating religious stories. These then become the subject of* rational thought. *And therein lies* their capacity to explain data in a self-evidently valid way."

These two scholars see the world differently, each in accord with his academic discipline. The one reads books: the other reads living people. The reason for the difference? Rabbi Neusner studies texts handed on through tradition, and these are written down long after the experience to which they refer has taken place. The religious experience is mediated to us through the words written down and preserved afterward. Father Greeley studies religious life today, and contemporary religious life consists of religious experiences, imagery, story, and event to which we have immediate access. In sociology of religion he is concerned with experience, image, story—the elements of religion that occur before doctrine takes shape.

Studying different sorts of things in different ways, each of the authors asks his own questions and develops his particular perspectives. But what joins the authors together is that they learn from and teach each other. For neither of the two models of religion excludes the other. Both authors readily recognize the validity, the necessity, and the utility of the other's model. True enough, if the truth be told, each has a preference for his own. But in this book the two distinct approaches complement one another.

But since we do differ in religion, the one a rabbi, the other a priest, and also in scholarship, the one a humanist, the other a social scientist, you must wonder what draws us together. It is not merely mutual respect but a shared respect for religion, for the integrity of humanity's religious experience in its quest for God.

In addition, both of us affirm the holiness of the same revealed Scriptures, which Christianity knows as the Old Testament, within the Bible made up of the Old Testament and the New Testament, and which Judaism knows as the written Torah, within the one whole Torah made up of the written Torah and the oral Torah (about which more in chapter 1). These are terms we shall spell out in a moment. Here it suffices to say that the Bible and the Torah meet in the Scriptures of ancient Israel, and we, priest and rabbi, meet in those sacred writings, which we revere as God's word. Father Greeley, like many other Christian scholars, now uses the terms Jewish Scriptures and Christian Scriptures, a terminology we will adopt in this book.

Both of us revere not only religion and the religions of the West, Judaism and Christianity, we also begin with shared convictions that join Judaism and Christianity. Specifically, we jointly affirm, priest and rabbi together, the stout conviction that God made the world, rules history, and loves us. True, each of us expresses matters in his own distinctive way, true to the traditions of Christianity and Judaism, respectively. And these are not the same.

As Father Greeley frames matters, the correct definition of Jesus Christ is "the ultimate revelation of God's love."

Rabbi Neusner frames matters in line with Judaic tradition that sees the human being as God's image and likeness and that points to the fact that we are told we are in God's image and after God's likeness as evidence of God's love. So Judaism says, R. Aqiba would say, "Precious is the human being, who was created in the image [of God]. It was an act of still greater love that it was made known to humanity that humanity was created in the image [of God]. As it is said, 'For in the image of God he made man' (Gen. 9:6)."

Both of us affirm the one God, who loves humanity and takes on the form of humanity: God incarnate for the Christian faith, humanity "in our image, after our likeness" for the Judaic faith.

The recognition of each that the other is possessed of a genuine religious faith leads each to respect the faith of the other in its expression in sustained learning. The rabbi knew the priest as sociologist and novelist long before he met him. An admirer from afar, the rabbi found in the priest's writings on sociology a clear, true message that religion today thrives. In the setting of the academy, which takes for granted that religion is a mere relic of another age or that religion is personal and private, with no bearing on the public interest, the priest's scholarship bore the clarion ring of truth.

The rabbi then turned to the priest's fiction and found in it genuine religious conviction given form in the flesh and blood of the lives of real people. In that fiction, religion—Roman Catholic Christianity, the life of holiness mediated through sacraments—is not explained, surely not explained away. That religion lives in the real people made up by the priest in his own mind. It takes incarnate form in the everyday affairs of engaging people. The rabbi was drawn to this odd mixture of scholarship and honest religious feeling and belief and only later on found, on meeting the man himself, the joining of wit and intellect that makes faith not only admirable but interesting.

The priest, accustomed to having his scholarship and his fiction bashed, or ignored, by his fellow priests, was astonished when the rabbi rode over the hills, guns blazing, to defend both. Then he learned from the rabbi's scholarship the fascinating story of how at the same time Christianity was taking shape, the Judaism that is normative, which the rabbi explains is the Judaism of the dual Torah, was forming itself. It would be fun, the priest thought in characteristic Irish fashion, to argue with this man.

And the rabbi, not famed as either irenic or a flatterer, took up the challenge of an equally pugnacious and equally adventurous intellect: one he admired from afar and from many angles before he ever met the man.

The priest is the most prolific writer in Roman Catholic Christianity, the rabbi in Judaism, and the meeting was natural and, both now think, necessary. This book—a kind of *Abie's Irish Rose* for the twenty-first century—is the result. It is as if, when the Beast from Twenty Thousand Fathoms met Godzilla in Tokyo Bay, they went out for sushi and a good argument about theoretical physics.

Both of us have written a fair number of books. But this book is different from any that either of us has ever tried to write. Not only this, but we think it is different from any book ever written. We engage in a kind of dialogue of faith through shared learning and sensibility such as, as far as we know, no rabbis and priests have yet undertaken in the writing of a book together.

So far as we know, in two thousand years of the coexistence of Christianity and Judaism in Western civilization, while priests and rabbis occasionally cited Scripture to one another or supplied information needed by one another, we mark a new beginning in the relationships between believing

Christians and faithful Jews. For, it would appear, we are the first priest and rabbi to set about reading the Scripture together and then writing a book about what we have taught and also learned. We think that fact makes a statement about the United States, since we maintain this book could have been written only in this country. And since we both come from minorities, in a nation with a Protestant majority, we shall spell out what we think we have learned, both of us, from Protestant Christianity.

We agree on much more, since both of us are book writers and like telling people things. Each has learned important lessons from the writing of the other. And we both like each other. But that does not explain why we decided to read Scripture together, since we are not scholars of Scripture exchanging information. A sociologist and a historian of religion are not scriptural authorities or even theologians. We are something else; we are religious men, both of us, and that is why we want to meet and learn from the faith, expressed through Scripture, of one another.

For the faith represented by each of us, Christianity and Judaism, appeals to the common Scriptures, the ancient Israelite writings revered by Christianity as the Old Testament of the Bible and followed by Judaism as the written part of the Torah. Since we read the same words, we share a common bond. Since we do not agree on what these words mean and how they should shape the world today, we also have something to talk about—and can teach one another things that, on our own, we might never have grasped.

We work together because we like and respect one another's faith. The rabbi sees in Christianity a straight, true road to God, and the priest sees in Judaism the living religion of God's first love, Israel, the Jewish people. The rabbi admires Roman Catholic Christianity for its recognition of the power of tradition to convey religious truth and its emphasis that religion is something we do together as a group, a society, not merely something that we have, privately and personally, in our individual hearts. The rabbi identifies in Roman Catholic Christianity, with its emphasis on works as well as faith, the counterpart of Judaism that holds God sanctifies us through the commandments that we carry out, not only through truths that we affirm.

That, of course, is not the whole story. For neither one of us reads Scripture by itself. The priest reads Scripture as the Catholic church has framed it, and that means Jewish and Christian Scriptures, or, as better known, the Old and the New Testaments, seen as the word of God, the Bible. And that is the work of Christianity, not Judaism.

The rabbi reads Scripture as holy Israel, the Jewish people, has defined it, and that means the Torah, the one whole Torah revealed by God to Rabbi ("my lord") Moses at Mount Sinai. That whole Torah comes to Israel in two forms, one in writing, which the Christian world knows as the Old Testament, the other through memorization and oral transmission, hence orally a part and form of the Torah that the Christian world does not know at all.

So we begin with disagreement, and be warned: every page of this book bears its message not only of mutual respect and esteem but also of ongoing debate.

For one thing, can a rabbi read the New Testament as a work not of human imagination and affirmation, admiring Jesus as a great man for instance, but as the word of God?

For another, can a priest encounter the entirety of the Torah, oral and written, and not only respect the ingenuity of the ancient sages who wrote down the originally oral Torah, but also affirm that they have found in the words of the Scripture truth and abiding revelation?

These, then, form the starting points in our encounter, together with the rather odd collection of writings Christianity has given to humanity as the Bible and with the equally odd, but asymmetrical, collection of writings Judaism has given to the world as the Torah.

Now, how do we meet one another? Does a rabbi read Scripture in a way different from the way a priest reads it? Is it not the same Bible, and are not the words pretty much identical?

No, quite the opposite. What the priest, as a Christian, knows as "the Bible," the rabbi, as a believing Jew, reads as "the Torah." And, as we hinted before, these are different writings, though they do intersect.

So let us tell you how a priest and a rabbi read the Bible. Because each reads in his own way, in accord with traditions of Judaism and Roman Catholic Christianity, respectively. And, down the pike we'll tell you what we think each of us has also learned from Protestant Christianity, which, after all, taught us both to reread the Bible and explain what we find there.

—Andrew M. Greeley
University of Chicago
University of Arizona, Tucson

—Jacob Neusner
University of South Florida, Tampa
Bard College, Annandale-on-Hudson

1

NEUSNER

How a Rabbi Reads the Torah

Judaism reads not "the Bible" but the Torah. And the Torah and the Bible are not the same thing. The Bible comprises the Old Testament and the New Testament. Judaism receives what Christianity calls the Old Testament as "the Torah." But the Torah encompasses not only the Scriptures, it also includes an oral component, which comes down from Sinai in oral formulation and oral tradition, only to be written down much later on in the Mishnah and Midrash compilations, and two Talmuds, of the first seven centuries A.D. Accordingly, I read "the Torah" whole and complete, the written part and the oral part. For the Torah came to Israel, the holy people, in two media. One part was in writing. The other part was formulated orally and handed on in memory. Judaism, then, is the religion of the Torah.

What story does Judaism tell about the Torah? When Moses received the Torah at Mount Sinai, God gave that Torah, or revelation, in two media, the one in writing, the other formulated and transmitted only orally—that is, in memory and not written down. So the Torah is dual: written and oral. The written part of the Torah corresponds to what Christianity calls the Old Testament. The oral part is not familiar to the world at large. But the oral Torah—*Torah she-be-al-peh*, Torah that is memorized—is that half of the one whole Torah revealed by God to Moses at Mount Sinai that came down, from then to late antiquity, formulated and transmitted by memory alone. The oral Torah serves to complement and complete the written one—and vice versa.

When we read the Bible together, it is not Jack Neusner, friend, intense admirer, and unindicted co-conspirator of Andy Greeley, but Rabbi Jacob and Father Andrew, priest of the Diocese of Chicago. So here I want to give you not my personal opinions but what I conceive to be the Judaic reading of Scripture, the written Torah. How do I do that?

When I claim to speak for Judaism, it is because I consult the one whole Torah of Moses, our rabbi, the written and the oral parts, and set forth the result, as I understand it. This is Judaism in its authoritative and authentic version, and as a rabbi, I represent that Judaism in these pages. So when I

1

read what Christians call "the Old Testament part of the Bible," my reading is guided through the mediation of revelation in a dual form, and when I interpret passages of the Bible for you, what I do is join the oral to the written parts of the Torah and set forth the result.

In describing myself in this way, as a rabbi teaching the Torah, I speak for all positions in Judaism today: Orthodox certainly, but also, though of course in different ways and nuances, Reform and Conservative as well. Every rabbi who proposes to speak in the name of the Torah appeals to the same sources: the oral to inform the written, the written to construct the oral, the one whole Torah of our rabbi, Moses, at Sinai.

When and where do I study the Torah? It is in the synagogue on the Sabbath, as well as on Monday and on Thursday. Then the Torah scrolls are removed from the holy ark and displayed to the entire congregation with the proclamation, "This is the Torah which Moses set before the children of Israel at the instruction of the Lord."

The Torah is read a few verses at a time, and for each reading, a member of the congregation of Israel comes up and recites a blessing before and afterward. When we go up to the Torah to hear a passage read in the synagogue on the Sabbath, as well as on Monday and Thursday mornings, holy days, and festivals, there is a blessing said before the reading and one said afterward.

Since you, Father Andy, are Catholic in the Eucharist before you are Catholic in the church as an institution and value the church because of its gift of the sacraments, so I am Judaic in the liturgy of the synagogue before I am a Jew in the street and in the office. So I appeal to the words of prayer. And when the Torah is read, what do I say? "Blessed are you, Lord, our God, who has chosen us from all peoples by giving us the Torah. Blessed are you, who gives the Torah." And afterward: "Blessed are you, Lord, our God, who has given us a true Torah, so planted within us life forever. Blessed are you, who gives the Torah."

And what I find in that language—the whole of Judaism, really—is present tense: *gives, here and now, today, this morning, to us, to me.* Revelation is not an issue of historical time if it is everyday and here and now. It is an event in eternity: forever the same, however different the circumstances in which the Torah is read and intervenes.

But the Judaism of the dual Torah, written and memorized, encompasses in its vision not Israel alone but all of creation, to the outer reaches of uncharted space and the entirety of humanity, traveling companions of all times on earth. All nations, all creatures through the revelation of the

Torah come into relationship with God, creator of heaven and earth, ruler of the world, redeemer and savior of all being.

When God revealed the Torah to Moses, what was at stake? The Torah was revealed to tell the people, Israel, about themselves and their holy tasks. It was to explain to them what God wanted of them—and of humanity, for which, in relationship to God, they stood. We can understand the this-worldly form of revelation best when we ask ourselves, How is God to speak to us? And the obvious answer can only be, In language we can understand. That must mean, in terms and categories and issues of our everyday circumstance, the here and the now of life. And this meant, and must mean, In my language, in my issues, in my world's petty details—and in yours and in hers and in his.

When God called Moses on high and told him what Israel was to be and to do, God spoke in the language of human beings, about the things that we can touch and see and feel: do this; don't do that. And God lives in those details. God speaks on high, seeing all things all at once. I respond down here, seeing only a few things here and now. The Torah comes to us in concrete ways, which relate to the here and the now, and that is how God speaks and I understand. And whether the Torah took shape in the time of Moses or of Ezra or of the holy sages, called rabbis, of the Talmud in the first seven centuries C.E., it is always God speaking from Sinai. And wherever I am, I stand in the lights and shadows of Sinai.

And this brings us to the here and the now of the Torah: what it means to live by it. It explains why, Father Andy, I don't eat meat in your house, and it is why I don't mix milk with meat or eat shellfish. It is not because your meat is not nourishing, cream sauces on veal are wicked, or lobster is distasteful. It is because God has given a commandment, and I have no choice.

But God lives in the details, and the here and the now of the Torah come to us every day. The written Torah broke into time at Sinai but (so scholarship generally holds) took the forms of the here and the now only in the time of Ezra. And the same is true of the oral part of the Torah. It speaks from Sinai, but it speaks to Israel, the Jewish people, in the land of Israel, not in the wilderness, and then in the first seven centuries of the Common Era. Naturally, when the oral Torah was written down, it was set forth in the language and in terms of the issues of the age in which it was written, just as the written Torah speaks, to begin with, in the language that people of that time could understand and just as, today, we rabbis speak in the language and to the issues of our own day.

And that brings me to the main point and one I think you will accept. The Torah is not a history book; it is the record of what God wants of us—and that is us the living, here and now—in our language, concerning the challenges and opportunities that we confront in our lives. The issues of the Torah are not historical fact but theological truth, and as the Talmud says, God wants the heart. But then it takes a rabbi who has knowledge of the Torah, written and oral, and also faith in God and understanding of the traditions of Torah learning through discipleship to set forth what that rabbi proposes as the Torah for the here and the now. Then does the Torah twist and turn through the ages? No, the Torah doesn't, but Israel does, the life of the everyday does, I do.

My "being religious" is analogous to your being religious, Father Andy, but it also is different. It is not better, not worse; not holier, not less holy; it is different. God endows us all with gifts, but each one's gifts are unique, as much as his or her chromosomes. And everyone makes of those gifts what he or she will: we are responsible for what we are because we bear the burden of what we do, and we are what we do. The key to understanding holiness is that the Torah wants me to be "like God," and that means holy like God. Now what does that mean? I can state the fundamental truth very simply: we are what we do, and God cares about what we are and do.

Therefore, the Torah cares about how I treat my neighbor and also about what I eat. But I care, too, and in my particular corner of things that is something that bears deep meaning to me. It is something I control: private, personal. But it is also something public and unchanging: social and communal and corporate.

I've read and loved your books, Father Andy, and I know that within them you plant a profoundly Christian, deeply Catholic message: you know God when you love and are loved. You find God in the here and the now. I find myself moved by that message, changed by it, because it is a profoundly Judaic message, something I hear at Sinai: you find God in the details of the here and the now, in the everyday, in what you eat, how you gesture, what you say about other people, how you do your business, whether you see in the face of the other the image and likeness of God that is there.

These messages—yours with its emphasis on love, which can shade over into the sentimental, mine with its emphasis on the deed, which can shade over into a kind of formalism and religious behaviorism—are congruent. They share the conception that God not only made the world but lives in the world and through humanity. But they differ in important ways as well. After two thousand years, I suppose even as stubborn a person as I am must admit God surely wants that difference. And after two thousand years, your church has come to concede that same thing of us: God wants us as we are.

That's why we can talk together, not because secular reason makes it possible and not because difference does not matter. It is because God wants the difference: you to be you, imitating Christ, with the sacrament of love in the here and the now standing for God's love, and us to be us. And that means, with the *mitzvoth*, the religious deeds, in the here and the now standing for God's power to make us holy and God's demand that we become holy. And to be holy is certainly also to love and to be loved. But love is not what consecrates.

So much for how "I as a rabbi" read the Torah. I won't use the language "I as a rabbi" anymore. I am never only, or mainly, "a rabbi." I am merely me, and you are always to me Andy, and I study with Andy rather than with Father Andrew. How do I combine the "I" of Jack Neusner with the "Rabbi Jacob Neusner" who is ordained to teach Torah to Israel, the holy people, by the Jewish Theological Seminary of America? It is through a process of give-and-take, and in order to study the Bible together, both of us, as a matter of fact, are going to give and take a great deal. That process in Judaism is called midrash. Let me tell you about my half of the give-and-take that studying the Bible together demands.

2

GREELEY
How a Priest Reads the Bible

I read the Bible as a love story, an account of a passionate romance between God and God's people.

In subsequent chapters I'll talk about the love aspect of the story. In this chapter I propose to explain why I read the Bible as a story. I do not suggest that it is the only way to read the Bible. Nor do I argue that it is the best way. I maintain only that the story approach is one of the necessary ways to read Scripture.

It follows that there are a number of common ways in which the Bible is read that do not interest me:

1. I do not read Scripture to find texts with which to bash others in controversy.
2. I do not go through the Bible searching for passages with which I can impose moral and political obligations (either liberal or conservative) on others.
3. I do not go through Scripture looking for proofs for doctrines that developed after the books of Scripture were written. I accept the infallibility of the pope, for example, but not because of quotes from Saint Matthew's Gospel.

I am not rejecting (necessarily) the propriety of these approaches. I am merely asserting that they are not my way of reading Scripture.

Moreover, I want to emphasize that my style of reading the Bible is that of one particular priest and not the way all priests read the Bible. I do not intend in this book to teach Catholic doctrine or to offer "official" Catholic interpretations of Scripture. I am not a bishop or a theologian or a Scripture scholar, and I will not usurp the roles of those teachers. (I will make use of the work of Scripture scholars and clear my use of that work with one of them to make sure that I have used it properly.)

I hasten to add that I do not reject either the necessity of doctrine or Catholic doctrines. Since humans are reflecting creatures, they must formal-

6

ize their religious reflections in doctrines. Moreover, the Catholic doctrinal system provides the window frame through which I look at the story of the Bible. But my training and skills are not in the presentation of doctrinal propositions. (Anyone wishing to study Catholic doctrinal propositions can find them in one of the new Catholic catechisms.)

I am a sociologist interested in religion as experience, image, and story and a storyteller who attempts to tell religious stories, tales of God at work in the world. If I have a special contribution to make to the way others might read the Bible, it is from the perspective of a sociological storyteller.

My "model" of religion is a four-part paradigm: experience, image, story, and community. This model is not the only and not necessarily the best way to look at religion, but it is one that I have found useful both as a sociologist and as a storyteller. Religion begins with an experience that renews hope and restores direction and purpose to life; it is encoded in a memory trace of the experience that continues to provide purpose and direction for life and hence can be called a symbol; it is shared with others through a story that touches parallel experiences in the lives of those who listen to the story, usually with members of the community who share the repertory of images of the storyteller.

A new father, discouraged and disheartened with career problems, looks at his firstborn son. Beholding the wonder of that small and noisy assertion of life, he finds himself smiling. The worries slip away. Life goes on. The experience remains in his memory. He shares it with others, perhaps by saying, "It was just like looking into the crib at Bethlehem." Thus he invokes a religious picture to share his story with those who share the picture with him.

The origins and raw power of religion, then, begin in the religious experiences of our life, the experiences that renew our hope and point to an order and purpose in existence. These experiences can be dramatic and overwhelming or gentle and seemingly insignificant—reconciliation after a quarrel, renewal of love, the touch of a friendly hand, a child toddling across the floor, the clash of cymbals in a symphony, a sunset, a frozen winter lake. But if they renew human hope and restore direction and purpose they are by definition religious.

The community of shared imagery is the custodian of a religious heritage that not only provides the images with which to share the experience and the audience who listens to the experience, it also so shapes the "receiving mechanism" of the mind and the imagination that the person is predisposed not merely toward a hope-renewal experience but a particular kind of hope-renewal experience. The new father mentioned above is predisposed—explicitly or implicitly—toward the kind of experience that links what happened to him as he views his son to what happened at Bethlehem.

Religion, then, is experience and story before it becomes doctrine and creed. Humans must have doctrines and creeds (and catechisms and philosophy and theology) because they are reflective beings. Doctrines emerge very soon after the primary religious experiences that shape a heritage. All the books of the Christian Scriptures are books of doctrinal reflection on the formative experience the early Christians had of Jesus. Humans must not only tell their stories ("He is risen!") but explain what the story means. Doctrine and story are equally important, but story comes first.

For most of human history religious heritages have been passed on by stories—told by parents to their children or around the campfire at night. Even today, much of the Jewish religious tradition is passed on initially at the seder and much of the Christian story around the Christmas crib. The most fascinating parts of the Scriptures are the stories. Not many of us read the Book of Numbers or the Book of Revelation, but we are enthralled by the tales of Joseph and David and by the parables of Jesus.

We humans love stories because they arrange the puzzling and mysterious events of our lives into a pattern that has meaning. The child's cry, "Mommy, tell me a story!" is a plea at the end of the day for the child's mother to make sense out of all that has happened. We are all storytellers, narrating the story of our lives, a story in which we are the protagonist, the narrator, the hero, and often the only admirable character, a story that has a beginning, a middle, and a trajectory toward fulfillment. When asked who we are, we usually tell our story in some form. When asked what our story means, we are likely to narrate those crucial life experiences that give us meaning and hope and direct our life toward purposeful goals.

Even those who insist that there is no meaning in life still will tell their stories.

Religion is experience and story before it is anything else.

The Scriptures tell the story of the relationship between humans and God, a relationship that was first experienced at Sinai when God said, "I am YHWH, your God!"

Period. Paragraph. End of revelation.

All else is commentary and explication.

Uninvited and often unwelcome, YHWH, a pushy old Jewish desert warrior God, elbowed his way into the human condition.

And, like it or not, that was that.

She* returned again to say the same thing, in richer and more powerful language, when the angel announced at the tomb, "He is risen! He is not here!"

It is these two experiences, Sinai and Easter, about which the Bible was written. They are not the same experience, but they are experiences of the same God. At the most primal level of experience and story, the two religious heritages of which the rabbi and I are writing are one religion because they share the same God and the same story. Easter does not rewrite or eliminate Sinai. It merely deepens and enriches the earlier experience in its promise that life is stronger than death. It is another chapter in the same never-ending story.

The ragtag band of disparate desert warriors gathered around Sinai experienced themselves as having been constituted as a people, not by anything they had done but by the intervention of a God who, whether they wanted it or not, had appointed himself their God.

And an equally unprepossessing band of the followers of Jesus, much against their will, experienced that he who was killed was not dead but alive through the power of God.

Exactly what happened in these two momentous events can be argued by others and will doubtless be so argued till the end of human history. For my purpose it is enough to say that the Bible was written to tell the story of those two overarching religious experiences. In both cases the story is of a sudden, astonishing, implacable intervention of a powerful and powerfully loving God, the same God.

No one else around like her.

I am not saying that the two religions that emerged out of the matrix of Second Temple Israel and were shaped and formed in the early centuries C.E. are the same religion. Obviously the doctrinal formulations, the ritual practices, the historical experiences are different. But just as obviously, I think, both heritages are rooted in experiences of the same God and tell the same basic story of that God's relationship with us.

That truth ought never to be forgotten, but, unfortunately, all too often has been forgotten.

We are all YHWHists.

---

*God is neither male nor female, both male and female, which is to say that the attributes we predicate of men and women are found combined in God. It is therefore appropriate to imagine God either as male or female, so long as we realize the limitations of both metaphors. See my chapter below, "The Womanliness of God" (chapter 34).

Let us not forget that. Ever again.

I don't ask the reader to accept this approach to the Bible as the only approach. I merely ask him or her to accept it as a useful and illuminating approach.

But could not any sociological storyteller read the Bible that way? What, if anything, does my role as a Catholic priest add to the way I view the never-ending story?

I watch the biblical drama unfolding through a window whose frame is shaped by the doctrinal propositions of the Catholic heritage and whose transparent stained glass is patterned by the Catholic imagination.

The other three religions of YHWH, Islam, Judaism, and Protestantism, tend to emphasize the absence of God, the discontinuity between Creator and his creation. Catholicism tends to emphasize the presence of God, the continuity between Creator and her creation. Catholicism believes in the "sacramentality" of creation; it believes that the world and all the objects and events and people in it are metaphors for God, revealing what God is like.

The other religions are inclined to say that God is radically unlike the world and its events and objects and people. Catholicism is inclined to say that God is radically like the world.

These two religious emphases need one another, but the difference between them is both real and important. Only Catholicism, for example, has statues and stained glass windows with pictures and souls in purgatory and an elaborate system of honor to angels and saints and especially Mary the Mother of Jesus. These practices are not the result of superstitions by which Protestants (especially) are horrified and certain elite Catholics are embarrassed. They are rather manifestations of the "sacramental" instinct of the Catholic religious sensibility. Those practices that seem to differentiate Catholicism from the other heritages of YHWH are the result of this different sensibility. Moreover, it is the appeal of the Catholic emphasis on ceremony, community, and the continuity between nature and God that constitutes the principal appeal of Catholicism to its adherents.

Judaism, I hasten to add before the rabbi corrects me, is more like Catholicism in its sacramentality than are the other two traditions. But you still don't have statues and honor to Mary the Mother of Jesus.

This difference, I must emphasize, is not a difference of doctrine (though it has doctrinal implications); it is a difference of sensibility, a disagreement about how much God discloses himself in and through creation, about how much at ease one can be with the instinct that the world and all its creatures are metaphors for God.

Thus I read the Bible in search of metaphor, in search of stories of God that enable me to say what God is like and how God loves.

A distinguished Protestant theologian once remarked that the only sacrament we have of God (the only valid metaphor) is Jesus Christ and him crucified.

The Catholic response is that Jesus crucified (and risen) is the metaphor *par excellence* of God's love, but that all creation is also metaphor for God.

In order that some realities be sacraments (as in Catholicism's seven sacraments) everything must be a sacrament—capable of telling us something about God.

Everything is grace.

Grace lurks everywhere. In Richard Wilbur's words, it is the "Cheshire smile which makes us fearfully free."

Hence my earlier reference to YHWH as a "pushy old Jewish desert warrior God" was neither irreverent nor exaggerated.

The story in that image is the story of a fierce, powerful desert chieftain who storms around the desert, protecting his friends and routing his enemies. Then at the end of a weary day, with passionate tenderness he forces his way into the tent of his beloved young bride, who is both timid and eager, claims her for his own, and embraces her in a love affair that will endure . . . how long?

Forever.

That's what the story is all about.

3

NEUSNER

Is Not My Word like Fire?

I read the Torah in the light of the way Judaism reads the Torah, and that is the way called midrash. Midrash means "search, inquiry," and it refers to the Judaic way of interpreting the Hebrew Scriptures. You can understand what I see only when you look through my glasses. You can understand how Scripture comes to life for me only when you know how the method we call midrash brings Scripture to life and life to Scripture. So what is this way of reading Scripture that Judaism calls midrash? The answer to the question matters, because if you want to know how Scripture becomes Torah, you have to know how midrash *turns* Scripture (the written part of revelation) into Torah.

That method is captured in the way in which we read a passage in which God says to Jeremiah, "Is not my word like fire, and like a hammer that breaks the rock into pieces?"

On this passage the holy rabbis of the oral Torah comment as follows: "Just as a hammer strikes the anvil and kindles clouds of sparks, so does Scripture yield many meanings, as it is said, 'Once God spoke but I heard two things' (Ps. 62:11)."

The point is that Scripture contains many meanings, and it is the task of study to discover some of those many meanings. Scripture is determinate, Torah indeterminate. Scripture comes from some specific time and place. Torah speaks out of eternity for all times and places. The work of midrash is to find in Scripture some of those meanings that have been treasured out of eternity for our particular time and place.

Christians know midrash when they see it, because throughout the New Testament are examples of midrash. Indeed, much that we find in the Gospels is fully comprehensible only when we understand that the Evangelists in part are working out a midrash on the Old Testament in terms of the life of Jesus Christ.* One important trait of midrash as the rabbis of the first

---

*I speak of "Jesus Christ" in the context of Christianity, "Jesus" the man in the context of Judaism.

seven centuries work out midrash exegesis is to cite a verse of Scripture and then say what you think it means in light of events of today. That is to say, we turn the everyday world into a commentary upon the received and written Torah or Scripture. To give an example familiar to you, let's look at the second chapter of Matthew.

The Evangelist is trying to explain to his fellow Jews what has happened to the world because of the life, death, and resurrection of Jesus Christ. In the setting of Matthew, that is the here and the now. We must not forget that simple fact, because if we miss the immediacy, for the Evangelist, of Jesus alive and of Christ risen from the dead, we do not understand what questions he brings to Scripture or why he wants to read the received Bible at all. His problem is to make sense of the then in light of the now—that is, to reread the Torah in light of what he now understands to be its real meaning. And what is that "real meaning"? It is what Scripture has always meant, but it is a sense that only now we have uncovered. In this sense, the everyday turns out to form part of revelation: it serves to clarify the sense of the received revelation of Sinai.

That is the process of midrash. It is, as I told you, the work of bringing life to Scripture and Scripture to life. How does Matthew do it?

Let's take events that are critical to the life of Jesus as Matthew has received and now sets forth the story: Jesus' birth to the Virgin, the slaughter of the innocents, and the proclamation of John the Baptist. These for Matthew are facts. But only the Torah can tell me what they mean, what they have to mean. So this is how he sets them out:

> Now the birth of Jesus Christ took place in this way. When his mother Mary had been betrothed to Joseph, before they came together she was found to be with child of the Holy Spirit. And her husband Joseph, being a just man and unwilling to put her to shame, resolved to divorce her quietly. But as he considered this, behold, an angel of the Lord appeared to him in a dream, saying, "Joseph, son of David, do not fear to take Mary your wife, for that which is conceived in her is of the Holy Spirit; she will bear a son, and you shall call his name Jesus, for he will save his people from their sins." All this took place to fulfil what the Lord has spoken by the prophet: "Behold a virgin shall conceive and bear a son, and his name shall be called Emmanuel" (Is. 7:14), which means, God with us. When Joseph woke from sleep, he did as the angel of the Lord commanded him. He took his wife, but knew her not until she had borne a son, and he called his name Jesus.

What has happened here? Matthew has taken the fact of the birth of Jesus Christ to the Virgin and asked the Torah—here, prophecy—to explain that fact.

Matthew does not cite Scripture as a proof text—that is to say, as evidence for a proposition he wishes to establish as fact. Not at all, not at all. The virgin birth is the fact. What does the fact mean? Isaiah answers that question by linking the fact of the day to the truth of the ages: God has done this thing; this event now realizes what the prophet long ago had prophesied. The power of Isaiah is not to validate or verify. The power of Isaiah is to be renewed and empowered by the realization of Isaiah's prophecy in the fact of the virgin birth.

Does midrash seen in this way take place only occasionally? No, I think we are dealing with a fundamental perspective, a principle that teaches us how to read in a new, and the right, way. Let us ask Matthew to show us a pattern. Let me give two more examples of the same manner of midrash. The first concerns the slaughter of the innocents:

> Then Herod, when he saw that he had been tricked by the wise men, was in a furious rage, and he sent and killed all the male children in Bethlehem and in all that region who were two years old or under, according to the time which he had ascertained from the wise men. Then was fulfilled what was spoken by the prophet Jeremiah: "A voice was heard in Ramah, wailing and loud lamentation, Rachel weeping for her children; she refused to be consoled, because they were no more" (Jer. 31:15).

The fact of the day? Herod's murder of the infants. But what does it all mean? In finding the sense in Jeremiah's picture of Rachel weeping at Ramah, Matthew has written into the life of Jesus the entire tragic history of Israel. It is as though he wants to signal that Jesus' life, from the very beginning, will embody the life of Israel, his people. He will live out each chapter of the life of God's first love.

For what does Rachel represent? Buried near Bethlehem, Rachel is portrayed by Jeremiah as weeping at the exile, in 586, of the Jews from Jerusalem to Babylonia. They were marched north from Jerusalem via Ramah, the place at which Rachel sees them. So Rachel wept. And now, what has this to do with Jesus' life? When Herod undertook to murder the infants, Joseph and Mary fled to Egypt, as they had been told, "Take the child and his mother and flee to Egypt and remain there till I tell you." That is the fact. What is its meaning? Going into exile, Jesus with his parents acted out Israel's exile. Then the return must mark in the new age a counterpart to an event in the age of destruction and renewal.

And that is precisely what Matthew finds out. For he knows the contemporary fact of John the Baptist, preaching the advent of the kingdom of heaven. And what can this mean? Matthew again turns to the received

Scripture, the Torah, and his mind reaches out to the counterpart, to the return to the Holy Land on the part of Jesus and his parents. This he finds in the return to Zion of Israel after the exile to Babylonia. And what marked the moment? It was Isaiah's prophesy: the road home is open; come home:

> In those days came John the Baptist, preaching in the wilderness of Judea, "Repent, for the kingdom of heaven is at hand." For this is he who was spoken of by the prophet Isaiah when he said, "The voice of one crying in the wilderness: prepare the way of the Lord, make his paths straight" (Is. 40:3).

John makes sense in light of Isaiah's prophecy: the world now read in light of the Torah. But the road runs in both directions. The Torah then is read in light of the world now.

Midrash is the road that leads me to what the Torah says today. And that is a matter of not mere scholarship about the facts of this and that, but the exercise of taste and judgment, sensibility, and, above all, vocation: faith in God who gives the Torah through Moses, our rabbi, and thereby—in the language of the liturgy of Judaism that I quoted in chapter 1—"plants eternal life in our midst," in the midst of Israel, the holy people.

Since the written Torah comes in the hand and voice of Moses (called in Judaism "our rabbi," meaning "our lord") in historical time and since the oral Torah comes in the name of later authorities than that, a faithful Jew reads Scripture and the oral Torah as well not as a set of historical statements pertaining to a particular time and place but as statements that are supposed to speak to all time and everywhere. We therefore have to sort things out the way the blind Isaac did when he gave his blessing to Jacob: the hand is the hand of Esau; the voice is the voice of Jacob. We live in the West, the modern and secular world of Esau. Finding our way in our blindness, from touch and feel we know that the hand that wrote the words was the hand of men who lived in a particular place at a certain time. But the voice—that is another matter. For we hear in ways in which we do not feel and touch.

The word not tangible, not in the storm and not in the fury, is the voice *current* of silence, thin and sinewy. The voice *is* (not was) the voice of God, who *speaks* (not spoke) through Moses, *our* rabbi (not only theirs, long ago). This same God of Sinai through time and today has spoken and now speaks through sages who have mastered and now stand for and exemplify God's Torah to Moses at Sinai. The Torah creates for holy Israel, the supernatural entity, an eternal present, here and now as much as there and then.

Midrash is not merely an approach to Scripture. It refers to a particular body of writing. That writing, books comprising compilations of readings and interpretations of the written Torah, forms an important component of the oral Torah, which I introduced to you in chapter 1. And in referring to particular books, I mean to introduce to you the main guidelines that direct me in the study of the Torah. For just as Matthew was trying to read one particular thing in light of another specific thing—not life in general but the life of Jesus in particular, not received Scriptures in general but the prophets in particular—so I am doing the same thing. What part of the everyday and the here and now do I wish to bring to Scripture and in the light of which I want to read the Torah? What for me is the counterpart to Matthew's life of Jesus—birth, flight to Egypt, return from Egypt—is the life of Israel, the Jewish people. And what for me plays the role of Matthew's reading of the prophets Jeremiah and Isaiah? It is the five books of Moses, the Pentateuch, which we read through the year in the synagogue. The word *Torah* encompasses many things, but it begins with that one thing: the five books of Moses.

So midrash for me becomes real and concrete when I can read the Torah in the synagogue and discover sense and meaning in my own life. But that study also means that I bring my own life to the Torah and impart new sense to Scripture out of what I have discovered out there, in the world of the everyday. So much for me, your friend Jack. But for me, Rabbi Jacob, there is yet another dimension of the study of Torah we call midrash. There are particular books called midrash compilations (*midrashim* in Hebrew).

There are three ways of reading Scripture in the manner of midrash. These I call midrash as paraphrase, midrash as prophecy, and midrash as parable or allegorical reading of Scripture. This third way is the one I find compelling, as you will see in my reading of every biblical passage I set forth and explain in this book.

In the first of these, the exegete would paraphrase Scripture, imposing fresh meanings by the word choices or even by adding additional phrases or sentences and so revising the meaning of the received text. This I call midrash as paraphrase because the fresh meaning is imputed by obliterating the character of the original text and rendering or translating it in a new sense. The barrier between the text and the comment here is obscured, and the commentator joins in the composing of the text. Midrash as paraphrase may also include fresh materials, but these are presented as if they formed an integral part of the original text.

In the second, the exegete would ask Scripture to explain meanings of events near at hand, and Scripture would serve as a means of prophetic reading of the contemporary world. Midrash as prophecy produces the identification of a biblical statement or event with a contemporary happening.

Torah = present tense

prophecy

Here the scriptural verse or text retains its particularity, being kept distinct from the commentary or exegesis. But in its substance, as against its form, midrash as prophecy treats the historical life of ancient Israel and the contemporary times of the exegete as essentially the same, reading the former as a prefiguring of the latter. Through midrash as prophecy, therefore, Scripture addresses contemporary times as a guide to what is happening even now.

Do I really mean this? Isn't this how "the fundamentalists" read Scripture? Yes I do, and yes it is. All they are asking of Scripture is that it speak to them. I don't think that's asking something Scripture does not promise. If God reveals Torah ("Blessed are you, Lord, who gives the Torah"—present tense!) then it must be to the here and the now. Then can I ask no less than answers to my questions? When people read Psalms and come across the verse, "The Lord is my shepherd," they find themselves. And why not? And when I come to prophecy, as I do, with a heart broken by the murder of the Jews of Europe in my own lifetime, and I read in Isaiah's account of the return to Zion meanings about the renewal of the life of Israel, the Jewish people, in the land of Israel, I do no less. So yes, I do mean that Scripture addresses contemporary times as a guide to what is happening even now.

parable / allegory

But back to the exposition. In the third type of midrash as process, which for the sake of convenience I call midrash as parable, though the categories of allegory or metaphor also pertain, the exegete reads Scripture in terms other than those in which the scriptural writer speaks. Scripture, for instance, may tell the story of love of man and woman in the Song of Songs, but Judaic and Christian exegetes hear the song of the love of God and Israel or God and the church.

Scripture in Genesis speaks of the family of Abraham, Isaac, and Jacob, while in Genesis Rabbah, a fourth-century compilation of midrash interpretations of the Book of Genesis, the great Judaic sages read the history of the children of Israel, down to the present time as they knew it. Scripture in the book of Leviticus speaks of the sanctification of Israel. Leviticus Rabbah's framers transformed the book of Leviticus into an account of Israel's salvation.

This third type of midrash process or hermeneutic I call allegorical, meaning simply reading one thing in light of some other, or parabolic, for the same reason, or metaphorical. The basic principle of midrash as allegory is that things are never what they seem. Israel's reality is not conveyed either by the simple sense of Scripture or by the obvious realities of the perceived world. A deeper meaning in Scripture preserves the more profound meaning of the everyday world of Israel even now. This third type characterizes the rabbinic exegetes. The upshot, as I present Judaism, is to insist that Scripture speaks not only to us but also about us: our situation, our problems, our sanctification, our salvation.

Precisely where do we find these midrash compilations? In theological terms, how do I locate the written-down version of the oral Torah? As a matter of historical fact, as I said, the oral Torah reached written form between the second and the seventh centuries, in a series of documents produced by the Judaic sages, or rabbis, of the land of Israel and of Babylonia (present-day Iraq), beginning with the Mishnah, a philosophical law code of about A.D. 200. The explanations of the Mishnah begin with the Tosefta, a corpus of supplementary sayings, and continue with the Talmud of the land of Israel, ca. 400 C.E., a systematic exegesis of the Mishnah, and the Talmud of Babylonia, also a systematic explanation of the Mishnah, ca. 500–600 C.E.

A separate body of exegesis—the one that concerns us here—concentrates on Scripture, first of all, books of the Pentateuch, of five books attributed to Moses. These include Genesis Rabbah, on the Book of Genesis, commonly regarded as a work of ca. 400, and Leviticus Rabbah, on the Book of Leviticus, ordinarily dated as ca. 450. These two books deal with the family history portrayed in Genesis and the lessons for the life of the family set forth in passages of Leviticus, respectively. There are systematic amplifications of those passages of Exodus, Leviticus, Numbers, and Deuteronomy that instruct Israel on how to conduct its life.

These books, *Sifra,* on the Book of Leviticus, *Sifré Numbers,* and *Sifré Deuteronomy,* of indeterminate date but probably of the later third or fourth century, provide a verse-by-verse reading of those important passages. What they aim to do, in general, is to take the case described by the written Torah and turn it into a general rule of conduct for the purposes of the oral Torah. Yet another work, Mekhilta, imputed to R. Ishmael, on Exodus, generally held to derive from the same period, combines the interests of the two distinct types of midrash compilations, the ones concerned with what I called family history and moral conduct, Genesis Rabbah and Leviticus Rabbah, and those interested in rules for the life of Israel, the family that is a community, *Sifra* and the two *Sifrés.* All of these are in English; I have translated them.

There were various other writings of the same age, for instance, *Pesiqta deRav Kahana,* a collection of exegeses of verses of Scripture important on special occasions, following the style and conceptual program of Leviticus Rabbah, and *The Fathers According to Rabbi Nathan,* an amplification of the Mishnah tractate, *Tractate Avot* (in English *The Fathers*), in which stories about sages are told to enrich the mishnah tractate's account of sayings assigned to sages. In a later chapter, we shall meet these very authorities and consider some of their teachings. All together, these and related contemporary writings constitute the oral Torah, as it had reached writing by the end of late antiquity, signified by the Muslim conquest of the Christian Middle East. To learn and then to teach how the oral Torah mediates the written Torah to us is a rabbi's task. It is what makes a rabbi a rabbi, as much as the bishop's ordination makes a priest a priest.

What is important in these books that compile midrash teachings is that they answer the questions of salvation, of the meaning and end of Israel's history. The age—the early Christian centuries—demanded answers from Israel's sages: What does history mean? Where are we to find guidance to the meaning of our past—and our future? Sages turned to the written Torah read in light of the oral Torah. For example, they looked to Genesis, maintaining that the story of the creation of the world and the beginning of Israel would show the way toward the meaning of history and the salvation of Israel. So they proposed to explain history by rereading the book of Genesis. There they found the lesson that what happened to the patriarchs in the beginning signals what would happen to their children later on. And Jacob then is Israel now, just as Esau then is Rome now. And Israel remains Israel: bearer of the blessing.

Let me ask a question that Christians always address to Judaism, the messianic question. What about the messiah claim of Israel? In the written Torah or Scripture, sages found a simple answer. Israel indeed will receive the Messiah, but salvation at the end of time awaits the sanctification of Israel in the here and now. And that will take place through humble and obedient loyalty to the Torah. So sages in the oral Torah counter the claim that there is a new Israel in place of the old. This message sages found by rereading the book of Leviticus, with its message of sanctification of Israel, and finding in that book a typology of the great empires—Babylonia, Media, Greece, Rome. And the coming, the fifth and final sovereign, will be Israel's messiah.

In these ways, the rabbis or sages of Judaism addressed the points in conflict with Christianity in particular. The points important to Christianity were, and are, these: history vindicates Christ, the New Testament explains the Old, the Messiah has come and his claim has now been proved truthful, and the Old Israel is done for and will not have a messiah in the future. The rabbinic system in reply laid stress on the priority of sanctification in the here and now through carrying out the requirements of the Torah. Salvation would come whenever sanctification was attained. They further found in the dual media by which the Torah came forth from Sinai the messianic dimension of Israel's everyday life. And they uncovered in the one whole Torah of Moses, our rabbi, ample proof of the permanence of Israel's position as God's first love.

In the first Christian centuries, as in our own day, Jews and Christians alike believed in the Israelite Scriptures and so understood that major turnings in history carried a message from God. The shared program brought the two religions into protracted confrontation on an intersecting set of questions. The struggle between the one and the other—a struggle that would continue until our own time—originated in the simple fact that, to begin with, both religions agreed on pretty much everything that mattered. They differed on little, so made much of that little.

Scripture taught them both that vast changes in the affairs of empires came about because of God's will. History proved principles of theology. In that same Torah prophets promised the coming of the Messiah, who would bring salvation. Who was, and is, that Messiah, and how shall we know? And that same Torah addressed a particular people, Israel, promising that people the expression of God's favor and love. But who is Israel, and who is not Israel?

So Scripture defined the categories that were shared in common. Scripture filled those categories with deep meaning. That is why, to begin with a kind of dialogue—made up of more than two monologues on the same topics—could commence. And because of the new setting, which has no precedent in the shared histories of Christianity and Judaism in the West, this rabbi and this priest want to undertake a new kind of dialogue: arguing in love, disagreeing in friendship, above all undertaking that kind of confrontation that profound mutual respect, not only personal but religious, makes possible.

4

NEUSNER

Beginning "In the Beginning"

When God began to create heaven and earth—the earth being unformed and void, with darkness over the surface of the deep and a wind from God sweeping over the water—God said, "Let there be light," and there was light. God saw that the light was good, and God separated the light from the darkness. God called the light Day, and the darkness He called Night. And there was evening and there was morning, a first day.

Genesis 1:1–5

The heaven and the earth were finished, and all their array. On the seventh day God finished the work that He had been doing, and He ceased on the seventh day from all the work that He had done. And God blessed the seventh day and declared it holy, because on it God ceased from all the work of creation that He had done. Such is the story of heaven and earth when they were created.

Genesis 2:1–4

The first thing I notice in the story of creation—and I think it is what the story wants me to notice—is that the seventh day, the Sabbath of creation, is the climax of the beginning of creation. Everything is aimed at that one thing, which commemorates and celebrates creation, all in a single sentence: "And God blessed the seventh day and declared it holy, because on it God ceased from all the work of creation that He had done." That contains the entire message of "in the beginning":

1. God made the world.
2. God declared the world of nature to be good.
3. Nature exhibits order and purpose, signified by all things having the right name.
4. Nature is to be celebrated as the holy work of God.
5. The seventh day of the week, the Sabbath day, serves to celebrate creation, and the rest that I take on that day is like the rest that God took to mark the wholeness and completeness of creation.
6. God made holy, or sanctified, the time, the seventh day, in response to the completion and wholeness of creation.

These six lessons come to me from the six days of labor in which God made the world and all that is in it. I remember them on the seventh day, the Sabbath.

But I know about creation more than that there is a world. I also know some of the things that have happened in creation and since the beginning. Can I place into the context of beginnings these events in the sacred story of holy Israel? That is precisely the question that the rabbis of Judaism answer for us.* They ask how, in the account of beginnings, I can uncover the presence of things that took place later on. They therefore want me to see in the story at hand the entire history of the world, up to the coming of the Messiah and the redemption of humanity. So "in the beginning" encompasses the middle and the ending as well. What we shall now see is how the great moments in the afterlife of creation are discovered within creation itself: the sin of Adam, the murder committed by Cain, the generation of Enosh, the time of the flood, but then Noah, Abraham, Isaac, Jacob—and then Esau, too.

Precisely how do I want you to follow the story of creation? What am I going to read into what? I want to treat each verse of Scripture as a point of illumination, a color, to be combined with other verses of Scripture, all of them shedding light on one another, forming a composition of colors, a new picture. Every fact of Scripture exists at a single moment, on a single plane, and this vast tableau permits us to set side by side what in Scripture comes to us only in sequence and order. One verse from here, one verse from there, and all things are set into a new arrangement.

The first passage of midrash I want to lay out shows us how one thing is read in light of everything and vice versa. Rabbi Judah son (=b.) of Rabbi (=R.) Simon wants the story of creation to point toward the future history of humanity, meaning, Adam, then Cain, then the generation of Enosh (the ones who built the Tower of Babel), then the generation of the great flood. So much for the downward spiral. But then R. Judah b. R. Simon calls to mind the upward ascent, from the depths to Sinai. So he finds in the creation story Abraham and then Jacob, and that points onward and upward.

What he does is cite a verse in some later passage that he thinks is implicit in the earlier one. That is the work of making connections to which

---

*My source is Genesis Rabbah, the fourth-century commentary to the Book of Genesis, written by sages in the land of Israel (aka Palestine) in the century or so after Emperor Constantine, when the Roman Empire adopted Christianity and made it the state religion. My translation of the Genesis Rabbah is published by Scholars Press, Atlanta, Georgia, 1987. All passages in this chapter come from Genesis Rabbah, chapter 2.

I referred in the last chapter. First let's walk through the passage as it comes to us in the great collection of midrash interpretations of the Book of Genesis called Genesis Rabbah; then I'll go over what has happened in the passage.

"And the earth was unformed . . . " (Gen. 1:2):

R. Judah b. R. Simon interpreted the verse as referring to coming generations [as follows]:

" 'The earth was unformed' refers to Adam, who was reduced to complete nothingness [on account of his sin].

" 'And void' refers to Cain, who sought to return the world to unformedness and void.

" 'And darkness was upon the face of the deep' (Gen. 1:2) refers to the generation of Enosh: 'And their works are in the dark' (Is. 29:15).

" 'Upon the face of the deep' (Gen. 1:2) refers to the generation of the flood: 'On the same day were all the fountains of the great deep broken up' (Gen. 7:11).

" 'And the spirit of God hovered over the face of the water' (Gen. 1:2): 'And God made a wind pass over the earth' (Gen. 8:1).

"Said the Holy One, blessed be he, 'For how long will the world make its way in darkness. Let light come.'

" 'And God said, "Let there be light" '(Gen. 1:3).

"This refers to Abraham. That is in line with the following verse of Scripture: 'Who has raised up one from the earth, whom he calls in righteousness to his foot' (Is. 41:23).

" 'And God called the light day' (Gen. 1:5) refers to Jacob.

" 'And the darkness he called night' (Gen. 1:5) refers to Esau.

" 'And there was evening' refers to Esau.

" 'And there was morning' refers to Jacob."

The rabbi links each of the elements of the set of verses of Genesis to other biblical figures. The heroic or evil figures who will occur are prefigured in the elements of creation. Time and again the sages make the same point, that there is a close correspondence between the creation of the world and the history of Israel or, later on, between the lives and deeds of the patriarchs and the salvation of Israel in history and at the end of time. When a rabbi claims that we Jews read Scripture as a commentary to our own time and our own time as a commentary to Scripture, this is what is meant. Creation contains within itself the entire history of humankind. That is what a rabbi reads in "in the beginning."

To understand what happens next, you have to know that, for any rabbi reading Scripture, Jacob stands for *Israel,* meaning, the holy people of God, the Jewish people, and *Esau* stands for Rome, perceived as the brother and the enemy. That enemy, Esau, for the fourth- and fifth-century sages is none other than Christian Rome. *Christian* meant "brother," because Christians revered the same written Torah. *Rome* meant "enemy." Hence the story of humanity in the rabbi's reading of Scripture is the tale of the love-hatred of the brothers who are enemies, Israel and Rome.

Holy Israel, so the rabbi knows, forms the centerpiece of creation, the aim and goal of the making of the world. Therefore, the history of Israel is to be discovered in "in the beginning." And that requires attention to what happens in historical time. The first rabbi asked us to read the creation as an account of the coming generations. The next one reads the same verses as a story of the history of the world, and by that he means the four kingdoms that would rule. For Scripture there are four great empires, leading up to God's rule. These are the ages of Babylonia, Media, Greece, and Rome. And after Rome comes the rule of the King-Messiah.

> R. Simeon b. Laqish interpreted the verses at hand to speak of the empires [of the historical age to come].
>
> " 'The earth was unformed' refers to Babylonia, 'I beheld the earth and lo, it was unformed' (Jer. 4:23).
>
> " 'And void' refers to Media: 'They hasted [using the letters of the same root as the word for void] to bring Haman' (Est. 6:14).
>
> " 'Darkness' refers to Greece, which clouded the vision of the Israelites through its decrees, for it said to Israel, 'Write on the horn of an ox [as a public proclamation for all to see] that you have no portion in the God of Israel.'
>
> " '. . . upon the face of the deep' refers to the wicked kingdom [of Rome].
>
> "Just as the deep surpasses investigation, so the wicked kingdom surpasses investigation.
>
> " 'And the spirit of God hovers' refers to the spirit of the Messiah, in line with the following verse of Scripture: 'And the spirit of the Lord shall rest upon him' (Is. 11:2)."
>
> On account of what merit will the Messiah come? [It will be on account of the merit represented by the verse:] ". . . over the face of the water" (Gen. 1:2).
>
> It is, specifically, on account of the merit of repentance, which is compared to water: "Pour out your heart like water" (Lam. 2:19).

The reading of "in the beginning" leads us through time and beyond, to the coming of the Messiah. And what will bring the coming of the Messiah and the triumph of holy Israel over its sorry history? It is repentance, return to God. But these are not historical matters, not at all, not at all. They are things that we do. So what the rabbi is saying to us is that we are party to creation. Historical time, meaning an age in which the empires rule, connects to the everyday lives of real people. Three things then intersect: the creation of nature in the Genesis story; the history of humanity, in the linking of the Genesis story with the generations from Adam to Noah to Abraham, Jacob, and then Sinai; and, finally, the secular history of the great empires. And when these things intersect, the climax comes with repentance and return to God. So what is that "beginning" that the "in the beginning" explains? It is the immediacy of the human condition that I experience. So we see that the rabbi carries forward a strong interest in finding the historical, human points of correspondence to the components of nature that are at issue. We move from creation to the patriarchs to the history of Israel, a complete account of the three components of the world in which we Israel live.

What have I found out about how to read the Bible? The story of creation gives a good example. It is to find in the Bible—which for me means in the written part of the Torah—God's answers to humankind's questions. That applies first of all to creation. If we come to the story of the creation of the world with the right questions, the story illuminates life as God's perspective upon us. If we ask the wrong questions, we gain from the story only a set of "facts" that are not facts. For what the Bible says about creation and how the Bible says it have to be sorted out. And what I want to know about the creation of the world is whether or not God knew what was going to happen from then to now and to the end of time. For creation has not led to the things that I would have wanted.

That set of questions may sound pretty obvious to you until you remember how other people bring a different set of questions to these same important passages. In fact, because of creationism, which holds that the biblical account concerns questions of astronomy, geology, paleontology, and the natural history of the world, I suppose you and I are supposed to be slightly apologetic about the biblical stories of creation, and at this point we should begin to backtrack. We should assure the readers we're not asking them to believe the world really was made in six days, with God's resting on the seventh or the Sabbath day. Or (if you want a different audience) we should try to persuade our readers that when the story says six days, it really means six something-else's, like six billion years. Or whatever.

But I'm not going to apologize for reading Scripture my way, which is the way of Judaism. And the question that Judaism maintains Scripture addresses in telling the story of the creation of the world is right there in the story. It concerns, first, the nature of time, reaching its climax in the

Sabbath; second, the nature of the world, reaching its perfection in God's pleasure with what God had created, God's blessing and sanctifying creation; third, the character of humankind, man and woman, perfect in God's image, like God, but tragically flawed, too. That is there. How can we admit to our conversation trivial questions, which our author cannot have regarded as urgent, about where the dinosaurs came from or how come fossils? Creationists seem to me not to affirm the perfection of the Bible as God's inerrant word, but to misread the perfect message. I am not going to apologize for my reading of the same words, nor am I going to concede they are more "orthodox" or "perfect in faith" than I am. I think they're wrong, that's all.

What then are my questions to creation? I want to know how to fit together creation with the story of humankind, with Adam, Cain, the generation of the flood, but also with Abraham, Isaac, and Jacob. Creation did not end on the sunset of the sixth day. Creation bore within itself humankind as well. The story of the beginnings of creation tells me, therefore, about us: humankind, what we are, and who we are meant to be. That explains why I think some of today's concerns—creation in seven days, not in aeons of immeasurable time, and the story of creation as a handbook for geology, not a theology of humanity in God's plan and program—strike me as monumentally beside the point.

At issue is not history in the sense that the world really was made in six days, but eternity: that God sanctifies and rests on the seventh, the Sabbath of creation. At stake is what Scripture teaches us to make of what is happening now. All of us for nearly two hundred years have suffered from the abuse of those who think that Scripture answers a set of historical questions: did it really happen? But the questions that draw us to Scripture are not questions about what happened long ago, but rather what is happening now and what, in Scripture, God wants of me. And to people who ask Scripture to explain what is happening now the lessons and example of the sages of Judaism have much to say. That is what I want to find out in studying Scripture with my priest.

But then what troubles me in creation? It is the condition of the world. To see just what corner of the world I mean, I have to stand back for a moment and remind you that the story of creation is part of a much larger picture of the world and that world is one that, for every writer of the written Torah, finds one land as holy, which is the land of Israel, one ordering of time that is holy, and that is the ordering of time that identifies the Sabbath day as the climax of creation, and one ordering of space that is holy, and that is the ordering of space that sees Jerusalem as the highest place in the world and the Temple that once stood in Jerusalem as the highest place in the highest place. The written Torah is the story of Israel: its space, its time, its service. What precisely begins in the beginning? It is the beginning of the world as Israel, holy Israel, encounters it. As soon as I speak of beginnings, I have to account for the holy time, the holy place, and the holy service of Israel: Sabbath, Jerusalem, Temple worship.

I hinted that that is where matters were heading when I pointed out the climax of the creation story: the sanctification of the world at the moment of the advent of the Sabbath day. So it is that whole conception of the world, with God's revelation to Israel at Sinai, with the holy way of life of the Torah as the heart and soul of matters, that the story of creation draws upon in framing its picture of beginnings. What begins in the beginning is humanity, culminating at Sinai, as the first day of creation points toward the seventh.

And you know that, Father Andy, because that is precisely how the Bible—the Christian Bible, with its Old Testament and its New Testament—represents matters. So when we come to talk together about Paul, we're going to have to sort out just how the written Torah got to be the Old Testament of the Bible of Christianity (which, I remind you, is not the same as the written Torah and the oral Torah that form the one whole Torah of Moses for Judaism).

And that makes me wonder: if the purpose of creation was to lead to the sanctification of the seventh day, the Sabbath, and if the Sabbath is sanctified by holy Israel in particular, then what has happened to holy Israel? For Israel celebrated creation through offerings of the gifts of creation back to the creator, and this it did in a Temple. We remember then a Temple to offer sacrifices to the service of God and that the Temple was destroyed. We remember that Israel had a dominion of its own, but it fell under the rule of the great empires of the world, in biblical times meaning Babylonia, Media, Greece, and Rome. Creation contains within itself everything that happened then, and much of what happened turns us back to creation for an explanation: we want the reason why things are the way they are, if that is how they started out.

All of this from "In the beginning God created the heaven and the earth"? Well, yes, as a matter of fact. For this return to beginnings has to explain how things now are, and when Ezra brought together the received traditions and made the Torah, it was in a Jerusalem that had been destroyed and rebuilt. And he was part of an Israel that had gone into exile to Babylonia in 586 b.c. and returned to Zion around three generations later, in ca. 500 b.c., so, when he put the Torah together, in ca. 450 b.c., the issues were clear: "how did the world begin" meant, "how was the world so made that Israel served God in a Temple that was destroyed and now is rebuilt, in a land that was lost and now is regained, in a holy way of life that was set down from Sinai, violated, but then recovered and renewed, here and now, in the Torah."

So there you have it: creation of what, for what? Of a world in which there would flourish a Cain and a Sodom, as well as an Israel and a Temple? Of a world in which those who celebrate creation on the Sabbath day will suffer the rule and, we now know, the depredations unto annihilation of those who do not? At stake in my reading of creation is whether or not at creation God's rule encompassed history, too. Now the real beginning of "When God began to create heaven and earth" is within. It is who is beginning. When I begin the account of beginnings, there are many things I already know about the world long before I begin "in the beginning." So in no way is "in the beginning" news: the story of creation in six days. The issues are other.

Coming to Scripture is not the beginning or the ending, but rather a moment of continuity in a life of sanctification beginning with birth into the holiness of Israel, the holy people of God, and ending with the death in the hope for the resurrection and a share in the world to come. The one thing that does not begin with "in the beginning" is holy Israel's life with God. Accordingly, what I want to know from the story of the beginning of the world is a different matter altogether.

You as a Catholic can understand that, because you affirm that Scripture is the gift of the church. First there was the church, with the Eucharist and the other sacraments. And the church before Scripture possessed and handed on traditions. Then, after three hundred years or more, came Scripture—the Bible of Christianity, made up of the New Testament and the Old Testament—as part of the heritage of the church, hence Scripture and tradition. But I think Protestants, with their reverence for Scripture and their insistence that all truth is verified by Scripture alone, without appeal to tradition, can understand my reading of Scripture as Torah, that is, in the already-present reality of the holy way of life of Judaism. Protestants too appeal to religious experience to which Scripture also attests; and that is to God in the here and now of direct encounter, not solely God mediated by Scripture. Well, Jews' direct encounter with God is through the Torah; that is where we meet God, by studying the words of the Torah.

So the story of creation is not merely a chapter in a book. It is a record of all of human existence as Israel understands it: everything in one thing. When I read any passage of Scripture, I read the whole of Judaism writ small. So here too, in reading the story of the celebration of creation in the Sabbath day, I find the entire history of holy Israel within humankind. That means, specifically, to read the creation story in terms of, first, righteous and wicked men, generation by generation. Then come the conventional "four monarchies," that is, four periods in the history of Israel, Babylonia, Media, Greece, and Rome, leading to the coming of the Messiah. This has its parallel, finally, in the three ages in the history of the Temple, building, destruction, and, when the Messiah comes, rebuilding. And how does Adam—that is to say all humanity, us included—fit into all this?

5

GREELEY

The Lovers in the Song—Creation

The Egyptian love songs and the Song of Songs are first of all poems about love. The poets reveal their views of love not by speaking about love in the abstract, but by portraying people in love, making lovers' words reveal lovers' thoughts, feelings, and deeds. The poets invite us to observe lovers, to smile at them, to empathize with them, to sympathize with them, to recall in their adolescent pains our own, to share their desires, to enjoy in fantasy their pleasures. The poets show us young lovers flush with desire and awash in waves of new and overwhelming emotions. We watch lovers sailing the Nile to a rendezvous, walking hand and hand through gardens, lying together in garden bowers. We come upon them sitting at home aching for the one they love, standing outside the loved one's door and pouting, swimming across rivers, running frantically through the streets at night, kissing, fondling, hugging and snuggling face to face and face to breast, and—no less erotically—telling each other's praises in sensuous similes.

—Michael V. Fox, *The Song of Songs and the Ancient Egyptian Love Poetry*

How is one to understand the Song in terms of human and divine love? It is we moderns who have difficulty with this question. But the bible suggests that these loves are united and not to be separated. Israel, it is true, understood that YHWH was beyond sex. He had no consort; and the fertility rites were not the proper mode of worship for him. Yet the union between man and woman became a primary symbol for the expression of the relationship of the Lord to His People. The covenant between God and His People is consistently portrayed as a marriage.

—Roland Murphy, O. Carm.

Whatever answer one may give to the problem . . . One cannot be unaware of the fact that even if it is only an anthology, in the vision of the final redactor (unless he be taken for a simpleton), Canticles does not end: true love is always a quest of one person for another; it is a constant straining toward the unity of the one who is preeminently the beloved with the companion who is the unique one.

—Daniel Lys, *Le Plus Beau Chant de la Creation*, trans. Michael V. Fox

The Bible is a love story, often a romance. It is a story of an intimate relation between God and his people and then a story of an intimate relation between God and the individual person.

Often this intimacy is pictured as romantic love, a marriage, even a love affair between God and us.

30

Love is not the dominant theme of the Bible in the sense that there are no other emotions in it. The books were not written or collected to fit any single theme. There are more than six thousand incidents of violence in the Scriptures. Love is often overwhelmed by ambition, anger, and hatred.

But the Bible is nevertheless about God and his people and, more precisely, about the persistence in God's relationship with his people. If love is not its dominant theme, it is nonetheless the theme that explains what the Bible is all about.

At the beginning of chapter 20 of Exodus, as God is portrayed as issuing the Ten Commandments, he says, "I am YHWH YOUR God. . . . I am a passionate God. I will not have you whoring with false gods."

The word that is here translated as "passionate" is used elsewhere in the Scripture to describe a bridegroom "panting" for his bride. The passage might just as well read "I am an aroused God."

The exact formulation of this prelude to the Decalogue came long after the experience of the Hebrew people at Sinai. However, the Scripture scholars assure us that the sentiment, the emotion, the "feel" of that event is faithfully recorded. The disparate collection of tribes who felt themselves molded into a people by God remembered that experience as the work of a God who *desired* them the way a man desires a woman (and vice versa, we would add now).

It is a powerful metaphor, one that would shock the prudish for a couple of millennia and one that translators of the Bible would tone down as best they could. While the Hebrews did not have the sexual hang-ups that Platonistic philosophy would introduce into Christianity, it was not a metaphor that they would easily use, especially since they were fighting the fertility cults that worshiped fertility itself as a God.

They described their Sinai experience as being like that of a woman obviously and implacably desired by a man because it was the only way to depict the overwhelming emotion that surged back and forth between them and their God. They felt flattered, frightened, delighted, embarrassed. He seemed demanding, tender, enraptured, pleasingly violent.

An eager bride and a groom who was not to be denied.

Unfortunately, the emphasis in the education most of us received about the Ten Commandments was on the "false gods" and not on the passion that excluded the false gods. Indeed, the word we translate as "passionate" was rendered as "jealous," a word that puzzled many grammar school children of my era: jealousy, we knew, was not a nice emotion; how come God felt it?

But the point was not the possessiveness of God. Rather, the meaning was that just as in the delights of the preliminaries to lovemaking there can be no thought of anyone else, so the love between God and his people excludes the possibility of infidelity.

The people would nonetheless be unfaithful and thus false to the experience and actions of their original union with their lover. But the lover was implacable and would not be turned away even by infidelity. We see here the first hint of a God who is madly in love, a theme that would be developed and expanded in the parables of Jesus. Human lovers would eventually be turned off by a bride who repeatedly gave herself to other lovers. But God is so possessed by desire for his people that he will never back off on his commitment. His passion has driven him to behave with an indulgence that would be considered mad in human lovers.

God is aroused to a frenzy of love by his people, and he will not be denied this fury to possess them, no matter how unfaithful they might be.

These are not interpretations forced on the passage as an afterthought; they are rather meanings that lurk in the metaphor itself. This sense has often been missed because teachers and translators are frightened by the sexual ambience; it is a heavy price to pay for squeamish prudery because we lose the feeling of being the object of passionate tenderness that shaped the experience of the Hebrew people at Sinai.

This feeling is the theme of a whole book of the Hebrew Bible, the Song of Songs (also called the Song of Solomon and the Canticle of Canticles). The Song (as I shall call it) is on the face of it an account of a passionate love affair, a richly detailed exploration of the erotic imaginations of a young man and a young woman who are mindlessly in love.

It is worth noting in passing that although they clearly engage in sexual intercourse (the key enters the door in the poetic description), they are apparently not yet married, although they are in their own hearts pledged irrevocably to one another. The point is not that premarital sex is acceptable but that sex makes marriage sacred rather than, as we were often taught, the reverse.

Despite metaphors that are hard for us to understand and terrible (and sometimes dishonest) translations, the erotic nature of the Song is patent. Many have wondered what it is doing in the Bible. Some Christians have simply dropped it from the Bible. Others, especially Catholics, cope with its eroticism by simply ignoring the existence of the Song.

For much of Jewish and Christian history, the problem of the blatant eroticism of the Song has been dealt with by allegorizing it. The poetry is not, according to this approach, about human lovers at all. It is about the love between God and his people or the love between God and the soul. There is no human passion in it at all.

While this interpretation was dominant for a thousand years and more, it is not easy to sustain, because the love described in the Song is so obviously and in such rich detail the love between man and woman. Contemporary Scripture scholarship has routed the allegorical interpretation: the Song is secular love poetry, a collection of love songs gathered around a single theme (about which theme there is much debate). It was probably drafted in its final version (from preexisting materials) rather late in the years before the beginning of the Common Era by a woman, perhaps for a funeral service, but more likely for a wedding celebration.

It was placed in the canon of the Scriptures because it was so well loved by the Israelite people that the Scriptures seemed a good place to preserve it. While some scholars believe that there was nothing religious about it originally, others suggest (more probably, it seems to me) that the author (or the editor) was conscious of its religious implications—that human love was a metaphor for divine love and, as Saint Paul would later insist, vice versa.

Thus at the end of the Song the woman describes her love for her man as being like "YHWH's flame": the love between them will not only be as strong as death; it will be as strong as YHWH's love for his people.

This is a bold metaphor. In religious symbolism flame is the male organ, water the female organ. The author of the Song seems fully aware of this meaning. But she dares, nonetheless, to describe her heroine not only as speaking of the (always potent) male organ of YHWH but, as it were, appropriating it for herself. She presents her woman as saying, in effect, I can be as tough and aggressive in maintaining our romance as you can and even as tough and aggressive as YHWH himself.

The Song then can be seen as a reverse metaphor or, perhaps better, a double metaphor. Not only is God's love like human love, the author is implying, but granted that, our love, yours and mine, is like God's love. Once God had approved of the metaphor, human love must be seen as sanctified because it is like God's love. The author feels that in the context in which she is writing, she can assume that to be true and indicate it with only one allusion. In her world secular poetry and sacred poetry cannot be sharply divided because the secular is an image of the sacred. The Song then can be interpreted as implicitly religious from beginning to end precisely because of the metaphorical relations between the two loves. But unlike the allegorical interpretation, the metaphorical interpretation does not interpret away human love. Rather, it sacramentalizes it: human love is a hint of divine love, and divine love is a hint of what human love can really be.

Religious teachers and educators, nonetheless, shy away from the Song. It is too vivid, too graphic, too sensual. It might give people dirty thoughts.

So we pretend that it doesn't exist, or translate it so that its sensuality is suppressed.

Thus when the man is glorying in the naked beauty of his beloved, he presents a detailed description of her body from the feet up. Between her thighs he describes an area of her anatomy surrounded by wheat and lilies that the translators describe as her "navel." An edition of the Catholic Confraternity Bible (issued before the Vatican Council) footnotes this passage with the comment that wheat and lilies are fertility symbols, so naturally they are associated with the parts of the body involved in reproduction.

The navel?

Someone has to be kidding!

The Good News Bible, perhaps because of its fundamentalist orientation, is honest. It uses the word "cleft." Professor Holt is more medical; he translated it as "vulva." Father Roland Murphy believes that the proper word is "valley"—a euphemistic metaphor, in keeping with pubic hair being described as wheat and lilies, which is, in fact, more erotic than the clinical terms.

Why would translators try to hide the fact that the woman has reproductive organs and that her man (as the woman author imagines him) delights in the beauty of those organs?

God obviously must be guilty of an artistic error for providing women with such organs and men with the feeling that these organs are beautiful.

The same antisexual sensibility has torn from the Catholic Easter Vigil service the obvious sexual interpretation of the plunging of the candle into the baptismal waters. Now the candle "may" be placed in the water. And it is no longer said, "May this candle fecundate these waters."

Such "cleaning up" of the tradition, I am told by Scripture scholars, abounds. This chapter is not the place to detail this bowdlerization or to refute it. Indeed, it ought not to be necessary to argue with those who engage in such sick practices. The Bible is the word of God (however one may choose to define revelation). Playing games with the word of God in the name of not shocking "the people" is dangerously close to blasphemy. It reveals not the sexual inhibitions of "the people" but rather the problems of sexual identity that beset the game players and the environment in which they work. Those who were educated in such an environment and are so emotionally attached to it that they cannot reconsider it will be quite incapable of accepting the interpretation I am making of the Scripture. I do not propose to argue with them. For those who are shocked at the word "breast" and appalled at the metaphor "valley," no argument is possible. I merely assert that their prudery drains the Scripture of much of its meaning.

The Song is uninhibited (one might almost say wanton) erotic poetry, written by a quite uninhibited (one might almost say wanton) woman who finds the metaphorical relationship between the two loves reason to delight even more joyously in human love.

The woman is by far the more interesting of the two actors in the story. Her response to the lover is so rich in its detail that scholars conclude that it was written either by a woman or by someone who had a remarkable insight into the psychology of a woman. While either of the lovers can be interpreted as representing God, the woman is the more implacable, the more determined, even the more passionate of the two.

She is, indeed, fragile, tearful, and, at times, sulky. But she is also determined, brave, aggressive, and wantonly seductive. She pouts that she has taken off her nightgown and her lover has yet to appear. Surely, she says, she cannot be expected to put it back on. She has set her cap for this gorgeous young man and is determined to have him for her own, no matter what she has to do to get him, including rushing about the town in her deshabille at night. He has no more chance of getting away from her than we have of escaping from YHWH.

The portrait of the young man convinces me that the author of the Song is a woman. Only in stories written by women are men treated as likable but irresponsible little boys. The young man in the Song is charming, very attractive, and a tender and passionate lover. But he disappears without warning and without any consideration of what his absence may mean to his beloved.

How like a man!

(If a man wants to know how women really think about us, he should read half a dozen contemporary novels by women. Men, as a woman political scientist remarked to me, are conceited vulnerability.)

Moreover, the story traced in the Song suggests that the young woman took serious risks in search of her lover, suffering not only the taunts of her family but abuse by the police, abuse from which she was rescued probably by her family and not by the absent lover.

The story of this love affair is like the story of most young loves—ups and downs, highs and lows, dreamy passion and angry hurt. It works out in the end—their commitment is final and definitive, as strong as death, as powerful as YHWH's fire. The same rhythms that manifested themselves in their premarital love will be present in their continued postmarital romance. Presumably the author knows that and realizes that, nonetheless, love is still strong as death.

The subtle psychology of the relationship between the sexes suggested by the Song is proof that our religious ancestors were not naive or unsophisticated about human love. Moreover, their recognition, in the context

of the metaphor of the two loves, of patterns of ebb and flow, of tenderness and misunderstanding, in love indicates that they saw no reason to
pretend that there were not parallel patterns in the relationships between
humans and God.

The Song, then, can be described as an exuberant romp through the
metaphor of the two loves. One can easily speculate that the author is
recalling her own youthful romance and that, with an imagination like hers,
she must have been a pure delight to her man in bed, if a stern taskmaster in
the other dimensions of their life.

Which, it might be said, is what being a wife and having a wife is mostly
all about.

The basic symbol of the Song is taken from the pagan symbolism of fire
and water, the plunging of the male fire into the female water in chapter 4
and the reenactment of that union at the end in which the woman becomes
the fire and the man the water—standing the pagan image on its head. The
metaphor of human and divine love, a unique Hebrew image, is combined
with pagan symbolism to cause power and depth and surprise: there is
nothing in the relationship between man and woman that does not tell us
something about the love story between God and humans and nothing in
the tumultuous passion between man and woman that is not illumined by
the love of God for us.

Did the author of the Song perceive these meanings? Did she intend this
interpretation?

She was a poet and a storyteller, manipulating with practiced craft and
profound insight the symbols and the metaphors of her belief system. She
need not have understood explicitly all the implications of her artistic
vision. (An author rarely does.) But it is not illegitimate to find these
meanings in her work. As the scholars would say, such meanings are "in
front of the text," They mean that they are not extrinsic to the metaphor the author is using, not added arbitrarily from the outside, but
rather lurk in the images and pictures and emotions that possess the
author.

We can draw a number of important conclusions from the Song:

1. Our religious ancestors were not prudes. To the extent that we are (and
   our treatment of the Song even today suggests that we still very much
   are prudes), they were more mature than we.
2. They could be exuberantly erotic within the context of the metaphor of
   the two loves and feel little shame or embarrassment and no sense that
   they were doing violence to God.

3. The context of their faith and of the metaphor made their erotic poetry different from that of their neighbors. Neither the Babylonian nor the Egyptian love poems, similar to the Hebrew poems in many ways, imply the depth of feeling or the dogged persistence of love that permeates the Song. The metaphor of divine and human love had already shaped human erotic love among the Hebrews.

4. For all the patriarchal tone of the Hebrew laws and their deep and nasty chauvinism, the relationship between man and woman in the Hebrew culture could be and sometimes was quite different from the theory.

5. The Song is written in perhaps conscious counterpoint to Genesis. The love story is an idyll acted out in Paradise. But it differs from the Genesis story in two important respects. In the Song love triumphs over sin—however transiently and imperfectly. Moreover, in the Song the generosity and the self-sacrifice of the young woman purchases happiness, however incomplete, for both the lovers. The theme of "salvation" through generosity and self-giving to be repeated in the Jesus experience is already present in the never-ending story. The bride is a Jesus figure.

6. Finally, in the Song we find a perspective on the religious life of the ordinary Hebrews that is only hinted at in most of the rest of the Bible. The winners write the history books. The prophets were the winners, so they shape our view of the history of Israel. There is nothing incompatible between the exuberant celebration of the Song and the stern moralism of the prophets. But from the latter we would never know the former if it were not for the Song.

For all these reasons the Song is one of the most important books in the Bible and not, as it has inexplicably been regarded, simply an odd and embarrassing bit of love poetry. Its inclusion can only be seen as the result of a providential intervention designed to illuminate the rest of the Scriptures with a controlling metaphor of enormous importance. The attempts of a couple of thousand years to translate or to interpret away the imagery of the Song, to in effect destroy the metaphor, are not only misguided; they are dangerous violations of the intent of God. One cannot understand the Bible without understanding the Song.

When I try to make this argument in other contexts I encounter embarrassed outrage from conservative Catholics and sneering contempt from secularists. For the latter there is less excuse. Scholarly work on the Bible is available to them; by their own standards they should take such work seriously. But in addition to their own personal sexual hang-ups, such secularists cannot tolerate that religion, which they have written off, can enjoy such powerful and passionate metaphors.

To both sets of objections I respond that, whether they like it or not, this is what, according to the best scholars of our time, the text says.

I do not expect any of the religious traditions to embrace such interpretation any time in the near future. So much the worse for them.

The author of the Song may have more in common with us than she does with men and women of the thousands of years between her time and our own. Like us, she can talk freely about sex (and use beautiful imagery of which we are not capable). Unlike us she seems more relaxed, more exuberant, more joyous about sexuality than we are able to be.

We have a lot to learn from her.

In an effort to make the Song available for contemporary readers, I have attempted a paraphrase. I have used English poetic forms, rhyme and rhythms, and tried to find parallel metaphors for those that are not part of our world. I am not a scholar of scriptural languages, but I have asked a number of those who are to assure me that there is nothing in this paraphrase that does violence to the intent and the spirit of the Song.

First Song

Beloved:

A captive enslaved by your amorous lips,
A prisoner of your sweet embrace,
Drawn after you in passionate chase,
Helplessly bound by your searing kiss,
Dark is my skin, I know, and slim my waist,
My breasts, dear brothers tell me, inferior.
Yet I undress swiftly when you draw near.
Of my prudish modesty you see no trace.
I am yours, my love, for what I am worth,
Play with me, I beg, however you will,
Fondle me, use me till your pleasure is filled.
I live only for your delight and mirth.

Lover:

But I am the one enraptured as slave,
Captured completely by your form and face.
Chained forever to your numinous grace
O mistress of love whose favor I crave.
Firm and full your bosom, an exquisite gift,
Your slender legs lead to a perfumed cave.
I am, that I might draw near that sacred nave,
A meek servant to your slightest wish.

Duet:

Lay your head against my breast,
Soothe me with your azure eyes,
Heal me with you gracious thighs,
In my arms forever nest.
You are as soft as raisin cake,
You're as warm, dear, as new-baked bread.
You are a blossoming apple grove,
And you a sandalwood treasure trove.
Drink me like expensive wine!
Consume me, I am only thine!
Beneath this star-dense sky,
Lie quiet now on my chest.
Then again, after a little rest,
Drown me in your happy sighs.
My wondrous love, softly sleep.
Your gift tonight I'll always keep.

Song 1:1–2:7

Second Song

Beloved:

On my garden path a hint of eager feet,
At the window ardent eyes strive to see,
Then my lover's arms reach out strong for me,
My sick and defeated heart begins to beat!

Lover:

Rise up, dear one, the snow is gone,
We are drenched in lemon-scented dew,
The lake again is melted blue,
See, flowers bloom and green the lawn.
Time, I insist, to play and sing and dance,
Let me see once more your laughing face
As together we run our ardent race
And, with darkness gone, we renew romance.

Beloved:

My lover left, quiet with the morning breeze,
Back to the city's busy squares and streets.
On my bed I shivered in icy air,
Unclothed, frightened, alone—what if I freeze!
All day, I pined, I missed him so,
At dusk wanton and wild, I ran to the gate.
"Welcome, my darling, I could hardly wait,
I've caught you now, I'll never let you go!"

Lover:

Enough of your running, my darling, my dove,
Ah, off with your dress, and lie at my side,
My woman now I claim you, and my bride,
In triumph I possess you and seal our love!

Song 2:8–3:5

Third Song

Beloved:

On my bed in the dark of night
I took off my gown for the one I love.
I prayed to God and the saints above,
But he did not come, my life, my light.
So I sought him everywhere in town,
In alleys, streets, and decrepit bars.
Recklessly I begged the unfeeling guards,
"Tell me, my love, where he is to be found?"
I lost all I had, freedom, hope, and fame,
Those who were my friends cruelly pulled me down.
I still wait for him, cold and harshly bound,
Stripped, humiliated, and ashamed.

I dream of him.

Lover:

In the silent, windless heat of day,
Wine sparkling in our goblets, you and me,
Two alone under the eucalyptus tree,
Still your lips, listen to what I must say.
While we recline in our aromatic bath
And my teeth your taut nipples gently bite
Let me sing, dearest, of your blazing lights:
As my fingers roam your fertile garden paths:
Your lips are chocolate, dark for a feast,
Your mouth is as sweet as honey and milk,
Your unblemished skin the finest silk,
Your clear eyes sunrise shining in the east.
Your hair is as smooth as lace.
Your complexion glows like the rising moon,
Irish linen your flesh and roses in bloom.
An artist's miracle your lovely face.
Your ivory throat, lithe, supple, and clean,

Your elegant shoulders shapely and bare,
Invite me to a bed warmed by loving care,
A house of grace where I'll be free to dream.
I take your round breasts, one prize in each hand,
Generous and rich, thick cream in my mouth—
I suckle and drain them, thirsty after drought.
Your hips sweet flowing hills round for my hand,
Your belly a peach sugared to my tongue.
Your flanks burnt cinnamon tart to my teeth
Then a mountain forest, fragrant and neat,
Whose depths I'll explore before I am done.

Beloved:

I am deprived of my sense, dear poet mine,
Swept away by the winds, the song in your voice.
Here are my poor favors, what is your choice?
I am your harvest, darling . . . reap me and dine!

Song 3:6–5:1

Fourth Song

Beloved:

My lover came to unlock the secret door—
Bathed, fragrant, and unveiled I waited on my bed—
"Unfold, O Perfect One," he gently said,
Hand in the keyhole, his forever more!
I was powerless, mere putty to shape,
He opened me up, skilled master of the game,
Filled me with his incandescent flame,
And lighted a fire I'll never escape

Then, my turn to attack, I disrobed my man.
I devoured him, uncovered, full length,
Explored, then reveled in his youthful strength
And traced his wonders with my eager hand.
I tickled and tormented my poor darling one,
Embarrassed him, aroused him, drove him quite mad.
"Don't squirm, dearest, you're cute when you're nude;
I'll stop teasing you only when I'm done.
You are clever, good, and kind, I admit,
And also belly, arms, and loins rock hard,
A tree, a mountain, a fiercely loving guard,
In my body and plans I think you might fit.

"Black hair, blue eyes, tawny sunrise skin,
Demanding hands, determined virile legs—
And also an appealing, trustful babe,
Savage chest outside, wounded heart within.
Lie here quietly on my garden couch,
I'll encircle you with affection and love.
My lilies and spices fit you like a glove,
It's fun to torment you with my giddy touch.
On you pleasured smile I complacently gaze,
Oh! . . . Stay here, my dear, be with me all my days!"

Song 5:2–6:3

Fifth Song

There are many girls, but you're my special one,
Fierce and passionate woman, kindest friend,
Without you my hours never seem to end,
Where have you been, my sun, my moon, my dawn?
There's no escape now, I'm holding you down.
Do not pretend that you want to flee,
Tremble at my touch, you belong to me,
Be still while I slip off your frilly gown!
You were sculpted an elegant work of art,
Dark hair falling on snow-white chest,
Honeydew, your high and graceful breasts,
One taste enough to break my heart.
In the curve of your wondrous thighs:
A deep valley flowing with perfumed wine
Around which wheat and blooming lilies twine
Whose sweetness invites my enchanted eyes.
I will seize the fruit, press them to my teeth.
Then, famished, impassioned, and lightly deft,
Explore the valley's tantalizing cleft
And your delicacy savor, drink, and eat!

Beloved:

I will be dry white wine to slake your thirst
And a tasty morsel to tease your mouth.
A trembling prize from the misty south,
A plundered vessel for your nightly feast,
A submissive trophy you can carry off
To a cool treasure house in your magic lands,
A most willing slave to your artful hands,
A total gift, passionate, loving, soft!

Lover:

She sleeps now, my innocent little child,
Wake her not, good winds, adore her radiant smile!

Song 6:4–8:4

Sixth Song

Beloved:

Let my breasts be towers for you to scale
Above my belly's captured ivory wall
Climb them again each day, my love, my all
As I your victory forever hail.
Let my face be branded on your heart
That you may feel my heat in every breath,
My love, implacable as death,
My passion like YHWH's raging fire,
Impervious to the storm and flood
Of deadly friction and foolish strife
And the insidious anxieties of life,
A burning need forever in my blood.

Song 8:5–8

6

NEUSNER

God and Israel—the Lovers

Father Greeley's understanding of Scripture runs parallel to the reading of the Song of Songs by the great sages of the Torah, who read every verse as a metaphor for a relationship, either of God's love for Israel or of Israel's love for God. In a great compilation, Song of Songs Rabbah, they read the Song of Songs as a metaphor, which is to say a picture of an "is " concerning an "as if"; this *is* like that, *as if* it were that. We understand the "that" better because we can envisage it through the "this is." The *is* of the metaphor is the love of man for woman and woman for man, the yearning, the passion. The *as if* is the love of God for Israel and of Israel for God—the same yearning and passion. So far as our sages work out the meanings of the *is* in response to the messages of the *as if,* in these pages we see with great clarity the outer limits of their labor. For here the *is* is the love of man for woman and woman for man, and the *as if* is the love of God for Israel and Israel for God. But that is leaping from metaphor to metaphor, and that is precisely what our sages have done in reading the Song of Songs; like a hart, like a gazelle.

So real and concrete is that poetry that understanding its implicit meanings, identifying its hidden messages as an account of the lovers, God and Israel, and the urgency of their love for one another, these represent a triumph of the *as-if* mentality over the mentality of the merely *is*. But, we rapidly realize, the poem is the metaphor, the reality, the tangible and physical and material love of Israel for God and of God for Israel: the urgent, the never fully satisfied desire. Given the character of the Song of Songs, our sages' power to grasp its wholly other meanings and plausibly to state them attests to the full givenness of their affirmations of God and Israel as the principal figures in contention—as the lover and the beloved must always contend—in this world.

Let me give a concrete example of how our sages read the Song of Songs. The passage is Song 1:2, and it concerns the phrase "your love is better than wine." To our sages, the "wine" refers to the Torah, which is the supreme expression of God's love for Israel. Then the exposition follows:

"For your love is better than wine:"

Words of the Torah are compared to water, wine, oil, honey, and milk. To water: "Ho, everyone who thirsts come for water" (Is. 55:1).

Just as water is from one end of the world to the other, "To him who spread forth the earth above the waters" (Ps. 136:6), so the Torah is from one end of the world to the other, "The measure thereof is longer than the earth" (Job 11:9).

Just as water is life for the world, "A fountain of gardens, a well of living waters" (Song 4:15), so the Torah is life for the world, "For they are life to those who find them and health for all their flesh" (Prov. 4:22); "Come, buy and eat" (Is. 55:1).

Just as water is from heaven, "At the sound of his giving a multitude of waters in the heavens" (Jer. 10:13), so the Torah is from heaven, "I have talked with you from heaven" (Ex. 20:19).

Just as water [when it rains] is with loud thunder, "The voice of the Lord is upon the water" (Ps. 29:3), so the Torah is with loud thunder, "And it came to pass on the third day, when it was morning, that there were thunderings and lightnings" (Ex. 19:16).

Just as water restores the soul, "But God cleaves the hollow place which was in Levi and water came out, and when he had drunk, he revived" (Judges 15:19), so the Torah [restores the soul], "The Torah of the Lord is perfect, restoring the soul" (Ps. 19:8). . . .

Just as water leaves the height and flows to a low place, so the Torah leaves one who is arrogant on account of [his knowledge of] it and cleaves to one who is humble on account of [his knowledge of] it.

Just as water does not keep well in utensils of silver and gold but only in the most humble of utensils, so the Torah does not stay well except in the one who treats himself as a clay pot.

Just as with water, a great man is not ashamed to say to an unimportant person, "Give me a drink of water," so as to words of Torah, the great man is not ashamed to say to an unimportant person, "Teach me a chapter," or "a verse," or even "a single letter."

The same things that our sages say about the Torah, in comparing it to water, you can find said of Jesus as Christ in Christian faith. The Song then provides metaphors for love, each faith in its own context. In our context, it is God's love for Israel, expressed through the gift of the Torah.

That is what God has given to Israel, and it is Israel's praise of the gift of the Torah. How does God respond with a love song for Israel? In the following poem, on Song 1:15, "Behold, you are beautiful, my love, behold you are beautiful," our sages compose a hymn to Israel's holy life, as God sings that hymn:

"Behold, you are beautiful, my love; behold, you are beautiful; [your eyes are doves]:"

"Behold you are beautiful" in religious deeds,

"Behold you are beautiful" in acts of grace,

"Behold you are beautiful" in carrying out religious obligations of commission,

"Behold you are beautiful" in carrying out religious obligations of omission,

"Behold you are beautiful" in carrying out the religious duties of the home, in separating priestly ration and tithes,

"Behold you are beautiful" in carrying out the religious duties of the field, gleanings, forgotten sheaves, the corner of the field, poor person's tithe, and declaring the field ownerless.

"Behold you are beautiful" in observing the taboo against mixed species.

"Behold you are beautiful" in providing a linen cloak with woolen show-fringes.

"Behold you are beautiful" in [keeping the rules governing] planting,

"Behold you are beautiful" in keeping the taboo on uncircumcised produce,

"Behold you are beautiful" in keeping the laws on produce in the fourth year after the planting of an orchard,

"Behold you are beautiful" in circumcision,

"Behold you are beautiful" in trimming the wound,

"Behold you are beautiful" in reciting the Prayer,

"Behold you are beautiful" in reciting the Shema,

"Behold you are beautiful" in putting a mezuzah on the doorpost of your house,

"Behold you are beautiful" in wearing phylacteries,

"Behold you are beautiful" in building the tabernacle for the Festival of Tabernacles,

"Behold you are beautiful" in taking the palm branch and etrog on the Festival of Tabernacles,

"Behold you are beautiful" in repentance,

"Behold you are beautiful" in good deeds,

"Behold you are beautiful" in this world,

"Behold you are beautiful" in the world to come.

The Torah contains commandments—the recitation of the Shema ("Hear O Israel, the Lord is our God, the one God"), building a tabernacle (sukkah) on the Festival of Tabernacles, carrying out in loyalty and obedience the religious deeds of the Torah. And these, we now see, are the marks of beauty and grace that adorn Israel; so God says in this poem.

The Song of Songs is the holiest book of the Torah; so our sages taught, and now we see why. It is the book of the Torah in which the private and personal is set forth in metaphors that are private and personal, the feelings of love, the sentiments of affection, the powerful emotions of passion that join God to Israel and Israel to God. These are now set forth in the only way in which we can fully grasp them, in terms of emotions we are going to recognize and feelings we are going to know. For our relationship to God, creator of heaven and earth, draws us into a world beyond this world. How are we to follow if we speak of things we have never known? In our quest for God without the Torah we strike out into the unknown, like blind people not able to imagine color, like deaf people not able to describe music. The Torah then reaches down into the world we do know to guide us into a world we do not know but must explore.

Now as I look back on Father Greeley's reading of the same Song, a reading I so admire that I included his translation-rendition of the Song of Songs in my translation of Song of Songs Rabbah, I find everything familiar but nothing quite the same. For he reads the Song in its own terms, but I read it in terms of the Torah. He reads it "out there," a representation of the generality of things. I read it "in here," an account of who we, Israel, are. We, Israel, and I, a rabbi in Israel, cannot read the written Torah/Old Testament with Christianity because I can read the written Torah only as part of the one whole Torah that, in the end, we must call "Judaism."

We who believe in the Torah and so practice Judaism (whether Orthodox or Reconstructionist or Reform or Conservative or Feminist or Hasidic or whatever other shaping we impart to the Torah) read the Torah, written and oral, as God's love letter to us in particular. How different a reading it is from Father Greeley's! And that underlines the point of difference between us, a point that will come out at the end of this book. I think religious people can talk together but religions cannot. And he thinks religions can communicate, too. I think his chapter and my chapter on the same book of the Bible prove I'm right, and I am sure he thinks the two chapters prove he's right, and, rabbi and priest pray together, may God grant we're both right.

7

NEUSNER

Let Us Make Man

And God said, "Let us make man in our image, after our likeness. They shall rule the fish of the sea, the birds of the sky, the cattle, the whole earth, and all the creeping things that creep on earth."

And God created man in His image, in the image of God He created him; male and female He created them.

God blessed them and God said to them,"Be fertile and increase, fill the earth and master it; and rule the fish of the sea, the birds of the sky, and all the living things that creep on the earth."

God said, "See, I give you every seed-bearing plant that is upon all the earth, and every tree that has seed-bearing fruit; they shall be yours for food. And to all the animals on land, to all the birds of the sky,

"And to everything that creeps on earth, in which there is the breath of life, [I give] all the green plants for food." And it was so.

And God saw all that He had made, and found it very good. And there was evening, and there was morning, the sixth day.

Genesis 1:26–31

Humanity in our image? Is the Bible joking? Father Andy, you and I share the single faith in humankind that this stunning passage sets forth: we are in God's image, after God's likeness. You find in Jesus Christ what it means to be in God's image, after God's likeness: God in the flesh. And I find in the picture of what it means to live a holy life, to be a holy human being, the image and the likeness. And you and I both find God in the face of the other—at least, we try. But then you and I have to face an incredulous world. And the world's unbelief is right: not much we can point to validates this faith of ours, we Jews, we Christians, that we are what God is like, only mortal.

But how are we like God, in the image, after the likeness? For we rebel and we sin. Midrash turns the Torah into an indictment. When we think of how Moses broke the tablets of the Ten Commandments, when you think of how Jesus Christ was crucified, you and I realize that is the only way revelation—Torah—can come to us: as a challenge to what we are.

So "Let us make man in our image, after our likeness"—indeed, indeed.

The right question, in response to our dreadful century, the twentieth, is:

Adam, *what* are you? For what has Adam done! Now, finally, we have seen it all, we who have survived this century of factories constructed to produce death, of governments instituted to murder their populations, of a million dead in a single battle of a single war, and of six million dead by reason of their birth alone. And we, Israel, ask and have the right to ask, no more, no less, than do Armenians and Cambodians and Ukrainians and all the citizen-victims of their own governments: who or, better, what is this thing, this monster that God has made and set in creation? No question presses more urgently; none proves more critical to sentient life. And that is the question that the Bible answers in the story of beginnings.

And what the Bible says is that humankind is like God: "in our image and likeness," "And God created man in His image, in the image of God He created him; male and female He created them." But the Bible also contains the painful words "I will blot out from the earth the men whom I created—men together with beasts, creeping things, and birds of the sky; for I regret that I made them" (Gen. 6:7). So let us contemplate humankind on high, in the moment of creation, before Eden and the fall from grace, before the awful judgment, "I regret that I made them." So the story of humankind, of God's perspective upon Adam and Eve, begins, but does not end, with Scripture's account of creation and of Eden.

And that means what does it mean to be "like God," in God's image, after God's likeness? And where shall we find humankind who are in the image and after the likeness of God? The Torah contains God's picture of humankind: God's image of humanity, as much as of humanity in God's image. And what a sad story, for the tragic hero of the Torah is none other than God: God in search of a humanity worthy of being in God's image and after God's likeness. These questions trouble us. And they also bothered the rabbis of Judaism, and, quite naturally, they sorted them out in an orderly way. So we too shall follow the sages—we call them "our sages of blessed memory," and we can share them as "our sages"—as they work their path through the written Torah's facts of human life.

First of all, they wondered, does that mean both man and woman are like God? Indeed so, God is both male and female, that is to say "androgynous." That is stated explicitly by R. Jeremiah b. Eleazer, who says: "When the Holy One, blessed be he, came to create the first man, he made him androgynous, as it is said, 'Male and female created he them and called their name man' (Gen. 5:2)." So God's image is male and female. The Torah teaches that humanity is one in God: male and female both. This nonsense that God is male or that it is more normal to be male than to be female because God is male has no roots in the Torah, even though, in today's world, people think that "orthodox" (meaning, true-to-the-faith) Judaism holds just that view. But back to the main point.

If the scriptural passage tells us about God, does that mean that from the image and likeness of humankind we discern the image and likeness of God? The answer is a resounding yes, and that forms the principal reading of the creation of Adam and Eve that I derive from the Torah: we are in the image and after the likeness of God, and, it must follow, when we see one another rightly we see God. This radical reading of Scripture scarcely conforms to the perceptions our century provides to us, but it is the point of emphasis and insistence. The following passage expresses the matter with great force:

> Said R. Hoshiah, "When the Holy One, blessed be he, came to create the first man, the ministering angels mistook him [for God, since man was in God's image] and wanted to say before him, 'Holy, [holy, holy is the Lord of hosts].'
>
> "To what may the matter be compared? To the case of a king and a governor who were set in a chariot, and the provincials wanted to greet the king, 'Sovereign!' But they did not know which one of them was which. What did the king do? He turned the governor out and put him away from the chariot, so that people would know who was king.
>
> "So too when the Holy One, blessed be he, created the first man, the angels mistook him [for God]. What did the Holy One, blessed be he, do? He put him to sleep, so everyone knew that he was a mere man.
>
> "That is in line with the following verse of Scripture: 'Cease you from man, in whose nostrils is a breath, for how little is he to be accounted' (Is. 2:22)."

I find this reading of the Torah simply stunning. The angels could not tell the difference between God and humankind! Does that mean that God can become incarnate? I think it does. Does it mean that I should regard Jesus Christ as God incarnate? Yes, but. But not uniquely so. Jesus is God incarnate just the way you and I are, or can be, God incarnate. You can claim that Jesus Christ is the best incarnation possible, and I am not so sure that I would argue you're wrong (for reasons I'll tell you, from a very personal point of view, when later on I talk about Jesus). But when you enter the claim of "uniqueness," we have to part company. For, we see in the oral Torah, to me incarnation means all of us can be, some of us may be, but none of us alone is "like God."

But back to the passage at hand. Since man—Adam and Eve together— is in God's image, the angels did not know man from God. Only that man

[margin note: Jesus and we as God incarnate]

sleeps distinguishes man from God. I cannot imagine a more daring affirmation of humanity. Accordingly, "in our image" yields the view that the complete image of man is attained in a divine union between man and woman, and, further, the syllogism that what makes man different from God is that man sleeps and God does not sleep.

What exactly does God look like? And, if in God's image and after God's likeness, then who in particular is the human being who is like God, that, through that person, we may know God? Judaism answers that question in this way:

> The Holy One, who is blessed, appeared to them at the sea like a heroic soldier, doing battle, appeared to them at Sinai like a teacher, teaching the repetition [of traditions], appeared to them in the time of Daniel like a sage, teaching Torah, appeared to them in the time of Solomon like a lover . . .

This same matter occurs in connection with the Ten Commandments, which begin with God's self-identification: "I am the Lord your God." So I did not exaggerate or misrepresent when I told you that for me God is incarnate in us all: in God's image, after God's likeness. But why? That is, how come God introduces matters in that way?

> "I am the Lord your God:"
>
> Why is this stated? Since when he appeared at the sea, it was in the form of a mighty soldier making war, as it is said, "The Lord is a man of war" (Ex. 15:3),
>
> and when he appeared to them at Sinai, it was as an elder, full of mercy , as it is said, "And they saw the God of Israel: (Ex. 24:10),
>
> and when they were redeemed, what does Scripture say? "And the like of the very heaven for clearness" (Ex. 24:10); "I beheld until thrones were placed and one that was ancient of days sat" (Dan. 7:9); "A fiery stream issued" (Dan. 7:10),
>
> [so God took on many forms.] It was, therefore, not to provide the nations of the world with an occasion to claim that there are two dominions in heaven,
>
> that Scripture says, "I am the Lord your God [who brought you up out of the land of Egypt, out of the house of bondage]:"
>
> [This then bears the message:] "I am the one in Egypt, I am the one at the sea, I am the one at Sinai; I am the one in the past and I am the one in the age to come, the one in this age is the one in the world to come: "See now that I, even I, am he" (Dt. 32:39); "Even to old age I am the same" (Is. 46:4); "Thus says the Lord, the king of Israel and his redeemer, the Lord of hosts: 'I am the first and I am the last' " (Is. 44:6); "Who has wrought and done it? He who called the generations from the beginning. I the Lord who am the first and with the last I am the same" (Is. 41:4).

When it comes to God, God is incarnate in the representation of God as teacher, warrior, lover of the congregation of Israel. Does this mean that God is everyone and everything? No, there is one and only one God. We are like God. We are incarnations of what God is like. But there is one that is unique, and that is God alone, God always, God everywhere:

> The Holy One, who is blessed, said to them, "You see me in many forms. But I am the same one who was at the sea, I am the same one who was at Sinai, I [anokhi] am the Lord your God who brought you out of the land of Egypt" (Ex. 20:2).

The qualification of the foregoing yields no difficulty. God appears in diverse models of incarnation. It is one and the same God.

I love these texts, and I love the ways in which these amazing, these radical rabbis are ready to read them. So bear with me while someone else says the same thing in his own way. I think you can find the patience because, after all, we're dealing with a reading of the Bible that you don't get every day, not at all, not at all:

> Said R. Hiyya the Elder, "It is because through every manner of deed and every condition he had appeared to them [that he made that statement, namely:]
>
> "he had appeared to them at the sea as a heroic soldier, carrying out battles in behalf of Israel,
>
> "he had appeared to them at Sinai in the form of a teacher who was teaching Torah and standing in awe,
>
> "he had appeared to them in the time of Daniel as an elder, teaching Torah, for it is appropriate for Torah to go forth from the mouth of sages,
>
> "he had appeared to them in the time of Solomon as a youth, in accord with the practices of that generation: His aspect is like Lebanon, young as the cedars (Song 5:15),
>
> "so at Sinai he appeared to them as a teacher, teaching Torah: I am the Lord your God who brought you out of the land of Egypt" (Ex. 20:2).

When portrayed as a warrior, teacher, sage, and lover, God is represented in incarnate form. Incarnation now is fully exposed, and an explicit and intentional statement of God in human form is set before us.

My God is not an abstract being, but some one, One, whom we can know and with whom we can identify and whom we can love. These are not the only passages in the writings of the sages of Judaism that maintain we look like God, therefore God looks like us. Quite to the contrary, the incarnation of God forms a constant theme and defines Judaism's theory of what humankind is. It is the single most profound and most elevated conception that I could hope to offer from Scripture. God can take the form of any one of us, however humble—and did and does just that.

Then back to where we started: what kind of thing is humankind, like God? For what kind of God can have made such a mess of something that started out so well, as humanity has made of this world that God created, sanctified, and blessed? The act of faith is not that God can take the form of humanity. It is that humanity is in God's image, after God's likeness. Does the oral Torah take account of that obstacle, that unconquerable mountain blocking the path of faith? Once more, is it possible that the Torah is making fun of us?

Consider, after all, the descendants that were going to come forth from this Adam and this Eve. The oral Torah claims that God did just that. So alongside the question is the answer: "in our image, after our likeness" encompasses Adam and Eve and their sin and all the sinful descendants of Adam and Eve, that is, all humanity. God had to decide whether it was worth making humanity "in our image" when humanity itself would corrupt the image of God engraved in the flesh of woman and man. Did God know? God knew, God decided, God affirmed:

> Said R. Berekhiah, "When God came to create the first man, he saw that both righteous and wicked descendants would come forth from him. He said, 'If I create him, wicked descendants will come forth from him. If I do not create him, how will the righteous descendants come forth from him?'
>
> "What did the Holy One, blessed be he, do? He disregarded the way of the wicked and joined to himself his quality of mercy and so created him.
>
> "That is in line with this verse of Scripture: 'For the Lord knows the way of the righteous, but the way of the wicked shall perish' (Ps. 1:6).
>
> "What is the sense of 'shall perish'? He destroyed it from before his presence and joined to himself the quality of mercy, and so created man."
>
> R. Hanina did not explain the cited verse in this way. Rather [he said], "When the Holy One, blessed be he, proposed to create the first man, he took counsel with the ministering angels.
>
> "He said to them, 'Shall we make man?' (Gen. 1:26).
>
> "They said to him, 'What will be his character?'
>
> "He said to them, 'Righteous descendants will come forth from him,' in line with this verse: 'For the Lord knows the way of the righteous' (Ps. 1:6), meaning, the Lord reported concerning the ways of the righteous to the ministering angels . . .
>
> " 'But the way of the wicked shall perish' (Ps. 1:6), for he destroyed it [to keep it away] from them.
>
> "He reported to them that righteous descendants would come forth from him, but he did not report to them that wicked descendants would come forth

from him. For if he had told them that wicked descendants would come forth from him, the attribute of justice would never have given permission for man to be created."

God's act of creation represented a demonstration of God's merciful and loving character. That is the critical proposition, against anyone who holds that the creator-God was evil. Quite to the contrary, God created human-kind as an act of love, fully recognizing the truth about the descendants of Adam and Eve.

There is another way to draw the same picture of a loving God, a God who in creating the world knew what was going to happen to God's own image in the world, what humanity would do to make that likeness into a caricature. That way is to make up a debate, a kind of dialogue:

> Said R. Simon, "When the Holy One, blessed be he, came to create the first man, the ministering angels formed parties and sects.
>
> "Some of them said, 'Let him be created,' and some of them said, 'Let him not be created.'
>
> "That is in line with the following verse of Scripture: 'Mercy and truth fought together, righteousness and peace warred with each other' (Ps. 85:11).
>
> "Mercy said, 'Let him be created, for he will perform acts of mercy.'
>
> "Truth said, 'Let him not be created, for he is a complete fake.'
>
> "Righteousness said, 'Let him be created, for he will perform acts of righteousness.'
>
> "Peace said, 'Let him not be created, for he is one mass of contention.'
>
> "What then did the Holy One, blessed be he, do? He took truth and threw it to the ground. The ministering angels then said before the Holy One, blessed be he, 'Master of the ages, how can you disgrace your seal [which is truth]? Let truth be raised up from the ground!'
>
> "That is in line with the following verse of Scripture: 'Let truth spring up from the earth' (Ps. 85:2)."

Creating man and woman "in our image," after our likeness, God ex-pressed special love for them. Then how account for the evil that humanity would do? Truth knew the truth all the time. God dismissed truth and acted in utter mercy. Then the twin traits of humankind—extraordinary capacity for mercy, unfathomed depths of evil—were known from the start. That's small comfort, but it does give us the important reassurance that there is rationality, a logic, that permits us to understand things. And that recalls creation, which is the Torah's way of saying things make sense. There was chaos; there is order. God created out of unformed void, bringing every-thing into its right place. And now, in the recognition that humankind would corrupt God's image but that God knew it right from the start, we find the same message: there is sense, order, in the chaos we see in the world.

You know, I wonder whether anything so challenges common sense as these radical claims for the world: sense, not nonsense, order, not chaos. Anyone can compile a big, fat telephone book of facts that contradict our shared faith.

And yet every time someone says, "Why me? Why here? Why now?" we hear the faith of the Torah: there is justice and a judge; there is reason, order, explanation. And deep in our hearts, in the very foundations of our being, we affirm meaning, order, sense: Why me? Because . . .

So what's the answer? God did right; we did wrong. We are in God's image. Look what we have done to ourselves! The Torah's picture of humanity invokes the matter of sin and death. And as soon as we call to mind sin, we think of Adam in the Garden of Eden, which is why that is going to be our next stop on our journey through the Torah. But here, even before we come to Adam, a rabbi tips us off:

> R. Tipdai in the name of R. Aha: "The Holy One, blessed be he, said, 'If I create him solely with traits of creatures of the upper world, he will live and never die, and if I do so solely with traits of creatures of the lower world, he will die and not live. Instead, I shall create him with traits of creatures of the upper world and with traits of creatures of the lower world.
>
> " 'If he sins, he will die, and if not, he will live.' "

Sin makes the difference, Humankind has traits of angels and traits of beasts. When they are righteous, their angelic and heavenly traits mark them as in God's image, and when they sin, then, not in the likeness and the image of God, they die. Whence sin? Why death? The story of humankind in Paradise, that is, Adam and Eve in the Garden of Eden, answers these questions.

8

NEUSNER

Adam, Where Are You?

The two of them were naked, the man and his wife, yet they felt no shame. Now the serpent was the shrewdest of all the wild beasts that the Lord God had made. He said to the woman, "Did God really say, 'You shall not eat of any tree of the garden'? "

The woman replied to the serpent, "We may eat of the fruit of the other trees of the garden. It is only about fruit of the tree in the middle of the garden that God said, 'You shall not eat of it or touch it, lest you die.' "

And the serpent said to the woman, "You are not going to die, but God knows that as soon as you eat of it your eyes will be opened and you will be like divine beings who know good and bad."

When the woman saw that the tree was good for eating and a delight to the eyes, and that the tree was so desirable as a source of wisdom, she took of its fruit and ate. She also gave some to her husband and he ate. Then the eyes of both of them were opened, and they perceived that they were naked; and they sewed together fig leaves and made themselves loin cloths.

They heard the sound of the Lord God moving about in the garden at the breezy time of day; and the man and his wife hid from the Lord God among the trees of the garden. The Lord God called out to the man and said to him, "Where are you?"

He replied, "I heard the sound of You in the garden, and I was afraid, because I was naked, so I hid."

Genesis 2:25, 3:1–10

What went wrong in Eden? It is a simple thing: the one thing God did not choose to shape "in our image, after our likeness" was the will of humanity. Notice, after all, the odd omission of incarnation: the sages never say we are like God in our hearts. The angels can't tell us apart from God, because we look alike. But that means only we are like God in form.

But what should make us like God is not only our form bur our inner being. God is free to choose, and so are we. Like a parent who raises children to be responsible in their choices and their actions, so God gave us freedom even to sin.

And that explains what happened in Eden. Because we are free to choose, we make wrong choices. So if we are not like God in our will and attitude and intentionality, that is because we are like God in our freedom to choose. God made us so that, like God, we can do what we want. But I

56

wonder—the Torah wonders—whether God knew just what that would mean. And the answer is, Yes and no. God asks, "Where are you?," so God didn't know. But God knows how we are like God: "knowing good and bad." We know the difference; we are free to choose.

And God cannot command choice and still accomplish the goal of creation: to make humanity in our image. God is free, and so are we. So God can command love, but if we do not obey, there is no love. We command our attitudes, our feelings, give or withhold our love, after all. So God commands, "You will love the Lord your God with all your heart, with all your soul, with all your might," as we say in the creed of Judaism, the Shema. But then we have the choice: to love or not to love is to be like God, knowing the difference between good and evil and choosing what we will.

I suppose that is why there have to be among us some who in soul and heart show what it is like to be like God. We call them "the thirty-six righteous," perfect in their righteousness. And you call him Jesus Christ. More like God? Surely in the one way that counts, which is willing obedience, a heart made of love.

From "in our image and likeness" to "Where are you?" how swiftly do the mighty fall, and what has happened to humankind? These questions in the language of the biblical story penetrate into the heart of life in our fading century. To read the story in any other way is to miss its message. And we who come to the end of an age and look backward find in the fall of Adam and Eve the story of ourselves and our own time: how rapidly has humankind fallen!

Here is the other half, then, of creation: fall from grace. And in this story I find the biblical equivalent to the twentieth century, with its challenge to the very conception that humanity possesses any worth at all, let alone forming the counterpart to none other than God on high. The way forward, from creation, led downward, from Heaven. The biblical story then takes up the progress of humanity from promise of creation to tragedy in the fall from Eden. Had the story stopped with creation, no one can have believed it. For, after all, it would have told the tale of the creation of perfection—humanity "in our image, after our likeness." And I don't think anyone believes that we are perfect. If you're going to tell the story of beginnings, with the premise that things can be explained and so make sense, you'd better not say we are like God and leave it at that.

But to say we are only Adam and Eve, disobedient and willful, craven and weak, hardly gains credence either. For we know full well not only our weakness, but also the glory and the wonder: giving, caring, courageously enduring—these too are ours. So the story cannot stop with our entering

Eden, and it also cannot conclude with our fall from there. So what's the point? Recognizing full well what humankind is, the Torah will begin to tell the story of what humankind can become. For creation failed but can be made to work. Humankind not only sinned, but also found its way back. The full promise of creation, not kept by Adam and Eve, would be kept. Without the story of the fall from Eden, the Torah would have presented us with an incredible picture: human perfection in the model of divine perfection. And who can have believed that, even in the best of times? But we do not live in the best of times.

The fall from grace, from Eden, affirms humanity's likeness to God. For, I remind you, the fall is explained in the thing that makes humankind what it is: its power to choose, freely, but also to bear responsibility for free choice. And that bears the heartening and hopeful message that we are free to choose life, too. There is no story more brutal in its truth, none more comforting in its message about who we are and where we are.

The Torah's story then focuses upon our power to decide, and that means to exercise free will: to hear commandments and to decide whether or not to obey them. Everything depends upon our own attitude, upon our heart and sentience and intellect and imagination: how we see things and, consequently, decide things. In terms of the story at hand, the infinite power of God confronts its limitation in the competing power of the human will: attitude and intention given the status of cosmic force, standing against God's power. God commands; humankind decides.

Then we by our disobedience to God's commandments sin and bring on evil. Now there are many ways in which disobedience takes place. One is to disobey what God demands; another is to disobey what God has not demanded, that is, to form an attitude of disobedience, whatever one has done. These two things add up to arrogance: not to obey or to pretend to a great obedience. And that is the Torah's main point: to be arrogant is to defy God, and that may be as much by obedience as by disobedience. I like to think that Jesus had that deeply Jewish message in mind when he criticized his confreres, the Pharisees, for a piety he found showy. Obedience must come from love, from reverence, but not from love of self and awe at one's own power—not at all, not at all.

So where do I find the arrogance? In the story of Eve's conversation with the snake we notice, for instance, that Eve does not say to the snake exactly what God has said to Adam and Eve. God has said not to eat the fruit. But there was no admonition not to touch it. Yet what does Eve say? "You shall not eat of it or touch it." Here is how sages point up the error of an excess of piety:

". . . of the fruit of the tree which is in the midst of the garden" (Gen. 3:3):

That is in line with this verse: "Add not to his words, lest he reprove you, and you be found a liar" (Prov. 30:6). [God had said nothing about not touching the tree, but the woman said they were not to eat of the fruit of the tree or even to touch it.]

R. Hiyya taught, "It is that one should not make the fence taller than the foundation, so that the fence will not fall down and wipe out the plants.

"So the Holy One, blessed be he, had said, 'For on the day on which you eat from it, you shall surely die' (Gen. 2:17). But that is not what she then said to the snake. Rather: 'God said, "You shall not eat from it and you shall not touch it."' When the snake saw that she was lying to him, he took her and pushed her against the tree. He said to her, 'Have you now died? Just as you did not die for touching it, so you will not die from eating it.'

"Rather: 'For God knows that when you eat of it, your eyes will be opened and you will be like God' (Gen. 3:5)."

See the discrepancy between God's instruction not to eat the fruit of the tree and the woman's report that God had forbidden even touching the tree. What is at stake in such a minor detail? It is what I said just now: the conception of the arrogance of humankind. The underlying motif is that it is arrogant for man to demand more than God had already laid down. The story is made to focus upon the dangers of human arrogance—here, even in a good cause.

What follows is yet another such statement, now that man should not compete with God in ruling over creation. The upshot was that Adam and Eve gained knowledge, but of what? It was that they had lost not innocence but access to God. The fall from grace is frequently identified with the discovery of our sexuality. But nothing could be further from the truth. What is gained is knowledge that they were naked, and what is lost is something else entirely, namely, closeness to God. That, at any rate, is what our sages find here when they comment on the clause: "And they knew that they were naked" (Gen. 3:7). They remark: "Even of the single religious duty that they had in hand they were now denuded." The word *naked* is associated with "being clothed by the merit accruing from the performance of religious duties."

You don't have to read too closely to notice another striking discrepancy. Eve added to what God had commanded. But God, on the other hand, seems to have forgotten altogether what was at stake. God had said, "If you eat the fruit, you die." But they ate the fruit. And they didn't die. Did God forget? No, that's hardly the point. A mark of the merciful love of God in relationship to humankind is that Adam and Eve did not die, though God had said that they would. How make sense of this? The angels thought that God had gone off to take the lives of Adam and Eve. But that is not exactly what happened.

> Said the Holy One, blessed be he, to them, "[He will die] but with the respite of a day [for the Hebrew translated 'in the cool of the day']. Lo, I shall provide him with the space of a day. So did I say to him, 'For on the day on which you will eat it, you will surely die' (Gen. 2:17).
>
> "But you do not know whether it is one day by my reckoning or one day by your reckoning.
>
> " 'Lo, I shall give him a day by my reckoning, which is a thousand years by your reckoning. So he will live for nine hundred and thirty years and leave seventy years for his children to live in their time.' [So God's statement that man would surely die if he ate the forbidden fruit in fact did come to fruition. Adam lived a period of 930 years, and each subsequent Adam gets seventy years.]"
>
> That is in line with this verse of Scripture: "The days of our years are threescore years and ten" (Ps. 90:10).

So much for humanity in general. This looks to me like one of those simple statements with many meanings that my original description of midrash promised. On the surface all we are doing is harmonizing details that don't match. But underneath—there we see the real message. God found excuses for not doing what God had said would happen. And that loving Mother-God rings true: threaten, but never do, at least, not exactly what you threaten. There is always room, with God, for second chances.

And following the Torah's story of humanity, that brings us to the formation of Israel, counterpart to Adam, humanity's second chance. That may sound pretty strange until you look again at the whole of the Torah and not one story at a time. And we surely cannot leave the story of the fall of humanity as though nothing happened thereafter. The story goes forward, leading from the fall downward, for ten awful generations, to Noah, and then upward, for ten hopeful generations, to Abraham. So the Torah prepares the way for the rebirth of humanity in Noah and the rise of humanity to Sinai through Israel. That is the way of midrash: making connections, drawing conclusions. And the connections are made when everything happens in each important passage: Eden, flood, Noah, Abraham, Sinai.

What really answers the question: "Adam, where are you?" It is not the tergiversation of Adam: "I heard the sound of You in the garden, and I was afraid, because I was naked, so I hid." That is really beside the point, because all Adam explains is why God has to ask, "Where are you?" He doesn't answer, "Here I am, over here." He answers, "I heard . . . I was afraid . . . I hid." Then who answers "Where are you?" It is the one who says, "Here I am." That is Abraham, Jacob, Moses: Israel. To put this together in the all at once and the here and now of the midrashic way of reading the Torah is easy. The answer to "Where are you?" is: Here I am, once in Eden, then wiped out by the flood, then from Noah through Abraham, Isaac, Jacob to Moses and Sinai. Where are you, humanity? En route—the Torah says—to Sinai. Eden is the tale of freedom exercised in the wrong way, Sinai freedom engraved on the tablets (as the play on words, *herut*, for "freedom," and *harut*, for "engraved," tells our sages). So what freedom means is freely to bring our heart to love God, in full responsibility to accept the Torah and its covenanted responsibilities. All of that in this little, awful story? Well, yes, it's all there.

But to find it all there, to tell that story, the sense of the question "Where are you?" has to be spelled out. What is it that has brought about the catastrophe? It was disobedience. Then what will bring about reconciliation is obedience. But for Judaism, the story of Eden is also the story of Israel in the land of Israel. Then Israel is like Adam; it too had Eden but lost it. So the two realms of being, humanity in general, represented by Adam, and Israel in particular, draw together and are to be compared. And the point of comparison will be Adam's disobedience and Israel's disobedience, the consequences for Adam, the consequences for Israel. In both cases, it is the loss of Eden. And I have to tell you I find in this reading of Eden one of the glories of the Torah: everything in one thing, all time in one moment, the choice is clear.

So why—the Torah explains—has Eden slipped through our grasp? It is because of the disobedience that has come of our arrogance. And in what does that arrogance consist? It is the fact that we have followed not God's plan but our own. And how are we to right matters? It will be by following not our will but God's: the Torah that at Sinai reveals what God wants of humanity and demands, to begin with, of Israel. How then am I to read the story of the fall? In light of the story of the ascent. From Eden to hell to Sinai, that marks the progress of humanity.

If then we wish to compare the history of disobedient humanity with the history of sinning Israel, this is how it goes:

> "And the Lord God called to the man and said to him, 'Where are you?' " (Gen. 3:9):
>
> [The word for "Where are you" yields consonants that bear the meaning] "How has this happened to you?"

[God speaks:] "Yesterday it was in accord with my plan, and now it is in accord with the plan of the snake. Yesterday it was from one end of the world to the other [that you filled the earth], and now: 'Among the trees of the garden' (Gen. 3:8) [you hide out]."

The die is cast: yesterday I planned; today the snake does. And look what has happened! But that is mere prologue. The real comparison is between Adam and Israel, and that is drawn in these words:

R. Abbahu in the name of R. Yose bar Haninah: "It is written, 'But they are like a man [Adam], they have transgressed the covenant' (Hos. 6:7).

" 'They are like a man,' specifically, like the first man. [We shall now compare the story of the first man in Eden with the story of Israel in its land.]

" 'In the case of the first man, I brought him into the garden of Eden, I commanded him, he violated my commandment, I judged him to be sent away and driven out, but I mourned for him, saying "How . . ." [which begins the book of Lamentations, hence stands for a lament, but which, as we just saw, also is written with the consonants that also yield, 'Where are you'].

" 'I brought him into the garden of Eden,' as it is written, 'And the Lord God took the man and put him into the garden of Eden' (Gen. 2:15).

" 'I commanded him,' as it is written, 'And the Lord God commanded . . .' (Gen. 2:16).

" 'And he violated my commandment,' as it is written, 'Did you eat from the tree concerning which I commanded you' (Gen. 3:11).

'I judged him to be sent away,' as it is written, 'And the Lord God sent him from the garden of Eden' (Gen. 3:23).

" 'And I judged him to be driven out.' 'And he drove out the man' (Gen. 3:24).

" 'But I mourned for him, saying, "How . . ." ' 'And he said to him, "Where are you" ' (Gen. 3:9), and the word for 'Where are you' is written, 'How . . .'

" 'So too in the case of his descendants [God continues to speak,] I brought them into the Land of Israel, I commanded them, they violated my commandment, I judged them to be sent out and driven away but I mourned for them, saying, "How . . ." '

" 'I brought them into the Land of Israel,' 'And I brought you into the land of Carmel' (Jer. 2:7).

" 'I commanded them.' 'And you, command the children of Israel' (Ex. 27:20). 'Command the children of Israel' (Lev. 24:2).

" 'They violated my commandment.' 'And all Israel have violated your Torah' (Dan. 9:11).

" 'I judged them to be sent out.' 'Send them away, out of my sight and let them go forth' (Jer. 15:1).

" '. . . and driven away.' 'From my house I shall drive them' (Hos. 9:15).

" 'But I mourned for them, saying, "How . . ." ' 'How has the city sat solitary, that was full of people' (Lam. 1:1)."

I am moved by both readings of Genesis 3:9. The first simply contrasts one day with the next, a stunning and stark statement, lacking all decoration. The stark, the simple—there is the truth.

The more complicated exposition says the same thing in a richer way. For the other compares the story of man in the Garden of Eden with the tale of Israel in its land. All of this rests on the simple fact that the word for "Where are you" may be expressed as "How . . . ," which invokes the opening words of the book of Lamentations. So Israel's history serves as a paradigm for human history, and vice versa. Then Israel stands at the center of humanity. And that is the centerpiece of my reading of the Bible. For a rabbi, Scripture tells the story of humanity embodied in Israel, the holy people, who bear the gift of God to all humanity, which is the Torah.

The story of humankind in Adam in Eden is the story of Israel in the land and after its loss. But that is a story of the fall from grace because of the sin of disobedience. And I cannot leave matters there, with so general an observation that what happens to humanity at large reflects the fate of Israel, the holy people. For that is not the message of the Torah, only part of that message. The other part concerns the reconciliation of humanity with God, signified, in the life of Israel the people, by the salvation of Israel; signified, in a supernatural framework, by the restoration of the people to the holy land and the rebuilding of the Temple of Jerusalem for the divine service. The story of humanity, captured in the story of the holy people, Israel, is the tale of not only the fall but also the rise. Then it encompasses not only estrangement but the renewal of love, alienation and reconciliation.

This cannot sound strange to you, Father Andy. You surely find in him whom you know as Jesus Christ just that renewal of love, that reconciliation of God to humanity, that I evoke. But how does that come to expression for me? The answer lies in the conception of the Shechinah, which refers to God's presence in the here and now of the world. Note that in Hebrew that is a feminine form and here God is she. The love of mother for child conveys the love of the Shechinah, God really present in the world, for us all. We then may compare the love of a mother for a child with the love of God for us. And in making that comparison we may find a worldly way of conveying otherworldly truth. And what is the truth? It tells of separations that are not for always, of the ever-present possibility of return.

How does this work in the Torah, this possibility of return (in Hebrew the word is *teshuvah*, which is translatable by either "return" or "repentance")?

With the disobedience and fall of Adam and Eve, the presence of God drew away from the world, becoming more remote. It rose ever higher from humankind with Cain, the generation of Enosh, the generation of the flood, the dispersion at Babel, the sin of Sodom; then the bad conduct of the pharaoh of Egypt with Abraham brought the presence of God to the highest point away from humanity. And what is it that brought God's presence back to earth? The righteous, the counterparts of the wicked, restored God's presence to dwell among humankind. And where is that return/repentance portrayed in the Torah? It is in the road to Sinai. Here is how the whole of the story of God in the relationship to humankind takes shape from the perspective of the Torah:

Said R. Abba bar Kahana, "The word is not written, 'move,' but rather, 'walk,' bearing the sense that [the Presence of God] leapt about and jumped upward.

"[The point is that God's presence leapt upward from the earth on account of the events in the garden, as will now be explained:] The principal location of the Presence of God was [meant to be] among the creatures down here.

"When the first man sinned, the Presence of God moved up to the first firmament. When Cain sinned, it went up to the second firmament.

"When the generation of Enosh sinned, it went up to the third firmament.

"When the generation of the Flood sinned, it went up to the fourth firmament.

"When the generation of the dispersion [at the tower of Babel] sinned, it went up to the fifth.

"On account of the Sodomites it went up to the sixth,

"And on account of the Egyptians in the time of Abraham it went up to the seventh.

"But, as a counterpart, there were seven righteous men who rose up: Abraham, Isaac, Jacob, Levi, Kahath, Amram, and Moses. They brought the Presence of God [by stages] down to earth.

"Abraham brought it from the seventh to the sixth,

"Isaac brought it from the sixth to the fifth,

"Jacob brought it from the fifth to the fourth,

"Levi brought it down from the fourth to the third,

"Kahath brought it down from the third to the second,

"Amram brought it down from the second to the first.

"Moses brought it down to earth."

On the surface what we explain is the meaning of the work *walk*. It does not bear the corporeal sense; it bears an altogether spiritual meaning. While the wicked (Gentiles) drove God out of the world, the righteous (Israelites) brought God back into the world. This theme links the story of the fall of man to the history of Israel, with Israel serving as the counterpart and redemption. Then how does Israel set forth its understanding of its task? It is by obedience, since the fall of humanity came about through disobedience.

Here is one way of expressing the calling of holy Israel—which is in humility freely to obey, to love by reason of the commandment, that is, to love in response to the love bestowed by God—that the Torah records:

> Judah b. Padaiah interpreted, "Who will remove the dust from between your eyes, O first man! For you could not abide in the commandment that applied to you for even a single hour, and lo, your children can wait for three years to observe the prohibition of the use of the fruit of a tree for the first three years after it is planted. 'Three years shall it be as forbidden to you, it shall not be eaten' (Lev. 19:23)."

Here again we compare the character of Israel to the character of the first man, calling Israel "descendants of the first man" and pointing out that they can observe a commandment for a long time. The example is apt, since Israel observes the prohibition involving the fruit of a newly planted tree, and does so for three years, while the first man could not keep his hands off a fruit tree for even an hour. This of course states with enormous power the fact that Israel's history forms the counterpart to the history of humanity. But while the first man could not do what God demanded, Israel can and does do God's will.

Can you identify with this insistence of mine that the fall of Adam marks the rise of Israel, that from the depths of the disaster of Eden humanity rises to the ascent at Sinai? Shall I now apologize for the ethnocentrism of my reading of the fall of humanity? For after all, what have I set forth if not an account of how I read myself as "Israel" into the story of the very essence and meaning of humanity: the definition of humankind as disobedient and sinful! Then am I holier than you, because I am Israel and you are not?

No, my reading of Scripture tells me, I am humanity because I am sinful and disobedient. But I can be "Israel," the medium and vehicle for reconciliation with God, because to me the Torah has been given. Then the contrast between sinful Adam and obedient Israel is not a statement of pride, let alone a claim that that is how things really are. It is an effort to say what we can be and are supposed to be, all of us, which is obedient as Israel is supposed to be obedient. For Adam lost Eden, but, our sages underline, so too Israel has lost the land. And the history of Israel, the holy people, in its humble details then stands for the history of humankind, in the far reaches of creation.

9

GREELEY

Adam

All religions have creation myths, but the stories in the myths are different. The important fact about the stories of Adam and Eve contained in the first chapters of the Book of Genesis is not that there is some similarity between them and the other creation myths one can find in the ancient Middle East, but rather the striking differences between the Adam and Eve story and the other stories. It's not the humans of Genesis who are different, but the God of Genesis.

Before I can discuss the story of a different kind of God, I must create a context by describing how I approach the Hebrew Scriptures (or the TNK, as they are properly called).

1. I accept the rabbi's* position that Christianity and Judaism are cousin—or, perhaps better, sister—religions, both descended from the religious matrix of ancient Israel. Hence Christianity does not approach the TNK as a daughter approaching the sacred books of her mother but as a co-heiress approaching sacred books that she shares with her sister.

I realize that this position is disconcerting to many Jews and many Christians, but I find the historical arguments in favor of it conclusive and agree completely with the rabbi in this respect.

2. I understand revelation to be the self-disclosure of God—through creation, through history, and through interpersonal relationships. Such revelation takes the form of doctrinal propositions only indirectly and derivatively as those who have experienced the self-disclosure of God reflect on their experiences and try to articulate their propositional meaning for themselves and for others. The central experience of God that binds Christianity and Judaism together is the experience of God as one who makes promises, the promises of a lover.

In the ordinary course of human events, the self-disclosure of God is

---

*The rabbi is always called "The Rabbi" in my office because he is "our" rabbi, in the sense in which a Jewish congregation calls a rabbi "our" rabbi. He is welcome to call me "The Priest"—especially since he cannot call me "The Monsignor"!

"natural"; that is to say, it occurs in the wonders of the cosmos, the unfolding of history, and the surprises of human love. However, unlike those who subscribe to the philosophy of scientism, I also believe in the possibility of "supernatural" interventions of God. I prefer the "ordinary" and "extraordinary" (or "special") for these two kinds of revelations, and I picture them as not discontinuous but rather as shading off into one another. To what extent the experience of the Hebrews at Sinai (about which I will write in a later chapter) was "ordinary" and to what extent it was "extraordinary" is a question that we cannot resolve except by saying that both kinds of self-revelation of God were probably present. Christians believe that Jesus represents a "special" intervention of the self-disclosing God in history; but most Catholics today also acknowledge the "ordinary" nature of the human nature of Jesus—like us in all things save sin.

The Catholic tradition officially has always been reluctant to assume the presence of special marvels and hence has been skeptical of so-called private revelations. Are there not enough marvels in creation, history, and human love without postulating as necessary even more marvels, which often are not all that marvelous?

Similarly, does not the presence of God in Jesus, which we call the incarnation, radically validate the whole of ordinary creation as a sign of God's presence?

On the one hand against the fundamentalists, I believe that most revelation is "ordinary"; that is to say, one does not need to require a "special" intervention of God. On the other hand, against scientism, I believe in an "open" universe, that is to say, one in which remarkable events are possible and do occur. The belief that the cosmos is "closed" and that therefore no special interventions of the creator are possible is a "scientific" dogma, an a priori assumption for which there is no scientific proof.

It is also based on the curious notion that whoever was responsible for producing the universe somehow does not have the power to intervene in it. I suspect that the truth is that s/he normally does not need to intervene in it.

The distinction between "natural" revelation and "supernatural" revelation, between "ordinary" and "special" self-disclosure of God, is a view from our perspective. It ignores the fact that anyone with the power to launch the universe can scarcely be excluded from its processes and that from the viewpoint of the creator such distinctions have no meaning.

How God works through history and through the events of the ordinary life of a person ("divine providence") is an issue I do not feel competent to discuss.

The history of revelation is a history of increased understanding of the "promise" of God, the promise of a passionate lover. The increase in our understanding of the nature of the promise is not so much the result of the piling up of new promises as it is the result of a deeper insight into the promise itself, or rather of the promising God. Revelation must be imagined as "going deeper" instead of "spreading out." The history of revelation is not the story of the piling up of new doctrines, but rather the story of richer and fuller experiences of the promise of the Divine Lover (an experience that is explicated in doctrinal propositions but precedes them).

The human race need not have experienced either the Sinai event or the Jesus event to have perceived the possibility that life is a promise from one who loves. Hints of that truth abound both in creation and in human intimacy. We sense at least intermittently in our lives that we are caught up in a protective envelope of intimate love. Sinai and Jesus disclose to us more powerfully and more fully that which already in our better moments we suspect and/or hope may be true. "Special" revelation may be usefully conceptualized as a confirmation of our most expansive suspicions and our brightest hopes. Thus "special" and "ordinary" revelation are inextricably linked with one another as part of the ongoing dialogue between two parties in a love relationship about a promise that has constituted the relationship.

3. By inspiration I mean the presence of God in the act of creation of the books of the Scriptures so that a given scriptural work will make its proper contribution to the ongoing dialogue between God and his people. Because of inspiration, no book of the Scriptures can err in its development of the story of God's promise. From this it follows, in the Catholic perspective, that the "literal interpretation" of a scriptural book means the search for what the author actually meant to say, for the experience of God about which the author is telling a story, a search that is sometimes difficult because the authors lived in different eras and in different cultures than our own.

Catholics do *not*, therefore, accept the notion of "verbal inerrancy" to which fundamentalists are committed, a concept that requires God to be involved directly and specially in the choice of every single word the author puts down on paper (and therefore in interpretation of every single word by subsequent readers). Such a notion involves a proliferation of miracles for which there is no basis in the Bible itself and which turns the ordinary processes of human behavior into an empty sham. In the Catholic tradition God normally works through these ordinary processes and accomplishes her/his goals gently, subtly, and delicately instead of through constant and violent intervention, which turns human writers and readers into automatons.

Both scientism and fundamentalism are dogmatic positions. Scientism excludes special interventions without any proof from science. Fundamentalism requires constant special interventions without any proof from Scripture.

Fundamentalism makes two errors about history that have caused enormous problems for those who would read the Bible.

First, it thinks that every sentence of the Bible is history the way modern history books recount history. Thus one reads Genesis for a precise and accurate description of how the universe was created and how the human species came to be. Moreover, every sentence of the Bible is of equal importance as historical description—the Adam and Eve story in every detail is as "true" as are descriptions of the trial of Jesus.

Such an approach does terrible violence to the patently different literary forms of various books of the Bible and the patently different intent of the human authors.

Moreover, the fundamentalist fallacy also ignores the different historical contexts in which the various books of the Scriptures have been written. On the one hand it wants everything to be history in the strict sense of modern history, and on the other it ignores the effect of history on the actual composition of the text.

The Genesis story of God's promise as we have it was assembled from (it would seem) four antecedent texts in the time after the return of the remnants of Israelite elites from their captivity in Babylonia, thus within the half millennium before the coming of Jesus. It thus describes events that occurred long before the actual composition but from the religious perspective of a later era. Genesis in its current form is more recent than the prophets and is heavily influenced by the prophetic insight about God and the meaning of God's promise. It presents not the religious vision of the patriarchs whose deeds it recounts, but the religious vision of the era of its final composition (an important point, as I will note in my comments on the Abraham/Isaac story in a subsequent chapter). Genesis is in fact a story of the religious experiences of the Jewish people half a thousand years before Jesus and not the religious experiences of their predecessors—which later are seen through lenses of postcaptivity Israel and are recounted in the religious language of this later era.

In the strict sense "inspiration" can be claimed only for the final edition of the work in which the four sources (themselves compilations of earlier sources, some of them very old indeed) appear, but many scholars believe that the immediate sources may also claim "inspiration" insofar as they represented dialogue between God and his community.

To complicate matters even more (for us if not for the original readers of Genesis, whose agenda was not our agenda) there are different levels of "history" in the TNK. The Adam and Even story can properly be called myth (about which word more shortly). The accounts of the deeds of the patriarchs are folklore: the patriarchs (Abraham, Isaac, and Jacob) were real people about whose era and lives we know something (though not much). The stories we are told about them, however, at least in their details are tales that were passed on by oral tradition and which have often changed to teach different religious lessons at different times in their own history (most notably, it would seem, in the Abraham/Isaac story).

We might compare the stories of the patriarchs to legends of King Arthur—an actual king who did hold the line in Roman Britain against invaders, but the stories about whom were put together and edited by later authors to make their own points and teach their own convictions.

We have a much clearer picture of Moses and his personality, life, and work than we do of his predecessors, but in his story, too, there is much legend and folklore; moreover, much of the subsequent work of elaborating the laws of Israel was attributed to him so as to invoke his authority (and not illegitimately, because he had begun the process of law giving).

Finally, in the stories of the kings of Israel and Judah we have accounts that are much more like histories written by the Romans and Greeks; the authors of these tales tried to give precise and historically accurate details, but they often lacked documentary evidence and had to rely on oral traditions, legends, and folktales.

When we read the books of the TNK, then, with modern historical patterns in our head (and since we are moderns we can't help but read them that way), we must understand that the TNK and indeed many of its individual books are collections of very different genera of storytelling, often edited together (*redacted* is the word the experts use) from the religious perspective of an era later than that which purports to be the setting of the tale.

Why does it have to be this way?

Because that is the way we humans have compiled the stories of our heritages and traditions. If Jesus is human in all things save sin, surely the Scripture must also be human in all things save errors about the nature of God's promise.

The fundamentalist temptation—which would reject virtually everything I have written so far in this chapter—is by no means limited to Protestants. Thus the Roman church, in one of its worst failures, condemned the work of Galileo because of a gratuitously fundamentalist interpretation of the account of the sun "standing still" in the Book of Exodus. One need only to have encountered hard-core Catholic charismatics to know that they can be as dogged in their fundamentalism as any Protestant.

The humanity of the Bible is an affront to all fundamentalists, whatever their religious or nonreligious orientation.

My casual reference to "myths," "folklore," and "legend" in the TNK will appall fundamentalists because they refuse to admit that different literary genres can exist in the Bible just as they do in other heritages and traditions. Just as some of them would deny the humanity of Jesus because of the presence of the Divinity, the fundamentalists would deny the humanity of the Bible because of the presence of God through "inerrancy."

It is useless to debate against those who deny the humanity of the Bible. Their theology has no basis in the Bible itself, but their dogmatic presuppositions prevent them from realizing that the authors of the books that have been handed down to us clearly and obviously made use of a wide variety of source genres to put together their religious stories of the promising God.

I will content myself with saying that such is the position of the Catholic church as taken officially at the Second Vatican Council.

I must also note the presence of what I would call secular fundamentalists in the national media—men and women who do not accept the "special" origins of the Bible but who nonetheless interpret the Bible stories in fundamentalist fashion to confront biblical stories with modern science.

Periodically one will read in the *New York Times* or *Time* magazine or hear on network TV that a new theory of science either tends to confirm or tends to refute biblical theories of creation. Thus it is said that if the universe continues to expand and will never contract (because new matter is being introduced through "continuous creation") then the biblical account of creation has been refuted. On the other hand, it is also asserted that if the big bang theory is confirmed and if the universe will eventually contract because there is no continuous creation, the biblical account of creation will be supported.

I suppose one has to say that the redactor of the Book of Genesis and the authors of the sources that he incorporated could not have cared less about a big bang theory and that to attempt to refute or support their religious vision by scientific data of an expanding or nonexpanding universe is ludicrous. Contemporary scientists and TNK authors were writing utterly different genres. Comparing them is like trying to measure the religious and human truth of the legend of the Holy Grail by archaeological research about the Britain of King Arthur.

Moreover, it may be understandable that the geneticists who are able to postulate a woman ancestor of all currently living humans would call that creature Eve. That our species (*Homo sapiens sapiens*) began with a single woman some quarter-million years ago is an interesting and useful fact, but she was not the Eve of Genesis, who was a mythological rather than an archaeological or genetic being. *

What do I mean when I say that the stories we have about Adam and Eve in the current form of Genesis are "myths"? I certainly do *not* mean that they are "not true." I mean rather that they are stories that tell us important religious truths about the nature of the human condition and about the relationship between God and humans.

According to the *Harper Biblical Commentary* there are five characteristics of myths: the language is narrative and dramatic, the actors and participants are supernatural agents, the action is characterized by remoteness in time and space, the myths are related to communities for which they order human experience by providing a vision of the underlying structure of reality, and the goal is "salvation," broadly understood as whatever contributes to human well-being.

The *Commentary* suggests that since there is so much discussion about the proper definition of myth, one might also call the Genesis stories parables— "theological narratives whose intention is to present the Israelite view of the meanings of such fundamental realities as God transcendent and immanent, the creation, blessed humankind, the frustration of God's design by human sin, and the restoration and renewal of humanity by divine grace."

That's a nice summary of what the Adam and Eve story is about. For my money, calling it a parable raises more questions about the definition of parable than calling it a myth raises about the definition of myth. The reader can choose any term he or she wants so long as it is understood that the Adam and Eve story is about the fundamental realities of God, creation, human nature, sin, and grace.† Only the most dogged fundamentalist can

---

*When did the "prehominids" and the "protohominids" become "human"? Archaeologists suggest that the ability to reflect on one's behavior requires language. Consciousness and language developed hand in hand, each move forward in one requiring a move forward in the other. How much consciousness and how much language was required for the presence of a human soul? Was the Lucy, the little protohominid discovered by Donald Johansson, capable of consciousness? Did she have a soul? Or did we have to wait for modern humans to emerge with "Eve" for the soul to be present? Clearly there are no answers to these questions. We would perhaps be both wise and humble to extend our definition of full religious humanity as broadly as we can.

†Which is undoubtedly how they were understood before modern scientific sensibilities and the fundamentalist response required a detailed discussion of the literary genre of the Genesis story. Unfortunately the churches, put on the defensive by science, lacked the resources and the understanding that would have been required to make clear the difference between scientific explanation and religious interpretation of the origins of the universe. Now the nonfundamentalist churches can make this distinction. But the fundamentalist response to science is so widespread and, as I have said, so prevalent even in those who reject the Bible as a source of religious truth that one must begin any exploration of the Bible with definitions and clarifications of the sort I have attempted in this chapter.

argue that scientific questions about the origin of creation are more impor-tant than questions about its meaning and its relationship to its creator and about the nature of human nature and the purpose of human life.

That brings us back to the issue raised at the beginning of the chapter: the critical question about Adam and Eve is not about how the elements of their story are similar to other creation stories—even to the use of similar vocabulary—but how they are different.

How did the redactor some five hundred years before Jesus (and to some extent the authors of the sources he used) interpret the meaning of creation, of God's relationship with the world, and of the nature of human nature?

In a nutshell, he said the same thing that Saint Paul would later say (in a somewhat different context): God does not repent of the promises he has made.

The Genesis story, properly understood, is the most optimistic of all possible creation myths: the world is good, human nature is good, God is involved with his creation and especially with his human creatures, human sin interferes with the working out of God's plan, and God's grace will overcome sin.

The promise, in other words, is stronger than sin.

That is very good news indeed.

The differences between Genesis and other creation stories can be sum-marized as follows:

1. The God of Genesis is utterly transcendent. Unlike all the other cre-ators, he is completely independent of his creation. He creates easily and with a simple command.

2. Unlike many other creators (especially those in the world religions that were emerging at the time of the prophets and with which the final redactors of Genesis had to deal), the utterly transcendent God, the lord of creation, is also personally involved with his creatures. He is as transcendent as the God of any of the world religions, but as involved as any of the local gods of the nature religion. Here one may find the genius of the Hebrew religion: a combination of divine transcendence and presence that no one else had or has ever attempted.

3. Everything God created is good. In contrast with many other creation stories, in Genesis creation and fall are not the same event. The troubles that afflict the world and humanity do not represent God's final goals.

4. Despite its flaws, human nature is good. Human sinfulness may be powerful and pervasive; God's grace is more powerful and more perva-

sive. Salvation is not only possible, it is an absolute promise from a God who keeps his promises.

5. The love between man and woman is not a corruption of human good-ness but part of God's plan.

Since the Reformation (indeed, since sin-obsessed Saint Augustine) much of the discussion about the sin of Adam and Eve has focused on the mode of its transmission from them to us. However, it would seem that the author of Genesis was not particularly concerned about the dynamics of human sinfulness or about its prevalence (as Martin Marty once remarked, one need only read the front page of a newspaper to see proof of sinfulness), but about the promise that God's grace would triumph over the fatal flaw in human nature. The Genesis author was interested in making as clear as he could the power of the promise over sin.

Catholics would also add (and I believe Jews would agree) that the author also thought that whatever its flaws, human nature (and human nature as sexual) was more good than evil, wounded by sinfulness perhaps, but not perverted by it. *

This chapter—and indeed this book—is not the proper place to discuss in detail the theology of Original Sin. It suffices to say that the human propensity for evil seems to result from the fear of death in the only creature (about whom we know) that is conscious of its own mortality. Adam and Eve eating the fruit are trying to break the bonds of human finitude and hence escape death. They choose to opt for their own powers over the uncertain (to them) powers of the God who made them and loves them. They are hedging their bets against mortality, against the possibility that the promise might be a trick, that God may not (or may not be able to) deliver on the promise.

In this respect Adam and Eve are truly everyperson. Their story is not a tale of an event in the distant past that cursed all of us, but rather a tale of how everyone acts in daily life. Human sinfulness ultimately seems to be a lack of trust (or an inability to trust) in God's loving promise.

Leaving aside the complex (and not unimportant) theological controver-sies, this seems to be a not unreasonable interpretation of what the final author of Genesis was trying to say about the nature of human nature and of

---

*The classical Reformation theory, following Augustine more literally than the Catholic counter-reformation was willing to do, put much more emphasis on the inherent sinfulness of the human condition, a position that reading Professor Marty's front page might lead us to think is not unreason-able. But classic Catholicism does not despair of the fundamental goodness of human nature, especially when it is given an opportunity to respond to God's grace.

the human condition in his creation story, one that is unique not for its account of humankind's fallen nature but rather for its emphasis on God's promise—a promise that becomes more explicit as the author turns from Adam and Eve to subsequent patriarchs.

Again one must ask what is more important to know—how human sinfulness is transmitted across generations or that God's loving promise is stronger than human sinfulness.

Only the most rigid fundamentalist will choose the former motif.

10

NEUSNER

"I Regret That I Made Them," but Noah Found Favor

The Lord saw how great was man's wickedness on earth and how every plan devised by his mind was nothing but evil all the time. And the Lord regretted that He had made man on earth, and His heart was saddened.

The Lord said, "I will blot out from the earth the men whom I created, men together with beasts, creeping things, and birds of the sky. For I regret that I made them."

But Noah found favor with the Lord.

Genesis 6:5–8

For the imagination of man's heart is evil from his youth.

Genesis 8:21

No century proves the truth of God's judgment of humanity more powerfully than our own. Rivers of blood, oceans of tears, a million dead at the Somme, six million here, five million there, three million somewhere else, half the population of a whole country murdered by its own government— does anybody have reason these days to doubt that "the imagination of man's heart is evil from his youth"? And would anybody blame God for saying, "I regret I made them"? But what does that say about God, in whose image, after whose likeness, we are made? These questions draw us downward, into dark reflections at the waning light of a dreadful century.

The story of Noah and the flood tells the tale of humanity's second chance. It is a way of conveying the sense that God is like a father and also like a mother to us all. If God is only father, there is no end to the horror of justice. The flood tells it all: "I will blot out from the earth the men whom I created, men together with beasts, creeping things, and birds of the sky. For I regret that I made them." If God is only mother, then there is no end to the excess of our self-indulgence: "every plan devised by his mind was nothing but evil all the time." How then to bring the two together in that holy matrimony of the one God who gave the Torah?

Have I gone too far? Since, the Torah explicitly says, God made humanity in God's image, male and female, I am not claiming more than the Torah says when I compare one aspect of God's life with us to a mother's love for her children: there always is a second chance. But there is the other aspect, and it is a father's love, which is full of expectations. Mercy and justice wed in God's making humanity. But that too was not a Catholic marriage: they split.

And with the story of the flood we see what happens in two near divorces, the one of God's justice and God's mercy, the other the near divorce of God and humanity. But we know that is not the end: there is no divorce, but reconciliation. The Torah sets forth the story of the expanding knowledge of God concerning humanity, and of humanity concerning God. Out of this story is forged a more mature knowledge. On whose part? On humanity's part, it is knowledge of what God wants and is perfectly capable of doing to get what God wants. But, too, on God's part, it is knowledge of the meaning of what humanity is: our limitations, our promise as well. We are free to choose, and we can, and generally do, choose wrongly, "for the imagination of man's heart is evil from his youth." But we can atone, for Noah, after all, found favor. And, the Torah makes clear, Noah is where it all began: Noah, not Adam. Don't forget that.

But this starts out as God the Father's story, not God the Mother's, and these are terrible words: "I regret that I made them" and "For the imagination of man's heart is evil from his youth" (Gen. 8:21). God, who made heaven and earth, formed humankind "in Our image, after Our likeness," but then declares regret for having done so. Ten generations from Adam to Noah had produced nothing of merit. A child who hears from a parent, "I'm sorry I ever had you," such a one alone knows the full horror of the sentence spoken by God. It is a sentence of death in life. The horror of the story cannot be missed.

God who made humankind denounces what God himself has done. That is how the Torah understands these terrible words:

"For the imagination of man's heart is evil from his youth" (Gen. 8:21):

Said R. Hiyya the elder, "Miserable is the dough concerning which the baker herself testifies that it is no good: 'For the imagination of man's heart is evil from his youth.' "

Abba Yose the potter said, "Miserable is the yeast concerning which the one who kneaded it testifies that it is no good: 'For he knows our evil passions, he remembers that we are dust' (Ps. 103:14)."

Rabbis say, "Miserable is the planting when the one who planted it testifies that it is no good: 'For the Lord of hosts, who planted you, has spoken ill of you' (Jer. 11:17)."

Dough, yeast, planting—humankind had been intended as the foundation of civilized life but had ended up the cause of its destruction.

The Torah's account of all humanity treats Noah as the progenitor of us all: "But Noah found favor." After the flood, we are not the children of Adam and Eve alone, but Adam and Eve via Noah. And that has made all the difference. We survive our origins. For we are the children of a new beginning, not of Adam but of Noah. Then all humanity derives from the one decent family that ever was, not from the sin of Adam but the grace shown to Noah. And heirs to grace, we look forward, not backward.

And that brings us to Noah, who found favor. Why Noah in particular? The Torah says that Noah was righteous in his generation. That can mean he was all right by the standards of his generation, but had he been a contemporary of Abraham, Isaac, and Jacob, he would have been found wanting. Or the statement in the Torah can be an absolute judgment. Consider, though, the trial that Noah had to endure. Everyone else ignored the warnings; he heeded the commandment and so saved his own life and the lives of his family.

The final judgment lies with the sage Rabbi Jonathan, who says Noah was chosen because he was strong:

> "The Lord tries the righteous, [but the wicked and him who loves violence his soul hates" (Ps. 11:5)]:
>
> Said R. Jonathan, "A potter does not test a weak utensil, for if he hits it just once, he will break it. So the Holy One, blessed be he, does not test the wicked but the righteous: 'The Lord tries the righteous' (Ps. 11:5)."
>
> Said R. Yose bar Haninah, "When a flax maker knows that the flax is in good shape, then the more he beats it, the more it will improve and glisten. When it is not of good quality, if he beats it just once, he will split it. So the Holy One, blessed be he, does not try the wicked but the righteous: 'The Lord tries the righteous' (Ps. 11:5)."
>
> Said R. Eleazar, "The matter may be compared to a householder who has two heifers, one strong, one weak. On whom does he place the yoke? It is on the one that is strong. So the Holy One, blessed be he, does not try the wicked but the righteous: 'The Lord tries the righteous' (Ps. 11:5)."

Noah was chosen because God knew he could stand the test. And what was the test? As we now realize, for the Torah the test will always be of faith shown through obedience or of distrust shown through disobedience.

The Torah's perspective upon humankind comes to the fore once again. The perspective is the struggle between God's will and humanity's free will. God's power meets its outer limit in humanity's freedom. But God makes the rules, and we bear responsibility for what we do. That is why we need

God's love and forgiveness. The generation of the flood disobeyed, but Noah listened and did what he was told, and that is what made all the difference.

> R. Yudan in the name of R. Aibu commenced [discourse by citing the following verse]: " 'In the transgression of the lips is a snare to the evil man' (Prov. 12:13):
>
> "On account of the rebellion of the generation of the Flood against the Holy One, blessed be he, their downfall came.
>
> " 'But the righteous comes out of trouble' (Prov. 12:13) refers to Noah: 'Go forth from the ark' (Gen. 8:5)."

Noah was found able to withstand the trial and so was proved righteous. The contrast between Noah's obedience, going into the ark when told, coming out when told, explains why he survived the flood while the rebels, who did not accept God's word, perished. But Noah was free to disobey, and they were free to obey. All were humanity.

But what good did it do Noah, for when he came out of the ark what did he find? No friends, no familiar scenes, utter desolation. The reward that Noah got was his own life and the lives of his family. Everything else was gone—not much of a world to inherit. So if we consider Noah's situation when the flood was over, we must find more astonishing his obedience after the flood than before it. So commences the story of God the Mother.

Imagine the world when Noah opened the windows of the ark! There was nothing whatsoever, no cities where there had been cities, no roads, no buildings, none of the marks of civilization; no beasts, no birds, nothing of nature had survived but what was in the ark. Where there had been human-kind there was now devastation. Who would want to have been saved, and for what had Noah been saved? If we were sent as the last of the human race to save civilization and rebuild it on Mars, we should require more courage to get out of our spaceship than to get into it. Looking backward, we could feel sorrow but hope, But looking outward? Nothing.

No wonder, then, that the sages of the Torah point to Noah's obedience in leaving the ark as a mark of his wisdom and also his loyalty to God:

> "To every thing there is a season and a time to every purpose" (Eccles. 3:1).
>
> There was a season for Noah to enter the ark, "Come into the ark, with all your household" (Gen. 7:1),
>
> and there was a time for him to leave the ark: "Go forth from the ark" (Gen. 8:15).
>
> "Go forth from the ark" (Gen. 8:15): [Why did God have to order Noah to leave the ark?]

He said, "Should I go forth and procreate only for a curse [and produce children who will be subject to divine wrath]?"

Only when the Holy One, blessed be he, took an oath to him that he would never again bring a flood, as it is said, "For this is the waters of Noah to me, for as I have sworn that the waters of Noah should no more go over the earth," (Is. 54:9), [did Noah agree to leave the ark,] and then he engaged in further acts of procreation.

God had to order Noah to leave the ark, thus indicating that Noah did not wish to leave and had to be told to do so. It was now not a mark of obedience to God but of Noah's own independent judgment. And that brings us to the nub of the matter.

Seeing all that horror and destruction, Noah could have decided to make himself the end of the human race. What good, after all, can come of this life that is no life, a life in conflict with God? In the ark, sages maintain, sexual relations were forbidden Noah. That is in line with the formulation of this verse: "You shall come into the ark, you, your sons"—and that means, males by yourselves, "your wife and your sons' wives"—by themselves. Now when he left the ark, sexual relations once more were permitted. That is in line with the formulation of this verse: "Go out of the ark, you and your wife" (Gen. 8:16). Now Noah was instructed not only to go forth but also to bring forth "every living thing that is with you of all flesh, birds and animals and every creeping thing that creeps on the earth" (Gen. 8:15). Why so? "That they may breed abundantly on the earth" (Gen. 8:17).

That resumption of procreation carries us to the heart of the matter. Noah stands for the new start for humankind. Just as the first beginning, with Adam, involved one religious duty or commandment, not to eat of the fruit of the tree of knowledge, so Noah had to address himself to his duties. And these were seven, for sages discover in Scripture seven religious duties or commandments. These were the tasks of all of the children of Noah, and, for us Jews that means all of humanity, east and west, of all races and religions.

All are expected by God, so the Torah tells us, to keep these seven rules. And if they keep no others but these, they are loved by God, are held to be obedient and loyal to God, and will inherit the world to come. Israel, the holy people, have many more tasks but in the end gain no greater response from God in all eternity than do those beyond the limits of Israel, those "others," different from Israel, who keep only these seven rules. And the rules form the counterpart of natural law in the sense that, so far as the Torah knows, these rules apply by nature, not by revelation, to all nations and every people.

This brings us to the single most important element in the story of Noah and the flood: the commandments that, through Noah, God has assigned to all of humanity. The children of Noah, that is, everybody except for holy Israel, must obey only these seven commandments, and if they do, God is satisfied with them and regarded them as fully in good standing. These seven commandments are the minimum requirements for a decent society:

> The children of Noah received seven commandments, specifically those prohibiting [1] idolatry, [2] fornication, [3] murder, [4] blasphemy, [5] enjoining the establishment of good government ["courts of justice"], [6] stealing and [7] cruelty to animals ["cutting a limb off a living beast"].

What are the minimal requirements that God requires of all civilizations? These represent the absolute demands: family, property, life, humanity to animals, fair and legal government.

The seven duties or religious obligations of all nations and peoples cover conduct toward God, women, other human beings, property, animals, and society at large. Humankind must worship one God, not idols, and must not blaspheme God's name; that means people must not, for example, take oaths by God's name and then violate those oaths. There must be stable families, not fornication. The life of every person is to be protected, hence no murder. Everyone has a right to property, hence no stealing. Animals too have rights; cruelty to animals is forbidden. Finally, all civilizations must establish and protect the social order, which, after all, makes possible the life of family, property, and equity and fairness among persons.

Five of the religious duties that are incumbent on all humanity, so Scripture says, the ones prohibiting idolatry, fornication, murder, blasphemy, and stealing, are among the Ten Commandments. These then pertain not only to holy Israel, as, for instance, the Sabbath does. All of humankind must establish for itself the conditions of civilized life, therefore, and sustain the sanctity of the family, life, and property. Rights extend to dumb animals, who must be treated humanely. Finally, God's name must be honored; there can be no relationship with God without honor for God's name.

In the Torah Noah stands for all humanity. There is then a covenant between God and Noah that covers every nation, race, and civilization. If God has revealed the Torah, it is to us and through us to everyone. Accordingly, here at the very outset I present that theory of the "other," or the outsider, that for the Torah is meant for all time. Everyone has a portion in God and in the world to come, and the tasks of all persons and societies are of the same order: obedience to God, carrying out God's will, and that means the building of an orderly world of justice and love. And that's all. To serve and love God everybody does not have to do it my way, not at all. And, frankly, I wish Christianity would learn that one lesson from us.

When Christianity brings further demands to the peoples of the earth, asking that they not only keep the religious requirements of civilization but further accept a salvation accorded by faith in Jesus Christ, that seems to me to exhibit the very ethnocentric trait that is imputed by some Christians to the Torah. For—like Christianity—we maintain that God's will and therefore concern and love extend to all humanity equally. But, we hold, in doing the seven religious duties God assigns to everyone, all humanity equally carry out God's will. To know God and find salvation humanity need not enter into the circle of sanctification formed by the Torah's requirements for holy Israel. Israel is different, but not better, holy in a different way and aspect, but not holier in God's perspective.

Christianity wants everybody to adopt their image and their likeness. When reading the religions of others, therefore, Christianity judges everybody by their own standard, pigeonholes everybody their way. For its part, Judaism expresses toward the whole of humanity—the rest of humanity—a much greater respect, holding, as it does, that God loves you as you are: in God's image, after God's likeness. What that means is justice for all, humaneness toward animals, not stealing, not fornicating, not lying—in all, establishing a just social order. The reason Judaism did not set out to conquer the world, in the way in which Christianity and Islam have tried to do, is that Judaism did not think that is what God wants. God does not ask everyone to be like everyone else, all in a single uniform model. God does ask everyone to do justice and love mercy, and that suffices. In this respect, the rather limited message that Judaism sets forth to the rest of humanity proves the more universal, and the universal love that Christianity wants to realize by changing everybody into itself proves the less universal and, I think, much less loving than Christians suppose. We really do like being what we are, and we understand that that is so for everybody.

One last point that the story of the flood calls to mind: is there going to be another one? I suppose in the nineteenth century people could not have imagined such a thing. But after Hiroshima, who can perish the thought? So we wonder, *What of the future?*

Do I think the Torah answers that question? Well, yes, I do. For if in the Torah we gain God's perspective upon the present, we may also come to a surmise about God's plan for the future. And surely at stake in the story of Noah is an issue vivid for us in the twenty-first century. Will there ever again be another flood? The flood in Noah's time raised a possibility that humanity before then could not have imagined and that humanity afterward can never forget: the mass destruction of all of civilization. And the age of genocide, which all of us have survived so far, makes us wonder whether the flood is not, after all, the story of humanity.

Can it happen again? Of course it can. So the sages of the Torah maintain when they read the verses before us:

> "While the earth remains, seedtime and harvest, cold and heat, summer and winter, day and night shall not cease" (Gen. 8:22):
>
> R. Yudan in the name of R. Aha: "What were the children of Noah thinking? Was it that the covenant with them ['neither will I again destroy every living creature,' Gen. 8:21)] would last forever?
>
> "Rather, only so long as heaven and earth lasted would the covenant with them endure.
>
> "But when that day should come concerning which it is written, 'For the heavens shall vanish away like smoke, and the earth shall be worn out like a garment' (Is. 51:6), then: 'And [the covenant] will be broken in that day' (Zech. 11:11)."

Yes, it can happen again. The future of humanity is not secured. Why not? Because the conditions that brought about the flood remain: stipulations of obedience and of the consequence of disobedience. The covenant is a contract that imposes upon both parties not only restrictions but also responsibilities. There are, after all, the seven religious duties assigned to all humanity. When the heavens vanish, when the earth is worn out, then the covenant will be broken, then humanity will vanish. And will there be another Noah? And whether or not there is, will anyone care?

In the meantime, we can discern evidence of how well, or how poorly, we for our part carry out our duties. The evidence is in death, sickness, and natural disaster. These storm warnings fly even in calm seas and prosperous times, and they are perpetual:

> Said R. Aha, " 'What is it that made them rebel against me? Was it not because they sowed but did not reap, produced offspring and did not have to bury them?'
>
> "Henceforward: 'Seedtime and harvest,' meaning that they will give birth and then have to bury their children.
>
> " 'Cold and heat,' meaning they will have fever and ague.
>
> " 'Summer and winter,' meaning: 'I shall give the birds the right to attack their summer crops,' in line with this verse, 'And the ravenous birds shall summer upon them and all the beasts of the earth shall winter upon them' (Is. 18:6)."
>
> Another interpretation: "While the earth remains, [seedtime and harvest, cold and heat, summer and winter, day and night shall not cease]" (Gen. 8:22):

R. Yudan in the name of R. Aha: "What were the children of Noah thinking? Was it that the covenant with them ['neither will I again destroy every living creature,' Gen. 8:21)] would last forever? Rather, only so long as day and night endured, would the covenant with them endure.

"But when that day comes, concerning which it is written, 'And there shall be one day which shall be known as the Lord's, which is not day and not night' (Zech. 14:7), then: 'And it will be broken in that day' (Zech. 11:11)."

Two distinct readings of the statement of Genesis 8:22 present themselves. The first emphasizes the limitations of the covenant made with humankind—that is, that covenant lasts up to the end-time but not beyond. The second reads the statement as essentially a curse—namely, humankind had rebelled under conditions of prosperity, so now they will have to endure "hot and cold," "seedtime and harvesttime," interpreted as misfortunes.

Let us end our meeting with Noah just where we began, with the question, Whence then the saving "but"? Why Noah in particular? The Torah's account gives us God's picture of humanity, and that picture portrays a constant struggle between what God wants and what humankind does of its own free will. Noah did what Adam did not do: he obeyed God. In generation after generation a few persons stand out for their loyalty and obedience, above all for their faith. And yet even those few, we see now and shall see with Abraham, Isaac, and Jacob, as well as Israel at the sea, stumble and fall, sin and atone, undergo a constant test of a failing faith. And so it is with Noah: best of a bad lot, but acceptable.

So the human condition finds its boundaries between obedience on the one side, the willful exercise of the power of disobedience on the other, and the dynamic of the human condition derives from humanity's freedom, even to sin. Then the story of humankind will be the story of the exercise of freedom under God, and that means the tension between the word of God and the will of humankind. What will resolve the tension? Loyalty to, trust in God. And, as we shall see, when it comes to the best of the lot, Abraham, Isaac, Jacob, founders of Israel, the holy people, it is simply one test after another: God tests them, but they test God, too. It is a story that demands and promises a happy ending but does not have one yet. On to Abraham and Sarah, ten generations after Noah, twenty generations from Adam, and the first generation of Israel.

And—let's not forget—of Christendom and Islam, too. Since we have the Torah, the Bible, and the Qu'ran, all locate our forebears in Abraham and Sarah.

11

GREELEY

Noah

Almost as many traditions have flood myths as creation myths. The flood myth of Genesis differs from other flood stories not because it is a story of wrath, destruction, and survival, but because it is a story of a renewed promise, now one signed by the rainbow. One might even say that the whole story is about the rainbow metaphor.

I'm always taken aback when I encounter a flood story similar to the Noah story in a culture one could not reasonably think has been influenced by the Hebrew religious tradition.

I find myself speculating that maybe sometime, long, long ago, the children of Eve (the geneticists' Eve, not the biblical Eve) did encounter a massive flood from which they escaped to begin their migration around the world. Were the grasslands of Africa where Eve and her children probably lived subject to repeated disastrous floods?

If this possibility—a tradition almost a quarter of a million years old—is anything more than a flight of fancy (and I don't really think it is anything more than that), it would follow that the search for Noah's ark ought not to take place on Mount Ararat but somewhere in African foothills near banks of prehistoric rivers. *

More likely (much more likely) is that the similarity of flood myths around the world is based on similar human experiences of the destructiveness of water—especially among agricultural peoples. The world is wiped out by water, and then, after the flood recedes, life begins again. Such an experience might not be quite inherently religious, but it certainly makes

---

*The periodic expeditions to Turkish mountains in search of Noah's ark—usually undertaken with much fundamentalist funding—is about as meaningful as a search for the Garden of Eden. What if a boat was found in some unexplored crevice (should there be such) of an Anatolian mountain? So what? One would still be faced with the problem of how such a craft would hold all the creatures of the earth, two of each kind (save for the unicorn, if one is to believe the Irish Rovers). Such exercises in hyperliteralism make as much sense as Saint Brendan's pious expectation that he would find Paradise by sailing the Western Seas.

men and women think about the meaning of life and death, both of which can be caused by water.

So flood myths, I am convinced, are based on the (nearly) universal human experience of the life and death potential in water—water destroying and then water renewing.

In the story of Noah and his family we certainly have a classic story of water destroying and water renewing. The old is wiped out; the new begins.

The Noah myth differs from most flood stories both because it is another variation on the theme of promise that preoccupies the author of Genesis and because the cause of the flood is human moral evil.

The tradition out of which the Book of Genesis was composed was eminently practical and profoundly ethical. It cared little for theological theory, much less for scientific speculation. It was not concerned (as we are today) to find a response to the "problem" of evil. It did not ask why physical disasters like floods were permitted by an allegedly good God. It did not even wonder, as Job and the Psalms would later on, why God permitted evil people to flourish. Rather, it pondered the possibility that the world was so bad and the people in it so evil that God would regret his creation and wipe out everything.

Or, as we would say in our modern concern about the self-destruction of the species, are we not so benighted, so greedy, so selfish, that we have embarked on political and environmental and economic policies that will devastate the planet and everyone who lives on it?

It's a nice theological question: will God permit human freedom to go so far that it will destroy itself?

Some theologians answer "yes" to that question. I think they're wrong, but I have to acknowledge that there are times when human behavior seems so perverse that I have to conclude that the Holy Spirit more than earns her salary for her work in protecting us from ultimate self-destruction.

I find it very hard, however, to conclude that the God who was experienced by the tradition that embodies its cosmology and anthropology in Genesis would tolerate final and complete human self-destruction.

Such an optimistic thought should not cause us to relax in the face of the threat of planetary destruction. It would seem that once before the species started out with only one female. * Doubtless, if need be, God could make do with the same situation again.

---

*Should the "Eve" about whom the geneticists have argued be called female or a woman? Since I want to extend "humanity" back as far as I can to our ancestors, I'd be inclined to call her a woman. Incidentally, I think the only possible answer to the question of whether an intervention of God was required to

The author of Genesis suffered no illusions about human evil or about the possibility that such evil could lead to destruction. His answer to the challenge proposed by human evil was that God's promise was stronger. The human species might come dangerously close to destruction; God's promise, nonetheless, would guarantee its renewal. The theme of death and rebirth through water, later to be echoed in the baptismal liturgy, was already understood and offered as a symbol of the struggle of humankind to respond to the promise.

God would turn any event and every event to the realization of his promise.

Again, since he was not a theorist, the author of the final version of Genesis did not propound a theological explanation of how God's promise would be achieved, he did not explain how God's plan works out in history, and he did not explain why God permitted so many obstacles to his plan. In almost a "skin of the teeth" response, the author of Genesis asserted with deep faith that, come what may, God's promise would be kept.

We may be more theologically sophisticated today and even perhaps more religiously mature, but when faced with evil and sin, including our own evil and sin, we too cling to our faith by the skin of our teeth.

A reader of the Noah story notices almost immediately that some events seem to be narrated twice. This phenomenon is one of the classic proofs of the "source" theory on which most biblical scholars now agree. The editor of the final version of Genesis often combined his sources instead of editing out the repetitions. Source theory is not important to the ordinary reader of the Bible, save in that it explains such seeming contradictions and illustrates how the authors of the final version of the book worked.

One would have to ask the proponents of word-for-word inspiration why God permitted such repetitions. Doubtless they would have an explanation, but hardly one that a reasonable person would take seriously in the face of the likelihood that a human editor was simply combining different sources.

Such a possibility can be rejected only by those who have the a priori conviction that the Bible is not a human book, but rather a book that was written directly by God, with the human author making no more contribu-

---

produce Eve is "yes." Was it a "special intervention" of the sort I discussed in chapter 9? Or part of the ordinary process of evolution (both of which would be acts of God's creativity)? I will leave that issue to theologians. My only comment is that creation of this prime ancestor—however it was accomplished—was a remarkably ingenious accomplishment. Moreover, the ingenuity of that accomplishment ought to be the ultimate response to those who think that somehow God's creativity is called into question by evolutionary theory. For a discussion of the most recent theories of the "directionality" of evolution, see my novel *Angel Fire*.

tion than my Microsoft Word word processing program makes to the writing of this book.

One can only say that there is not a shred of proof in the Bible for such a model of Bible composition. It is rather a preconceived dogmatic assumption that is imposed on the Bible.

The author of Genesis provides more than a confident assertion that God will keep his promises. He also adds in Noah a delightful example of how humans ought to respond to God's promise.

Most mythological heroes act like heroes. They are brave, resourceful, dominating men. Not so Noah, who displays human faults, including a propensity for, as the Irish say, "too much of the drink taken" and also a certain craftiness in figuring out whether the floodwaters are receding.

In many of the stories that are told as elaborations of the terse Genesis account, Noah is depicted as the target of ridicule from his neighbors and even from his wife and family. Moreover, he is often portrayed as a man who has his own doubts about the strange commands God has given him.

No expanded version of the Noah story is more charming than the famous Bill Cosby routine in which Noah complains and complains and complains—until the rain starts. Then he prays fervently, "Just you and me, Lord! Just you and me!"

These "extrapolations" of the Noah story are based on the insight that, despite his faithful obedience to God's commands, Noah must have often wondered and doubted. How could he have been human and not doubted the bizarre instructions God gave him? Yet, for all the doubts he might have had, Noah responded the way all must, according to the author of Genesis, respond to trouble and obscurity: you do what you believe God wants you to do and trust in him.

As absurd as it might have seemed, Noah built the ark. He believed in God and trusted most in God. So God renewed his promise with Noah.

How should we react when the world seems absurd, when life seems meaningless, when there appears to be no sanity, no purpose, no rationale for continuing to exist?

We must simply cling to our faith in God's promise of love.

Contemporary followers of the biblical traditions understand the difference in the various literary genres in the TNK; they realize that the Noah story is a folktale invested with religious meaning; they ask elaborate questions about the problem of evil. But when push comes to shove, they have no better answer to the troubles of human life than that which Genesis presents concretely in the behavior of Noah: you hang onto your faith, do what you have to do, and trust in God's loving promises.

Somehow, some way, the rainbow will appear and God will renew his covenant.

So the flood story in the TNK continues the theme of the creation story and makes it more explicit: God will not be defeated by human sinfulness. His promise will continue and be renewed no matter what humans may do.

The author of the text (or, more likely, of the sources in this case) is skillfully developing and expanding the theme of God's promise to prepare the way for an explicit promise to Abraham that will begin the history of the Hebrew people.

The word "covenant" (or "testament") appears at the end of the Noah story. The rainbow is a sign of the covenant God has made with Noah—he would never again destroy the world by flood. It is a modest promise, but it outlines the style of the relationship between God and his people that will structure the rest of the Torah. The covenants God will make repeatedly with his people in successive episodes of the story will become more explicit and more detailed. The author of Genesis sees history as a progression in the detail of divine "grants" to humans. It can just as well be seen as a progression of human understanding about the nature of God and the promise that seems to be implied in human experience of God.

The author of Genesis, then, is well aware of religious evolution. The relationship with God depicted in his earliest sources is not the relationship available in later sources, much less in the religious environment in which he was writing. From the human viewpoint there is progress in God's self-disclosure. From God's viewpoint, perhaps, there is progress in understanding the promise that is disclosed in creation and history and human relationships. The dialogue between God and humankind continues.

The covenant metaphor seems to have been taken from secular grants made by human rulers—unilateral privileges given by someone with great power to someone who lacks power. The ancient Near Eastern covenant was a one-sided treaty in which the one who made the grant bound himself regardless of the behavior of the grantee. Conditions were imposed unilaterally by the grantor, but even if the conditions were not honored the grant was still valid. "I am YHWH, your God, regardless of what you do. I expect you to be a faithful people, but even if you're not, I am still your God."

Thus did postexilic Israel experience its God and thus did it interpret the experience of its predecessors—quite reasonably, given the data to be found in the sources. God was determined to see that the work of creation reached its designed goals. He made a promise by the very work of creation and to humans specifically by creating them. No obstacles would deter him from fulfilling that promise. God is a ruler who would not revoke his grant because the grantee failed to honor the conditions imposed. Nor was he a lover who would regret his love because the beloved proved unfaithful.

The covenant image would dominate the stories of the patriarchs and in part even the story of Moses. By the time of the prophets (before the exile) Israel would discover the pathos of God, and the image of God as a lover would grow stronger. In both images the theme of a promise that would never falter is the essential religious experience of Israel.

Christianity would use the metaphors of Adam and Noah to describe its primal experience of Jesus. He was the new Adam who was the father of the renewed humanity. He was the new Noah who presided over another survival and another covenant between God and his people.

Or to put the matter differently, for early Christians both Adam and Noah "prefigured" Jesus and prepared humankind for later renewals of God's promise, for "new testaments."

Such "figurative" interpretations of the TNK do not deny the importance, much less the validity, of earlier experiences and earlier stories of God. The Noah story is valid in itself and does not exist merely to anticipate Jesus. It is, however, part of the same story of God's promise that is manifested again in Jesus. It represents a theme that will recur again and again as God continues to renew his promise. Noah and Jesus, each in his own way, share in the work of revealing and renewing the promise.

And both show us how to live in confidence of God's ultimate triumph, no matter how grim the immediate prospects may be.

12

NEUSNER

And Abram Put His Faith in the Lord

Some time later, the word of the Lord came to Abram in a vision. He said, "Fear not, Abram, I am a shield to you; your reward shall be very great."

But Abram said, "O Lord God, what can You give me, seeing that I shall die childless, and the one in charge of my household is Dammesek Eliezer!"

Abram said further, "Since you have granted me no offspring, my steward shall be my heir."

The word of the Lord came to him in reply, "That one shall not be your heir; none but your very own issue shall be your heir."

He took him outside and said, "Look toward heaven and count the stars, if you are able to count them." And He added, "So shall your offspring be."

And because he put his trust in the Lord, He reckoned it to his merit.

Then He said to him, "I am the Lord who brought you out from Ur of the Chaldeans to assign this land to you as a possession."

And he said, "Lord God, how shall I know that I am to possess it?"

He answered, "Bring Me a three-year-old heifer, a three-year-old she-goat, a three-year-old ram, a turtledove, and a young bird."

He brought Him all these and cut them in two, placing each half opposite the other; but he did not cut up the bird.

Birds of prey came down upon the carcasses, and Abram drove them away.

As the sun was about to set, a deep sleep fell upon Abram, and a great dark dread descended upon him. And He said to Abram, "Know well that your offspring shall be strangers in a land not theirs, and they shall be enslaved and oppressed four hundred years; but I will execute judgment on the nation they shall serve, and in the end, they shall go free with great wealth. As for you, you shall go to your fathers in peace; you shall be buried at a ripe old age. And they shall return here in the fourth generation, for the iniquity of the Amorites is not yet complete."

When the sun set and it was very dark, there appeared a smoking oven and a flaming torch which passed between those pieces. On that day the Lord made a covenant with Abraham, saying, "To your offspring I assign this land, from the river of Egypt to the great river, the river Euphrates; the Kenites, the Kenizzites, the Kadmonites, the Hittites, the Perizzites, the Rephaim, the Amorites, the Canaanites, the Girgashites, and the Jebusites."

Genesis 15:1–21

What makes Abraham so appealing that Judaism, Christianity, and Islam trace themselves back to him: all part of his family and Sarah's descendants?

If I only knew the story and not the history that begins there, would I predict that the man and wife portrayed here would so enchant so much of humanity? Well, yes, I think I would. The reason is that, with Abraham and Sarah, people we can believe really lived and breathed enter the story. Adam and Eve, Noah—these stand for beliefs, but they are not really believable as flesh-and-blood people. They don't say much; they don't seem to feel; they just do things.

But Abram and Sarai, whose names get changed to Abraham and Sarah—these are real people. Why do I say so? Because, like the rest of us, they doubt as much as they believe, maybe more. Like the rest of us, they want things, they hope, they worry, they feel, they love, they hate—they're human. I'd like to say they could be figures in one of Father Greeley's novels, except, after all, they're not Irish. They're Jewish, and everyone can make them whatever they want from that starting point!

What makes humanity human? It's not strength but weakness, not the saint but the sinner. At the patience of the saint the world can marvel, but with the impatience of the doubting sinner I can identify. And Abraham and Sarah matter because, doubting and troubled, they nonetheless believe. Never fully persuaded, testing God and being tested by him, Abraham muddles through. All they really seem to want most of the time is a place to stay in a life of wandering and children to raise for these barren parents. And these God has called to greatness: Islam, Judaism, Christianity all begin with a man who challenges God, "What can you give me anyhow, seeing that I shall die childless?" But there is that answer: "None but your very own issue shall be your heir."

That's a pretty humble exchange. But the stakes prove cosmic: "And because he put his trust in the lord, the Lord reckoned it to his merit."

Is that all it took? Yes, but it was hard, so it was enough: to believe in a heart filled with doubt, to overcome anxiety, to affirm and not deny, even when nothing out there gives you reason to believe—that is an act of courage. It is the hardest thing that most of us ever have to do: to believe, to affirm, to say yes, yes to ourselves and those we love and who love us and to God. That is why belief is worthy of merit, because it runs against the everyday, not because the here and now confirm that faith. No wonder Christianity, Islam, and Judaism reach back to Abraham. You begin with where, and with what, we really are: full of doubt, occupied with purely personal concerns, yet able to affirm and serve when God calls, as God calls us all.

Strange story, human story, honest story, real story about real people. The bearer of the blessing of God for humanity, Abraham, progenitor of Israel, the holy people, doubts but believes, not once but many times. His entire life is a test, and what puts him to the test is faith in God's promise. "What can you possibly give me, if I have no heirs and continuators?" So Abraham doubts with good reason, for God promises this and that, each promise contradicting the facts of the world.

We think of God in cosmic terms; we don't realize that God is in the here and the now and this is the only place we shall know God. That world in which God makes promises and demands comprises these homely facts. God rips a wife and husband out of their homeland and family and says they will have a homeland and a family. Why bother? Just leave them where they are. God promises descendants to a childless couple, long past fertility. How so? God promises a land to a landless wanderer. When and where? God promises a future to the enslaved children of a pariah on the earth. Can it ever be? Whatever God promises is paradox and ridicule of what now prevails. But Abram believed, putting his trust in the Lord, and that represented Abram's merit. But the believing was never very easy, and the doubts were many indeed.

We start with Abraham's discovery of God. How did he know, without being told, that God had made the world and was to be served? Our sages find striking the power of Abram to deny his father's house, his home and country, to become an immigrant, a person of no standing and no place:

> "Now the Lord said to Abram, 'Go from your country and your kindred and your father's house to the land that I will show you' " (Gen. 12:1):
>
> R. Isaac opened [discourse by citing the following verse of Scripture]: "Hearken, O daughter, and consider and incline your ear; forget also your own people and your father's house" (Ps. 45:11).
>
> Said R. Isaac, "The matter may be compared to the case of someone who was going from one place to another when he saw a great house on fire. He said, 'Is it possible to say that such a great house has no one in charge?'
>
> "The owner of the house looked out and said to him, 'I am the one in charge of the house.'
>
> "Thus since Abraham, our father, [took the initiative and] said, 'Is it possible for the world to endure without someone in charge,' the Holy One, blessed be he, [responded and] looked out and said to him, 'I am the one in charge of the house, the lord of all the world.' "

Abraham came to God before God came to Abraham; that is how the Torah sees this stunning call to leave "your country and family and father's house and go to some distant place." Abram went looking for God, even before God found Abram. And the Torah tells the story of that search, each for the other.

Abraham and Sarah went in search of God. Were they the first? Well, as a matter of fact, they were. A verse in Jeremiah is read by our sages to say just that. What about the generations between Noah and Abraham? Why have they not responded as Abraham did?

> R. Azariah commenced discourse [by citing the following verse of Scripture]:
> " 'We would have healed Babylon, but she was not healed' (Jer. 41:9).
>> " 'We would have healed Babylon' refers to the generation of Enosh.
>> " 'But she was not healed' refers to the generation of the Flood.
>> " 'Forsake her' refers to the generation of the dispersion.
>> " ' . . . and let us go every one to his own country' (Jer. 51:9):
> "Thus: 'Now the Lord said to Abram, "Go from your country and your kindred . . . to the land that I will show you" ' (Gen. 12:1)."

How come Abram left Babylonia? Why did God not have him do his work there? God had done the work, with the generation of the flood and of the dispersion, and it had done no good. The peoples who had formed one people gave up and returned to their own countries, so God had Abram leave Babylonia for the land of Israel. Linking Abram's call to the generation of the dispersion not only ties the threads of the narrative. It also contrasts Israel's loyalty to the land with the cosmopolitan character of the generation of the dispersion, shown by its willingness to abandon its ancestral homeland.

And why Abraham in particular? First, because Abraham sought both justice and mercy for the Sodomites. Therefore, Abraham was a worthy founder for Israel. Second, because Abraham held God to the same rule that applied to humanity: "Will not the judge of all the world do justly?" (Gen. 18:25). God is bound by the rules of the Torah. God is restricted by the covenant that is in force with Noah. So Abraham is the right person to set forth on the journey that would rise to the height of Sinai and the meeting with God. No wonder Christendom and Islam find in Abraham their roots and beginnings as much as Judaism does: to Abraham, God is the judge of all the world, bound by one set of rules for all peoples. Here is the founder, the one who loves righteousness and hates wickedness. He may not be rich in acts of faith, so his capacity to believe through his doubt is what is noteworthy. But he surely is rich in acts of mercy and justice, and that is what counts:

> R. Azariah in the name of R. Aha commenced [discourse by citing the following verse of Scripture]: "You have loved righteousness and hated wickedness" (Ps. 45:8).
> R. Azariah in the name of R. Aha interpreted the verse to speak of our

father, Abraham: "When our father, Abraham, stood to seek mercy for the Sodomites, what is written there? 'Far be it from you to do such a thing' (Gen. 18:25)."

Said R. Aha, "[Abram said to God,] 'You bound yourself by an oath not to bring a flood upon the world. Are you now going to act deceitfully against the clear intent of that oath? True enough, you are not going to bring a flood of water, but you are going to bring a flood of fire. If so you will not carry out the oath!' "

Said R. Levi, " 'Will not the judge of all the earth do justly?' (Gen. 18:25). 'If you want to have a world, there can be no justice, and if justice is what you want, there can be no world. You are holding the rope at both ends, you want a world and you want justice. If you don't give in a bit, the world can never stand.'

"Said the Holy One, blessed be he, to him, Abraham, 'You have loved righteousness and hated wickedness. Therefore God, your God, has anointed you with the oil of gladness above your fellows' (Ps. 45:8).

" 'From Noah to you there are ten generations [that is, that lived from Noah to Abraham].

" 'Among all of them, I spoke only with you.' "

"And the Lord said to Abram, 'Go from your country and your kindred and your father's house to the land that I will show you' " (Gen. 12:1).

The element at issue now is the singling out of Abraham, and that is on account of his love of righteousness. On that basis the world can endure. But there is another element in Abraham's advantage. He also trusted God, and that was shown at each stage in his long and troubled life. At the very outset, for instance:

" 'To the land that I will show you:' but why did he not inform him [in advance where that would be]?

"It was so as to make it still more precious in his view and to give him a reward for each step that he took [in perfect faith and reliance on God]."

Abraham trusted in God from the outset to the end, and that—as I pointed out to begin with—was his merit. What makes me think so? Because it also was the most difficult task assigned to him. For believing despite the evidence of this world, affirming God's love for Israel despite Israel's sorry condition in the world, acknowledging God's rule of the world even when that rule appears to permit unspeakable horror—trust in God is more difficult, even, than love for God. And Abraham is the model and the paradigm.

Now what is strange in the story of the covenant between the parts that is portrayed at my starting point is this: Abram really doesn't believe at all.

God says, "Your reward shall be very great," and Abram says, "I have no children." God states: "Look toward heaven and count, so shall your off-spring be." Abram says nothing at all. But "he put his trust in the Lord," and "the Lord reckoned it to his merit." Abram doesn't believe, because he sees himself as not only the first but also the last to believe in God. He sees no future. Despairing, Abraham thinks he is not only the first but also the last Jew on earth!

Israel begins with Abraham, and in him I see the trait of eternal Israel: a hopeful people always on the edge of despair. And in that trait eternal Israel stands for many of us in the everyday world: hopeful amid disappointment, going forward through life even though unsure there is a future to go to. That painful story of how Abraham responds to God's statement captures the condition of Israel, the Jewish people, because it portrays what it means to be human: "Since you have granted me no offspring, my steward shall be my heir." That explains why Abram, whom we know was the first of Israel, Islam, and Christendom—the first Jew, who also is the first Christian, who also is the first Muslim—thinks he is going to be not only first but last. Nobody ever said faith was easy. The Torah says it's the hardest thing in life.

For this conversation with God shows us the despair of the man who heard the commandment, "Go from your land . . . to a land that I shall show you," and the one who expects to be the last of his line shows us both sides of Israel's faith. On the one side, Israel sees itself in the Torah as the holy people, of old, of now, of all time. On the other, Israel sees itself on the brink of death, every generation expecting to be the last generation. A great theologian, Simon Rawidowicz, called Israel "the ever dying people." By that he meant Israel is a people that always thinks it's dying. He said this after the Holocaust, and he meant that Israel has to accept its own eternity. And so do all of us.

The merit of Abraham comes because for him, as for us all, faith is not easy but hard, and trust, the highest form of faith, also is the hardest religious duty that we know. Well did God reckon that trust of Abraham as merit; in that attitude the human being sets forth whatever he or she has to give, and God receives whatever God is going to get that is truly ours to give. God can command love. God can exact affirmations of faith in this and faith about that. These speak from the surface of things. Faith that God is one, belief that God demands that we not murder and not steal, and obedience to those demands—these we can offer without ourselves being changed. They are matters of actions and verbal affirmations. But attitudes form us and express what is particular about us, and our attitude is what ultimately takes shape in the form of deed and in the expression of conviction. So it is that trust in God that is to Abraham's credit in particular, since that is what has to have been the most difficult thing to offer.

Well, Abraham has gained his merit. And what of the future? You cannot be surprised to learn that our sages find in this story not only a day long past, but the future history that Israel will endure. This, as a matter of fact, involves the nations of the world, not Israel alone. Abraham is told that through him all nations of the world will be blessed. But where do we hear about the nations of the world? No one has mentioned them just yet. The nations, it turns out, rule by reason of Israel's failure, and the return of Israel to its land, in God's good time, will mark the right relationship between God and Israel.

In this story of Abraham's faith and the merit that his trust earns we gain a grand vision of all of human history. No wonder Islam and Christendom as much as Judaism identify with Abraham. For in this passage of the Torah all the nations find their place and order, organized around God's plan and program for Israel, the holy people. Our sages review the history of the great empires, in relationship to the life of Israel: Babylonia, Media, Greece, then Edom, which is Rome, then ruling. In our day we might insert France, Germany, Britain, and the United States in sequence through Napoleon, Bismarck, imperial England after World War I, and our own country after World War II. It is as if we were to claim that everything that has happened to world history for the past two centuries gains meaning, makes sense, only in relationship to what happened to one of the smallest and least important peoples in the world:

"[And it came to pass, as the sun was going down,] lo, a deep sleep fell on Abram, and lo, a dread and great darkness fell upon him" (Gen. 15:12):

". . . lo, a dread" refers to Babylonia, as it is written, "Then was Nebuchadnezzar filled with fury" (Gen. 3:19).

". . . and darkness" refers to Media, which darkened the eyes of Israel by making it necessary for the Israelites to fast and conduct public mourning.

". . . great . . ." refers to Greece.

". . . fell upon him" refers to Edom, as it is written, "The earth quakes at the noise of their fall" (Jer. 49:21).

"Then the Lord said to Abram, 'Know of a surety ["that your descendants will be sojourners in a land that is not theirs, and they will be slaves there, and they will be oppressed for four hundred years; but I will bring judgment on the nation which they serve, and afterward they shall come out with great possessions"]' " (Gen. 15:13–14):

"Know" that I shall scatter them.

"Of a certainty" that I shall bring them back together again.

"Know" that I shall put them out as a pledge [in expiation of their sins].
"Of a certainty" that I shall redeem them.
"Know" that I shall make them slaves.
"Of a certainty" that I shall free them.

Here are the choices before Israel, humble choices, homely fates. The Israelites are scattered but can be brought back together again. They sin but can atone and be redeemed. They are slaves but can be free. And how are all these things brought about? If the answer were to appeal to some sort of national virtue, then I doubt Islam and Christendom could identify with so parochial a conception of God's relationship to the world. But we now see Israel is humanity writ small. What happens to Israel happens everywhere and to everyone, because of what is at stake. The issue in the end draws us back to the home and hearth: what we are, what we believe, what we do, in the private space in which we live.

First we learn that Israel's fate is in fact in its own hands. If they do their duty, by obedience to the Torah and by sustaining the offerings, they will be spared the suffering of the rule by the nations.

". . . behold a smoking fire pot and a flaming torch passed between these pieces" (Gen. 15:17):

Simeon bar Abba in the name of R. Yohanan: "He showed him four things, Gehenna, the [four] kingdoms, the giving of the Torah, and the sanctuary. He said to him, 'So long as your descendants are occupied with these latter two, they will be saved from the former two. If they abandon two of them, they will be judged by the other two.' "

Then what is the upshot if the Israelites do not do what they should? They suffer one of two penalties, and God and Abraham have made the choice:

"He said to him, 'What is your preference? Do you want your children to go down into Gehenna or to be subjugated to the four kingdoms?' "

R. Hinena bar Pappa said, "Abraham chose for himself the subjugation to the four kingdoms."

R. Yudan and R. Idi and R. Hama bar Hanina: "Abraham chose for himself Gehenna, but the Holy One, blessed be he, chose the subjugation to the four kingdoms for him."

R. Huna in the name of R. Aha: "Now Abraham sat and puzzled all that day, saying, 'Which should I choose?'

"Said the Holy One, blessed be he, to him, 'Choose without delay.' That is in line with this verse: 'On that day the Lord made a covenant with Abram' (Gen. 15:18)."

R. Yudan and R. Idi and R. Hama bar Hanina said in the name of a single sage in the name of Rabbi: "The Holy One, blessed be he, chose the subjugation to the four kingdoms for him, in line with the following verse of Scripture: 'You have caused men to ride over our heads' (Ps. 66:12). That is to say, you have made ride over our heads various nations, and it is as though 'we went through fire and through water' (Ps. 66:21)."

F. R. Joshua said, "Also the splitting of the Red Sea he showed him, as it is written, 'That passed between these pieces' (Gen. 15:17), along the lines of the verse, 'O give thanks to him who divided the Red Sea in two' [in which the same word, the letters for pieces, occurs as 'in two'] (Ps. 86:13)."

The upshot is that what happens to Israel is not accident but choice, and not the choice of an ordinary person but the will of God in consultation with Abraham. The special interest is in Israel's suffering later on, with the particular stress on God's choosing subjugation to the nations as the appropriate penalty for Israel's failures to come. In fact, Abraham is made party to the entire future history of Israel, even choosing, in dealing with God, the penalty for their sin and their mode of atonement. But, on the other side of suffering, the gift of the land awaits: "To your descendants I give this land."

Why do I insist that this is a story about everybody? Because the issue is sin and suffering, atonement and reconciliation. And these are things that each of us does and all of us seek. True, the issue is framed in terms of not every person but a whole people, quite distinctive and particular. Suffering is set forth in national terms: exile, subjugation to foreigners. But the reason for the need to atone lies in what I have done and you have done, in the here and the now. So the nation stands for each person, and the history of the nation corresponds to the lives of everyone. That is how the story of Abraham finds its way into the hearts of one and all. And that explains why the Torah can also enter the Qu'ran and the Bible. Islam and Christendom understand that, then and now, there was and is "Israel," meaning the Jewish people. But in Abraham they find their origins, and that is because the story of Israel serves as the account of how things are for everyone.

But we should not forget, and we Jews have not forgotten, the particulars of the story. In the story before us, the land is the centerpiece. The story of Abraham's covenant between the parts takes the form of an account of Israel and the land of Israel. It is in that relationship between holy people and holy land that God's relationship to humanity finds its paradigm. So, in the details of the covenant, it is in the loss by Israel of the land of Israel and the restoration of the people Israel to the land of Israel that the origins of the people in its land took on their cogent meaning. That very private and particular, almost personal picture of things yields a principle that everyone can grasp.

Starting with the particular, it is this. Even when the land is promised, it is also promised under conditions. Israel can have the land but can lose it, too. So on the one side, Israel then began with its acquisition of the land, through Abraham. Israel attained its identity as a people through the promise of the land, in the covenant of Sinai, and the entry into the land, under Joshua. But even to begin with, Abraham is warned, the land is not a given, but merely a gift. The Torah recast Israel's history into the story of the conditional existence of the people, their existence measured in their possession of the land upon the stipulation of God's favor. Everything depended on carrying out a contract originally made with Abraham, Isaac, and Jacob: do this, get that, do not do this, do not get that—and nothing formed a given, beyond all stipulation.

So much for the particularization of a truth I think universally pertinent. How can I express matters in a way that everyone can find personal? It is very simple: the land for Israel stands for life for all of us. And life is not a given but a gift. It is not to be taken for granted but to be treasured. The nation restored to its land may be compared to a person healed from a life-threatening illness. To such as these nothing loses its astonishing quality. Once one has recovered, to such a now-well person nothing ever can look the same as it did before. Life cannot be taken for granted, as a given. Life becomes a gift, each day an unanticipated surprise. Everything then demands explanation, but uncertainty reigns.

So with Abraham we receive the story of nationhood for Israel, life for us all, subject to condition and stipulation, forever threatened with desolation, always requiring renewal. For the Torah teaches the picture of society subject to judgment. And nothing is secure. And the same lesson illuminates the lives of us all. And why not, when we remember that the whole issue concerned whether or not an old woman and an old man could have a baby? I can't think of anything less national, social, and public, more private, more rich in pathos, than household gossip about childlessness. So what holy Israel has found through history is the same as what ordinary you and me find in life. It is that everything is subject to conditions and no gift ever is a given.

13
GREELEY
Abraham

The architectonic theme of God's unconditional promise—and hence unconditional love—explodes in the Genesis story of Abraham. Humans continue to engage in behavior that puts God's promise in jeopardy. God continues to fend off humans' stupidity and weakness to sustain his promise. The promise becomes more explicit and detailed and hence more subject to human resistance and recalcitrance. God, however, continues to stand by his commitments.

The redactor of Genesis reads his own theology back into the accounts available to him in his remote sources. Yet the theme of promise is already available in the sources, early records of the prehistoric experience of the ancestors of Israel.

Perhaps the oldest documentary account of the ancient experience of Israel is contained in a prayer that Deuteronomy urges Israel to pray to YHWH:

My father was a wandering Aramean. He went down into Egypt to find refuge there, few in numbers, but here he became a nation, great, mighty and strong. The Egyptians ill-treated us, they gave us no peace and inflicted harsh slavery on us. But we called on YHWH the God of our fathers. YHWH heard our voice and saw our misery, our toil and our oppression; and YHWH brought us out of Egypt with mighty hand and outstretched arm, with great terror and with signs and wonders. He brought us here and gave us this land, a land where milk and honey flow.

The word *promise* is not used but is implicit in this ancient segment (so ancient that it does not seem to know even about the Sinai experience). Israel justifies its appeal to YHWH in terms of his existing relationship with their fathers. The Israel of the exodus (immediately after the exodus, if this text is as old as the scholars think it is) already claimed a special relationship with God, a relationship which he had already established.

As Genesis tries to arrange its data around the theme of promise, it sometimes selects materials that have to be stripped of their original meaning and converted to mean something quite different than they once did.

The classic example of this—and one very important for our understanding of how the TNK works—is the story of Abraham and Isaac. In its origins it was almost certainly a folktale used to condemn human sacrifice. It has been converted to mean that God will honor his promises even if he seems to have put an insurmountable obstacle in the way of the fulfillment of the promise.

One might wish that the author had chosen another folktale to make his point, so great has been the confusion and misunderstanding it has produced.

The point of the story (in its context in Genesis) and the only point is that God fulfills his promise regardless of what happens. Attempts to justify the behavior of God in the story are fruitless. The author of Genesis (or the source from which this context is taken) is not concerned to explain the utter irrationality of God's command, nor to defend God from the accusation of being cruel and irrational. He does not praise Abraham for an obedience that is sinful by our standards (and by those of his time, too). Nor does the author care about excusing God from the charge of demanding an obedience that is sinful. None of these matters is on the author's mind. They are irrelevant to what he intends—and what the author intends and only what he intends is what a segment of the Bible means.

All the author of Genesis intends to convey is that nothing can stand in the way of God's promise—that and no other interpretation is valid for the story in its context in Genesis. No matter what obstacles humans put in its way, the promise will be fulfilled.

This is the constitutive theme of the story of Abraham and his descendants, of the Torah from Abraham down to Exodus. It is difficult if not impossible to make sense of many of the stories of family conflicts and personal misbehavior in these chapters of Genesis 12–26 unless one understands the fundamental "story line" that God's promise survives no matter what humans do. Attempts to rationalize or justify the often crude and savage actions of the patriarchs are foolish because the author of the book does not approve of their behavior either. The patriarchs are no better than their religious descendants, Jewish or Christian, and that is exactly what the Genesis storyteller is trying to teach us: just as the sinful humanity of the fathers of Israel—often a base and cruel humanity—could not invalidate God's promise, so too our flawed and errant humanity cannot block God's overwhelming love.

The emphasis, then, is not on the greatness of Abraham and Isaac and Jacob but on the implacable commitment of the God of Abraham and Isaac and Jacob—a God who to them was a Semitic warrior God but to the author of Genesis the simultaneously transcendent and immanent God of the prophets: a lover who never turns away from the beloved. To understand Genesis one must read Hosea's story (about which more later) back into the story of the patriarchs. That requires that we break ourselves of the habit of imagining that Hosea was written after Genesis because the latter tells of deeds in olden times. In fact, the final synthesis of Genesis was written centuries after Hosea and with the prophetic image of the "pathos" of God very much in mind.

Gerhard von Rad, perhaps the greatest of the modern scholars of the TNK, sums up the message this way:

> The era of the patriarchs as a whole is understood as the time of promise, an elaborate preparatory arrangement of the creation of the people of God and for its life. What is new in this view is not the use of the idea of promise in itself. . . . The promise of a land and of children already formed a part of the oldest traditions deriving from the patriarchal age. What is new is rather the theological employment of this twofold promise as a word of God which set in motion the whole of the saving history down to the conquest under Joshua. Behind this conception lies a prolonged and insistent reflection upon herself on Israel's part. The Israel which had become conscious of her peculiarity now felt the need to visualize how she came into being. Thus, there lies behind the patriarchal history in the Hexateuch* a mighty amazement at the far-reaching preparations which YHWH had made to summon Israel into being.†

Abraham is promised at the beginning of his story that he will be the father of a great people, a promise that is repeated a number of times in the story as the author brings together his various sources. There are serious problems with the promise. First, Abraham's wife, Sarah, is beyond the childbearing age. However, she is not so far beyond childbearing, it would seem, that her husband does not fondle her in public and that she does not attract the desires of the pharaoh, who takes her into his harem because of the cowardice and deceit of her husband. Abraham's betrayal of his wife and giving her over to slavery (an act as despicable at the time Genesis was written as it would be today) endangers the fulfillment of the promise. At that point, the author says in effect, it looks as though the promise is in great trouble (as are the crew of the starship *Enterprise* when they are beamed down to a strange planet and promptly arrested by the resident aliens). Then God intervenes and the pharaoh learns that Abraham has lied to him: the mature but appealing Sarah is his wife, not his sister. Egypt is

---

*Von Rad includes the book of Joshua together with the first five to form a "Hexateuch."
†*Old Testament Theology*, Vol 1. New York: Harper & Brothers, 1962, 170.

suffering plague because the pharaoh is guilty of adultery. Back goes Sarah to her husband, presumably with appropriate comments from her about what she thinks of this liar and coward to whom she is married.

The first setback has been overcome; however, as in all good stories, there must be three conflicts before the denouement. Sarah is still childless and now even older than when she was traded to the Egyptian. The angel of YHWH shows up and announces that, age or not, she will still conceive a son. Sarah overhears the promise and laughs at the prospect of further dalliance (at her age!) with her husband—although she has returned from sustained dalliance with the king of Egypt. Despite her laughter, she does indeed sleep with her husband, conceives, and gives birth to Isaac. The second conflict situation is surmounted.

Then we come to the most serious problem of all. Abraham's having a son is essential for the fulfillment of the promise, but it would appear that the son must die. The suspense is now at its height as the story crashes towards a conclusion. God intervenes and forbids the sacrifice, and the reader sighs with relief. Just as the crew of the *Enterprise* blast off at warp factor nine toward another adventure, so God and his promise survive until another day and another challenge from humans who stand in his way.

God is the protagonist of these chapters of Genesis, and the antagonists are the patriarchs whose stupidity and venality and obduracy constantly provoke him and almost but not quite frustrate his plan (which is not at all the same as their plans).

Read this way, Genesis is a series of variations on the theme of God drawing straight with crooked lines. The author of Genesis, however, is not interested in presenting a theology that demonstrates good being drawn out of evil. Rather, he is asserting simply and absolutely that God will accomplish what he has set out to accomplish, that he will, come what may, fulfill the promises that he has made.

In our terms God, having disclosed himself as a God of promise, will not back off on that self-disclosure.

What, however, is the nature of the promise? For the patriarchs it took the form of a guarantee of land and people. For Moses, as we will see, it was a covenant between God and a special people he had made his own. For the prophets and the Hebrew religious tradition (including Genesis) that they shaped, it was an intimacy between the individual (as well as the community) and a God who was totally transcendent and yet bound to them so intensely that he suffered with and because of them.

All of these are metaphors/stories for an experience of God that on the one hand is universal and on the other hand developed in a unique direction in ancient Israel.

At its most simple, the experience of a God who promises merely means that life has meaning. The promise is a pledge of a meaningful life. John Haught rephrases the question to which the promise is an answer in terms that might have meaning for moderns:

> Is the universe alone? Have the galaxies struggled in absolutely solitary silence throughout the ages of their evolution? Has evolution been completely unaccompanied by any principle of care and concern? Has life on earth labored along for two or three billion years in lonesome struggle eventually to produce the human species only by accident?

Often it seems that the answers to all of these questions is surely "yes," just as it seemed to those who heard the story of Abraham and the promise of a people to him and his descendants that the answer would have to be "yes" to the question, Must we abandon hope for the promise because the matriarch is a helpless slave in the harem of an Egyptian king?

Professor Haught describes the grounds for the modern "yes," a despair as profound as that which the enslavement of Sarah seemed to justify: "According to such modern thought the absolute indifference of the universe is the basis from which all honest thinking must begin."

Perhaps some of the most recent and advanced speculations of theoretical physics would provide a more hopeful view: in the first tiny fraction of a second of the exploding universe (when it was still so small that one would have needed a microscope to see it) the biopolymers—the raw materials from which life would eventually develop—were already present.

Yet the conviction that the universe is essentially empty is powerful and persuasive—and did not require modern scientific skepticism for justification. Often life does seem foolish and meaningless.

Yet as Professor Haught responds:

> Followers of the biblical tradition . . . believe that they have heard a "word" speaking out to us in our apparent lostness, a light shining in the darkness, a divine voice telling us that we are not alone and that the cosmos has from the beginning been delivered from its apparent companionlessness . . . for the Christian the person of Jesus of Nazareth constitutes the decisive breaking in of the promise of fulfillment felt long ago by Abraham. *

The promise, so conceived, seems modest enough—a life of purpose, a life of fulfillment. Does not such a possibility occur to almost everyone who

---

* "Revelation," *The New Dictionary of Theology* (Wilmington, Del.: Michael Glazier, 1987), 887.

is human? What is so special about the experience of Israel? Could not any people have argued from the virtually universal human experience of "promise" that human life is an invitation to a passionate love affair with a suffering and implacably loving God?

Right! Any people could have come to that conclusion. Any people might have reasoned from its experience of life as possibly meaningful and fulfilling to a God who was both immanent and transcendent, as supreme as any God of the world religions and as involved as any desert god of winds and storms.

However, the Israelite people, who by the admission of their own history were often not very much, were the only ones who did reason to such a God. However one might choose to explain the image of God that burst on the human scene in the time of Hebrew prophets, the appearance of such an image was an astonishing phenomenon, especially when it appeared among such a crude and unpromising people as the Hebrews.

Or again in yet more elaborate fashion, the Christian would say, in such a ragtag band of ne'er-do-wells as the disciples of Jesus.

Note that in its essence as a hint, the possibility of a promise is a fact of human experience. Thus neither the "Sinai event" nor the "Jesus event" represents experiences which are totally new and unexpected in the human condition. They deepen and enrich human understanding of the promise and powerfully confirm it. They do not tell humans anything so totally new that they had never before expected its possibility.

Is the self-disclosure of YHWH of the prophets the result of "ordinary" or "special" revelation? Probably a mixture of both, says the person of faith— and the "special" revelation was probably necessary to confirm that the incredible good news of a supreme creator who was also passionately involved was not too good to be true. This image of God could have been guessed without "special" help; indeed, it has always lurked in the human condition as a faint possibility. But it hardly could have been embraced with the passionate and total seriousness of the prophets in the face of all the contrary evidence unless Israel had experienced a totally unique encounter with such a divine presence.

For that experience we must turn to Moses, who shaped the religious tradition out of which came the prophets and subsequently Judaism and Christianity. Moses, the rabbi says speaking for Jews, is "Our Rabbi." I'm sure he will grant me that we Christians can and must make the same claim for him.

14

NEUSNER

The Abraham of the Bible and the Abraham of the Torah

The one thing I read when I read the Torah that Father Greeley does not read when he reads the Bible is the story of my family. Our sages read the Torah as genealogy, family history, and Abraham is "our father, Abraham," Sarah, "our mother, Sarah." That way of reading Scripture as Torah, our Torah, God's personal letter to us, Israel, about us and our family, is so profound that at every turning in life we reread that letter and find in it sentences written as though this morning.

And while Father Greeley and with him the church that formed him explore the depths of meaning, it is not our meaning, because it can't be. He begins his reading of Abraham with the human condition; he speaks of humanity, but we hear Israel; he speaks of the promise, but we know the covenant. That is why the point of origin of a story in the Bible is unimportant in understanding an event in the Torah. For us this is an event in the here and now of the Torah, so whether or not there was some "original," this-worldly meaning, imputed by a long-ago author or storyteller, is monumentally irrelevant. That is why, for me, the point of the story cannot be located in the context of Genesis but in the context, only, of the holy and eternal life of Israel, God's people.

Abraham is a case in point. Abraham was ready to offer up his son, Isaac. In the terrible years from 1939 to 1945, when the Germans murdered most of the Jews of Europe, there was not one Abraham; there were many thousands, hundreds of thousands. And it was not Abraham alone, but it was Sarah. The Germans made Jews choose which of their children would live—for the Germans read the Bible, most of them having been raised as Protestants or Catholics (though their Nazi ideology perverted and corrupted Christianity and destroyed it). So they had fun telling Jews, "Pick a son, any son, and the others can live." How people responded you can imagine. So, too, the Germans sent the mothers and the children from the freight car to the gas chamber, and the mother had to choose which of her children she would hold in her arms, as she and the child suffocate in the gas. Pick a daughter, any daughter. And the others can die without the mother's embrace. No wonder, then, that after the war we found scraps of paper, prayers to God: "Abraham chose one and was ready to offer him but didn't, and I chose them all and they all died."

My point is simple. We cannot read Scripture as the story of long ago, and you cannot. But we also cannot read the Scripture as the story of the human condition, and you can and do. To us the story is the story of the God of Abraham, who is our grandfather, and Jacob, after whom we are named Israel. Read in this way, Genesis is a series of variations on a theme, as you say, but the theme is God patiently teaching our family how to live. There I find a real difference between us: the intensely personal Torah as against the (to me) rather general "human condition." Still, you can claim, and I would surely concur, that in the man Jesus there is another figure who, like Abraham or Jacob, in word and deed showed specifically and concretely what it means to be Israel. Of course he was a rabbi—what else? But, if a rabbi, then nothing else.

15

NEUSNER

"Take Your Son, Your Favored One, Isaac"

Some time afterward, God put Abraham to the test. He said to him, "Abraham," and he answered, "Here I am."

And He said, "Take your son, your favored one, Isaac, whom you love, and go to the land of Moriah, and offer him there as a burnt offering on one of the heights that I shall point out to you."

So early next morning, Abraham saddled his ass and took with him two of his servants and his son Isaac. He split the wood for the burnt offering, and he set out for the place of which God had told him.

On the third day, Abraham looked up and saw the place from afar. Then Abraham said to his servants, "You will stay with the ass. The boy and I will go up there; we will worship and we will return to you."

Abraham took the wood for the burnt offering and put it on his son Isaac. He himself took the firestone and the knife, and the two walked off together.

Then Isaac said to his father, Abraham, "Father!"

And he answered, "Yes, my son."

And he said, "Here are the firestone and the wood, but where is the sheep for the burnt offering?"

And Abraham said, "God will see to the sheep for His burnt offering, my son."

And the two of them walked on together.

They arrived at the place of which God had told him. Abraham built an altar there; he laid out the wood; he bound his son Isaac; he laid him on the altar, on top of the wood. And Abraham picked up the knife to slay his son.

Then an angel of the Lord called to him from heaven: "Abraham! Abraham!"

And he answered, "Here I am."

And he said, "Do not raise your hand against the boy or do anything to him. For now I know that you fear God, since you have not withheld your son, your favored one, from Me."

When Abraham looked up, his eye fell upon a ram, caught in the thicket by its horns. So Abraham went and took the ram and offered it up as a burnt offering in place of his son.

Genesis 22:1–13

Abraham belongs to everybody. But Isaac is ours, because Isaac is us, Israel in particular. Isaac is the victim, who dies—or is supposed to die—to prove someone else's point. We Jews identify with Isaac, because we see ourselves as the ever-dying people, always on the verge of extinction. So to us life is a gift: "*Lehaim* [to life]" is what we say when we drink. Not (merely) to health, but to life. Isaac had it all: son of a famous, rich man, favorite son at that. He stayed home (our sages say he was studying the Torah) with his mother and father, and when he got married his father arranged that, too. Easy life, no?

Well, not really. Keep in mind what his father had had in mind for him. That is something a Christian can understand, since Christianity too appeals to the figure of a willing victim, a weak man, someone who was "done to" but who did nothing: done in by his times, by his friends, by his father. And he too went willingly: "if this cup not pass . . . ," and "your will be done." So if in the story of the binding of Isaac on the altar Israel finds itself, in that same story the church finds Jesus Christ. Isaac arose from the altar and lived, and Jesus Christ arose from the cross and lived.

But we, Israel, are Isaac not only in general but in our own age in particular. For Isaac, the victim in the last trial that God imposed upon Abraham, stands for Israel, the people, in this most terrible trial of our long tale among the nations. It is no accident that, when Elie Wiesel went looking for a word to contain and capture the Judeocide—the murder of Europe's Jews by the Germans and their allies in World War II—he turned to the language of the sacrificial cult in Jerusalem's Temple and came up with the word for an offering that was wholly consumed on the altar's fires, which is *holocaust*. So the Judeocide became the Holocaust. And that is ours, isn't it?

A Roman Catholic Christian can hardly concur. For here, too, you invoke not only the death and resurrection of the new Isaac, Jesus, on his altar, but the sacrifice of the Eucharist, in which (in the language of the Letter to the Hebrews) the perfect victim is offered up by the perfect priest in the perfect sacrifice. Jesus become Christ is the sacrifice of the Eucharist. A holocaust? The word is not all that inappropriate.

But I have gotten ahead of my story. Why invoke the sanctifying experience of Christianity, the formative moment of Judaism, in speaking of the odd and frightening relationship of a father to his son? I have made the move from Scripture to the present moment without dwelling sufficiently on Scripture itself. So first comes Isaac, then comes the contemporary moment to lend new light to the ancient tale. The story is a simple one. God told Abraham, "Take your son, your favored one, Isaac, whom you love, and go to the land of Moriah, and offer him there as a burnt offering on one of the heights that I shall point out to you." So he did. Or he was ready to. That's the story, almost.

This last, most difficult trial demanded that Abraham overcome his natural love of his son, his honesty with his wife, Sarah (whose son, after all, Isaac also was), and his supernatural trust in God. God had promised Abraham descendants through Isaac. Now he is to slaughter Isaac as an offering. Everything from the call to leave Ur and come to the Holy Land is then to be declared naught. At the threshold of the grave, now surely beyond even the miracle of making new children with Sarah in his dotage, Abraham is now asked to repudiate what he wanted most in his life, his son by Sarah.

No wonder that Christians and Muslims as well as Jews identify Abraham as the beginning of their faith. For what can be a greater act of trust than to give up one's entire life and being to a demanding, incomprehensible God, One who gives and takes away? Sages capture the situation in very simple language, leaving open the question, Who would want to identify with Isaac, the gift?

> If someone should say, "He gives riches to whomever he wishes, and he impoverishes whomever he wishes, and whomever he wishes he makes king [all this without justice], and so too as to Abraham, when he wanted, he made him rich, and when he wanted, he made him king [and all this without justice]," you may reply to him, saying, "Can you do what Abraham did?"
>
> "Abraham was a hundred years old when Isaac, his son, was born to him" (Gen. 21:5). And after all that anguish, it was stated to him, "Take your son" (Gen. 22:2).
>
> And he did not demur.

Like Noah's, Abraham's trust in God overcame all doubt. But Noah held onto his family, and Abraham in the last trial gave up his future. So, as the sages say of Noah, the same applies to Abraham: "The Lord tries the righteous" (Ps. 11:5).

But precisely what was it that God wished to test in Abraham? Surely not trust, for Abraham had placed his trust in God. Nor could it have been loyalty, faith, commitment; these he had shown in abundance. Then the test is of a different sort altogether. Subject to the trial were both Abraham and Isaac, the one to give up, the other to be given up. Can the two walk together to a common end? That is the question that is answered. Yes, they can; yes, they did; yes, they do: it is how our family is.

And the main point as I see it, concerns not Abraham alone, but Isaac, especially Isaac. Abraham was ready to give up his son. Isaac was ready to give up his life. Abraham is the hero. But is Isaac merely a victim? No, I think not. Abraham is a man of power, who by his own will leaves his family and by his own courage travels as an immigrant to a distant land and by his own faith trusts in God to make it all work. But is Isaac a mere son, an accident, a nothing? He did not create the comfort in which he lived, nor the glory that being son of Abraham brought to him, nor the trust and confidence the father's life endowed upon the son's. He is passive. But no, Isaac went willingly, as Israel through all ages walked willingly with God; through fire and water, through torture and gas, God's will was done to us. Isaac is the hero, more than Abraham.

In this regard, I read the Torah in a manner a Christian will understand. For I see the victim as one who also brings a gift, makes an offering of suffering and pain, a concept Christians understand from Christ on the cross. In that same way as the pope has said he sees Israel's suffering in our century as our hour upon the altar, bound upon the altar as was Isaac, but then made into the Holocaust: the burnt offering of the age.

Why Isaac, not Ishmael? Because Isaac sinned through arrogance and therefore was given the chance to atone through obedience: the perennial truth of Israel's life as our sages read that life. Now let us see how sages represent Isaac's offering:

> Isaac and Ishmael were arguing with one another. One said, "I am more beloved than you, for I was circumcised when I was thirteen years old."
>
> The other said, "I am more beloved than you, for I was circumcised sooner, namely, on the eighth day."
>
> Ishmael said to him, "I am more beloved than you, because I could have objected but didn't."
>
> At that moment Isaac said, "Would that the Holy One, blessed be he, appeared to me and told me to cut off one of my limbs. I would not object."
>
> Said the Holy One, blessed be he, to him, "If I should tell you to offer yourself up to me, you would not refuse."

Isaac becomes the centerpiece of the story, the trial is his, as much as it is Abraham's. But the reason is that Isaac boasted to Ishmael about what he would do and that is enormous arrogance. So Isaac had to show his humble obedience. And wherein lay the test? It was not to do what God had said. It was to be prepared to do it. The real test consisted of the three days of journeying, which gave Abraham plenty of time to think about what he was going to do. If you doubt it, talk with a dying cancer patient or a young man with AIDS. Thy will be done, indeed!

The conversation between God and Abraham sets the stage. Each detail, each step in the way, stands for a trial and gives Abraham and Isaac an opportunity to show their trust and gain merit on that account.

"And he said, 'Take, I pray you, your son, your only son, Isaac, whom you love, and go to the land of Moriah, and offer him there as a burnt offering upon one of the mountains of which I shall tell you' " (Gen. 22:3):

". . . your son."

He said to him, "Which son?"

He said to him, ". . . your only son."

"This one is the only son of his mother, and that one is the only son of his mother."

". . . whom you love."

"Where are the dividing walls within the womb? [I love them both.]"

"Isaac."

Why did he not tell him to begin with? It was so as to make Isaac still more precious in his view and so to give him a reward for each exchange.

Not only in the exchange with God but also in his actions Abraham showed eagerness to do what God told him. He had plenty of servants. But he himself saddled the asses. It was out of love. This is Abraham; the same Abraham who walked out on his mother, his father, his homeland, who took his wife away from her family, is ready now to kill his son—some faith! But our strength is our pathos, and the faith of Abraham is his merit.

Has Isaac inherited the faith of Abraham? Yes, I think so. He is the one who carried the wood and, the sages of Judaism notice, "It is like one who carries his own cross on his shoulder." So Isaac is compared to one who is crucified, a common Roman mode of execution, and in this context, Judaism may observe, Isaac is compared to the One who was crucified. This too will come back, since Isaac is also compared to one who rose from the dead on the third day; the comparison wrought by the Judaic sages then is not to be missed. And throughout, it was willingly and knowingly:

"So they went both of them together" (Gen. 22:6):

This one went to tie up and the other to be tied up, this one went to slaughter and the other to be slaughtered.

Whence then the merit accruing to the two? For Abraham it was the torment of giving up the son, for Isaac of giving up his life.

Are these real people, living real lives, or mere made-up models of perfect faith, a trust that no one can hope to emulate? The answer is that Abraham was tempted not to obey and Isaac was tempted to run away. But Abraham obeyed God, and Isaac offered himself willingly. So these are people with impulses we share, self-love we understand, models for us because they are like us, but models of that perfect faith of which we too are capable. For the devil had a conversation with each, both father and son, and that conversation tells us we deal with people like ourselves. That is to say Abraham and Isaac went through all the torments that we would, were we in their places:

> Samael [the devil] came to our father, Abraham. He said to him, "What sort of nonsense is troubling your heart? The son that was given to you at the age of a hundred are you going to slaughter?"
>
> He said to him, "Indeed so."
>
> He said to him, "And if he tests you still further than this, can you stand the test? 'If a thing be put to you as a trial, will you be wearied' (Job 4:2)?"
>
> He said to him, "And still more."
>
> He said to him, "Tomorrow he will [reverse himself and] tell you that you are a murderer, and you are liable."
>
> He said to him, "Indeed so."

That is how Abraham withstood the trial. It is not merely giving up the son; it is also being ready to plead guilty to the charge of murder, if need be. Come what may, come what may!

And what of Isaac? A mere boy, has he no pity for his mother? No self-pity? What does Samael say to Isaac? The devil is clever, he knows just what to say.

> When he saw that he could accomplish nothing with him, he came to Isaac. He said to him, "Oh son of a miserable mother. He is going to slaughter you."
>
> He said to him, "Indeed so."
>
> He said to him, "If so, all those lovely cloaks which your mother made will be the inheritance of Ishmael, the hated one of her house."
>
> If a word does not make its way entirely, it makes its way in part. That is in line with this verse: "And Isaac said to his father, Abraham, 'My father' " (Gen. 22:7). [That is, Isaac began to waver in his faith.]
>
> Why does the verse state, "And Isaac said to Abraham his father and said, 'My father' "? Why thus: "his father . . . my father"?
>
> It was so that he should be filled with mercy for him.

Isaac wavered, but Isaac went willingly nonetheless. For so the story proceeds, answering our question about whether the victim is martyr. By an act of will Isaac is a martyr, not merely victim.

I have said time and again that to study the Torah requires us to bring the words of the Torah into our work of understanding the world as it is, the world we know into the task of explaining the Torah. And over and over again, like every other Jew today, the world I bring to the Torah encompasses the awful pain of immediate memory, the Judeocide of our own day. But no passage of Scripture so demands a reading in light of the Holocaust as does this one. For Abraham had to be ready to give one, but mothers and fathers in our own times gave all. And Abraham was commanded by God, but Israel in our time was compelled by Satan. Then where the binding of Isaac in particular?

In all the stories of the dignity of the victims of the Holocaust, the ones I find most moving are the memories of families, with the men selected for killing labor, the women and children for immediate killing: "I remember them, as they walked off hand in hand." "The last sight I had of my wife and my daughter was their walking toward the gas chambers, hand in hand." "I remember his little red coat, as he ran after his mother." These are not victims alone; they are martyrs: "God will provide himself a lamb for a burnt offering."

> And he said, "Behold the fire and the wood, but where is the lamb for a burnt offering?"
>
> " 'God will provide himself the lamb for a burnt offering,' and if not, then: 'the lamb for the burnt offering will be my son' " (Gen. 21:8).
>
> "So they went both of them together" (Gen. 22:6):
>
> This one went to tie up and the other to be tied up, this one went to slaughter and the other to be slaughtered.

But as our sages read the story, matters do not rest there. Abraham's resolve was implacable. That accounts for the phrasing of the angel's outcry:

> "He said, 'Do not lay your hand on the lad or do anything to him, for now I know that you fear God, seeing you have not withheld your son, your only son, from me' " (Gen. 22:12):
>
> Where was the knife ["Do not lay your hand"]?
>
> Tears from the ministering angels had fallen on it and dissolved it.
>
> Then he said, "So I shall strangle him."
>
> He said to him, "Do not lay a hand on the lad."
>
> Then he said, "Then let us at least draw a drop of blood [symbolic of the offering]."
>
> He said to him, " '. . . or do anything to him.' "
>
> ". . . for now I know [that you fear God]:"
>
> "Now I am telling everybody that you love me: 'seeing you have not withheld your son, your only son, from me' (Gen. 22:12)."
>
> "And do not claim, 'Whatever sickness does not affect one's own body is no sickness,' for I credit the merit to you for this action as though I had said to you, 'Offer me yourself,' and you did not hold back."

The dialogue for God and the angel and Abraham shows us the true resolve that Abraham exhibited out of the angel's statement. Abraham's answers are worked out. Isaac is no longer the offering, but Isaac will forever stand for the one prepared to offer himself or herself:

> "And Abraham went and took the ram and offered it up as a burnt offering [instead of his son]" (Gen. 22:13):
>
> R. Yudan in the name of R. Benaiah: "He said before him, 'Lord of all ages, regard the blood of this ram as though it were the blood of Isaac, my son, its innards as though they were the innards of Isaac my son.' "
>
> R. Phineas in the name of R. Benaiah: "He said before him, 'Lord of all ages, regard it as though I had offered up my son, Isaac, first, and afterward had offered up the ram in his place.' "

That concludes the representation of the matter as a onetime event: this thing happened this day, for this reason, in this manner. But the Torah speaks not only of then but also of now—mainly of now. So we have to ask how Abraham stands for Israel and how Isaac represents Israel.

The answer lies in our sages' portrait of the conversation that God and Abraham had when the binding of Isaac had drawn to a close with the sacrifice of the ram:

> "So Abraham called the name of that place 'The Lord will provide,' [as it is said to this day, 'On the mount of the Lord it shall be provided']" (Gen. 22:14):
>
> R. Bibi the Elder in the name of R. Yohanan: "He said before him, 'Lord of all ages, from the time that you said to me, "Take your son, your only son" (Gen. 22:2), I could have replied to you, "Yesterday you said to me, 'For in Isaac shall seed be called to you' (Gen 21:12),
>
> " 'and now you say, "Take your son, your only son" (Gen. 22:2). God forbid, did I not do it? But I suppressed my love so as to carry out your will.
>
> " 'May it always please you, Lord our God, that, when the children of Isaac will come into trouble, you remember in their behalf that act of binding and be filled with mercy for them.' "

That forms the link between Abraham and Isaac, in the beginning, and the life of Israel in enduring time. God will remember; God will forgive. At stake is the life of both the individual and the holy people: for all time, the binding of Isaac stands for God's mercy and love.

Holy Israel enters the account of the death and life of Isaac at just this point, when the ram takes Isaac's place. And the ram signifies the sacrifices of the Temple, which stands for Abraham's willingness to bind Isaac to the altar and to offer him as a sacrifice. In the coming ages, Israel will turn to God in penitence, having sinned and now seeking atonement, and will call to mind the binding of Isaac. This they will do through sounding the horn of the ram, the shofar, on the Days of Awe, the New Year and Day of Atonement, when in the synagogue they read once again the story of the binding of Isaac. Through Abraham's willingness to sacrifice Isaac, through Isaac's willingness to be sacrificed, Israel in all eternity gains atonement for sin, so our sages say explicitly:

> "And Abraham lifted up his eyes and looked, and behold, behind him was a ram [caught in a thicket by his horns. And Abraham went and took the ram and offered it up as a burnt offering instead of his son]" (Gen. 22:13):
> What is the meaning of the word for "behind"?
> Said R. Yudan, " 'Behind' in the sense of 'after,' that is, after all that happens, Israel nonetheless will be embroiled in transgressions and perplexed by sorrows. But in the end, they will be redeemed by the horns of the ram: 'And the Lord will blow the horn' (Zech. 9:14)."
> Said R. Judah bar Simon, " 'After' all generations Israel nonetheless will be embroiled in transgressions and perplexed by sorrows. But in the end, they will be redeemed by the horns of a ram: 'And the Lord God will blow the horn' (Zech. 9:14)."
> Said R. Hinena bar Isaac, "All through the days of the year Israelites are embroiled in transgressions and perplexed by sorrows. But on the New Year they take the ram's horn and sound it, so in the end, they will be redeemed by the horns of a ram: 'And the Lord will blow the horn' (Zech. 9:14)."

The issue is not individual sin alone, but Israel's situation among the nations. Not surprisingly, here again we invoke the binding of Isaac when we raise the issue of redemption, this time not of you and me from sin, but of all Israel from the nations:

> R. Abba bar R. Pappi, R. Joshua of Siknin in the name of R. Levi: "Since our father, Abraham, saw the ram get himself out of one thicket only to be trapped by another, the Holy One, blessed be he, said to him, 'So your descendants will be entangled in one kingdom after another, struggling from Babylonia to Media, from Media to Greece, from Greece to Edom. But in the end, they will be redeemed by the horns of a ram: And the Lord God will blow the horn . . . the Lord of Hosts will defend them' (Zech. 9:14–15)."

As always, the Torah means to link the life of the private person, affected by transgression, and the history of the nation, troubled by its wandering among the kingdoms. From the perspective of the land of Israel, the issue is not exile, but the rule of foreigners. In both cases the power of the ram's horn to redeem the individual and the nation finds its origin in the binding of Isaac. So when I read the Torah, I seek for the ways of linking the lives of the patriarchs to the life of the nation. In this manner I bring the narrative back to the paradigm of individual being, so from patriarch to nation to person. The path leads in both directions, of course, in a fluid movement of meaning.

When God has tested humankind, one time after another, there is a renewed covenant. Now I know; therefore . . . We recall that after the trial of Noah, there was an oath and a covenant, which bound God as much as Noah. Would Abraham have to go through another such test? And would Isaac and his descendants have to bear up under more trials?

> "And the angel of the Lord called to Abraham a second time from heaven and said, 'By myself I have sworn,' [says the Lord, 'because you have done this thing, and have not withheld your son, your only son, I will indeed bless you and I will multiply your descendants as the stars of heaven and as the sand which is on the seashore. And your descendants shall possess the gate of their enemies, and by your descendants shall all the nations of earth bless themselves, because you have obeyed my voice']" (Gen. 22:15–17):
>
> What need was there for taking such an oath?
>
> He said to him, "Take an oath to me that you will never again test me or Isaac my son."
>
> What need was there for taking such an oath?
>
> R. Levi in the name of R. Hama bar Hanina, "He said to him, 'Take an oath to me that you will never again test me.' "
>
> "The matter may be compared to the case of a king who was married to a noble lady. She produced a first son from him, and then he divorced her, [remarried her, so she produced] a second son, and he divorced her again, a third son, and he divorced her again. When she had produced a tenth son, all of them got together and said to him, 'Take an oath to us that you will never again divorce our mother.'
>
> "So when Abraham had been tested for the tenth time, he said to him, 'Take an oath to me that you will never again test me.' "
>
> Said R. Hanan, " '. . . because you have done this thing . . . '! It was the tenth trial and he refers to it as ' . . . this [one] thing. . . . ' But this also is the last, since it outweighs all the rest.
>
> B. "For if he had not accepted this last trial, he would have lost the merit of all that he had already done."

Abraham met the test when he said, "Here I am." And every subsequent "here I am" in Israel's history recalled the original readiness. But there would not have to be another—until today.

So much for Abraham and Noah. But what about that other representative of the human condition, Adam? There is nothing in common, from beginning to end. Contrast Abraham with Adam. What did Adam say when God called him? "The Lord God called out to the man and said to him, 'Where are you?' He replied, 'I heard the sound of You in the garden, and I was afraid because I was naked, so I hid.' " The one courageous, the other craven, the one silent and obedient, the other full of excuses. So there are these three: Adam, Noah, Abraham. Adam proved worthless, so God started fresh. Noah proved worthy, and God made a covenant with him: never again total destruction. Then finally came Abraham and Isaac, who formed holy Israel and who would stand in an eternal covenant, but one that to begin with announced "never again."

No wonder that the "here I am" would echo through the ages, forming yet another enduring reality transcending time. So Abraham became the model for Moses:

"And he said to him, 'Abraham!' And he said, 'Here I am' " (Gen. 22:1):
Said R. Joshua, "In two passages Moses compared himself to Abraham.
"God said to him, 'Do not glorify yourself in the presence of the king and do not stand in the place of great men' " (Prov. 25:6).
"Abraham said, 'Here I am.' 'Here I am, ready for the priesthood, here I am, ready for the monarchy.'
"He had the merit of attaining priesthood: 'The Lord has sworn and will not repent, you are a priest for ever after the manner of Melchizedek' (Ps. 110:4).
"He also had the merit of attaining the monarchy: 'You are a mighty prince among us' (Gen. 23:5).
"Moses for his part also said, 'Here I am' (Ex. 3:4). 'Here I am, ready for the priesthood, here I am, ready for the monarchy.' "

The upshot is to link Abraham to Moses and to show how the biography of the patriarch prefigures the life of the founder of the nation. Since Moses is usually represented as meek and mild, the comparison presents a certain irony.

The merit gained through the binding of Isaac would endure for all time. And what was the source of the merit? It was the act of prostration, which is to say the act of prayer:

". . . and we will worship [through an act of prostration or prayer] and come again to you" (Gen. 22:5):
Said R. Isaac, "And all was on account of the merit attained by the act of prostration.
"Abraham returned in peace from Mount Moriah only on account of the merit owing to the act of prostration: ' . . . and we will worship [through an act of prostration] and come [then, on that account] again to you' (Gen. 22:5).

"The Israelites were redeemed only on account of the merit owing to the act of prostration: And the people believed . . . then they bowed their heads and prostrated themselves" (Ex. 4:31).

"The Torah was given only on account of the merit owing to the act of prostration: 'And worship [prostrate themselves] you afar off'" (Ex. 24:1).

"Hannah was remembered only on account of the merit owing to the act of prostration: 'And they worshipped before the Lord' (1 Sam. 1:19).

"The exiles will be brought back only on account of the merit owing to the act of prostration: 'And it shall come to pass in that day that a great horn shall be blown and they shall come that were lost . . . and that were dispersed . . . and they shall worship the Lord in the holy mountain at Jerusalem' (Is. 27:13).

"The Temple was built only on account of the merit owing to the act of prostration: 'Exalt you the Lord our God and worship at his holy hill' (Ps. 99:9).

"The dead will live only on account of the merit owing to the act of prostration: 'Come let us worship and bend the knee, let us kneel before the Lord our maker' (Ps. 95:6)."

The entire history of Israel flows from its acts of worship ("prostration") and is unified by a single law. Every sort of advantage Israel has ever gained came about through worship. The Torah supplies those facts from which the governing law is derived. Israel gains its goals through prayer.

And yet we know that is not entirely the case. For how much did prayer avail or piety or study of Torah or acts of loving-kindness, when the Holocaust came and consumed holy Israel in Europe? Six million of holy Israel died there. Of what can Abraham boast, and whence can he take pride, for he gave up only one son, but Israel in Europe gave up a million!

Nor was it an accident; nor is it merely our retrospective view. It was intentional, it was planned, it was deliberate, and forgive them not, O God, for they knew exactly what they were doing. The German Nazis and their many allies, large numbers of them faithful Christians, also read the Torah, which they called the Old Testament of the Bible, and they turned it against Israel in Europe; in very cruel ways. Many of their acts of massacre, which they called actions, took place on Jewish holy days, for instance.

And, knowing the Torah in their evil way, they made many Abrahams. This they did by confronting a father and a mother with a choice: "You have six children. Here are ration cards for one. The others can starve to death. You have two sons. We shall take one to the gas chamber; the other will live. Which one? You choose." Abraham chose once, between Ishmael and Isaac. Abraham was ready to give up one son. But Israel in Europe chose a million times and gave up a million Jewish sons and daughters. Wherein your glory, Abraham? And why the merit for so paltry an act of trust and courage? In our time we have been many Abrahams, many Sarahs.

But, too, we recall, out of Israel in Europe was reborn the State of Israel, encompassing Israel from all countries. In this rebirth of the Jewish state we also see the resurrection of Israel, the ever-dying people, out of the gas chambers of Europe. The binding of Isaac today stands for the renewal of Israel in its life as a state and in its life, throughout the world, as a people. It is as though we have died and been reborn, for, if truth be told, we have died and we have been reborn. Our renewal is just as miraculous to us as the resurrection of the dead on the third day. No wonder then, that we find in the details of the binding of Isaac, as our sages read it, an account of what has happened to us and what is happening to us, in the here and now. Once more, I maintain, each detail of the story stands for Israel's history in time to come.

For the deed of the patriarchs and matriarchs serve as models for their descendants. The third day—which Christians count as the day of the resurrection—is the day on which Isaac rose from the ashes of the altar:

"On the third day Abraham lifted up his eyes and saw the place afar off" (Gen. 22:4):

B. "After two days he will revive us, on the third day, he will raise us up, that we may live in his presence" (Hos. 16:2).

C. On the third day of the tribes: "And Joseph said to them on the third day, 'This do and live' " (Gen. 42:18).

D. On the third day of the giving of the Torah: "And it came to pass on the third day when it was morning" (Ex. 19:16).

E. On the third day of the spies: "And hide yourselves there for three days" (Josh. 2:16).

F. On the third day of Jonah: "And Jonah was in the belly of the fish three days and three nights" (Jonah 2:1).

G. On the third day of the return from the Exile: "And we abode there three days" (Ezra 8:32).

H. On the third day of the resurrection of the dead: "After two days he will revive us, on the third day he will raise us up, that we may live in his presence" (Hos. 16:2).

I. On the third day of Esther: "Now it came to pass on the third day that Esther put on her royal apparel" (Est. 5:1).

J. She put on the monarchy of the house of her fathers.

K. On account of what sort of merit?

L. Rabbis say, "On account of the third day of the giving of the Torah."

M. R. Levi said, "It is on account of the merit of the third day of

Abraham: 'On the third day Abraham lifted up his eyes and saw the place afar off' (Gen. 22:4)."

The third day marks the fulfillment of the promise at the end of time of the resurrection of the dead and at appropriate moments of Israel's redemption. The reference to the third day at Genesis 22:2 then invokes the entire panoply of Israel's history. To Christians, the third day can mean only Easter, on which Jesus Christ rose from the dead. To holy Israel, we live in the third day, even now. We have suffered, we have died, and we renew life—right here in the twentieth century, right here in this free society, but also in that Holy Land, the land and state of Israel, of which the Torah speaks. For the Bible speaks of whatever the Bible speaks. But the Torah speaks of us.

16

NEUSNER
"Then Jacob Made a Vow"

Jacob left Beer-sheba and set out for Haran. He came upon a certain place and stopped there for the night, for the sun had set. Taking one of the stones of that place, he put it under his head and lay down in that place. He had a dream; a stairway was set up on the ground and its top reached to the sky, and angels of God were going up and down on it. And the Lord was standing beside him.

He said, "I am the Lord, the God of your father Abraham and the God of Isaac. The ground on which you are lying I will assign to you and to your offspring. Your descendants shall be as the dust of the earth; you shall spread out to the west and to the east, to the north and to the south. All the families of the earth shall bless themselves by you and your descendants. Remember I am with you. I will protect you wherever you go and will bring you back to this land. I will not leave you until I have done what I have promised to you."

Jacob awoke from his sleep and said, "Surely the Lord is present in this place and I did not know it."

Shaken, he said, "How awesome is this place! This is none other than the abode of God, and that is the gateway to heaven."

Early in the morning, Jacob took the stone that he had put under his head and set it up as a pillar and poured oil on the top of it. He named that site Bethel; but previously the name of the city had been Luz.

Then Jacob made a vow, saying, "If God remains with me, if He protects me on this journey that I am taking and gives me bread to eat and clothing to wear, and if I return safe to my father's house—the Lord shall be my God. And this stone which I have set up as a pillar shall be God's abode; and of all that You give me, I will set aside a tithe for you."

Genesis 28:10–22

Then Jacob resumed his journey and came to the land of the Easterners. There before his eyes was a well in the open. Three flocks of sheep were lying there beside it, for the flocks were watered from that well. The stone on the mouth of the well was large. When all the flocks were gathered there, the stone would be rolled from the mouth of the well and the sheep watered; then the stone would be put back in its place on the mouth of the well.

Genesis 29:1–3

The Torah speaks of humble people, full of doubt. Here comes Jacob, the third generation from Abraham, as skeptical and uncertain as his grandfather, still making deals. But if anything, he is the most human of them all, and being Jacob, I like this Jacob most of all. For I can identify with him. He should have come first, but he didn't. He should have been a real man, like his big brother, Esau: hunter and warrior, ravisher of women. But he wasn't. He was a mama's boy. And Isaac does not come to us as a strong father. And he couldn't even manage the politics of his father's household. His mother had to tell him how to get what he wanted: the birthright that Esau despised. So he got it. And then what? Then: nothing. He had to run away: some birthright, some victory!

The people, Israel, bear the name of Jacob, which God changed to Israel. They identify with this man, even more than with his father and his grandfather. And the Torah is the reason. For of Abraham we know only dramatic encounters with God and of Isaac we have access to a mute victim, someone done to, but not doing. In Jacob, by contrast, there is a life, a whole, rich, exciting life. Isaac's father sent his manager off to find a wife for him. Jacob went into exile and found his own. Isaac stayed home; Jacob went and worked for a stranger for twenty-one years before he could claim what was his. Isaac produced Jacob and Esau. Jacob and his wives, Rachel and Rebecca, had the twelve tribal progenitors: all Israel. Abraham struggled with petty chiefs, Jacob's son, Joseph, became metropolitan ruler of all the world, in behalf of Pharaoh. What a life! So with Jacob it is easy to identify.

Here is a case in point. Jacob is running away from his brother, Esau, whom Jacob has, after all, cheated. And Jacob is not all that certain that his father, Isaac, will miss him, for Jacob deceived his father, and his father knew it: "The hands are the hands of Esau, but the voice is the voice of Jacob." Jacob now is leaving the promised, holy land to return to that place from which his grandfather, Abraham, had fled. He is taking refuge with his mother's family. It is as if all his family's history is repeating itself, in reverse. No wonder that, at the very frontier, Jacob sleeps one last night in the promised land—and has a dream. And so do we all, on the turnings of the chapters of our lives.

Just as Jacob leaves the land, he has a vision, and then, and only then, he expresses his doubt in the form of a vow. Now, a vow is an act of a weakling; it is meant to coerce when there is no power but the power of persuasion. Here is the language of a vow: "If you do this, I shall do that, and if you do not do this, I shall not do that." It is what you say when you have no means of coercion at all except for your own will and attitude. You can't force the other; you can only bind yourself. Jacob, in doubt and in despair, fleeing with his life alone, has received a promise—and this is how he responds.

And in that sequence of events we identify the condition of faith: doubt, despair, constant search for reassurance. But why not? For God has given and gotten nothing, so God tests again and again. Just as God tested Abraham time after time, so did humankind test God over and over again. No test sufficed, for no results persuaded for very long. With Jacob, whose name became Israel, too, even after the vision of the stairway to heaven and God standing beside him, he still made a conditional vow: if this, then that. For Jacob lay down in much distress. He was a refugee, fleeing from his native land, the land of Israel. He was en route to take shelter with his mother's family, whom he had never known and from whom he did not know what to expect, and, as I said, leaving his father, whom he had deceived, his brother, whom he rightly feared wanted to kill him for stealing his birthright, and his mother, co-conspirator in his troubles, Jacob had good reason to sleep a troubled sleep. Would he ever come home?

Yes, God said, "I will protect you wherever you go and I also will bring you back here." Jacob acknowledges the dream and the promise and recognizes the awe of the place, in Hebrew called the house of God. And, after all that, he makes his conditional vow, that if God protects him and provides his needs and brings him home, then God will be his God. And if not, not. All God's love for Abraham, God's oversight of Isaac, protection for Sarah, his grandmother, given Isaac in her old age, and Rebecca, his own mother, these acts of caring and of love now gave way to doubt. The record meant nothing; the promises just now were just that—promises. If he kept them, well and good.

No wonder, then, that our sages so read the vow as greatly to raise the stakes in it. What is it that Jacob wanted from God? It was to be protected from gossip and the triplet of the mortal sins, the ones the Torah requires us to die rather than commit. These are fornication, murder, and idolatry.

> R. Abbahu said, " 'If God be with me and will keep me in *this way*' refers to the protection from gossip, in line with this usage: 'And they turn their tongue in the way of slander, their bow of falsehood' (Jer. 9:2).
>
> " '. . . will give me bread to eat' refers to the protection from fornication, in line with the usage: 'Neither has he kept back any thing from me, except the bread which he ate' (Gen. 39:9), a euphemism for sexual relations with his wife.
>
> " '. . . so that I come again to my father's house in peace' refers to bloodshed.
>
> " '. . . then the Lord shall be my God' so that I shall be protected from idolatry.' "

Rabbis interpreted the statement "this way" to speak of all of these.

[The rabbis' statement now follows:] "Specifically: 'If God will be with me and will keep me in this way that I go' [by referring only to 'way'] contains an allusion to idolatry, fornication, murder, and slander.

" 'Way' refers to idolatry: 'They who swear by the sin of Samaria and say, As your God, O Dan, lives, and as the way of Beer-sheba lives' (Amos 8:14).

" 'Way' refers to adultery: 'So is the way of an adulterous woman' (Prov. 30:20).

" 'Way' refers to murder: 'My son, do not walk in the way of them, restrain your foot from their path, for their feet run to evil and they make haste to shed blood' (Prov. 1:15–16).

" 'Way' refers to slander: 'And he heard the words of Laban's sons, saying, "Jacob has taken away" ' (Gen. 31:1)."

In light of this reading, in which Jacob asks God's protection to keep himself from sinning, Jacob's distrust directs itself toward Jacob. He asks for God's protection that he not sin. So the oral Torah imparts upon the written Torah's story a different shape. The story as we have it is of a frightened man, asking for protection. The story as it is handed on is of a pious man, asking for virtue. Scripture says, "If God remains with me, if He protects me on this journey that I am taking and gives me bread to eat and clothing to wear, and if I return safe to my father's house—the Lord shall be my God." All that is very particular to Jacob and his problems. He is going on a dangerous journey. He does not know where he will get food and clothing and cannot say for sure he will ever come home again. So Jacob is afraid and vows a vow, as if to coerce God in his own weak way.

Sages of the oral Torah see Jacob differently. He stands for them and their people, and his fears are theirs. But his situation also is not personal but exemplary. He stands for everybody. The Torah portrays a self-centered man, concerned for this-worldly things. Our sages know a virtuous man, who going out into the world for the first time asks for protection against those sins that the world makes easy: fornication, idolatry, murder—and common gossip. These are public, social sins. I can't imagine that any pious sage conceived of Jacob as a candidate for murderer, idolator, or fornicator. But sages cannot imagine a Jacob so trivial and irrelevant as Jacob Scripture portrays. So the Torah gives us a different Jacob, one who really does stand for Israel, the whole people, which is to say for the society of the Jews in the here and now.

That interpretation rehabilitates Jacob. Then what does Jacob really ask of God, since it can hardly be bread and clothing. Our sages can no more conceive of Jacob in particular, but only Jacob as exemplary, than they can imagine Jacob worried about his next meal. In light of the oral Torah's constant stress on Torah study in discipleship with sages, the allusion to "bread" deepens the re-visioning of Jacob. What he wants is Torah learning and the company of disciples of sages in the enchanted circle of the master:

> ". . . will give me bread to eat and clothing to wear."
>
> Aqilas the proselyte came to R. Eliezer and said to him, "Is all the gain that is coming to the proselyte going to be contained in this verse: ' . . . and loves the proselyte, giving him food and clothing' (Deut. 10:18)?"
>
> He said to him, "And is something for which the old man [Jacob] beseeched going to be such a small thing in your view, namely, '. . . will give me bread to eat and clothing to wear'? [God] comes and hands it over to [a proselyte] on a reed [and the proselyte does not have to beg for it]."
>
> He came to R. Joshua, who commenced by saying words to appease him: " 'Bread' refers to Torah, as it is said, 'Come, eat of my bread' (Prov. 9:5). 'Clothing' refers to the cloak of a disciple of sages.
>
> "When a person has the merit of studying the Torah, he has the merit of carrying out a religious duty. [So the proselyte receives a great deal when he gets bread and clothing, namely, entry into the estate of disciples].
>
> "And not only so, but his daughters may be chosen for marriage into the priesthood, so that their sons' sons will offer burnt-offerings on the altar. [So the proselyte may also look forward to entry into the priests' caste. That statement will now be spelled out.]
>
> " 'Bread' refers to the show-bread.
>
> " 'Clothing' refers to the garment of the priesthood.
>
> "So lo, we deal with the sanctuary.
>
> "How do we know that the same sort of blessing applies in the provinces? 'Bread' speaks of the dough-offering [that is separated in the provinces], while 'clothing' refers to the first fleece [handed over to the priest]."

Now a different Jacob comes before us, one who lives in the eternity of Torah learning and whose deepest concerns are not for himself but for his place within the circle of the Torah study. Even the outsider entering Israel, the proselyte, may hope through this kind of "bread" and "clothing" to have heirs within the priesthood, engaged in the service of God in the Temple. Surely there is no higher reward than that. So Jacob's vow is not for God's this-worldly protection, which he has already been promised. It is for God's help in the struggle against mortal sin, on the one side, and in the effort to acquire knowledge of the Torah learned in discipleship, on the other. Clearly we are moving out of the narrow limits of a "Bible story," and toward the broad and inviting plane of the world of the perpetual everyday. Jacob is an everyman, and that is why he matters to me, Jacob, too, and to us all.

Just as, for the church, Christ serves wherever the Christian calls upon him, so Jacob, like his mother and father, grandmother and grandfather, becomes people we know because he is like us, only an example for us to follow. This reading of Jacob's moment of despair shows once again how to receive the Torah not without the mediation of tradition but rather through sages' reading of it. Abraham, Isaac, Jacob—these patriarchs stand not for themselves but for the life of Israel, the holy people, and each incident in their lives resonates in the private life of each Israelite, every Jew.

You must wonder whether this way of studying the Bible works everywhere. Well, I think it can, if we make it work. In that regard, of course, I am fortunate to find a guide and a model in the oral Torah. But that model is for me to emulate and even improve upon, and the guide leads me on a journey that only I can undertake. That is what makes the study lively: an exchange of viewpoints, not just a heavenly episode of show-and-tell. Now I have to admit some passages engage more readily than others. Where I see despair, I can identify, and I know what it is to hope, to love, to cope with disappointment, betrayal, and doubt, too. All these are human experiences that any of us knows. When we bring the streets to Scripture and expand on Scripture's sense, when we read Psalms looking for comfort because we have walked through the valley of deep darkness and death, that journey takes us on a smooth and direct path.

But what about the barren spots? That brings us back to Jacob's journey through the wilderness. No passage in the Torah can promise less reward, I should imagine, than the simple, factual statement about Jacob's coming upon a well. Immediately following his vow, Jacob, having journeyed eastward, sees this scene:

> Then Jacob resumed his journey and came to the land of the Easterners. There before his eyes was a well in the open. Three flocks of sheep were lying there beside it, for the flocks were watered from that well. The stone on the mouth of the well was large. When all the flocks were gathered there, the stone would be rolled from the mouth of the well and the sheep watered; then the stone would be put back in its place on the mouth of the well.
>
> Genesis 29:1–3

What am I to make of it? All I have here is the story of how Jacob came across a well out in the open. There were flocks of sheep, a stone on the mouth of the well, and here is how the sheep are watered. How mundane, how arid—who can find life in such a trivial detail or bring to the picture of still sheep by a well any questions that count? Nothing much is happening here—a storyteller's artifice, not Torah, not revelation, you say? Well, look again.

What we shall now see is how the entire history of Israel, the holy people, is represented in this well. What happens to Jacob is a foretaste of what will happen to his children, the children of Israel, through the ages. And whatever happens to them finds its sense and meaning in the Torah as well. What Jacob saw in the encounter at the well is the whole future of his children—every motif, every important chapter, beginning to end, in the supernatural story of holy Israel. Here is everything in some one thing. So when I say that the Torah turns today into a model of all time and allows me to find everything that ever comes about within the words of the Torah itself, I'm not making things up as I go along. And I'm not free-associating. I have to admit the way our sages spell things out takes some time, but when you realize what is at stake, I think you'll see how the Torah is not tedious but engaging:

> "As he looked, he saw a well in the field:"
> R. Hama bar Hanina interpreted the verse in six ways.

That is, Hama divides the verse into six clauses and systematically reads each of the clauses in light of the others and in line with an overriding theme. This is what now happens. Jacob at the well sees Moses, Aaron, Miriam: the generation that received the Torah at Sinai.

> " 'As he looked, he saw a well in the field:' this refers to the well [of water in the wilderness, Num. 21:17].
> " '. . . and lo, three flocks of sheep lying beside it:' specifically, Moses, Aaron, and Miriam."

Next comes the life of Israel in holy time, the three festivals, celebrated in pilgrimages to the holy temple on Mount Zion in Jerusalem:

> " 'As he looked, he saw a well in the field:' refers to Zion.
> " '. . . and lo, three flocks of sheep lying beside it:' refers to the three festivals [Passover, Pentecost, Tabernacles, that is, Pessah, Shavuot, Sukkot].
> " '. . . for out of that well the flocks were watered:' from there they drank of the holy spirit.
> " '. . . The stone on the well's mouth was large:' this refers to the rejoicing of the house of the water-drawing."
> " '. . . and when all the flocks were gathered there:' coming from 'the entrance of Hamath to the brook of Egypt' (1 Kgs. 8:66).
> " '. . . the shepherds would roll the stone from the mouth of the well and water the sheep:' for from there they would drink of the Holy Spirit.

" '. . . and put the stone back in its place upon the mouth of the well:' leaving it in place until the coming festival. [Thus the second interpretation reads the verse in light of the Temple celebration of the Festival of Tabernacles.]

Now we turn to the life of the people on ordinary days, in the everyday of society and government. Jacob foresees the perfect government of his children, Israel, in time to come:

" '. . . As he looked, he saw a well in the field': this refers to Zion.

" '. . . and lo, three flocks of sheep lying beside it': this refers to the three courts, concerning which we have learned in the Mishnah: 'There were three courts there, one at the gateway of the Temple mount, one at the gateway of the courtyard, and one in the chamber of the hewn stones' [M. San. 11:2].

" '. . . for out of that well the flocks were watered:' for from there they would hear the ruling.

" 'The stone on the well's mouth was large:' this refers to the high court that was in the chamber of the hewn stones.

" '. . . and when all the flocks were gathered there:' this refers to the courts in session in the Land of Israel.

" '. . . the shepherds would roll the stone from the mouth of the well and water the sheep:' for from there they would hear the ruling.

" '. . . and put the stone back in its place upon the mouth of the well:' for they would give and take until they had produced the ruling in all the required clarity." [The third interpretation reads the verse in light of the Israelite institution of justice and administration.]

So much for the life of perfection. But what of historical time? Jacob's vision now turns to what would happen to Israel in its life among the nations:

" 'As he looked, he saw a well in the field:' this refers to Zion.

" '. . . and lo, three flocks of sheep lying beside it:' this refers to the first three kingdoms [Babylonia, Media, Greece].

" '. . . for out of that well the flocks were watered:' for they enriched the treasures that were laid up in the chambers of the Temple.

" '. . . The stone on the well's mouth was large:' this refers to the merit attained by the patriarchs.

" '. . . and when all the flocks were gathered there:' this refers to the wicked kingdom, which collects troops through levies over all the nations of the world.

" '. . . the shepherds would roll the stones from the mouth of the well and water the sheep:' for they enriched the treasures that were laid up in the chambers of the Temple.

" '. . . and put the stone back in its place upon the mouth of the well:' in the age to come the merit attained by the patriarchs will stand [in defense of

Israel]." [So the fourth interpretation interweaves the themes of the Temple cult and the domination of the four monarchies.]

The life on the outside is lived among the nations. But within, in Jacob's tents, Israel lives in the world of Torah study, sages with their disciples forming the inner court and true authority, by contrast to the nation's governance:

" 'As he looked, he saw a well in the field:' this refers to the sanhedrin.

" '. . . and lo, three flocks of sheep lying beside it:' this alludes to the three rows of disciples of sages that would go into session in their presence.

" 'for out of that well flocks were watered:' for from there they would listen to the ruling of the law.

" '. . . The stone on the well's mouth was large:' this refers to the most distinguished member of the court, who determines the law-decision.

" '. . . and when all the flocks were gathered there:' this refers to disciples of the sages in the Land of Israel.

" '. . . the shepherds would roll the stone from the mouth of the well and water the sheep:' for from there they would listen to the ruling of the law.

" '. . . and put the stone back in its place upon the mouth of the well:' for they would give and take until they had produced the ruling in all the required clarity." [The fifth interpretation again reads the verse in light of the Israelite institution of legal education and justice.]

Not only schoolhouse and Torah study but synagogue and prayer mark the life of Jacob's children, and this is the everyday of Torah reading on week-days and the Sabbath:

" 'As he looked, he saw a well in the field:' this refers to the synagogue.

" '. . . and lo, three flocks of sheep lying beside it:' this refers to the three who are called to the reading of the Torah on weekdays.

" '. . . for out of that well the flocks were watered:' for from there they hear the reading of the Torah.

" '. . . The stone on the well's mouth was large:' this refers to the impulse to do evil.

" '. . . and when all the flocks were gathered there:' this refers to the congregation.

" '. . . the shepherds would roll the stone from the mouth of the well and water the sheep:' for from there they hear the reading of the Torah.

" '. . . and put the stone back in its place upon the mouth of the well:' for once they go forth [from the hearing of the reading of the Torah] the impulse to do evil reverts to its place." [The sixth and the last interpretation turns to the twin themes of the reading of the Torah in the synagogue and the evil impulse, temporarily driven off through the hearing of the Torah.]

So there it all is, the whole of the eternal life of Israel; here is everything. The six themes read in response to the verse cover (1) Israel in the wilderness, (2) the Temple cult on festivals with special reference to Tabernacles, (3) the judiciary and government, (4) the history of Israel under the four kingdoms, (5) the life of sages, and (6) the ordinary folk and the synagogue. The whole is an astonishing repertoire of fundamental themes of the life of the nation Israel: at its origins in the wilderness, in its cult, in its institutions based on the cult, in the history of the nations, and, finally, in the twin social estates of sages and ordinary folk, matched by the institutions of the master-disciple circle and the synagogue.

Were I to stop here, you would rightly conclude that the Torah is something that happens out there, in the world at large, but not in here, to me personally. For I would not have gone on to tell you what I make of Jacob's dream and vision, his vow and his encounter at the well. But I maintain that the Torah is not "about" history. It concerns the perpetual and the ongoing, what I would call eternity in time. That explains in abstract terms why and how the Torah imparts its mark upon history. The onetime and everyday events of the here and now, that is to say, what we call history, scarcely form pertinent models for the kinds of events of which the Torah speaks. For what "history" is contained in the trivial information that there was a well with flocks gathered around it? None that I can see. But what kind of truth is contained in that same account we now recognize: all truth, that is to say every important element of the holy way of life of the holy people, Israel, in its maintenance of the social order in the here and now and in its service to God on high.

And if in Jacob's life we find our own, so in what goes on with us we identify new meaning for his life, too. If we see the Torah as an open book, on the pages of which we live out our lives, that is to say the Torah as a commentary on what happens to us and what happens to us as an illustration and amplification of the words of the Torah, too, Jacob is ideal. Seeing the Torah as a commentary on life and the everyday as a systematic exegesis of the Torah allows the experience of the everyday world to form part of revelation, too. And that is how we see our own lives; how else? But that then calls our attention to what matters in the Torah. And it is not the history of the Torah or even the historicity of the events portrayed in the Torah. Knowing those things is interesting but, for matters of faith, not determinative. What matters is the authority of the Torah, and that rests upon the community of the faithful today, not the events that (we may "prove") took place so long ago. This most of all is the approach to reading the Bible/studying the Torah that I want to offer to my friend, my priest.

That and one other thing: what do we Jews bring to the world and also to the Torah? It is, and can only be, our knowledge of the world as we have lived in it, in our time, in our place, in our condition. And to me, in the entire range of that knowledge of what we are and can be, I identify two commanding facts. And what these facts are presents no surprises by this point in my presentation of the Torah. The first is the history of the age, marked by the murder of nearly six million Jews in Europe for the sole reason that they were Israel, the holy people, or that they had one grandparent who was Israel. The second is the social fact of the age, defined, for us, by our life: we survive; we endure; we know tomorrow. That was not supposed to happen; all of us were marked for death.

But we outlived the mass graves, some of us, and among us were those who found even the strength for renewal. In the State of Israel—imagine those words; who in 1939 could have dreamed them for 1948, the *State* of Israel?—and in the democracies, where Jews freely chose to be Israel, we, Jacob's children, including this particular Jacob, renew life. That to me is the miracle of this time and of all time. And how could I open the Torah or study the Torah except in the light of that commanding fact: renewal beyond the grave. There is scarcely a line of the Torah that bears no meaning for that life that I live with memories of not dreams, like Jacob, but nightmares. Jacob dreamed a dream; this Jacob, along with all Israel, lived a nightmare. But Jacob came home, with Leah and Rachel and a tent full of children. And, for now at least, most of Jacob's and Leah's and Rachel's children are home—somewhere.

I can offer no more telling case of the way in which, in my view, the Torah addresses the world. It is to link the everyday we know to the paradigm of humanity represented by Israel's patriarchs and matriarchs. The Torah here is made into a commentary upon the everyday and the ordinary. But the here and the now also serve as a source for amplification and explanation of the Torah. The road is open in both directions, and much traffic moves, just as the stairway that Jacob saw brought those on high to earth and raised Jacob's vision upward, too. To a reading of stories in light of the sanctity of the Torah as principal component of God's revelation to Moses at Sinai, answers to merely historical questions are mildly interesting but simply irrelevant. What really matters is how the Torah lives, which is to say for us here and now. And that carries us to the crisis of the sea and the climax of Sinai.

17

NEUSNER

"I the Lord Am Your God Who Brought You Out of the Land of Egypt"

God spoke all these words, saying:

I the Lord am your God who brought you out of the land of Egypt, the house of bondage. You shall have no other gods besides Me.

Exodus 20:1–3

The Passover celebration, which commemorates the exodus of Israel from Egypt, is the single most widely practiced rite of Judaism. What do people do? Well, what happens is that family and friends sit down for supper. That is what Jesus did with his disciples, formed into a surrogate family, at the Last Supper, and that is what Jews do, nearly universally, at the same season at which Christians celebrate Easter.

How so secular an act as a supper party is turned into a highly charged occasion, rich in deeply felt meanings, we shall not find out if we simply review the words that are said. The meal consumed with ceremony turns people into something other than what they think they are and puts them down square into the path of an onrushing history.

In the presence of symbols both visual and verbal, in the formation of family and friends into an Israel redeemed from Egypt, people become something else, and words work that wonder. This is the key to how Scripture becomes Torah: God's revelation to Moses at Sinai, but, as the blessing we say when the Torah is read, an event of today: "blessed are you . . . who gives the Torah" here and now.

At the festival of Passover, which coincides with the first full moon after the vernal equinox, because they remember how some slaves ran off into the desert, Jewish families gather around their tables for a holy meal. There— speaking in very general terms—they retell the story of the exodus from Egypt in times long past. With unleavened bread and sanctified wine they celebrate the liberation of slaves from Pharaoh's bondage. There is, at the rite, a single formula that in words captures the moment, and, to understand how the "we" of the family becomes the "we" of Israel, how the eternal and perpetual coming of spring is made to mark a singular moment, a onetime act on the stage in the unfolding of linear time, we begin there: "For ever after, in every generation, *every Israelite must think of himself or herself as having gone forth from Egypt*" [italics added].

This is a curious passage indeed. It is one thing to tell Jews to think of themselves in one way, rather than in some other. It is quite a different thing to explain why Jews respond to the demand—and they do respond.

What is it that makes plausible for nearly all Jews all over the world the statement, "We went forth . . . ," and why do people sit down for supper and announce, "It was not only our forefathers that the Holy One, blessed be He, redeemed; us too, the living, He redeemed together with them"? I cannot imagine a more compelling invitation to derision and disbelief than that. We are not there. Pharaoh has been dead for quite some time. Egypt languishes in the rubbish heap of history. Wherein the enchantment? Why us, why here, why now? The answer derives from our power to transform the here and now into an intimation of the wholly other: to read the Bible as Torah, to read the narration of Passover as a story about us.

When we see the everyday as metaphor, that vision gives us a new sight of the Torah. For we perceive the deeper layer of meaning that permits us to treat as obvious and self-evident the transforming power of comparison, of simile applied to oneself: let's pretend, and what if? and why not? If you wonder just how this works when it comes to Israel at the sea and at Sinai, the Passover celebration shows us the answer. One theme stands out here: we, here and now, are really living then and there. That is an exact instance of midrash: Scripture imposing itself on the world today. So for example:

> We were slaves of Pharaoh in Egypt and the Lord our God brought us forth from there with a mighty hand and an outstretched arm. And if the Holy One, blessed be he, had not brought our fathers forth from Egypt, then we and our descendants would still be slaves to Pharaoh in Egypt. And so, even if all of us were full of wisdom, understanding, sages and well informed in the Torah, we should still be obligated to repeat again the story of the exodus from Egypt; and whoever treats as an important matter the story of the exodus from Egypt is praiseworthy.

And yet again:

> This is the promise which has stood by our forefathers and stands by us. For neither once, nor twice, nor three times was our destruction planned; in every generation they rise against us, and in every generation God delivers us

from their hands into freedom, out of anguish into joy, out of mourning into festivity, out of darkness into light, out of bondage into redemption.

This is how midrash does its work, shown in the way in which we leave slavery every year. If we ask, therefore, what experience in the here and now is taken up and transformed by enchantment into the then and the there, we move from the rite to the reality.

Where then do I fit in to the sea and to Sinai? The Jews are a minority, small in numbers, compensating in visibility. So far as they differ from "the others," a fantasized majority that is alike in all respects because everyone not Jewish is the same, that is, is (merely) Gentile, Jews confront not a critical but a chronic discomfort. To be different—whatever the difference—requires explanation; it provokes resentment; it creates tension demanding resolution and pain requiring remission. For the young, difference is deadly. For the middle-aged, difference demands explanation and compensation, and it may well exact the cost of diminished opportunity. For the individual may not be different from other individuals, but families always do retain that mark of difference from other families and that in the very nature of their existence.

Passover celebrates the family of Israel and is celebrated by the families of Israel. So Passover, with its rhetoric for rejoicing for freedom, plays out in a minor key the song of liberation: today slaves, next year free, today here, next year in "Jerusalem" (that is, not the real Jerusalem but the imagined, heavenly one). That is why, when they read, "We see ourselves as if . . . ," they do not burst out laughing and call for the main course.

And that brings us to Israel at the sea and the climax: the giving of the Ten Commandments. For, as we shall now see, in the Torah, the Ten Commandments are identified as the difference: what makes Israel different from all the other nations. They explain difference, as much as, in today's world, the Passover Seder invokes the exodus from Egypt to account for differences people feel in their everyday lives. That is not to say the Ten Commandments belong to us alone. But in the Torah they stand for what makes us what we are. These Ten Commandments, which Judaism shares with Christianity as the fundamental rule and requirement that God has set forth for us all, define tasks for both Israel and the nations, since, we recall, five of them are among the seven commandments that apply to all humanity, the children of Noah.

But we read them within our own setting, addressing to the passage questions that elicit the particular sense that we, holy Israel, seek. For instance, if these commandments are so important, why not put them at the head of the Torah? The following passage, which derives from a midrash compilation on the Book of Exodus called Mekhilta Attributed to R. Ishmael, answers that question:

> "[And God spoke all these words, saying,] 'I am the Lord your God, [who brought you out of the land of Egypt, out of the house of bondage]:' "
>
> How come the Ten Commandments were not stated at the very beginning of the Torah?
>
> The matter may be compared to the case of a king who came into a city. He said to the people, "May I rule over you?"
>
> They said to him, "Have you done us any good, that you should rule over us?"
>
> What did he then do? He built a wall for them, brought water for them, fought their battles.
>
> Then he said to them, "May I rule over you?"
>
> They said to him, "Yes, indeed."
>
> So the Omnipresent brought the Israelites out of Egypt, divided the sea for them, brought manna down for them, brought up the well for them, provided the quail for them, made war for them against Amalek.
>
> Then he said to them, "May I rule over you?"
>
> They said to him, "Yes, indeed."

No accident that the Ten Commandments find their place after God has saved Israel from the slavery of Egypt and the impending catastrophe at the Red Sea. Here, therefore, is the occasion for another covenant, or agreement, that binds God to Israel and Israel to God.

Like the covenant between the parts that Abraham made, like the vow that Jacob took, what we have is a set of rules that govern the relationship. That is to say, we have a covenant between God and Israel, between God and every Jew, between God and me. God's requirements are not without reason and rule and are not without limit. What God wants is moderate, accords with a rule of order and regularity, and produces a fair result if people obey. And people remain free to obey or disobey; that is the centerpiece of the whole. But God attends to what is public and also what is private. But the covenant at Sinai is with Israel as a whole. It is not with a private person, such as Abraham and Jacob, and his family. Accordingly, the question arises, Is the community or nation as a whole responsible for what is done in private, beyond the knowledge of the community? No, that is not the case. The covenant with the nation is public, and what individuals do will not affect the fate of the nation in its covenant with God:

> And it was not only what was overt alone that the Holy One, blessed be he, revealed himself to them to make a covenant with them,

but also over what is done in secret:

"The secret things belong to the Lord our God, and the things that are revealed" (Dt. 29:28).

They said to him, "Concerning what is done openly we make a covenant with you, but we shall not make a covenant with you concerning what is done in secret,

"so that one of us may not commit a sin in secret and the entire community be held responsible for it."

Accordingly, the private person bears personal responsibility for what he or she does, but the nation as a whole cannot take the guilt, though it may well accept the shame, for what is done privately.

Since both Judaism and Christianity affirm that the Ten Commandments represent the most important parts of the covenant between God and humankind and so belong to everyone, not only to Israel, can we find a clear statement that everyone is welcome to share in the Torah? Indeed we can. Our sages are explicit that there is nothing in the Torah that is particular to Israel, the holy people. What Israel has done is accept what is there for everybody:

To three things the Torah is compared: wilderness, fire, and water,

so as to say to you, just as these are there for nothing, for everyone in the world,

so teachings of the Torah are there for nothing, for everyone in the world.

And that leads us to the question that you must want to ask, "Why Israel? Why to "you" in particular? Beyond the covenant with Noah, the agreements in succession address only holy Israel. True, Israel, the holy people, do make ample room for newcomers. But we surely should ask our sages to answer that urgent question: "Why us—Israel in particular?" And then we want to return to what's really bothering me: "Why am I different? And why do (some) people hate me because of the difference? That is to say, why is there Jew hatred and anti-Semitism?" The Torah must answer that question for me, or it does not talk about the things that most affect me.

This question—the one of Israel's difference and the associated one of anti-Semitism—is answered in two parts. First of all, given the description of the giving of the Ten Commandments, in public, after dramatic events, we must know that other people knew what was going out. The Torah is explicit: "the earth shook," in line with this verse, "Lord, when you went forth our of Seir . . . , the earth trembled." Then how did the rulers of the world interpret these matters, and, again, why were they excluded?

> "[And God spoke all these words, saying,] 'I am the Lord your God, [who brought you out of the land of Egypt, out of the house of bondage]:' "
>
> When the Holy One, blessed be he, went and said, "I am the Lord your God, [who brought you out of the land of Egypt, out of the house of bondage]," the earth shook, as it is said, "Lord, when you went forth out of Seir, when you marched out of the field of Edom, the earth trembled" (Judges 5:4); "The mountains quaked at the presence of the Lord" (Judges 5:5); "The voice of the Lord is upon the waters . . . The voice of the Lord is mighty" (Ps. 29:3–4); "and in his palace, everyone says glory" (Ps. 29:9).
>
> Their palaces were filled with the splendor of the Presence of God. At that time all the nations of the world collected around the wicked Balaam and said to him, "Balaam, perhaps the Omnipresent is going to destroy his world with a flood?"
>
> He said to them. "Fools, the Holy One, blessed be he, has taken an oath to Noah that he will not bring a flood into the world, for it is said, 'For this is as the waters of Noah to me; for as I have sworn that the waters of Noah shall no more go over the earth . . .' (Is. 54:9)."
>
> They said, "Perhaps he will not bring a flood of water, but he may bring a flood of fire?"
>
> He said to them, "He is going to bring neither a flood of water nor a flood of fire. It is Torah that the Holy One, blessed be he, is giving to his people: 'The Lord is giving strength to his people' (Ps. 29:11)."
>
> When they had heard that from his mouth, they all turned around and each one went to his place.

The first point, then, is that the nations feared only a repetition of the events in the time of Noah, and this underlines the fact that the initial covenant was the only one that concerned them. But did they not have a chance to accept the Torah? Our sages proceed in this same account to allege that they did. But they all declined, each for his own reason.

Israel is different because other people did not accept the Torah—which they could have done. The reasons turn upon their local characteristics and customs, which contradicted the rule of the Ten Commandments in one way or another:

> Therefore the nations of the world were approached [to accept the Torah], so as not to give them an excuse to say, "If we had been approached, we should have accepted responsibility [for carrying out the Torah]."
>
> Lo, they were approached but did not accept responsibility for them, as it is said, "The Lord came from Sinai" (Dt. 33:2).

["The Lord came from Sinai" (Dt. 33:2):]

[When the Omnipresent appeared to give the Torah to Israel, it was not to Israel alone that he revealed himself but to every nation.]

First of all he came to the children of the wicked Esau. He said to them, "Will you accept the Torah?"

They said to him, "What is written in it?"

He said to them, " 'You shall not murder' (Ex. 20:13)."

They said to him, "The very being of 'those men' [namely, us] and of their father is to murder, for it is said, 'But the hands are the hands of Esau' (Gen. 27:22). 'By your sword you shall live' (Gen. 27:40)."

So he went to the children of Ammon and Moab and said to them, "Will you accept the Torah?"

They said to him, "What is written in it?"

He said to them, " 'You shall not commit adultery.' (Ex. 20:13)."

They said to him, "[The very essence of fornication belongs to them (us)], all of us are the children of fornication, for it is said, 'Thus were both the daughters of Lot with child by their father' (Gen. 19:36)."

So he went to the children of Ishmael and said to them, "Will you accept the Torah?"

They said to him, "What is written in it?"

He said to them, " 'You shall not steal' (Ex. 20:13)."

They said to him, "This is the blessing that was stated to our father: 'And he shall be a wild ass of a man' (Gen. 16:12) 'For indeed I was stolen away out of the land of the Hebrews' (Gen. 40:15)."

But when he came to the Israelites: "At his right hand was a fiery law for them" (Dt. 33:2).

They all opened their mouths and said, "All that the Lord has spoke we shall do and we shall hear" (Ex. 24:7).

He stood and measured the earth, he beheld and drove asunder the nations" (Hab. 3:6).

The answer to "Why Israel?" then is explicit. Israel alone was prepared to accept the Torah, unanimously agreeing to do whatever it was that they would hear. And the nations of the world would not give up those of their practices that contradicted God's will. Now, we recall, among those practices were murder, fornication, and thievery. These critical issues then separated the nations from God, since while not required to keep the Sabbath day holy, they were required not to murder, steal, or commit adultery.

Accordingly, sages observe, the nations could not observe the seven religious duties assigned to them and surely should not be expected to take up all of the sanctifying labors of the Torah. The following, from Mekhilta, attributed to R. Ishmael, addresses that question:

R. Simeon b. Eleazar says, "If the seven religious duties that were assigned to the children of Noah they could not uphold, how much the more so all the religious duties that are in the Torah!

"The matter may be compared to the case of a king who set up two administrators, one in charge of the supply of straw, the other in charge of the supply of silver and gold.

"The one in charge of the supply of straw was suspected of thievery, and he complained that he had not been appointed over the supply of silver and gold.

"They said to him, 'Fool! If you have been suspected of stealing from the straw-supply, how are people going to entrust to you charge of the supply of silver and gold!'

"Now this yields an argument a fortiori:

"If the seven religious duties that were assigned to the children of Noah they could not uphold, how much the more so all the religious duties that are in the Torah!"

What about the location? Why give the Torah in the wilderness, claimed by no nation? It was for the same reason: to explain why the Torah came to Israel in particular:

How come the Torah was not given in the land of Israel?

It was so as not to give an excuse to the nations of the world to say, "It is because the Torah was given in their land, therefore we did not accept responsibility for it upon ourselves."

So much for the setting and the audience for the Ten Commandments, which, it is clear, stand for the entire Torah. Since the Ten Commandments stand for the covenant between God and Israel, we have had first to explain why Israel in particular, and this question quite naturally has required us to account for the location of the covenant and the parties to it: not the nations, since it is alleged they could not keep even the most important of the seven religious duties assigned to them.

Once we have come this far, we turn back to the covenant with Noah. For all humanity are children of Noah, and when we speak of Sinai and its covenant—and the identification of Israel as different through the Ten Commandments—we find our way back to what makes the Ten Commandments different from the seven commandments of the children of Noah. And, we recall, God was happy with those: he was pleased with Noah's offering.

So that leads me to ask, When Scripture says that God was pleased with Noah's offering and therefore made the covenant never again to curse the world because of humankind, to what does the Torah make reference? Does this mean, I ask myself, that God responded to Noah without reference to me, Israel? The important verse is this: "And when the Lord smelled the pleasing odor, the Lord said in his heart, 'I will never again curse the ground because of man, for the imagination of man's heart is evil from his youth' " (Gen. 8:21). To what did God respond in the offering, or, in the language at hand, what exactly did God "smell"? To the merit attained through the faith and loyalty of Israel, and so our sages teach in this case, too.

God took note ("smelled") the gifts of the martyrs, the gift of faith:

He smelled the fragrance of the flesh of Abraham, our father, coming up from the heated furnace.

He smelled the fragrance of the flesh of Hananiah, Mishael, and Azariah, coming up from the heated furnace.

The matter may be compared to the case of a king, whose courtier brought him a valuable present. It was a fine piece of meat on a lovely plate.

His son came along and brought him nothing. His grandson came along and brought him a present. He said to him, "The value of the gift you brought is equivalent to the value of the gift your grandfather brought."

So God smelled the fragrance of the sacrifice of the generation of persecution.

Now in context we address those who accepted death by burning, equivalent to the burning up of the animals that produces the sweet smell God likes. So the blood sacrifice is turned into a symbol for Israel's sacrifice of itself in God's name.

Sinai is what made Israel different from Noah's children, everybody else. And that difference is our destiny and it explains why we are what we are. There is a commanding voice of Sinai. Emil Fackenheim, the great Jewish theologian of the Holocaust, speaks also of a commanding voice of Auschwitz, the commandment to Israel, the people: "Be! Live!" And with Fackenheim I see the course of the world as an ellipse running between two mountains, Sinai, the hill of the Torah, and—hear me out!—the mountains of corpses formed at Auschwitz and dozens of other high places made up of the shoes, the undergarments, teddy bears and dolls, the spectacles, of Jews. This happened, and it happened in our day, and it changes for all time the perspective and the aspect of the faith. So let me now say very simply that were I today to write these words, I would say: "God smelled the gas and the burning flesh," the fragrance of the sacrifice of holy Israel, in the gas chambers and in the crematoria of Europe, not only Abraham in the furnace of the Chaldeans, but Jacob in the fires of Auschwitz, not only Isaac on the altar—not only Israel at Sinai—but Isadore and Wilhelm in Mauthausen.

The martyrdom of Israel in God's name takes many forms, but it is always the same: "Such is the generation of those that seek after him, that seek your face, even Jacob." And the Torah speaks today to the world that remembers Auschwitz, as much as it speaks from Sinai: no less, no more, and, I claim, also no differently. It is the same world, under one God. But the tasks of affirmation, obedience, and faith in the Torah form a weightier burden than they did—all the more reason to undertake and carry them out. We are the generation of Abraham, promised heirs in old age, Isaac, on the altar, Jacob, driven from his home and homeland into an unknown wilderness, Israel, with the Egyptians behind them and the sea in front. Ours is the experience to which the Torah speaks, and ours is the challenge that the Torah sets forth. It is to us here and now: We are Abraham, Isaac, Jacob. We are Israel at the sea and at Sinai, we, after Auschwitz, unchanged and enduring, eternal Israel.

The entire history of Israel, the holy people, lies within the covenant of not only Abraham, Isaac, Jacob, and Sinai, but also of Noah, that is, the contract that secures for humanity the continuity of civilization. Here is how the matter is stated:

> "And surely your blood of your lives I will require. At the hand of every beast will I require it" (Gen. 9:5):
>
> This refers to the four kingdoms [who ruled in sequence over Israel before the coming of the fifth kingdom, which is God's: Babylonia, Media, Greece, and Rome, who are answerable for the murders that they commit.]
>
> "At the hand of man" (Gen. 9:5):
>
> Said R. Levi, "That means, from the hand of the Edomite [meaning, Rome]."
>
> "Even at the hand of every man's brother" (Gen. 9:5). "Deliver me, I pray you, from the hand of my brother, from the hand of Esau" (Gen. 32:12).
>
> "Will I require the life of man" (Gen. 9:5). This refers to Israel. "And you my sheep, the sheep of my pasture, are men" (Ez. 34:31).

Israel's history figures, with regard to both the sacrifice of one's life for God's sanctification and the role of the four kingdoms, with Esau/Edom/Rome at the climax. They are answerable for the blood that they shed. Then has Sinai and its counterpart mountain made us holier than Noah and the rest? Noah's sacrifices for all humanity are no less precious to God because Israel's sacrifices in its own flesh and blood, in the lives of its old people and its children, have risen to Heaven even in our own century. For the true sacrifices to God come from those who give their lives for his name. And, in the here and now, that means, to live life for God—by definition, to be different. But in what does the difference consist? The Ten Commandments spell it all out. And they therefore explain Auschwitz by appeal to Sinai. Let me say how.

How do the Ten Commandments form the occasion for making sense of the nonsense of anti-Semitism? And why do I approach Sinai by the road that passes through Auschwitz? To understand the context in which the oral Torah reads the written Torah in a way that we can make our own, I have to explain a moment of real history. For a brief spell, after a massive rebellion against Rome, in around 135 of the Common Era, the Roman government in Palestine, which Jews know as the land of Israel, prohibited the observance of some of the religious duties, putting to death people who kept them. That was not the Romans' usual policy, and it did not last long, but it made a profound impact. For under ordinary conditions, too, it was not always easy to keep the faith, living, as some people have done, among vast majorities who did not do so and among whom were some, even many, who despised Israel, the holy people, for doing so. Accordingly, the reading of the statement that God loves those who love God and therefore keep the commandments remained perpetually the same. Those who really love God do so even unto death:

> R. Nathan says, " 'those who love me and keep my commandments' refers to those who dwell in the land of Israel and give their lives for keeping the religious duties.
>
> " 'How come you are going forth to be put to death?' 'Because I circumcised my son as an Israelite.'
>
> " 'How come you are going forth to be burned to death?' 'Because I read in the Torah.'
>
> " 'How come you are going forth to be crucified?' 'Because I ate unleavened bread.'
>
> " 'How come you are going to be given a hundred lashes?' 'Because I took up the palm branch [on Tabernacles].'
>
> " 'Those with which I was wounded in the house of friends' (Zech. 13:6): these are the wounds that made me beloved to my father who is in heaven."

Alongside the Ten Commandments—right in the midst of explaining what they mean—comes an account of where and how they are kept. Judaism is the religion of only a small group, and Jewish people have to explain to themselves why it is that they are different from the others and less than the others in esteem. For we Jews never underestimate the power of that special hatred directed against us called anti-Semitism. Maybe we overestimate it. But in the twentieth century paranoia becomes understatement.

Anyhow, even if we wanted to, the history of our own century would not let us. Difference breeds dislike, dislike contempt, contempt hatred, hatred murderous hostility, which is acted out in horror in age succeeding age. Why? "Because I ate unleavened bread." "Because I took up the palm branch." "These are the wounds that made me beloved to my father who is in heaven." Anti-Semites may not know whether or not I eat unleavened bread on Passover, but they always know that I am different, a Jew, and they despise that particular difference: my being Jewish. In one way or another, small or large, these are the marks of "those who love me and keep my commandments." It is what we are. We can be nothing else. And we do not want to be. And that is why, and the only reason why, the German Nazis and their allies made the century that now closes the most perilous and painful that holy Israel has ever known. No wonder, then, that we cannot open the Torah without thinking of when we are and what has happened to us.

18

NEUSNER
The Ten Commandments

God spoke all these words, saying:

I the Lord am your God who brought you out of the land of Egypt, the house of bondage. You shall have no other gods besides Me.

You shall not make for yourself a sculptured image, or any likeness of what is in the heavens above or on the earth below or in the waters under the earth. You shall not bow down to them or serve them. For I the Lord your God am an impassioned God, visiting the guilt of the parents upon the children, upon the third and upon the fourth generations of those who rejected Me, but showing kindness to the thousandth generation of those who love Me and keep My commandments.

You shall not swear falsely by the name of the Lord your God; for the Lord will not clear one who swears falsely by His name.

Remember the Sabbath day to keep it holy. Six days you shall labor and do all your work, but the seventh day is a Sabbath of the Lord your God; you shall not do any work—you, your son or daughter, your male or female slave, or your cattle or the stranger who is within your settlements. For in six days the Lord made heaven and earth and sea, and all that is in them, and He rested on the seventh day; therefore the Lord blessed the Sabbath day and hallowed it.

Honor your father and your mother, that you may long endure on the land that the Lord your God is assigning to you.

You shall not murder.

You shall not commit adultery.

You shall not steal.

You shall not bear false witness against your neighbor.

You shall not covet your neighbor's house; you shall not covet your neighbor's wife, or his male or female slave, or his ox or his ass or anything that is your neighbor's.

Exodus 20: 1–14

The Torah makes Israel Israel, so the entire message of Scripture insists, and at the centerpiece of the covenant stand the Ten Commandments. When I was growing up, in a Reform Jewish temple in West Hartford, we were required to memorize the Ten Commandments (in English, of course; who in those dim days imagined Hebrew lived?) and recite them. But they seemed remote. After all, we Reform Jews did not remember the Sabbath day, except for a few of us who attended Friday evening services. But then the day was just an hour and a half, not twenty-four holy hours, set apart.

Of course we did not murder. True, we gossiped. Of course we did not commit adultery. True, it was only because we did not know what it was. Of course we did not steal, unless no one was looking or unless we didn't think a person's good name was covered by not stealing. Anyhow, we envied, we coveted, we had a million other gods apiece. And, as for images, we were surrounded by the things we really worshiped.

So, yes, the Ten Commandments were the heart of our faith, and no, they really had nothing to do with us, not at all, not at all.

The hell they didn't. The problem was, and still is, we didn't know that the Ten Commandments really are what they are cracked up to be: do this and you'll be about as good as a human being can get to be. But the "this"—there's the problem.

For the Ten Commandments are not ten different things. They are one thing in ten forms: "I am the Lord your God . . . ; therefore, don't do this, and do do that." The Ten Commandments are the details, the "I am the Lord *your* God," the main thing. So the Ten Commandments outline a path to follow to make God "your God." And to leave that Egypt that "the Lord your God" helps you escape: slavery in one form or another.

So we reach the heart of the matter of the Torah: how do the Ten Commandments define our relationship with God? The very order of matters will answer that question to begin with. God begins by announcing that Israel is to have only the Lord for God. Why start there? For the simple reason that, before one can agree to the details, one has to adopt the main point. And the principal part of the Ten Commandments is what comes first: that God rules and that Israel accepts God's dominion. On the basis of that fact, all else follows.

This point is made explicit in several ways. First of all, Israel has to affirm that it has already accepted God's rule, in which case it is instructed in the first detail of that rule, which is not to have other gods.

"You shall have no other gods before me" (Ex. 20:3):
Why is this stated?
Since it says, "I am the Lord your God."
The matter may be compared to the case of a mortal king who came to a town. His staff said to him, "Issue decrees for them."
He said to them, "No. When they have accepted my dominion, then I shall issue decrees over them. For if they do not accept my dominion, how are they going to carry out my decrees?"
So said the Omnipresent to Israel, "I am the Lord your God.
"You shall have no other gods before me.
"I am the one whose dominion you accepted upon yourselves in Egypt."

They said to him, "Indeed so."

"And just as you accepted my dominion upon yourself, now likewise accept my decrees: 'You shall have no other gods before me.' "

The same point is made again by Simeon b. Yohai, the great second-century sage, in a still more explicit way. What it means to accept God's rule is not to do what the Egyptians or the Canaanites do, but to do only in accord with God's commandments, hence starting with the Ten Commandments.

["The Lord spoke to Moses saying, 'Speak to the Israelite people and say to them, I am the Lord your God' " (Lev. 18:2):]

R. Simeon b. Yohai says, "That is in line with what is said elsewhere: 'I am the Lord your God [who brought you out of the land of Egypt, out of the house of bondage]' (Ex. 20:2).

" 'Am I the Lord, whose sovereignty you took upon yourself in Sinai?'

"They said to him, 'Indeed.'

" 'And just as you accepted my dominion upon yourself, now accept my decrees.'

" 'You shall not copy the practices of the land of Egypt where you dwelt, or of the land of Canaan to which I am taking you; nor shall you follow their laws.'

"What is said here? 'I am the Lord your God [who brought you out of the land of Egypt, out of the house of bondage]' (Ex. 20:2).

" 'Am I the Lord, whose sovereignty you took upon yourself?'

"They said to him, 'Indeed.'

" 'And just as you accepted my dominion upon yourself, now accept my decrees.'

"You shall have no other gods before me" (Ex. 20:3).

Accordingly, first comes God's rule, then come God's rules, in that order. But Simeon's point is so concrete that he turns what is abstract into something palpable. To be one thing, stop doing another thing. Give up "Egypt," that slavery that you have bound yourself to. Then "I am the Lord." It follows that first Israel recognizes that it is the Lord who has brought them out of slavery, then is instructed not to have other gods.

This is the last really abstract and intangible point. From here onward, everything is very concrete. And this is the point at which Catholics and Jews join forces. For we all believe that when God wants things from us, these are particular and concrete. Works matter. Faith matters. But we see faith without works as empty and works without faith as hypocritical.

Over the past two hundred years a good bit of Protestant preaching has ridiculed Judaism but meant Catholicism. Some preachers held that Judaism made us into robots, just doing things but not really feeling or believing them. And they had in mind the Catholics, whom they described as mindless soldiers of a distant pope. What makes me jump from Sinai to anti-Catholicism and anti-Judaism, which turn out to be the same thing? Because the rest of the Ten Commandments are rules and laws. Do this, and do not do that. Any claim that there is a "salvation by faith alone" without works contradicts the Ten Commandments. For right here we have a slew of works; take the Sabbath, for example! Do this; don't do that: these are works, acts of commission and acts of omission. Citing "the law kills, but the spirit gives life," and the insistence of Paul (whom we'll meet shortly, as I want to know him, too) that the route to being "Israel" after the spirit is faith, has made people belittle deeds of faith. But we are what we do, and deeds of faith define us.

And in Judaism these deeds are made very specific and represented as wholly obligatory. Rules and laws, such as Judaism finds in the Torah, are not mere generalizations or good advice. They are firm, detailed requirements. And God lives in the details. Any sense that the Torah speaks in generalizations, for instance, about love, without responsibility, justice, without judgment, loyalty, without costs, submission to God's will, without sacrifice—any representation of relating to God in intangible ways alone misses the character. That spiritualization of things dismisses the contents of the Torah.

We see how the Ten Commandments speak not in generalities but require careful and explicit application to all manner of situations. And, in all honesty, that is where I find the power of the oral Torah in its address to the written part of the Torah. The strength, but the poetry, too—both derive from a loyal literalism. And that means, If this is what God has said, then this is what we must do. And to do in the here and now requires not mere general principles but careful and explicit specifications. Let us see, for instance, how the oral Torah spells out what it means not to make a graven or carved image of God that the written Torah makes obligatory.

The Ten Commandments left by themselves, the way we received them in the synagogue before our Bar or Bat Mitzvah celebration, were just that: lists of things to remember, someone else's list. Those ten things were easy: they had nothing to do with me or anybody I knew. That is what Christians call cheap grace, which is to say, no grace at all. But what takes heart and soul and work? It is forming my own "oral Torah," that is, helping God live in the details that strike home.

When I insist that the Torah imposes its shape on the common life, this is how the oral Torah conveys the imprint: in detail, one thing after another, for what seems an unending list. But the list makes the point, not only of its contents but beyond them: this is what it means, in the here and now, to keep the Ten Commandments:

"You shall not make for yourself a graven image:"

One shall not make one that is engraved, but may one make one that is solid?

The Torah says, "or any likeness of anything."

One should not make a solid one, but may one plant a tree for oneself as an idol?

The Torah says, "You shall not plant an Asherah for yourself" (Dt. 16:21).

One may not plant a tree for oneself as an idol, but perhaps one may make a tree into an idol?

The Torah says, "of any kind of tree."

One may not make an idol of a tree, but perhaps one may make one of a stone?

The Torah says, "Nor shall you place any figured stone."

One may not make an idol of a stone, but perhaps one may make an idol of silver or gold?

The Torah says, "Gods of silver or gods of gold you shall not make for yourself."

One may not make an idol of silver or gold, but perhaps one may make one of copper, iron, tin, or lead?

The Torah says, "Nor make for yourselves molten gods" (Lev. 19:4).

One may not make for oneself any of these images.

But may one make an image of any figure?

The Torah says, "lest you deal corruptly and make for yourself a graven image, even the form of any figure" (Dt. 4:16).

One may not make an image of a figure, but perhaps one may make an image of cattle or fowl?

The Torah says, "The likeness of any beast that is on the earth, the likeness of any winged fowl" (Dt. 4:17).

One may not make an image of cattle or fowl, but perhaps one may make an image of fish, locusts, unclean animals, or reptiles?

The Torah says, "The likeness of any thing that creeps on the ground, the likeness of any fish that is in the water" (Dt. 4:18).

One shall not make an image of any of these, but perhaps one may make an image of the sun, moon, stars, or planets?

The Torah says, "lest you lift up your eyes to heaven" (Dt. 4:18).

One may not make an image of any of these, but perhaps one may make an image of angels, cherubim, or Ophannim?

The Torah says, "of anything that is in heaven."

Since the Torah says, "that is in heaven above, [or that is in the earth beneath, or that is in the water under the earth]," might one suppose that that involves only sun, moon, stars, or planets?

It says, "above," that is, not the image of angels, cherubim, or Ophannim.

One may not make an image of any of these, but perhaps one may make an image of deeps and darkness?

The Torah says, "or that is in the water under the earth."

We see a sustained and searching process by which a general rule is made specific and shown to cover every conceivable situation. This is not a generalization, left up to our own imagination. It is a literal and uncompromising inquiry. Not having graven images is the generalization; everything else is the detail, and again, God lives in the details.

But isn't this tedious? Why not deal only with the main point? It is because we live in the here and now, and if sages do not cover every possibility contained within the language of the Torah, you can be sure someone somewhere will uncover an exception that God will not have approved, a possibility that violates the spirit of the law. So—if the spirit of the law is to live—the "letter of the law" has to be a very long letter.

So does that mean that the Ten Commandments are concrete, specific, and literal? Well, yes, it does. That is why Ten Commandments are enough; we didn't need twenty or fifty or a thousand. Because if we read the Ten Commandments in a very literal way, interpreting them to cover a large number of possibilities that the commandments cover, ten will do it. Take the case now concerning honor of parents. What is involved? How do we do it right? The answers to these questions, like the elaboration of the rule against idolatry, show us how Judaism in a very patient and detailed way proposes to have us understand the intent and rule of the Torah:

"Honor your father and your mother [that your days may be long in the land which the Lord your God gives you]:"

Might I infer that this is with words?

The Torah says, "Honor the Lord with your substance" (Prov. 3:9).

That means, with food, drink, and fresh garments.—

Rabbi says, "Precious before the One who spoke and brought the world into being is the honor owing to father and mother,

"for he has declared equal the honor owing to them and the honor owing to him, the fear owing to them and the fear owing to him, cursing them and cursing him.

"It is written: 'Honor your father and your mother,' " and as a counterpart: 'Honor the Lord with your substance' (Prov. 3:9).

"The Torah thus has declared equal the honor owing to them and the honor owing to him.

" 'You shall fear every man his mother and his father' (Lev. 19:3), and, as a counterpart: 'You shall fear the Lord your God' (Dt. 6:13).

"The Torah thus has declared equal the fear owing to them and the fear owing to him.

" 'And he who curses his father or his mother shall surely be put to death' (Ex. 21:17), and correspondingly: 'Whoever curses his God' (Lev. 24:15).

"The Torah thus has declared equal the cursing them and cursing him."

[Rabbi continues,] "Come and note that the reward [for obeying the two commandments] is the same.

" 'Honor the Lord with your substance . . . so shall your barns be filled with plenty' (Prov. 3:9–10), and 'Honor your father and your mother that your days may be long in the land which the Lord your God gives you.'

" 'You shall fear the Lord your God' (Dt. 6:13), as a reward: 'But to you that fear my name shall the sun of righteousness arise with healing in its wings' (Mal. 3:20).

" 'You shall fear every man his mother and his father and you shall keep my Sabbaths' (Lev. 19:3).

" 'And as a reward?' 'If you turn away your foot because of the Sabbath, then you shall delight yourself in the Lord' (Is. 58:13–14)."

Rabbi says, "It is perfectly self-evident before the One who spoke and brought the world into being that a person honors the mother more than the father, because she brings him along with words. Therefore The Torah gave precedence to the father over the mother as to honor.

"And it is perfectly self-evident before the One who spoke and brought the world into being that a person fears his father more than the mother, because the father teaches him Torah. Therefore The Torah gave precedence to the mother over the father as to fear.

"In a case in which something is lacking, [The Torah] thereby made it whole.

"But might one suppose that whoever takes precedence in The Torah takes precedence in deed?

"The Torah says, 'You shall fear every man his mother and his father' (Lev. 19:3),

"indicating that both of them are equal to one another."

You've heard of the Jewish mother? Then what you know is, first, she is overbearing and aggressive in her love. Second, she raises Jewish American princes and princesses. Well, here is the truth: the Jewish son and daughter, who honor the mother and the father and respect them. And that is much more the truth than the caricature of a precious and beautiful relationship.

The daughter and son give, the mother and father receive, because the father and mother give, the son and daughter receive: an ever-flowing spring of love. True, love can shade off into aggression, giving, into control, receiving, into victimization. How to confront the possibilities of corruption even of the natural love within families? Through word and deed: 'Might I infer that this is with words? The Torah says, 'Honor the Lord with your substance' (Prov. 3:9). That means, with food, drink, and fresh garments."

When we ask the Torah to comment on today, we can do worse than draw on the Torah's perspective about families and their relationships. For here is something startling—the Ten Commandments reverse the order we in our world think natural: parents give to children. (But in large parts of the Catholic world, all of Latin America, for example, children give to parents.) In the holy Israel the commandments mean to construct, it is the children who owe something to parents. That is not tangible. It is honor. The Ten Commandments, finally, consistent with the story of the creation of Adam and Eve, form the first feminist platform. Just as "in our image, after our likeness" means "male and female, he made them," so here honoring parents means mother and father, not just love of mother and fear of father, but both, in perfect equality.

There's another side to family relationships in the Ten Commandments. Here we are told:

> "For I the Lord your God am an impassioned God, visiting the guilt of the parents upon the children, upon the third and fourth generations of those who rejected Me, but showing kindness to the thousandth generation of those who love Me and keep My commandments."

That's pretty strong stuff, and it forces upon the love and respect owing to parents an unwanted question: aren't there parents we're better off not having? And isn't there a God best dispensed with: one who blames me for what my father did! To state matters more bluntly, is the Old Testament God a jealous and vengeful God, by contrast to the New Testament God of love? Punishing people for what they didn't do, penalizing children for their parents: mean, vengeful, spiteful God, that Old Testament God! We hear this from both the Catholics and the Protestants and the Orthodox, too: a common Christian message.

That, after all, is the view of not a few Christians, forgetful that theirs is both the Old Testament and the New Testament, equally and indivisibly. They point to the explicit statement in the Ten Commandments that God is impassioned, often translated as *jealous*. So we note in the translation given above:

"I the Lord am an impassioned God, visiting the guilt of the parents upon the children, upon the third and fourth generations of those who rejected Me, but showing kindness to the thousandth generation of those who love Me and keep My commandments."

In the following statement of sages, let us revert to the more familiar rendition, "a jealous God," to hear with great clarity how Judaism's sages deal with this "vengeful, jealous" God.

"for I the Lord your God am a jealous God:"
"It is with jealousy that I exact punishment from idolatry.
"But as to other matters, 'showing steadfast love.' "

The jealousy pertains to those who violate the First Commandment, that is to say, those who maintain that the Lord is not the sole God. In all other ways, God forgives readily and quickly. But that of course is the heart of the matter: obedience to God depends upon loyalty, faithfulness, and trust, and these are principal.

And everything depends on the heart: on your attitude, not your parents', on your deeds, not your mother's or your father's. What you deliberately do is what you are responsible for and not what you do by inadvertence or what is done for you or before you, for that matter. In the law of the Torah as it pertains to the Temple we find a parallel conception. You recall that through the book of Leviticus there is the requirement, for various indiscretions, to bring a sin offering to atone for sin. The point of the Torah is this: a sin offering atones for sin that is done inadvertently, not deliberately. Then a sacrifice makes up to Heaven for what has violated the rule, not deliberately and willfully. But if one sins deliberately, then the mere sin offering has no value. An attitude of arrogance makes all the difference, and then Heaven has to intervene directly. The consequence is the penalty of early death, before one's time. For what you do deliberately you have to give up life, which God has bestowed, in payment for a deliberate act of disobedience to Heaven. *But that then ends the matter.* Even the willful sinner enjoys life eternal and the world to come after death; the sinner's death atones for deliberate sin, just as the animal's death atones for the inadvertent sin. The Torah consigns to perdition only those who by their own attitude demand it; for instance, those who deny that the Torah teaches that the dead will be raised are themselves not given resurrection and life eternal.

But the point is the same: everything depends upon one's own attitude. Here too the main point is that God will respond to a person's attitude; God and humankind share the same traits of heart and mind and soul such that if a person rejects God, then God passionately responds. If a person accepts God but violates any one of the commandments, God will readily forgive. So everything depends upon the basic attitude.

If so, why punish the children for what the parents do? That conception of collective punishment through generations violates the most elementary sense of justice: We are responsible for what we do, not for what others do. We can be punished only for our own sins or crimes. So our sages deal with the violent threat of punishing children for the sins of the parents:

> "visiting the iniquity of the fathers upon the children:"
> That is when there is no break in the chain, but not when there is a break in the chain.
> How so?
> In the case of a wicked person, son of a wicked person, son of a wicked person.
> R. Nathan says, "It is one who cuts down [the plantings], son of one who cuts down [the plantings], son of one who cuts down [the plantings]."
> When Moses heard this matter, "Moses made haste and bowed his head toward the earth and worshipped" (Ex. 34:8).

And whom does God love forever? It is "those who love me and keep my commandments," which then forms the mark of love. The Torah speaks in an eternal present. Therefore any passage refers to all other passages, and all the Torah addresses our situation.

My last question flows from the claim that everything is everywhere. How do I hold together a set of statements that—so I claim—can encompass all of my everyday life? If, as I say, the Torah speaks to the here and the now, then it must be infinite in detail, but then how does it all make sense? To answer that question, I can offer the method of the Torah, which is to look for points in common and correspondences. That method is expressed in a strange question: what do the Ten Commandments look like? People familiar with the symbols of Judaism will know that the Ten Commandments are set forth in two groups of five, facing one another.

So there are correspondences between the commandments, and that search for how this connects with that—a very intellectual search, since thought is thinking about the connections of things—brings us to the end of it all. The upshot of the search for a whole out of the parts is simple: the position that if you do one, the other follows. Violate one, and the other is broken as well. When we recognize these correspondences between each set of five commandments and the complementary ones, we grasp yet another layer of meaning in the passage under study.

"How were the Ten Commandments set forth?

"There were five on one tablet, five on the other.

"On the one was written, 'I am your Lord your God.'

"and opposite it: 'You shall not murder.'

"The Torah thus indicates that whoever sheds blood is regarded as though he had diminished the divine image.

"The matter may be compared to the case of a mortal king who came into a town, and the people set up in his honor icons, and they made statues of him, and they minted coins in his honor.

"After a while they overturned his icons, broke his statues, and invalidated his coins, so diminishing the image of the king.

"Thus whoever sheds blood is regarded as though he had diminished the divine image, for it is said, 'Whoever sheds man's blood . . . for in the image of God he made man' (Gen. 9:6)."

The whole of the Torah's picture of humankind is going to emerge in the Ten Commandments. We recall how the Torah insists that we are in God's image and likeness, and that means we look like God. Then murder diminishes God's image too.

So much for murder and God's image. Along these same lines, adultery represents a denial of God:

"On the one was written, 'You shall have no other god.'

"and opposite it: 'You shall not commit adultery.'

"The Torah thus indicates that whoever worships an idol is regarded as though he had committed adultery against the Omnipresent, for it is said, 'You wife that commits adultery, that takes strangers instead of your husband' (Ez. 16:32); 'And the Lord said to me, Go yet, love a woman beloved of her friend and an adulteress' (Hos. 3:1)."

Taking God's name in vain is the result of thievery. People often take oaths, so Judaism notes, in connection with the claim that they have not taken someone else's property. Hence, the correspondence:

"On the one was written, 'You shall not take the name of the Lord your God in vain.'

"and opposite it: 'You shall not steal.'

"The Torah thus indicates that whoever steals in the end will end up taking a false oath: 'Will you steal, murder, commit adultery, and swear falsely': (Jer. 7:9); 'Swearing and lying, killing and stealing, and committing adultery' (Hos. 4:2)."

What about the Sabbath? That is surely a commandment that has no counterpart, since it is (so it is seen by outsiders) a matter of pure "ritual," without ethical or moral implications. But, we recall, the Sabbath stands for creation and celebrates God's creating the world. There is nothing less narrowly ritualistic than the Sabbath, given its sense and meaning:

> "On the one was written, 'Remember the Sabbath day to keep it holy.'
> "and opposite it: 'You shall not bear false witness.'
> "The Torah thus indicates that whoever violates the Sabbath is as though he had given testimony before the One who spoke and brought the world into being, indicating that he had not created his world in six days and not rested on the seventh, and whoever keeps the Sabbath day is as though he had given testimony before the One who spoke and brought the world into being, indicating that he had created his world in six days and rested on the seventh: 'For you are my witnesses, says the Lord' (Is. 43:10)."

Is there a reward and punishment contained within the correspondences? So our sages maintain:

> "On the one was written, 'Honor your father and your mother.'
> "and opposite it: 'You shall not covet your neighbor's wife.'
> "The Torah thus indicates that whoever covets in the end will produce a son who curses his father and honors one who is not his father.
> "Thus the Ten Commandments were given, five on this tablet, and five on that," the words of Hananiah b. Gamaliel.

What Hananiah has done, we now realize, is to discover many of the basic principles of Judaism, that is, of the Torah, in these Ten Commandments.

The variety of themes that I locate in the Torah—creation and the celebration of creation, humankind in God's image and likeness, the covenant with all humankind through Noah, the covenant with holy Israel and its more particular requirements, the land, Israel among the nations, Israel's history—all of them have passed in review in this reading of the Ten Commandments. No wonder then that in the Torah sages through the ages have found in the Ten Commandments a simple and clear statement of everything that the Torah sets forth.

19

GREELEY
Moses, Our Rabbi

[handwritten: Moses = rabbi / Jesus = rabbi]

Just as we are forced to view Adam, Moses, and Abraham through the lens of postprophetic and postexilic Israelite religion, so we must view the work and the person of Moses, our rabbi, through the same lens.

The process can, perhaps, be compared to the phenomenon that we Americans tend to view George Washington, the founder of our country, through the lens of our view of the American history two centuries later. We know roughly the character and times of the man (less roughly than the Israelites who formulated the final redaction of the Torah knew Moses), but we are much more interested (unless we are professional historians) in the meanings of his words and deeds for our self-understanding as Americans today.

The final editors of the Torah were not so much interested in recording a precise description of the words and deeds of Moses (in many, if not most, instances they lacked the sources to do so even if they wanted to) as they were in explaining and interpreting Moses as his life and work was perceived to have relevance for their own religious situation and for their own understanding of what it meant to be Israel. *[handwritten: similar to Paul's writing of Jesus]*

In this chapter I will be typically modern and try to tease out from the various data available to us some information about "historical Moses." I will suggest—to paint with a very broad brush—that long before the rest of the world was able to develop the image of a transcendent deity, Moses did so—and in that respect at least he could be said to be the first monotheist. At the same time, however, as he launched a religious tradition that in some sense could claim to be the first "universal" (or "world") religion because of its image of a transcendent God, he also ensured the possibility that his successors (most notably the prophets and then Christianity and Judaism as heirs to the prophets) would be able to image (or conceptualize if you wish) that God was deeply involved with humans and suffering for and because of them (the "pathos of God," as Rabbi Abraham Heschel has called it).

The Moses of the Bible is presented as a great religious innovator, as founder of the religious tradition that the Torah records.

The "Moses of history" appears equally if not more important. He represents in its beginnings a decisive, perhaps the decisive, turning point in human religious history. He presided over the beginning of a tradition whose complicated, paradoxical, and yet profoundly appealing story of God has generated three great world religions (Judaism, Christianity, and Islam); a tradition that ingeniously and unexpectedly combines both nature religion and world religion; a God who is (often obnoxiously) present and a God who is utterly transcendent and supreme, the God beyond the Gods of Paul Tillich and at the same time the God of Abraham, Isaac, and Jacob, a religion that, as the rabbi asserts and as I can only agree, has an implicit demand for incarnation.

The first question is whether and to what extent Moses was the first monotheist, the herald of the monotheistic revolution that was to sweep the world in the millennium before the Common Era.

To answer the question we must understand what the religious situation had been since humankind began to reflect on its own mortality and to find that it could not help but hope that death was not the end.

Suspecting that there were powers in the universe greater than themselves and feeling dependent on those powers, men and women sought to worship such powers, which they identified as the forces of nature, of tribe, and of family. These gods and goddesses were as much part of the physical world as were the men and women who worshiped them, superior to their worshipers indeed, but still part of the natural processes by which the various species reproduced themselves or through which wind and storm affected human crops and flocks or which bound together in loyalty the tribe of the family.

All of these deities were to be found in the past of the Hebru, the wandering desert tribes whom, as we shall see, Moses bound together in covenant with God. Fertility gods and goddesses were especially important, perhaps because the desert was not that hospitable for reproduction of the flocks and the fields. The Passover festival, which came to represent the liberation of the Hebru from slavery in Egypt, seems to be the result of a combination of two earlier fertility festivals—the feast of the unleavened bread celebrated by the tribes who engaged in agriculture and the feast of the paschal lamb celebrated by tribes devoted to raising and tending flocks.

In the pre-Sinai era El Shaddai, or the God of the Mountain (perhaps the God of the Fruitful Mountain), was responsible for fertility, for the weather, and for protecting the tribe. He was thought to be a kind of male fertility principle and to live on the top of a high mountain.

The Hebru tribes were nomads and could find themselves wandering far afield from the mountaintop on which El Shaddai dwelt. On such occasions they turned to their family deity, an intimate and protective presence who had been chosen for the family by its patriarch, a kind of early version of a patron saint—not the chief god, surely, but a useful friend to have around on your journey.

Later Israel kept alive the memory of the gods of its patriarchs such as the Shield of Abraham, the Kinsman of Isaac, and the Mighty One of Jacob and combined them into one god—the God of the Fathers. But at the time that disparate and wandering tribes were first called by the term *Hebru*—at best a residual category and at worst a term of contempt (perhaps like "illegal alien"), their gods and goddesses were still a grab bag of fertility deities, mountain tribal gods, and family patrons. This Semitic pantheism was no different from that which could be found anywhere in the ancient world, save that like those who professed faith in them in the thirteenth century before the Common Era, the inhabitants of the pantheon were crude and inelegant.

A whiff of the monotheism that would sweep the world a couple of centuries later was already in the air. The Egyptian ruler Akhenaton (husband of the beauteous Nefertiti) had introduced worship of the solar disk as a substitute for Egyptian pantheism. Although the sun god was different from the God of Moses (and philosophically more elegant), it is possible that Moses was influenced by the religious reflections that went into this temporary religious reform. More likely both he and the pharaoh were products of the same culture of religious reflection, a culture perhaps of profound skepticism about the many gods and goddesses of the pantheon.

The God Moses encountered in his ecstatic experience in the burning bush was no solar disk. He had much in common with El Shaddai (met on a high mountain) and the family gods of the Hebru patriarchs. He was a demanding and intensely personal god—like all the family gods of antiquity. But he also made a unique claim: not only was he an acceptable god who would take care of his tribe; not only was he better than all the other gods; he was, in fact, the only god who really counted. He was so superior to the other deities that his people were to have nothing to do with them. For the God of the burning bush no compromise with pantheism was possible.

In one sense this notion represented only a slight movement away from the Semitic pantheism of Moses' ancestors. Was Moses a monotheist? Surely not a theoretical one as the later Greek philosophers would be. But the God of Moses was, if not the only god, the only one that mattered. He claimed to be the creator of everything, the source of justice, and superior to the forces of fertility and sexuality that he dominated (and hence without

[handwritten margin note: God = only god who counted]

sexuality of his own). He was equally powerful in Egypt, in the desert, and in Palestine, and (as W. F. Albright puts it) he existed in human form but invisible to humans and not susceptible to representation by human image.

The theoretical question of his transcendence did not arise, but practically he was superior to the world and all its natural forces. Yet he was deeply involved with the people that he had chosen freely to make his own—unlike the gods of the patriarchs, who had been chosen by family heads. Already in the time of Moses, the God of the burning bush had become the paradoxical God who was both (to use later terminology) totally other and yet deeply involved. The development of this paradox by the prophets several centuries after Moses was a logical conclusion of the religious insight of Moses.

Moses insisted on the absolute superiority of the God of the burning bush, the God who said his name was YHWH, which might have been (but also might not have been) a divine name with which the tribes were familiar. But the superiority of YHWH was not Moses' principal religious concern. The free choice by YHWH of the Hebru to be his people—quite independently of any invitation or response of theirs—was Moses' most important religious insight. *not superiority*

Previously gods had been chosen by families or tribes for various reasons related to expectations the families and tribes had of protection and help. You chose as powerful a god as you could find, so that your god might be more powerful than your neighbor's god, should you and your neighbor war against one another. You were a buyer in the marketplace of deities.

YHWH had to be superior to the other gods (and inchoately transcendent) because only a superior God could dare to reverse the roles and announce that he had chosen a people to be his own and that was that. Moses' great innovation, therefore, was not theoretical monotheism or a theme of philosophical transcendence. Rather, he gave to humankind the image of a God who was simultaneously free of the forces of nature and superior to them and at the same time deeply involved with his chosen people.

It was an experience of God and a story about him that was, as I have said, in one respect only a little bit beyond the notions of the deity that Moses had inherited. YHWH often seems only a combination of El Shaddai and the Mighty One of Jacob with an inflated self-image. Like so many great revolutionaries, Moses (and his successors) were still bogged down in the metaphors they had inherited. More important, however, than the metaphorical continuity with the past was the discontinuity. The image of a God superior to creation and yet deeply involved with a people may well be the most important religious innovation of human history. It combined the warmth and intimacy of the old nature religions with the power and majesty of the emerging world religions. The balance between the two has always been difficult to sustain, but the appeal of such a paradoxical image of God is so great that after Moses efforts would always be made to combine the twin images of God—transcendent yet immanent, superior yet deeply involved.

Almost certainly Moses developed his rough and ready theory of what God was like from his experience of God allying himself with the people despised by Moses—the Hebru (or Apriu), the illegal and rejected aliens of the time. Only a different God from any previously imagined would attempt such a manic stunt.

It would take centuries for Israel to deny all reality to other gods. YHWH was not the only God who mattered; he was the only God who had any reality at all. Yet more centuries would be required before men and women would conclude (first through experience, then through reflection on experience) that the involvement of God was not only with a people but with individuals. Still more centuries would elapse before men and women would come to see that YHWH was everywhere and loved individuals, *all* individuals. The Hebru had been chosen his people so that they could reveal his love to everyone else. (At least so the Christian would argue.)

All of these later experiences and insights were already latent in Moses' ecstatic experience with the burning bush.

What happened at Sinai (wherever the biblical Sinai may have been) that persuaded the Hebru to accept Moses' vision of God?

As best as one can reconstruct the historical situation, it looked something like this: there were a number of forced migrations of the unwelcome foreigners out of Egypt and into the desert. They combined and intermingled in the desert with other groups (perhaps too loosely organized even to be called tribes). Some of them drifted into the land of Canaan and formed alliances with other groups of unwelcome settlers to battle with those already in possession of the land (and hence the lack of reference to Sinai and Moses in the "wandering Aramean" prayer). Still others remained in the desert, where a group of them, some fugitives from Egypt and others who had always lived in the desert, camped at the foot of Sinai for some time. This camp was not a political entity or even a loose confederation of groups or semitribes, but a temporary juxtaposition of suspicious and diverse groups—I think of O'Hare Airport at holiday time. Under the influence of Moses and his family and allies, they began (perhaps suddenly) to experience themselves as a people. Moreover, they also experienced the God of Moses as the only possible cause of their unexpected and perhaps initially unwanted unity and Moses himself as the instrument for accomplishing and perfecting their new existence as a people.

Later when they moved into Palestine, still filled with fervent memories of their Sinai experience, these memories became the heritage of all the tribes that settled there and the core of the tradition that would develop into Israel.

Was there anything "miraculous" or "supernatural" about this experience in Sinai? It was surely intense. Moreover, it produced a sentiment of the sort that sociologist Emile Durkheim would have called effervescence, a kind of collective emotional high. The Sinai tribe (or tribes) may have been the first religious enthusiasts. But was their experience at Sinai at first political and secular and then only later interpreted as first liturgical and then miraculous? Or was it experienced as a marvelous supernatural event from the first?

Or was it possibly some combination of the two kinds of experience? In fact, do the distinction and the question not imply a perspective that would have made little sense to Moses and his followers and no more sense to a God bent on self-disclosure?

Whatever happened in Sinai, a people emerged from the experience, a people constituted, as they experienced themselves, not by their own choice but by God's choice. Moreover, the choice had been made by a special kind of God, the God whom Moses had experienced in the burning bush, the God who was superior to the world he had created but involved in a love relationship with those whom he designated as his own.

A precise explanation of the experience that produced Israel in Sinai is less important than the fact of the religious tradition that resulted from it. Given the unique nature of that tradition, one must say that it was a very powerful experience indeed—Moses' ecstasy in the burning bush writ large.

Moses is *our* rabbi—the rabbi of all those who are the heirs to the Sinai experience—because he was the first to teach about the God of the burning bush and because he began the process of organizing the human response to such a pathetically loving and imperiously demanding God.

The laws that evolved in the years after Moses are attributed to him because he began the tradition and probably because he also shaped the general outline of the legal components of that tradition—though obviously he did not write down in all the details later codifications.

Many of the laws were not original with the Hebru but were absorbed from preexisting legal traditions, including the Ten Commandments, which were hardly a Mosaic innovation (though the notion that moral behavior was a response to God's intervention in human life was perhaps original with him). Some of the regulations—dietary rules and even circumcision—

were public health measures that antedated Moses and Sinai and were later integrated into the emerging law of Israel. Eventually the law became a means of preserving the loyalty and the integrity of the followers of Moses and turned into the Law. Moses is rightly regarded as the lawgiver because he began the tradition of laws that would become the Law. His great contribution to his people and to the human condition is not law or the Law, but his vision of God. Moses was a seer before he became a legislator, and his vision is what makes him *our* rabbi.

We are so much the religious heirs of Moses that it is virtually impossible (without a visit to an animist tribe) to imagine the world without his religious insight, a world in which transcendence and immanence are not poised in delicate yet fascinating balance. Moses' contribution may be taken for granted in the same way we take for granted the atmosphere: it is so important and so much a part of our lives that we hardly notice it.

What, then, does it mean to say that Jesus is the "new Moses"? Did Jesus come to abrogate the law of Moses or to fulfill it? Or both? Or neither?

Those may not be the proper questions, although they have been asked so often that one must attempt an answer. Jesus was certainly impatient with some of the minute details of the Law, which seemed to him to violate its fundamental spirit, an impatience he shared with some of his contemporaries. Yet surely he did not think of himself as abrogating the Mosaic tradition. I doubt very much that he ate pork or even considered eating it. Moreover, he was certainly a Jew and so defined himself all his life, although he had broader ideas about the boundaries of Judaism than did his contemporaries. He believed that YHWH was the God of everyone, a belief with which some other Jews of his time agreed, even if they were not willing to push the belief as far in practice as Jesus and his followers, in his name, did.

Jesus was then unquestionably a Jew and a follower of Moses, who was Jesus' rabbi, too. He was not a Jew in the sense that the term would be defined in subsequent centuries by the Mishnah and the Talmud. However, none of his contemporaries were Jews in that sense either, because the issues and the contexts had not arisen that would make subsequent definitions possible and necessary. *

---

*Rabbi Neusner responds: Of course Jesus was unquestionably a Jew, and so were all the people around him. And, as Father Greeley rightly says, no one at that time was, or could have been, a practitioner of Judaism, which reached its full statement only in the Mishnah, midrash compilations, and Talmud. But even then the great conceptions of the oral Torah were being worked out in that process of tradition that had taken shape at Sinai. Many of the most important ideas that Jesus taught are held in common by the later writings of the oral Torah, and what that means is that the teachings of that part of the Torah were circulated and studied in the time of Jesus, too. All scholarship today recognizes that the great ethical

What Jesus did not deny, God save us all, was the central story of God that made Moses our rabbi and for which subsequent legislation was only a support and a codification. Moses' story was of the God in the burning bush. Jesus' story was of the very same God whom he described as his Father. The religious experience of Jesus would not have been possible without the religious experience of Moses. They are the same religious experience of a God who is both transcendent and profoundly involved. The experience of Jesus develops that of Moses not by adding to it, but by plunging deeper into its profundity, by disclosing just how far YHWH is willing to go to disclose himself to his people.

As far even as Bethlehem. As far even as the Upper Room. As far even as Golgotha.

Same story, more depth of detail.

---

teachings of Jesus in the Gospels correspond, point by point, to the message of the oral Torah, and none of them would have caused surprise or been found alien by the (other) great Judaic sages at the time of Jesus, Hillel, for example, who taught, "What is hateful to yourself, do not do unto your neighbor. That is the entire Torah. Now go and study" (Babylonian Talmud Tractate Shabbat 31a).

20

GREELEY

The Faithless Bride—
Hosea, Jeremiah, Ezekiel

The condemned woman was stripped naked in front of her children. She was cast out of the house, and her children with her, because her guilt was their guilt too. Then she was to be stoned to death and they became outcasts.

Not a pleasant event. But thus was adultery punished in Israel. The crime was not so much one of sexual "impurity" as we would think of it. Rather, the faithless woman had sinned against the basic social structure of her people because she risked producing a child who might inherit the family property though not, in fact, of her husband's seed.

Until Jesus, a man who slept with another man's wife was committing adultery in that he threatened that man's inheritance. But his action was not viewed as adultery against his own wife. She had no claim on his fidelity.

Since society was organized on the fundamental principle of inheritance, of raising up "seeds" to one's fathers and grandfathers, an unfaithful wife put in jeopardy the most basic principles of social order. If the punishment was terrible, so was the sin—so it seemed to those responsible for preventing society from tearing itself apart.

Obviously the woman was to blame—not her seducer or her husband. Or so it seemed then, if not later to Jesus.

The scene described in the first paragraph is taken from the prophet Hosea. Only, oddly enough, his wife Gomer, the shamed and condemned woman, is not stoned to death. Perhaps her punishment is mitigated. She is sold into slavery rather than stoned. Then she is reclaimed and restored to her family's home and her husband's bed. And her children are taken back, too.

Hosea does not honor the Law. He does not permit the execution of his guilty wife. Nor does he permanently exclude her from the family, the least he could do in the view of his friends and neighbors. Rather, he reinstated her in her full role as mother and wife. She is once more the honored woman of his household.

Hosea, patently, is crazy.

It's a dramatic scene: the naked woman is pulled away from the execution-ers, covered with a dress, and brought home in honor because her husband loves her so much he cannot live without her. The crowds of neighbors and friends taunt him for his folly. He does not seem to mind, not as much as he would have minded if he had lost her.

Still the neighbors must have continued to mutter. Were there no other women in the town that he could have for the asking? What was so special about Gomer that he should lose his dignity and self-respect because of his obsession for her? Surely she was not *that* good in bed, was she? Why did a sensible and reasonable man like Hosea permit himself to be enchanted by such a shameless slut?

It's only one of the many dramatic scenes to be found in the books of the Hebrew prophets, some of the most fascinating and baffling men who ever lived. It is impossible to summarize their work in a single chapter, and I will not try. (Perhaps someday the rabbi and I will have a try at a whole book on "prophecy" in our religious traditions.)

I chose the three prophets Hosea, Jeremiah, and Ezekiel because they each use explicitly the human love metaphor, which I am convinced is the most important image of God to be found in the Bible.

Indeed, they used it before the author of the Song and the author of Proverbs. Both the latter wrote after Israel was in exile in Babylon, while the three prophets wrote in the eighth, seventh, and sixth centuries B.C. respectively. I would not suggest that either of the more recent writers learned the metaphor from his predecessors. Rather I believe the image of God as lover was part of the matrix of Hebrew religious culture, readily available to anyone who wanted to use it and readily understood by those who heard it or read it.

Sexual intimacy was only one of the many metaphors the prophets used to describe what Rabbi Abraham Heschel called the "pathos of God"— God's passionate involvement with his people:

> To the prophet . . . God does not reveal himself in an abstract absoluteness but in a personal and intimate relation to the world. He does not simply command and expect obedience; He is also moved and affected by what happens in the world, and reacts accordingly. Events and human actions arouse in Him joy or sorrow, pleasure or wrath. He is not conceived as judging the world in detachment. He reacts in an intimate and subjective manner, and thus determines the value of events. Quite obviously in the biblical view, man's deeds may move him, affect Him, grieve Him, or, on the other hand, gladden and please Him. This notion that God can be immediately affected,

that He possesses not merely intelligence and will, but also pathos, basically defines the prophetic consciousness of God.

Many Catholics, raised in a religious educational environment dominated implicitly by Greek philosophy, will find this image of God hard to accept—for centuries Catholic catechesis if forced to choose between the Scripture and Greek philosophy invariably chose the latter. All one can say to those who reject the idea of pathos in God is that prophets are engaging in poetic talk; pathos is a metaphor for God.

But it is a metaphor that errs by defect: God is even more involved with us than the pathos metaphor would imply.

If it is true that those who win write the history, it is also true in this case that those who write philosophy shape history and thus win. The various prophetic movements were only one strain of the rich and varied Hebrew religion in Palestine during the early years of the millennium before Jesus. Yet the power of their religious vision and moral concern (one should probably say "visions" and "concerns," since Hebrew prophecy was pluralistic) was so great that the prophets were able to preempt centerstage during those years and influence not what everyone did, but what everyone would come to think of as the authentic worship of YHWH. Kings and priests acted out their dramas but always under the watchful ideas of the prophets. Sages studied their wisdom but did not dare resist the stern moral and religious demands of the prophets. The editors who gathered together the various strands of the tradition and put the books of the Torah in final shape did so in a religious atmosphere permeated by prophetic vision and enthusiasm.

Israel of the Second Temple era, the time of the coming of Jesus, was still a pluralistic religious culture and not yet a codified religion. But the shape and the direction of that pluralism had been dramatically affected by the prophetic response to the problems of the early and middle years of the first millennium B.C.

The rabbis who began the formation of the Mishnah were not prophets. (Perhaps Jesus was the last prophet, but the term fits him no better, as we shall see, than any of the other terms by which we try to constrain him.) But these rabbis were steeped in the moral fervor of the prophets, a jealous defense of the rights of YHWH over against his people. It was not the religion of the sages or the kings or the priests they were really trying to codify. Rather, if I may trespass ever so lightly on the rabbi's territory, they were trying to set down in their tradition the religion of the prophets.

If, as the rabbi rightly insists, Judaism today is a religion of moral obligation and sanctification, the reason is, I say subject to his correction, that the fervor of the prophets reaches down through almost three millennia now to influence the religious sensibility of the dual Torah even today.

The prophets (some more than others) have this remarkable influence because they were lucky enough to be present at two historical transitions—that of the Hebrew people from a collection of tribes to one and then two unsuccessful small kingdoms and that of humankind from an ancient materialism to spiritual and personal awareness.

The prophets—to oversimplify in order to make the point—inherited a religion that was mostly corporate, a religion of the relationship between God and the people considered as a body; they passed on a religion that was substantially influenced by the notion that God was engaged in a relationship not only with a people, but with individual persons. The prophets presided over the "personalization" of Yahwism at the same time they were defending Yahwism from the corruption of polytheistic pagan nature religion in the "folk religion" of the ordinary people.

Two qualifications must be made before I discuss the two critical turning points of which the prophets are a part and then return to the dramatic scene of Hosea and his faithless wife.

First of all, the prophets are not easy reading. Indeed, even with the help of the best modern commentaries, many prophetic passages range from opaque to impenetrable. The books are often collections of stories and oracles put together by disciples and admirers with little concern for consistency of integration of their accounts. Moreover, the editors often added their own comments, stories, observations, and interpretations without bothering to distinguish them from the utterances of the prophets. The prophets were often ecstatics, men who saw visions, and the imagery and the poetry of their visions are frequently wild and uninterpretable, partly because their culture is not our culture and partly because there is often a dreamlike, fantastical coloration to their language that one suspects baffled even their own contemporaries. Those of us who are not mystics usually find it hard to understand those who are even if we share a culture with them.

Finally, the text of many of the prophetic books leaves much to be desired. As the late Father Bruce Vawter (God be good to him!) remarks in his introduction to Hosea, "The Hebrew text of Hosea holds the distinction of being possibly the worst preserved of all the books of the Old Testament."

Thus the prophets are both extremely important to those of us who are their heirs and extremely difficult to understand.

Second, the prophets were not prophets.

When I say this August of 1988 that Michael Dukakis will win with at least 52 percent of the popular vote and that Jim McMahon will play the whole season without injury and lead the Bears to the Superbowl I am playing the prophecy game by predicting the future. The prophetic visions, however, were neither so precise nor so definite. The prophets were, of course, concerned about the future, about what would happen to Israel if it continued to be faithless to YHWH and what would happen if it returned to him. But their visions of the future were less predictions about what would happen than judgments on what was happening when they spoke. Prophecy was moral and religious judgment, not prediction.

We are inclined to think of their work as an attempt to anticipate in detail what Jesus would do because the Evangelists, especially Saint Matthew, speak of prophecies being fulfilled. But the Evangelists are using a pedagogic method of their era that was not so much concerned with precise forecasting as it was with finding patterns of God's action in the world. Only the most rigid fundamentalist now views the prophets as forecasters, and especially men who anticipated in their visions the events of the life of Jesus.

They are not predictors, then, not prophets in the sense in which we normally use the word. Rather they were visionaries, seers, men who *saw* the pattern of God's action latent beneath the events of ordinary life and, in particular, God's punishment for the religious infidelity and moral corruption to which Israel had succumbed. Amos, the first of the prophets whose oracles were written down in a book attributed to him, was a farmer. Isaiah was a courtier, it would seem. But both men, so different in other ways, *saw* in ecstatic visions God's judgment on a faithless people.

To use the language I introduced in an earlier chapter, they were men who claimed to see more clearly than others the implications for their own time of the principal metaphors of their religion. Indeed, they were men who were "snatched up" by and inundated in the depths of these metaphors even when they did not want to be. They were constrained by the power of God to explain what the metaphors meant even when such explication of their vision made them pariahs, outcasts, and criminals.

They saw too much, they spoke too clearly, they lived too strangely to be accepted by their ordinary fellows. Prophets were a danger and hence were often in danger.

Moreover, as I said before, they came along at just the right time.

A change of enormous importance occurred in many different parts of the world as the second millennium B.C. shaded over into the first. In China, India, Persia, Greece, and even, briefly it would seem, Egypt, humankind— or at least its great philosophers and teachers—discovered spirit and hence began to be dimly aware of the person and the personal responsibility. It was a complicated transition about which we still understand rather little. Nonetheless, the change had a tremendous impact on the future of the human race.

The human being, it was now understood, was more than just a body. Humans were spirit, too, capable of transcending their bodies; religious and philosophical ideas began to emerge that emphasized abstract beliefs and convictions, universally valid moral principles, and a deity who was spirit and independent of matter and of particular tribes and peoples. Nature religion (the worship of the powers of creation) was rejected in favor of the "world religions" worship of a god who transcended the world and who stood for universal ethics and wisdom. In many of the world religions, matter and body were rejected as evil because they restrained the freedom of spirit. Virtue was no longer defined as the ability to live in harmony with creation, but rather as the self-discipline necessary to transcend the body and become spirit.

This dramatic change at first had little effect on ordinary folk, whose religion continued to be a blend of superstition and nature worship—magic, shrines, sacrifices, auguries, and unpredictable gods and goddesses. It would require centuries before the purified world religions would triumph over the folk cults—if indeed that triumph is complete even today. Nonetheless, spirit had been discovered and humankind would never be the same.

The Hebrews did not have a vast empire to support philosophical speculation. They did not have any brilliant thinkers or religious and ethical leaders to compare with Buddha, Confucius, Zoroaster, the author of the Rig Veda, or Plato. What they did have was a God who somehow had already transcended time and space and demanded love in response for his love of them. He was still a particularistic God, involved with only one people, like all the other gods, but unlike the rest of them he was already the Lord of all creation. Like the gods of the other world religions, the God of the Hebrew prophets was spirit. Unlike the other spirit gods, he *cared*. He was not an indifferent, aloof spirit who, insofar as he acknowledged the existence of creatures at all, waited patiently for them to strip off matter and approach him. Quite the contrary, he continued to pursue his beloved people, just as he had when he was a god of the desert storms.

The God of the prophets, the God that we inherited and with whom we are still involved, is a spirit who cares. He cares that his people as a corporate body are loyal to him, but he also cares that the individual members of that corporate body, already emerging as responsible persons even with Amos, keep his moral and religious laws.

The prophets may move back and forth between personal and corporate responsibility, but by the time their era was over and Judah had been carried off into captivity in Babylon, religion and morality had become a personal responsibility. Not only was Israel the spouse; so was the individual person.

The prophets were not self-consciously founding a world religion. They cared rather little for abstract philosophical and theological speculations. They were preoccupied with two practical problems:

1. How could the people be recalled to moral virtue and to pure religion? How could they be rescued from the corruption of Canaanite pagan superstitions to the worship of YHWH?

2. How could they explain the fact that, although Israel was YHWH's people, it was little more than a powerless pawn in wars among the great powers of the time? How could YHWH betray his people into the hands of Egypt or Babylon?

The solution, echoed and reechoed by the various prophets, was that foreign invasion and domination was punishment for Israel's infidelity. YHWH's people ought not to put their faith in arms or politics. They would achieve greatness only if they returned to religious and moral righteousness.

In the short run the prophets were not successful. Folk religion was not routed. The political leaders of the nation did not give up military alliances. The land was overwhelmed by foreign invaders. The prophetic vision of Israel as a great nation was not achieved.

Nor would we today accept the causal link the prophets seemed to postulate between religious and moral righteousness on the one hand and political and military success on the other. Just because a people are virtuous, it does not follow that they will rout their enemies.

Yet Israel did survive and does survive, long after Babylon and Persia and Egypt have ceased to be great powers. YHWH did keep his promise after all, if not in the manner that they expected.

That was the final twist to the prophetic vision: if Israel became faithful again YHWH would restore her to glory. But even if she continued to be unfaithful, YHWH would not turn his back on her. Israel was still his people, no matter how unfaithful she might be.

That brings us back to Hosea and Gomer.

As best we can piece together the story from the confused and probably corrupted text, it is an autobiographical account of actual events in the life of the prophet himself. He married a woman with whom he was madly in love, even though she may not have been "any better than she had to be" (and we must remember that both husband and wife were almost certainly still in their teens). She was caught in infidelity, perhaps several times. He cast her out in shame and then reclaimed her, perhaps buying her back after he had sold her into slavery. He should have put her to death or at least left her in the humiliation of slavery. Instead he took her back to their marriage bed and begot more children with her.

It may even be, depending on what we make of the text, that she was caught in unfaithfulness again and forgiven again before Hosea's mixture of discipline and love finally triumphed over her sin.

Then Hosea, reflecting on the folly of his irresistible passion for this wicked but lovable woman, realized that it was a metaphor of God's passion for Israel.

Thus his prophecy: Hosea was a fool because of his love for Gomer. God is a fool because of his love for Israel. For both lovers the knowledge that they are fools only makes their passion stronger. They cannot live without the beloved.

Strong imagery indeed. The human lover who repeatedly forgives a faithless spouse, whose love is not turned off by an adulterous wife or husband, does seem a little mad. By human standards God is a little mad.

It is a theme that will recur often in the story of Israel and, as we shall see, in the teachings of Jesus.

In Hosea there is no direct and immediate conclusion for human relationships, no exhortation that we forgive those who offend against us in our intimate relationships, no call for generous self-giving to those we love. We see only the self-giving of YHWH to those he loves. In years to come, however, the successors to the prophets will begin to understand that we must strive to love even as we are loved.

Because we have heard the biblical metaphors so often we tend to think of them as exaggerations. The relationship between Hosea and Gomer is dramatic enough, and naturally it is an image of God's love for Israel and, by extension, for each of us. We are Gomer and God is Hosea. Sure. So what else is new?

We must remember that the love of God differs from the love of humans in that the former is more powerful and more implacable. God is even more of a fool than Hosea.

If we reflect on the Hosea story we might well conclude that Gomer, for all her faults, must have been an extraordinary woman to command such passionate devotion—extraordinary at least in the eyes of Hosea.

Are we, you and I, that extraordinary in the eyes of God?

And if we are not, why is he hooked on us?

Two later prophets, Jeremiah and Ezekiel, also use the metaphor of the faithless bride. The former (3:6–4:4) describes the two kingdoms, Judah and Israel, as playing the harlot in the mountain groves of the Canaanite cults and divorced from God's love for their sins but not permanently cast off. The latter (16:1–63) describes how he found his beloved naked in the dirt, lifted her up, and made her his beautiful queen, and then cast her off when she was unfaithful with harlots. Nonetheless, he will not permanently reject her but will eventually restore her to full dignity and love, because God does not withdraw from the commitments he has made.

In neither prophet is the folly of divine fidelity toned down. Regardless of the ingratitude of the beloved, God loves and that is that.

The romance image of the Sinai experience then continues and develops, not as the only prophetic metaphor but surely as the most poignant and vivid one. Unlike the furious and unforgiving Amos, Hosea, Jeremiah, and Ezekiel all see the faithless Israel as eventually forgiven, not because of her merit but because of God's love, which will simply not be turned away.

The prophets were wrestling, even as we do, with the problem of evil. Their solutions were no more adequate than ours. We cannot explain why a loving God permits bad things to happen to good people.

Their answer is the same as our answer: regardless of what happens, God loves us and that love will eventually triumph.

Another theme began to emerge in the later prophets, particularly in Isaiah: YHWH was not only the Lord of all the world; he was also the Lord of all the nations; all the people were his. He was the God of Israel, yes indeed, but the God of everyone else, too. Eventually all the nations would come to Jerusalem to worship him. This Hebrew form of the universalist change that was gradually moving across the world was expressed in figures of speech that were both vivid and vague. Israel at the time was in no position to make much of them, but they remained, leaven that would slowly grow and expand, even before the coming of Jesus.

We all know these universalist passages; they are the readings we hear at Christmastime and in Handel's *Messiah*. YHWH is lover of all nations and everyone. He wants Israel's response and that of all of the children of Israel. But he also desires all nations and every human.

The God of pathos, sometimes explicitly and always by implication, cannot be merely a God for one people, however much he may be involved in that people's history.

The story of the lover who pursues his beloved no matter what the beloved does is not meant to be merely an appealing if outrageous metaphor.

It is meant rather to be a template for life, an explanation of what life means—as all descriptions of who God is are in fact descriptions of what life is about and prescriptions about how we should live.

The image of God as a desire-crazed suitor seems almost too good to be true. The prescription, scarcely noted by the prophets, that we should be as generous with ourselves to those we love as God is, is too frightening to be taken seriously, is it not?

Yet those are the hints in the story, hints that would become more explicit as the story continued.

If the metaphor does not seem daring, reckless, outrageous, absurd, the reason is that either we have heard it too often or we have not paused to reflect on it.

It is embarrassing, after all, is it not, to think of God caught up in such a frenzy of obsessive love?

Yet it is how the three prophets experienced him, as did Israel often both before them and after them.

21

GREELEY

Who Is Lady Wisdom?

The Bible is a "tissue of metaphors." So speaks Australian scholar Mark Coleridge. At one level the statement is unassailable: one can only describe God through metaphors, since God cannot be known directly and immediately in this world. The Bible is about God and therefore it depends on comparisons to tell us what God is like.

But there is another and richer meaning to the insight that the Bible is a tissue of metaphors. Since metaphor is an attempt on the part of the imagination of the one who makes it to leap to the imagination of the one who hears it or reads it, the metaphors put us in touch with the imagination of those who wrote the books of the Bible. Before I explore the metaphor of wisdom and especially of Lady Wisdom, I must consider more in detail what a metaphor is and how it works.

Let us say that I assert, in a wild leap of my imagination, that God loves me the way I love my wife (assuming for the sake of discussion that I have one). You're startled by the comparison and are forced to consider the way you love your wife. My imagination has jumped across the barriers of cognitive discourse to stir your imagination. You and I share an experience of loving our wives that is part of the common human condition—the mix of affection, delight, bemusement, and patience that is common in all relationships between the sexes. So you sense what I'm talking about.

But you and I are different and our wives are different and our intimacies are different. There may, for example, be much greater sexual passion in one relationship and more intellectual sharing in the other. So the metaphor means something different to me than to you. Is only one meaning true, or are both true? The answer is that the symbol is rich, dense, and multi-layered. It admits of many different interpretations, all of which have some share of truth and none of which alone exhausts the truth.

As Father Coleridge says, "The task of metaphors in the Bible is to hold a range of meanings in unity and to keep them perpetually open to fresh interpretations."

Everyone who hears a metaphor must necessarily interpret it anew out of his or her own experience. Such a "fresh interpretation" does not imply, I must insist, that the metaphor can mean anything at all (as the modernists held). But just as there is a "range" (to use Father Coleridge's helpful word) of relationship styles between husband and wife, so there is a range of meanings, with infinite nuances within the range, in the metaphor of God loving me the way I love my wife.

If you and I live in the same era, the assumptions of our lives and the range of our experiences are such that we share similar, though not identical, experiences, even if the metaphor has different nuances of meaning for each of us—as well as the same basic meaning. But if we are separated by three thousand years of history and vastly different cultures, then we come to our common experiences with very different perceptions. The insights, the understandings, the wisdom of one era will draw a meaning out of the metaphor that had existed therein only in the most vague, hazy, and implicit way. On the other hand, a later era may lose some of the insights of an earlier era.

Thus the husband of the author of the Song could not understand the notion of complete legal equality with which you and I had better leaven our love of our wives. Viewing our beloved from the perspective of feminism, we know more about the meaning of the man/woman relationship than he did. (Our knowledge, as we will see later, was shared by Saint Paul.) On the other hand, it is very likely that, more confident of his eroticism than we are, the husband of the Song might be able to revel in wanton sexual celebration (of the sort his wife described in her poems) in a way that would be very difficult for us.

We may understand better than he the implication of some kind of rough equality with the beloved that God feels toward us. He might have been better able to understand how God revels in the delights of his passion for us. We might see the possibility of an Incarnation making God at his initiative our equal. He might reflect on the image of God delighting in sustained play with us as he delights in affectionate play with his wife.

The metaphor contains one truth, but a truth with an infinite variety of revelatory responses, all of them within the range imposed by the basic structure of the metaphor.

Both the images I suggest in the paragraph before last are startling. God making himself equal to us? God engaging in love play with us?

It is the nature of metaphor to startle and shock, to destroy old patterns of perception with surprising new insights that are then integrated into a revised and more illuminated pattern of perception. Metaphor is not one figure of speech among many others; it is the basic process of human knowing. It is the fundamental form of human thought and speech. We come to know from childhood on by making surprising comparisons, and then, having reflected on the wonder in the fact that one reality is like another yet different, we integrate that wonder into our understanding of the world in which we live.

From the child who learns that the electric light outlet is like the fire to the theoretical physicist comparing certain mysterious areas of the universe to a "black hole," comparison, surprise, and enhanced perception are the ordinary process of growing in knowledge. There is no growth in understanding without shock and surprise.

So, yes, it is shocking to say that God wills equality with us, but as the rabbi has argued in his work on incarnation in Judaism, this insight is a necessary consequence of what we believe about the personal love of God for us.

And, yes, it is startling to be told that God loves to play with us as a husband loves to fondle his wife. (And vice versa, because the metaphor is reversible: God loves us as a wife loves her husband.) But play is always both a cause and a result of love. God's play with us is different from the foreplay between man and woman but, and here is the essence of metaphor at work, not totally different.

The surprise that erupts from metaphor is a moment of both terror and delight—terror when our old perceptual structures crash and delight when we begin to see more clearly in the illumination that the metaphor provides. God plays with me the way I play with my wife? Dear God, how shocking! And how wonderful!

The philosopher Paul Ricoeur speaks of the "surplus of meaning" in a metaphor. By that he means that we can never exhaust the meanings to be found in a metaphor. New meanings are drawn out of it not by extending its range and inventing new meanings to add onto it but rather by plunging ever deeper into its mystery. We will never know all there is to know about the love between man and woman, and therefore we can never completely comprehend, never definitively exhaust, the meaning of the metaphor that God loves us the way we love our spouses.

It is in this sense that Father Coleridge speaks when he says that the Bible is always incomplete. Not only the individual person reading it but the whole community that has inherited it can always learn more about God by plunging deeper into the meanings of the biblical metaphors.

A wife delights in affectionately teasing her husband. Such play enhances her desire and his. It reinforces their mutual love, indeed it sets it on fire. It is great fun.

God is like this with us! How fabulous!

And, in a reverse twist of the metaphor (which would make Saint Paul stumble over his own words when he tried to say both at the same time), how much more fun it will be the next time I decide to tease God!

This is a new discovery about God! New for the woman who makes it and new for the community that learns it (again) after overcoming some of its prudery. But tacked on from the outside of the metaphor? Hardly. It was there all along, waiting to be discovered in a shocking, wonderful moment of discovery and illumination.

Movement in understanding the possibilities of a metaphor is generally circular and cumulative. We circle around the metaphor, examining time after time the possible links between the two realities involved in the comparison. We make our circuits, however, informed not only by our own personal insights and illumination, but by those of the community of which we are members, a community that has been circling the image for centuries and millennia.

Progress is neither inevitable nor one-directional. We tend to move ahead because we stand on the shoulders of our predecessors and benefit from their work and their insights, as well as from the growth of human knowledge. But some insights can be lost as cultures disintegrate and are reintegrated: the loss of comprehension of the Song proves that we do indeed move back one step at least when we take two steps forward.

The Bible is a work of the imagination—for both the writers and the readers. We must exercise our imagination as we read it to establish resonance between our imagination and theirs. If we do not understand the Bible as essentially a link between two profound imaginative enterprises, then we do not understand it at all.

It is not necessary to know what a metaphor is or even to describe the process of metaphorical knowledge to be caught up in the metaphorical experience. Only a rigid elitist would think that a graduate school course on metaphors is a requirement for metaphorical knowledge. Indeed, such a seminar might well be an obstacle. Men and women engaged in the metaphorical experience long before the Greeks thought up the name.

This is *not* a new way of approaching the Bible. Quite the contrary, while the self-conscious explanation of metaphor as a way of knowing may perhaps be new, the actual process of imagination responding to imagination in reading the Bible is as old as the Bible itself.

Indeed, it is the way most of us still read the Bible, however hesitantly and with however much fear that we might not be doing it "right."

Our modern obsession with "proofs" with which we can batter our adversaries, with the battle most narrowly defined between science and religion, with literalism in the most strict and rigid sense of the word, and with discursive, propositional knowledge to the exclusion of all else has blinded us to the obvious truth that poetic knowledge is superior and not inferior to prosaic knowledge.

(From which it does *not* follow that reflective philosophical religion is not absolutely necessary for reflective beings like humankind.)

Moreover, for those who fear the fancies of the "undisciplined" imagination, it must be said, first of all, that the imagination is never undisciplined; it is always shaped and focused by the life experiences of the person whose imagination is working. Moreover, the person reading the Bible is exercising imagination in the context of his or her own faith, a faith that guides and directs as it illumines. Finally, the faith community with its heritage also focuses on and directs our imaginative encounter with the Bible. Obviously, the imagination can on occasion run wild. But the power of faith and the faith community ought to eliminate most of the fears about manic reading of the Scriptures. Those who wring their hands about rampant imagination are usually only demonstrating their own fear of their fantasy processes.

All of this reflection on metaphors is a lengthy but essential prologue to a discussion of Lady Wisdom as a metaphor for a God who invites and attracts through creation (a discussion in which I rely heavily on the work of my friend, colleague, and mentor Father Roland Murphy O.Carm.).

Wisdom personified in Scripture is described by a feminine noun. But the translation of that noun as "Lady Wisdom" is mostly a modern innovation, and the suggestion that she represents the God who attracts is mostly modern insight.

But not entirely.

The possibility of such an interpretation lurks in the metaphor itself and could not have been completely absent from the imagination of those who used and developed the metaphor, even if it were of less explicit concern to them than it is to us, with our preoccupation with the equality of women. In fact, after a couple of millennia of patriarchy we may have come round to a sense of the image that was more explicit in the minds of those who first used the image than it has been in the minds of many of their successors.

The wisdom literature of Israel (and each of our canonical books has its own personality and its own perspective) is practical and pragmatic. It is oriented toward issues of how one might wisely and properly live rather than toward theoretical issues of what life means.

But, as anthropologist Clifford Geertz has observed, ethos is the flip side of mythos: how one lives is a reflection of what one believes life to be about. The "conventional wisdom" of how a person should live is a practical conclusion from a theory (or a story before the theory) of what life is about. Thus a world view, a story of the relationship between humans and God, lurks in each of the books of wisdom (a slightly different world view in each book).

Some scholars even suggest that the image of God that lurks in the wisdom literature is the most ancient form of Hebrew religion, antedating the more detailed and explicit developments in the books of the Torah. The Hebrew wisdom tradition has much in common with the other ancient wisdoms, but it is also strikingly different in some critical ways, precisely because Israel, even when it was fashioning its primitive expressions of wisdom, had a unique relationship with a unique God.

The critical issue that preoccupies the sages as they render their advice (sometimes managing to sound not unlike poor Polonius and not infrequently seeming to contradict themselves) is the nature of creation. Humans, they believe, must live in harmony with the world of which they are a part, but what is the nature of that world?

The question is subtly different from that which preoccupied the author of Genesis. The problem is not how the world began but what the world means now. In Father Murphy's apt summary, wisdom

> is as much an attitude, a dialogue with the created world as it is a set of admonitions or insights concerning various types of conduct. . . . The approach of the sage turns out to be a model for living, a style of operation that aimed at life, the gift of God.

When wisdom began to reflect on itself—that is, when the sages began to ask whence came their wisdom and what it represented—they fashioned the striking and wonderful and heroic metaphor of Lady Wisdom. They described wisdom as a person, a feminine person of imperious intelligence, vast experience, and great and fascinating beauty.

Here the reader should put down this book for a few moments, get out the family Bible, and read the eighth chapter of the Book of Proverbs. As you try to resonate with the imagination of the one who first set down the metaphor, permit yourself to see her as he must have seen her—as an absolutely dazzling and irresistible woman.

You should excuse the expression, but some dish, huh?

You wouldn't want to mess with Lady Wisdom.

There is considerable speculation about her origins. Some scholars compare her to the wisdom goddesses of the pagan nations around Israel. Others see her as a spiritualization of the Shechinah of YHWH, the "presence" or the "glory" of YHWH in the high religion of the prophets, but his consort, it would seem, in Hebrew folk religion both before and after Sinai, a consort who would continue to appear in some varieties of much more advanced Hebrew religion outside of Israel even at the time of Jesus.

While such speculation is interesting, it is rather beside the point. A writer who uncovers a metaphor does not check either pagan religions or his own nation's folk religion as a process in the discovery of the metaphor. Influenced indeed by the whole world around him and by all his own life experiences (including especially the experiences of women that have attracted him) he suddenly "encounters" Lady Wisdom. The metaphor explodes on him like the roar of a cannon, the boom of thunder above his roof, the aura of a lovely woman who strides briskly across his path.

He promptly falls in love with her. Such is the essence of his metaphor: the wise man falls in love with wisdom.

But who is she and what is she up to?

Some say that she represents the order that God has imposed on the world. Lady Wisdom is the self-revelation of God in the order and symmetry of creation.

Father Murphy, however, does not think this meaning goes far enough:

> The lyrical descriptions of Proverbs 8 [are not] adequately captured by the term order. The biblical metaphors portraying Lady Wisdom indicate a wooing, indeed an eventual marriage. Who has ever sued for or been pursued by order, even in the surrogate form of a woman? The very symbol of Lady Wisdom suggests that order is not the correct correlation. Rather she is to be somehow identified with the Lord, as indicated by her very origins and her authority. The call of Lady Wisdom is the voice of the Lord. She is, then, the revelation of God, not merely the self-revelation of creation. She is the divine summons issued in and through creation, sounding through the vast realm of the created world and heard on every level of human experience.*

Obviously she (or perhaps we really should say She) is related in some sense to the more benign mother goddesses of the pagan environment in which the Israelites lived. But what is striking is not the similarity between Lady Wisdom and, let us say, her neighbor Astarte, but the difference. The pagan goddesses are identified with the natural forces that they represent and on which they depend; she is the voice of YHWH, independent of

---

*The quotation is from Father Murphy's presidential address to the Society of Biblical Literature at the Palmer House in Chicago in December 1984. It is reprinted in the *Journal of Biblical Literature* 104, 3–11.

natural forces but manifesting her attractiveness in and through them. They must be persuaded and placated; Lady Wisdom merely invites. They represent the powers of the universe that are blind, capricious. She reveals through the beauty of creation the beauty of God.

Lady Wisdom represents the sacramentality of creation as revealing a God who attracts and calls. Such a meaning is simply not to be found in the pagan goddesses.

The Lady Wisdom metaphor takes the goddess symbolism and stands it on its head.

Here I agree with my teacher Mircea Eliade and my colleague Wendy O'Flaherty and disagree with Joseph Campbell: what is important about myths is not the similarity of their structure but the diversity of their substance, of the stories they tell.

Moreover, the Lady Wisdom metaphor is also a reversal of the image of God as passionate husband. Now God is presented as an attractive, demanding, exciting, seductive wife.

In Greek philosophy it is always the First Cause, the Prime Mover, the Uncreated Creator who seems important. The Final Cause—the end toward which the movement tends—is less important. In the philosophy many of us learned in college or the seminary the major emphasis was on the launching of creation. From the fact of creation we "proved" that God existed. Because creation is, therefore a creator is. But this argument, however useful it might be, deals with creation as a product that proves and not as an invitation that calls; it gives short shrift to the wonder and the power and the beauty of creation as we experience it. We were told that when we encounter such glory we are to conclude the existence of God. Much less frequently were we told that the glory discloses the seductive beauty of a God who calls, invites, and waits for us—as all lovers must at times wait for their beloved.

Yet in fact in our ordinary lives it is attraction that moves us more than inertial motion. The beautiful compels us more effectively than the true. The invitation affects us more powerfully than the instruction, the lover who wants us more than the boss who sends us on an errand.

Lady Wisdom is a restless gadabout, wheeling and dealing around the universe spinning for her wondrous invitations to follow after her in pursuit of the alluring lover that she represents and that in fact she is.

Any man who has ever been attracted by an overwhelming woman knows what the metaphor means—though he may find it difficult to think of God as like a woman who deprives you of sense and reason. Any woman who has fallen under the sway of a powerfully appealing man can adjust the metaphor to fit her experience—and she may find it easier to comprehend than a man because the image of God as woman is less common among us (though not, as we shall see later, completely uncommon).

The image of God as seducer is shocking—as it is meant to be, whether the seducer is pictured as male or as female. It is also illuminating because it suggests that all the gorgeous objects, events, and persons of creation are merely the veils behind which beauty lurks.

In the morning sunrise, then, and a northeast wind after a heat spell, in a frozen lake at winter twilight, in the goofy smile of a kid taking her first tentative steps, in a Mozart trio, in the smell of a rose garden, in a neat solution to an intellectual problem, in the touch of a friendly hand after a quarrel, in the body of a lover, in the tracery of green as trees explode into spring, in the taste of iced tea on a humid day—in all of these and all the other beauties of our lives, Lady Wisdom hides, attracting, inviting, calling.

Who would not follow someone who is steeped in such seductive hints of beauty?

Nor is she far off, distant and indifferent, waiting lazily for us to come after her.

Rather, as she says in Proverbs, her delight is to be with the children of men. So (chapter 9) she throws a great party and invites all to come to it.

22

NEUSNER
The Prophets

"I loathe, I spurn your festivals, I am not appeased by your solemn assemblies. If you offer me burnt offerings, or your meal offerings, I will not accept them. I will pay no heed to your gifts of fatlings. Spare me the sound of your hymns, and let me not hear the music of your lutes. But let justice well up like water, righteousness like an unfailing stream.

"To me, O Israelites, you are just like the Ethiopians," declares the Lord. "True, I brought Israel up from the land of Egypt, but also the Philistines from Caphtor, and the Arameans from Kir. Behold, the Lord has his eye upon the sinful kingdom: I will wipe it off the face of the earth. But I will not wholly wipe out the house of Jacob," declares the Lord.

Thus said the Lord, "For three transgressions of Moab, for four, I will not revoke it, because he burned the bones of the king of Edom to lime. I will send down fire upon Moab, and it shall devour the fortress of Kerioth. And Moab shall die in tumult, amid shouting and the blare of horns. I will wipe out the ruler from within her and slay all her officials along with him," said the Lord.

Thus said the Lord, "For three transgressions of Judah, for four, I will not revoke it: because they have spurned the Torah of the Lord and have not observed his laws; they are beguiled by delusions after which their fathers walked. I will send down fire upon Judah, and it shall devour the fortresses of Jerusalem."

Thus said the Lord, "For three transgressions of Israel, for four, I will not revoke it, because they have sold for silver those whose cause was just, and the needy for a pair of shoes.

"Hear this word, O people of Israel, that the Lord has spoken concerning you, concerning the whole family that I brought up from the land of Egypt: You alone have I singled out of all the families of the earth—that is why I will call you to account for all your iniquities.

"Seek good and not evil, that you may live, and that the Lord, the God of Hosts, may truly be with you, as you think. Hate evil and love good, and establish justice in the gate; perhaps the Lord, the God of Hosts, will be gracious to the remnant of Joseph."

The prophets present us with the most difficult pages of the Torah, because they seem to be telling us that God rejects what in the five books of Moses God commands. In the books of Leviticus and Numbers and Deuteronomy God tells Moses that God wants us to celebrate festivals, hold solemn assemblies, kill cattle and burn them up as burnt offerings, and throw grain on the altar fire as a meal offering. Now God speaks through

Amos and says that these are not only inappropriate, but offensive. Instead—instead, let justice well up like water. What has justice to do with liturgy, right with rite? Yet we read the prophets in the synagogue. Not only so, but first we read the Torah, meaning a passage in the five books of Moses, and then, as though commenting on that passage and explaining its importance, we read a passage of prophecy. That's why these are tough words.

But the love they bring is tough love: the Torah without prophecy can lead to sin. The sin can be one of pride: I'm doing what you want, so you do what I want. It can be the sin of self-righteousness: I gave an animal, so God loves me. Above all, it can be the sin of shallow and showy ritualism, by which we take the gesture we make to fulfill the obligation we bear. Then instead of caring for the other, we concentrate altogether too much on caring about proper conduct in ritual and, as rabbis through the generations have taught, we pay more attention to the food that goes into our mouths than the words—the killing gossip—that come out of them. The Torah contained in the five books of Moses requires the proper corrective. And if you were to say, Father Greeley, that much of the ethical and moral message of Jesus is prophetic, no one could disagree—because most of it is also rabbinic, and the rabbis of the oral part of the Torah are the true heirs and continuators of the prophets of the written part of the Torah.

Consider the conception that there are things God wants us to do: commandments we are to observe and to keep, this to do, that not to do. Seen as a search for humility, doing God's will with a whole heart, the notion that God wants us to do this or not do that yields pride and even arrogance. Keeping the Sabbath day, one of the Ten Commandments, done rightly forms an act of consecration, done in the wrong spirit becomes celebration of self, not holiness in time. It serves as a means for showing off one's piety. That turns the duties we owe to God into a kind of religious behaviorism, and we become robots of the law, not servants of the living God.

Prophecy was, and still is, radical and controversial. The prophets called into question attitudes fostered by a wrong, but very human, response to the written Torah as comprised by the five books of Moses. The two great principles of the Torah as Moses sets out that Torah are, first, God loves Israel, children of Abraham and Sarah, Isaac and Rebecca, Jacob and Leah and Rachel, and, second, God wants Israel to do certain things and not do other things. And each of those principles can be and commonly is corrupted by human arrogance. God's love becomes our pride, and God's will becomes our arrogance. When you see how this comes about, you understand that without the prophets, the Torah can make us self-important and self-absorbed. But then, in the life of the synagogue, the reading of the

Torah is in two parts, first, the five books of Moses, then, a passage of prophecy. Only together do we receive the Torah that morning.

If I have to choose the single most important teaching of prophecy, it is that God loves all humanity equally, in the same manner and in the same measure. If, therefore, we want to know how God feels toward everybody, we must see ourselves as an analogy: God's love for them is like God's love for us, and if we reflect on how God loves us, then we know how God loves the other. We are different. The Torah transforms difference into destiny. And so, too, are the Ethiopians, the Philistines, the Aramaeans, everybody. Then what purpose do we serve, who receive and fulfill the Torah? We provide a model, a metaphor: God's love for you is like God's love for us. In a deep sense we are among the peoples of the earth like the Song of Songs among the books of Scripture: a metaphor by which people may understand reality, the "as if" that illuminates the "is."

Making sense of the life of the group does not have to take the form that it does in the Torah. Other groups call themselves nations or peoples without telling themselves that God has identified them as special. Other people practice their customs and ceremonies without calling them commandments of God and acts of sanctification. Everybody is different from somebody else. Just as we are glad to be what we are, so most peoples are glad to be what they are. We conduct world-class arguments among ourselves on just who that is—and is not. So, in all, that intensity of belief that the Torah expresses when it takes the given of our common life and transforms it into the gift of God does mark us as odd. How odd to God to choose the Jews indeed: the most human of humanity, so flawed and frail!

That perception of Israel as metaphor, as an example of what it means to be "in our image, after our likeness," explains why in the words of the prophets we uncover that other half of the message of the written Torah, along with the five books of Moses, which all together make of the whole life-giving medicine and not poison. To me, the self-evident truth of the Ten Commandments is matched by the self-evident truth of the words of Amos. There can be no Torah consisting only of the Pentateuch without the prophets, just as there can be no Torah made up only of the written Torah without the oral Torah. The prophets guide us toward a balanced and honest understanding of the Torah as a whole. Without the prophets, the part of the Torah we know as the five books of Moses (Pentateuch, in Hebrew Humash) can yield an ethnocentric celebration of pride, not a quest of a whole community of faith for humility before God.

What this means in a concrete way is simple. The Israelites in the five books of Moses are told that they are God's first love, through Abraham, chosen with the giving of the Torah. But through Amos, God tells Israel that all that is well and good, but there is nothing all that special about them: "To me, O Israelites, you are just like the Ethiopians, declares the Lord. True, I brought Israel up from the land of Egypt, but also the Philistines from Caphtor, and the Arameans from Kir." Then to what end the story of election? "You alone have I singled out of all the families of the earth—that is why I will call you to account for your iniquities." Moab is no worse than Israel, and Judah is no better than Moab. They are all the same, except that Israel bears the burden of its sin: chosen for responsibility, exemplary in being called to account.

That is a radical faith indeed. The message of Amos is extreme because he asks jarring questions. You keep festivals—*but* . . . You are special—*but* . . . True, Amos rights the balance. He wants to hold together service of God through deed with humility before God in attitude. He sees Israel as elect—therefore accountable. Now, to be sure, the middle of the road is never crowded. But the prophetic writings are absorbed within the routine of everyday life. So they are made to serve our purposes, rather than provoking us to serve God's purposes. The result is that we treat prophecy as self-evident, but then routine and commonplace.

The first time I understood that the words of the Torah could stand for something other than self-evident truth, of course, was the one moment in my life in which I could hear, in the words of Torah, the voice of God. It was a very specific moment, a very immediate address, and thirty-five years later I can remember every detail of the occasion. It was a Sabbath luncheon, after morning worship, at the Jewish Theological Seminary of America in the middle 1950s. The professors and students assembled in honor of the chief justice of the U.S. Supreme Court, Earl Warren, and former president Harry Truman had come too, to honor Chief Justice Warren. A seminary professor, Shalom Spiegel, was called upon to speak. He spoke without a note. He told a story. I can still hear the majesty of his voice.

He told the story of a trial: the trial of Amos, brought to consider the charges of Amaziah. Here is the incident, as recorded in the Book of Amos:

Thus he showed me, Behold, the Lord was standing beside a wall built by a plumbline, with a plumbline in his hand. And the Lord said to me, "Amos, what do you see?" And I said, "A plumbline." Then the Lord said, "Behold, I am setting a plumbline in the midst of my people Israel, and I will never again pass by them. The high places of Isaac shall be desolate, and the sanctuaries of Israel shall be laid waste, and I shall rise against the house of Jeroboam with a sword."

Then Amaziah, the priest of Bethel, sent to Jeroboam, king of Israel, saying, "Amos has conspired against you in the midst of the house of Israel; the land is not able to bear all his words. For thus Amos has said, 'Jeroboam shall die by the sword, and Israel must go into exile away from his land.' "

Spiegel then told the story of how Amaziah "instituted legal proceedings for the deportation of an undesirable alien." Amos contested the suit, and a trial was under way. At the trial, Amaziah read Amos's speeches, as Spiegel says, "for example, the passage spoken in the sanctuary, while the priests were offering sacrifices and the people beseeching heaven to accept their alms and chants with favor." That is when Amos disrupted the affair with this radical statement:

"I loathe, I spurn your festivals, I am not appeased by your solemn assemblies. If you offer me burnt offerings, or your meal offerings, I will not accept them. I will pay no heed to your gifts of fatlings. Spare me the sound of your hymns, and let me not hear the music of your lutes. But let justice well up like water, righteousness like an unfailing stream."

This certainly disturbed the public peace and interfered with the rights of free worship. A series of witnesses contested Amos's allegations about God's will. Spiegel conjured up a woman "appearing on behalf of the Daughters of the Confederacy"—that is, the Confederacy of the Tribes of Israel. So Spiegel made her speech:

" 'To me, O Israelites, you are just like the Ethiopians, declares the Lord. True, I brought Israel up from the land of Egypt, but also the Philistines from Caphtor, and the Arameans from Kir. Behold, the Lord has his eye upon the sinful kingdom: I will wipe it off the face of the earth. But I will not wholly wipe out the house of Jacob, declares the Lord.'

"This seemed ill-bred, ill-tempered, and altogether illogical. Are we not Israel, and thus unlike the heathen in a very special and intimate and incomparable relation to the God of Israel? Of course, of course, since there is but one God, he must be the God of the whole world. But does this necessarily imply that God cares no more for the people of the covenant which he freed from bondage than he cares for their inveterate enemies, the uncircumcised Philistines? Naturally lines of communication must be maintained between the one God of the universe and all the peoples of the earth. We, the Daughters of the Confederacy, neither question nor deny any race equal access to the Lord, but cannot such access to the Lord be made equal but separate?"

The Hebrew Legion on behalf of the Veterans of the Israelitish Wars of Independence contended with Amos's announcement:

"You alone have I singled out of all the families of the earth—that is why I will call you to account for all your iniquities."

On this Spiegel's Hebrew Legion head:

"Such notions are plainly subversive of all soldierly and civic virtue, a threat to the security of the nation which had just emerged victorious from a long struggle with Aram."

Amaziah could have called on the Meat and Poultry Purveyors, the Dairymen's League, and the Consolidated Wholesale Florists of Northern Israel.

"Similarly he ignored frantic appeals made by powerful temple unions such as the Congress of Liturgical Organizations, which warned of disastrous unemployment, if the sanctuaries be closed."

Spiegel's main point was his own:

Amos found the divine signature in all men in their sense of justice. All men have an innate desire for the right, an inborn fear of arbitrary force, an instinctive response to wrong: it is not right! However failing or blundering, legal systems everywhere are but the attempt to articulate this desire for justice and to incarnate it in institutions capable of lifting from the brow of man the fright and curse of brutal force. . . . Amos vs. Amaziah makes justice the supreme command, overriding every other consideration or obligation. . . . Justice becomes the categorical imperative, transcending all the other requirements of the law. . . . Ritual is propaedeutic to religion, exercising and training for spiritual life, discipline in the restraints of holiness. Worship is meant to inspirit man with passion for justice, to purify and prepare him for an encounter with God.

That was Spiegel, not Amos, not Moses. And that radical message of balance concerned what matters most and what takes second place in a right ordering of all things. It was not the occasion that honored the man, Spiegel. In what he had to say, a true word of Torah, he honored the president of the United States, the chief justice, and the assembled masters and disciples of the Torah. All in the name of a shepherd and a trimmer of sycamore trees, Amos of Tekoa: subversive of the Torah, prophet of God, whose words are now Torah.

Then what does it all add up to? How are we to hold together the diverse and even contradictory messages that the Torah has brought and today brings to us? Just as, in the time of Jesus, people went about asking what they had to do in order to be saved, so through the ages people have tried to answer the question, What does it all mean? And just as Amos found his answer, "Let justice well up as waters," so, through the ages, prophets, rabbis, sages have formulated their answers. Can I tell you, in just a few words, what the Torah means—in definitions that Moses, in the five books of Moses, and the prophets, in their writings, can adopt? I certainly can, because in the oral Torah we find a full and comprehensive statement of the whole Torah.

It comes from Hillel, a Pharisaic sage who lived at the beginning of the Common Era, in the same time as Jesus. He once was asked by a Gentile to define all of Judaism while standing on one foot. Instead of regarding the man's question as impertinent, he replied:

> What is hateful to yourself do not do to your fellow-man. That is the whole Torah. All the rest is commentary. Now go and study.
> Babylonian Talmud tractate Shabbat, p. 31(a)

Hillel was neither the first nor the last to attempt a pithy definition of Judaism. He chose four elements for his definition. First, he selected, from among many available Scriptures, Leviticus 19:18: "You shall love your neighbor as yourself: I am the Lord." This commandment, Hillel held, summarized everything. Second, he referred to the central, dominating motif of the Judaic consciousness: Torah. He did not speak of Judaism but of Torah when referring to the tradition. Third, he regarded everything else in the tradition as "commentary"—that is to say, as illustration of this single, primary principle. So he did think a definition was possible. Finally, he told the man to go, not to the synagogue for prayer or to the temple for sacrifice; not to the contemporary Dead Sea monastery for meditation and for a holy life or to the zealot bands for a holy way to bring the messianic day; but to the schoolhouse for study of Torah.

Fifty years later, sometime toward the middle of the first century, Hillel's great disciple Yohanan ben Zakkai taught:

> "If you have done much in the study of Torah, do not take credit for yourself, for to this end were you created."

The purpose of man is to study revelation, truth—that is, Torah. Still a further definition of Judaism derives from much later rabbis of the Talmud.

The reason it is important is that, in the exposition of everything God wants from us, one of these scholars, Rabbi Simlai, expounded teachings of not the five books of Moses, but prophecy. He quotes David's Psalms, which are the work (in the view of the Torah) of the Holy Spirit; then he turns to Isaiah, Micah, Amos, and Habakkuk. So Rabbi Simlai, in the Talmud of Babylonia, which is the summa and authoritative statement of the Torah, both written and oral, that is, of Judaism, sees no problem in linking prophecy with the five books of Moses. He finds the one to state the point and meaning of the other:

> Six hundred and thirteen commandments were given to Moses, three hundred and sixty-five negative ones, corresponding to the number of the days of the solar year, and two hundred forty-eight positive commandments, corresponding to the parts of man's body. . . .
>
> David came and reduced them to eleven: A Psalm of David [Psalm 15]. Lord, who shall sojourn in thy tabernacle, and who shall dwell in thy holy mountain? (i) He who walks uprightly and (ii) works righteousness and (iii) speaks truth in his heart and (iv) has no slander on his tongue and (v) does no evil to his fellow and (vi) does not take up a reproach against his neighbor, (vii) in whose eyes a vile person is despised but (viii) honors those who fear the Lord. (ix) He swears to his own hurt and changes not. (x) He does not lend on interest. (xi) He does not take a bridge against the innocent. . . .
>
> Isaiah came and reduced them to six [Isaiah 33:25–26]: (i) He who walks righteously and (ii) speaks uprightly, (iii) he who despises the gain of oppressions, (iv) shakes his hand from holding bribes, (v) stops his ear from hearing of blood (vi) and shuts his eyes from looking upon evil, he shall dwell on high.
>
> Micah came and reduced them to three [Micah 6:8]: It has been told you, man, what is good, and what the Lord demands of you, (i) only to do justly and (ii) to love mercy, and (iii) to walk humbly before God.
>
> Isaiah again came and reduced them to two [Isaiah 56:1]: Thus says the Lord, (i) Keep justice and (ii) do righteousness.
>
> Amos came and reduced them to a single one, as it is said, For thus says the Lord to the house of Israel. Seek Me and live.
>
> Habakkuk further came and based them on one, as it is said [Habakkuk 2:4], But the righteous shall live by his faith.
>
> Babylonian Talmud tractate Makkot p. 24(a)

This long passage illustrates in both form and substance the very essential attributes of definitions of Judaism produced within the classical tradition. Ethical and moral deeds take pride of place. If *Torah* means "revelation," then according to the rabbis as much as the prophets, what was in fact revealed was mostly ethical teachings.

Yet to say the whole point is ethics is wrong. Ethics today is the union of casuistry and banality. People "analyze" a lot of cases and then say something we knew before we did the analysis. That is not what the prophets are saying, for after all, they are prophets of God, not professors of ethics. For prophets speaking in the name of God, the direction and goal (also) of ethics is not the good life but the search for God, and the good life consists of that search—"The righteous man shall live by his faith"—for in Hebrew, the word for faith is *emunah*, meaning trust, loyalty, commitment. We remember Abraham's covenant between the parts: "And because he put his trust in the Lord, He reckoned it to his merit." Thus what keeps a person alive, what renders life real and meaningful, is trust in and loyalty to God. All Christians will understand this Torah, since after all, it forms the foundation of Paul's letter to the Romans about what it means to be a Christian. The Protestants, especially, appeal to this same verse when they speak of "salvation by faith" in their prophetic critique of Roman Catholic Christianity. But, we see, the tensions within Christianity replicate the tensions between the five books of Moses and the prophets, and like Roman Catholic Christianity, Judaism holds the whole together.

Neither prophets in the written Torah nor sages in the oral Torah issued definitions of theological doctrines expressed as philosophical generalizations. They spoke in terms of Torah, commandment, moral requirements, attitudes of heart and mind such as loving-kindness and good-heartedness. They addressed themselves not to a self-conscious ethnic group seeking meaning for its peculiarity, transcendent importance for its customs and ceremonies, but rather to the condition of ordinary humanity. That explains why most of us Jews so intensely affirm—and even enjoy—being what we are.

23

GREELEY
Jesus—What He Said

Jesus was elusive. He still is.

When we finally think we understand him, when we have at last arrived at an adequate explanation of him, when we have eventually defined him precisely, when we have, after great effort, identified him with our cause, then we discover that he's not there anymore.

We can take it as axiomatic: when we have captured Jesus for our own side, then, whether we be curialists or liberationists, liberals or fundamentalists, whoever we have won to our cause and persuaded to bash our enemies, it isn't Jesus.

The early Christians piled up titles as they tried to articulate what the man was like that they had encountered. None of the titles quite did it. He was "like" Adam, "like" Moses, "like" David, "like" the Son of Man in Daniel the Prophet, "like" a messiah. But in each case he was also something more, something different, something more mysterious, something more disconcerting.

A Jesus who does not disconcert is not Jesus. A Jesus who disconcerts our adversaries but not us is most certainly not Jesus.

He was disturbingly evasive in his responses to questions about his origin and identity. In fact, he would not answer directly most of the religious and political questions put to him. His responses changed the agenda of the question from that of the one who asked it to his own. And often he answered questions that no one had asked and no one wanted to ask. He must have driven crazy those contemporaries who tried to figure him out, to pin him down, to categorize him, to capture him in neat and clear terms.

If he does not produce the same reaction of bemused frustration in us, then again it is not Jesus whom we are considering.

We have to take him on his own terms and grant him the right to be mysterious if we wish even to begin to comprehend him.

Many years ago a writer tried to explain Jesus in a book called *The Man Nobody Knows*. It was a good title, but the book failed precisely because the author thought that at the end of it readers would finally "know" Jesus. The only possible approach to the man nobody knows is one that ends up with him being more mysterious, more disconcerting, more fascinating, and more challenging than he was when we began to study him.

There are two ways one can approach the study of Jesus. One is called Christology from Above. In this method one takes the later theological definitions of Jesus and then goes back to the Gospels and arranges the data to fit the definitions. Such an approach is reassuring (in my denomination) to the nervous theologians who work for the Roman curia, because as they see it, there is no possibility of error. It does not seem to bother them that in this approach there is little that is useful for teaching and preaching to ordinary people who are neither theologians nor ecclesiastical bureaucrats.

The other approach, equally valid in the Christian tradition, is Christology from Below. It begins with a study of what Jesus said and what he did and then argues to what he must have been in view of what he said and did. In this model, Christology—who Jesus was—is derived from Soteriology—what kind of salvation he offered. It has the merit that it recreates the religious pilgrimage of the early Christians and can be as exciting to us as it is to them. Followed by men and women of faith within the community, such an approach is not likely to end up in error any more than the other approach is. It also treats Jesus on his own terms and not on the terms of philosophical debates of later eras. Finally, since it is not a search that is completely cut and dried beforehand, it grants to Jesus the mystery that was so much part of his personality and his appeal.

A word must be said about attempts by Scripture scholars to "recapture the historical Jesus," that is, to peel away the beliefs and convictions of the early Christians and get back to him the "way he really was."

It is now generally agreed that this search for the "historical Jesus" is problematic. Scholars, using stern and cautious rules, can now agree on a certain number of sayings and a few stories that are almost certainly directly from Jesus. But to achieve this they must reject most of the rest of the Gospels.

Without decrying the ingenuity and industry of those who pursue such a search and without denying the importance of their work (particularly on the parallels), most students of the Scriptures today are willing to say that we can know enough about Jesus from the Gospels as they give a pretty good idea of what he said and what he did. We need not, in other words, see the early Christians as a barrier to knowing him but rather as a help—especially when we can understand their own concerns in the contexts in which they lived.

In this chapter I will rely on the parables of Jesus—the authenticity of which is denied by practically no one.

To use my terms: there isn't much doubt about the metaphor Jesus was teaching and living. In fact, as a tentative pre-theological beginning, I would say that Jesus understood the metaphor of God's love better than anyone else before or since because he lived within the metaphor. It was this insight into the meaning of a metaphor shared with those who came before and those who would come after that made Jesus unique. In that most elementary sense he fulfilled all that had happened and anticipated all that would happen.

At first blush such an argument does not seem to be claiming much for Jesus at all. All right, he understood better than anyone else the meaning of the poetry by which his tradition understood God. What's so special about that?

It may not seem to be much, but as my friend the rabbi will admit (wondering perhaps how he ever got mixed up with such a tricky Irish Catholic priest), it really is everything.

The clearest expression of the religious vision of Jesus, of his experience of God, is the parables—short, powerfully disconcerting, deeply ambiguous stories with one and only one impact—but that one is a crash, a severe jolt, a knockout punch of surprise.

The parable is not an allegory, although the writers of the Gospels did allegorize many of Jesus' parables. Thus the story of the farmer sowing his seed has one and only one point: the harvest will come no matter what the obstacles. It is not completely illegitimate to provide an interpretation for each of the obstacles, but such an allegory usually deprives the parable of its most powerful punch.

A parable, to put is differently, is a metaphor turned into a stripped-down narrative with an economy of language and a powerful impact—although it is often difficult to put the impact, however deeply felt, into words. *Parable*

You either "get" a parable on hearing it or you miss it, no matter how many books on it you may read.

There are three kinds of parables—stories of surprise, urgency, and reassurance. I will concentrate in this chapter on four of the parables of surprise because they are the most important and the most dazzlingly original in the "story of God."

My thesis is that Jesus took the image of the madness of God and translated it from the man/woman relationship to other human intimacies. One might expect a man to become irrational in his love for his wife. But an employer with his workers? A father with his ne'er-do-well son? A Samaritan with a Jew? A judge with a guilty criminal?

God, Jesus would say in the parables of surprise, is even crazier in his dealings with us than anyone could possibly believe.

So it was harvest time and the agricultural proletarians, the landless day laborers, waited in the marketplace of the town for a farmer to come and hire them. It was a critical time for both parties to the transaction, because the farmer had to get his crops in before the hot weather withered them and the workers had to earn the money that would keep them alive for the rest of the year. There was usually a seller's market for the workers because there was so much work to be done in such a short time.

Farmers would hurry back and forth to the marketplace, hunting for laborers who might have come in from other fields or from other towns. No one needed to be idle long.

A young man in the midst of the harvest and short of workers hired new workers at the third and the sixth and the ninth hours. At the eleventh hour, concerned perhaps about getting as much as possible done before nightfall because the hot weather was already upon them, he rushed back to the marketplace and found the town loafers still standing around, men who made a fine art of just missing the employers who had come seeking more farmhands.

They were idlers, wastrels, men who avoided work whenever it was humanly possible—even though the food they and their families would eat that night and the rest of the year would depend upon their jobs at harvest time.

The chance of getting much useful work out of them was meager. Nevertheless, he invited them to come to his fields. Shamed by his insistence, they straggled after him, probably grumbling all the way to the farm.

When they arrived they spent most of their time shuffling around, "carrying on," and complaining about what they were probably going to be paid by the young farmer. He was lucky if he received fifteen minutes of halfhearted labor from them before sunset.

Yet, in a complete surprise, he pays them a full day's wages, perhaps taking pity on their own indolence and the needs of their wives and children.

Crazy. No sane businessman could possibly survive for long with that kind of human-resources policy. The young man's neighbors surely must have muttered that it was a terrible thing, the way he was risking his family inheritance by paying wastrels for doing hardly any work at all.

Yet, Jesus says with a smile, that's the way God works.

The emphasis in this story of surprise is entirely on the generosity of the farmer who reflects the generosity of God. It is not, as Sunday preachers have often tried to make it, a blueprint for a Christian management/

employee relationship. It is not a model for the way a farm or a business should be run. In fact, it says nothing at all directly about human relationships. The hardworking laborers are not part of the punch of the story, because the implication is that in relationship to God we are all workers of the eleventh hour.

Rather the point, the only point, of the parable is that God loves us even if we are wastrels and idlers and loves us with a generosity and a passion that, even if they were reflected in human intimacies, would be written off as sheer lunacy.

God can't be like that, you say?

Probably you're right. But the essence of the message of Jesus is that he *is* like that. The Father in Heaven, the God whom Jesus experienced, the God of the religion of Jesus is like that.

If men and women really believe in such a zany lovesick deity, will they not become even more idle and indifferent? Won't they stand around gossiping in the marketplace till a few minutes before sunset?

In other parables Jesus stressed the need to urgently seize the opportunity of the present moment—go to the wedding banquet while you still can. But for much of the nearly two millennia since he told this and similar stories, the leaders of the community of those who believe in him have been afraid to reveal the message of divine love in all its fullness. They believe, contrary to Jesus, that fear is a more important motive for generosity than love.

Or again a man is mugged on the road at night. Neighbors and acquaintances pass him by. Fearful of the dangers of the road, they scurry past him. Then a bitter enemy finds him, administers first aid, takes him to the hospital, and pays his bill in advance.

What the hell is going on! ? ! ?

In the kingdom of God's mercy, Robert Funk writes, there is always wonder and surprise.

The Good Samaritan story may perhaps be more of a model for behavior than the farmer story. But the Samaritan's behavior is excessive to the point of absurdity. Pay the bill? Doesn't the man have family and friends who will come and take care of him? Is not the Samaritan acting foolishly in picking up the tab for someone who does not need that kind of help, especially since the man is a Jew and hence an enemy—and a self-righteous and supercilious enemy at that?

All right, a black might take a white mugging victim to the hospital, but pay his bill? Doesn't the man have hospital insurance?

In its original and most important meaning the story tells us that God is a

God = Good Samaritan

crazy neighbor who is excessive in healing and caring love even for those who are or think they are his sworn enemies. God is the Good Samaritan.

One need hardly say that such a metaphor infuriated many of those who heard it.

A smart-aleck son demands his inheritance, goes off to a far place, lives the life of a hippie and a drug addict, sinks to the lowest possible level of existence, and then decides to come home, fake contrition, and live off his father again. He even rehearses the speech of phony sorrow he will recite when he comes to the old man.

The father has been sitting on the porch all day, every day, waiting—hoping against hope that the spoiled brat will return. Finally he sees him at a distance, and instead of waiting for the young scoundrel to come crawling to him (which the young man is fully prepared to do: it's better than sleeping in the gutters), he rushes down the road, embraces his son, cuts short his counterfeit apology, and proclaims a party of celebration.

Parents down through the centuries have been furious at the old man: That's no way to raise a child. Make him earn his way back in.

But the parable is not a model for domestic behavior any more than the story of the farmer is a model for labor relations. It is rather a story of God's love. The emphasis is not on the prodigal son but on the crazy father who reflects God just as the nutty farmer and the bleeding-heart Samaritan did. The postscript about the other son is almost certainly a later addition to appease those who were infuriated by the story, those who had missed the point completely.

resist moralization of parables

The temptation to moralize these parables has always been strong and must be resisted firmly. One surely would conclude from the stories that just as God is generous to us we must be generous to others. But Jesus was not in the business of imposing new moral obligations. (The beatitudes are not a new moral law to be added to the Decalogue; they are rather descriptions of how it is possible to live if you really believe in God's love.) Nor was he trying to set standards for human generosity that would apply to all times and all places. He was not particularly interested in detailing family or labor policy. Rather he was trying to tell us what God is like.

The final parable of surprise is the most outrageous of all—the story in Saint John's Gospel of the freeing of the woman taken in adultery. So subversive of domestic and social order was it thought to be that it was simply left out of many of the manuscripts of Saint John's text. Moreover, many scholars today suspect that it was originally a parable that the tradition modified into an event in the life of Jesus since it seemed less offensive as something he might have done than as a story he might have told.

Parables = stories of God's absolute love.

Jesus was a special representative of God, so it was all right for him to subvert the law. But he should not have told a story about a corrupt judge who ignored the obvious meaning of the law. Opinion heavily laden by human judgement

The woman was guilty, no doubt about it. She did not even try to deny her guilt. She should be stoned to death, should she not? The law was clear to the judge. He had no right to reinterpret it on the spot in the name of some new-fashioned legal liberalism. The law, after all, is the law, isn't it?

What would happen to society if a wife could commit adultery with impunity?

The judge doesn't care. He tricks her accusers and dismisses the indictment before the woman can even enter a plea for mercy.

It is hardly an accident that the story is in most ways an instant replay of the Hosea story. But while Hosea was thought to be a fool for taking back a harlot wife, at least it could be said in his defense that he was besotted with love for her. What can be said in defense of a judge who with no reason at all to feel pity for the criminal lets her go free anyway?

We do not have here a model of Christian jurisprudence. The story is not a cautionary tale about how judges ought to behave. It is not a plea for reform of the criminal justice system.

It is simply a tale of God's love. God is the indulgent judge just as he is the nutty farmer, the crazy father, the bleeding-heart Samaritan.

The lazy workers, the prodigal son, the mugging victim, the guilty woman are all overwhelmed by mercy because they are living in the kingdom of God's wonder and surprise.

Moreover, we are the workers, the son, the victim, the sinful woman. We live in the kingdom of mercy and surprise. The industrious workers, the second son, the woman's accusers, they are merely a part of the story and correspond to no one in the world— save in the minds of the allegorizers who try to tone down Jesus' wild imagery.

In the parables of assurance (the mustard seed, the farmer sowing the seed, et cetera) Jesus reassures his listeners that the stories of God's love he tells are true and will triumph eventually and certainly over all visions of the meaning of human life. In the parables of urgency (the wedding banquet, the garden, the treasure buried in the field, the jewel of great price) he warns those who listen—and through them us—to take advantage of the invitation implied in his stories while they still have time.

If one understands that the parables, in all their wild and manic imagery, capture the religious experience of Jesus, one can begin to comprehend (though not totally) everything else about him. Jesus really believed that God loves us that way and acted on his beliefs.

parables capture religious experience of Jesus

So Jesus did not take seriously the minutiae of the laws that the scribes tried to impose on the people. He could readily associate with tax collectors, prostitutes, and sinners because God loved them, too. He could defy religious and political authority because they did not understand, could not understand, God's love. He could spend much of his time caring for those who needed to be healed because that activity represented the presence of God's love in the world. He could refuse all titles that hinted at political revolt because that was not the purpose of his mission. He could face death bravely and confidently because he knew that such Love as he had encountered would not tolerate the permanent death of the beloved.

The stories—extravagant, fascinating, full of wonder and surprise, unmatched in all history for their dramatic impact—are surely the most important reason the crowds followed Jesus. They were intrigued by his signs, stirred by his teaching, overwhelmed by his charm. But they could not escape the fascination of his stories—and the enchantment radiated by a man who lived in the conviction that the stories were true portraits of God.

Sometimes and often later in his life they were infuriated by the stories and their powerful judgment on the religious and political goals of the people.

What kind of messiah is this who does nothing besides tell crazy stories about a crazy God when a messiah is supposed to restore Israel to the political glory it had in the time of David and Solomon? Besides, these stories often insult us, don't they? Well, don't they seem to sound like implied insults? And he won't ever really explain them. That's right, he doesn't claim to be a messiah. He doesn't claim to be anything. And he won't answer our questions about who he is or in whose name he preaches.

You know, he could be a very dangerous man.

It all seems a little too simple, doesn't it? After all the catechisms and theology books, after all the lectures and sermons, after all the debates and analyses, was Jesus only trying to tell us what God was like? Somehow that seems a little too simple.

Or perhaps only a little too dangerous. A Jesus that simple and that obvious was a troublemaker then and now. Better that we worry about rules and regulations, about how many angels can dance on the head of a pin and how extensive papal infallibility might be and the validity of infant baptism and when a dirty thought becomes a sin. Those are safe questions—and relatively undemanding ones. They do not require us to make a leap of faith into the arms of the manic God about whom Jesus preached.

Jesus was a visionary like the prophets, though a stable and solid vision-ary. He differed from them primarily in the wild splendor of his vision. It was a vision that then seemed too good to be true and still does. Finally, the vision was too subversive, too disturbing, too revolutionary, so, as Jesus probably understood early on, he would eventually have to die for it.

How willing are people then and now to die for the vision ???

24

GREELEY
Jesus—What He Did

I have this wonderful idea for a science fiction story. A group of young people invent a time machine. They plan to return to the Rome of Julius Caesar so that they can write the best term paper ever on the Rome of Julius Caesar. But they make a mistake in setting the controls and end up in Jerusalem on the fourteenth day of the month of Nisan in the year 30 c.e. (though of course that's not how it was being counted then).

Being good, solid Chicago Irish Catholics (the only kind of people I know well enough to write novels about), they don't propose to permit the execution of Jesus. They steal him away from the Praetorium of Pontius Pilate and out into the desert. The authorities are too frightened by this intervention to follow them.

They set up a little monastery by the banks of the Jordan to which people come to hear Jesus preach and to have their illnesses healed. A year later Jesus dies as he saves them from a desert sandstorm. The young people return to the present and find the world changed completely. Church and synagogue have never separated. Israel has not been fractured. All Christians are now Jews, the largest and most important (but not the only) component of the Jewish religious culture. The chief rabbi of Rome, the pontifex maximus, wears white and is called pope. As one of my colleagues would have remarked, Jews belong to all the country clubs now and there are no specifically Jewish country clubs.

The premise is that the fracture in Israel did not occur and the fantasy is what the world would be like if that had not happened.

(I hasten to add that I am not attributing the break between church and synagogue to the fact that Jesus died on the cross—save in this fantasy.)

I will never write the story because I believe it is impossible to adequately represent Jesus in a work of fiction. I cite it here not because I propose to discuss the fracture in Israel in this chapter (although I will later on). Rather, I use this story premise to illustrate the fact that while it was necessary for Jesus to die, since he was human, it was not necessary for him to die the way he did. The cross was not so much part of the plan of "redemption" that it must be considered essential.

By what he did Jesus showed us how to live and to die—both in the generous, self-giving service of others. Given the terrible hostility that his vision of God had stirred up, it may have been inevitable that the authorities would want to get rid of him. Knowing that they were determined to slay him, Jesus "set his face" toward Jerusalem after his religious experience on Mount Tabor. He chose to meet his fate in public in the Holy City instead of as a hunted fugitive, perhaps because he wanted the validation he was sure God would provide to also be a public event. There was an inevitability to the cross, but not an intrinsic necessity. *interesting*

I make this point because so many people seem to have been taught that God demanded this suffering from Jesus as a penalty for human sin and are horrified by what they conceive to be an unspeakably cruel demand. This understanding, as I shall explain, is based on allegorizing a metaphor and then interpreting the allegory literally.

The injustice, if there was one, was that Jesus had to die. But it is unjust that any being with a hunger for immortality should be frustrated in that hunger. It is unjust, or so it seems, that anyone should die.

If Jesus did not "expiate" in the sense of paying off a debt to God, then what did he do?

His followers knew after Good Friday and Easter that he had saved and healed them. About that conviction there could be no doubt in their minds at all. But how were they to explain to others what had happened?

They were filled with an exuberant sensation that they were both free and reunited with each other and with God. The history of the first century of Christianity is a history of luxuriant enthusiasm, of humans going forth to preach the good news that has filled them to overflowing. If we miss the joyous exuberance of those years, we fail to understand the most elementary fact about the first Christians.

What was the substance of their enthusiasm? Later theologians may dash in with theories of expiation and salvation to explain them, but the first Christians would not have found such rational and discursive explanations sufficient. Mere prose could not capture what they felt.

Father John Shea in his wondrous poem "The Story Teller of God" captures better than any prosaic theology the experiential environment in which the first Christians lived and which we sometimes still share with them.

> Now the sun,
> Which Ecclesiastes says always rises,

broke the night of the fierce debate
But no rooster greeted it
Instead
A stone the size of twelve men
moved like a mountain on its way to the sea
and on the fresh wind of morning
came the Son of Man,
His shroud a wedding garment,
His feet between earth and air in dance.
Death, Sin, and Fate poured rhetoric
into the stirring air about them
but the silent Son of God only danced
to music beyond their words
He whirled around Death
and with each turn
Death himself grew old
till with a last, unbelievable look
he saw no more.
Then wordless
Christ spun around the words of Sin
till a stammer started, sound choked
and finally there was only a mouth
without a voice.
Next Fate heard the risen footsteps
And frost formed on his tongue
As Christ leapt before him,
he froze in mid-syllable
iced by the warmth of God.
Now
there was only the morning
and the dancing man of the broken tomb
The story says
he dances still.

That is why
down to this day
we lean over the beds of our babies
and in the seconds before sleep
tell the story of the undying dancing man
so the dream of Jesus will carry them to the dawn.

This is something like what they felt—a dazzling sensation of wonder because Jesus had to rout death and sin and fate.

Do not underestimate or dismiss their mood of delighted surprise. If you miss that, you don't understand at all what "salvation" meant to them.

They chose two metaphors from their own experience to describe the saving and healing that had occurred.

One of the metaphors was the "redemption" of a slave. Generous men and women often purchased the freedom of a slave from the slave's owner. Sometimes a man purchased the freedom of his beloved so he could marry her. Or he bought the freedom of his wife and children. Or his brother and sister. Or his parents. Occasionally someone would sell himself into slavery to obtain the freedom of a loved one. "Redemption" meant "buying back," the freeing of a slave at a cost to oneself.

The followers of Jesus, like all of us, had lived with the sense that they were chained, imprisoned, enslaved by all the weaknesses of their own personalities and the limitations of imperfect human existence—ignorance, bad habits, weariness, physical and emotional weakness. As Saint Paul would later remark, the good we want to do we don't do and the bad we don't want to do, that we do.

But now the followers of Jesus were suddenly free of those chains. None of the weaknesses and limitations were swept away. None of the predispositions that constrained their lives were eliminated. But still they were free. Because of their encounter with Jesus they were convinced that they could struggle against their frailties and afflictions and eventually win. Moreover, in the power of God manifested in Jesus they could do extraordinary deeds despite their weaknesses.

So they said that they felt like freed slaves. By his life and death and resurrection, Jesus had paid the purchase price to win them their new freedom. Jesus had sacrificed himself for them.

Now as metaphor this was a perfectly valid description. They could say that they had been freed at the price of the blood of Christ and communicate to others that the sufferings of Jesus had set them free. The trouble arose when the metaphor was turned into an allegory and the question arose as to who was the slave owner to whom the price had to be paid.

Was it the devil, as some thought? Did the blood of Jesus satisfy the devil? Hardly.

Well, then, was it God the Father who would not free humankind from the bonds of servitude in which it had been entrapped until Jesus paid with his suffering for every last bit of debt humankind owed him?

What kind of God is that?

The kind of God, it is much to be feared, about whom many of us were taught in grammar school. Some theologians, not content with corrupting a metaphor into an allegory, had then derived from it a systematic thought structure of "redemption" that produced a monster God appeased only by the suffering of someone he loved.

The second metaphor was that of a reunion. Humans, then and now, are conscious of the disarray in which we find ourselves. All our relations are a mess—with our friends, our families, our parents, our children, our lovers, our fellow citizens, the world in which we live, and the God who made all. We find our normal condition to be alienation.

In their exuberant enthusiasm, the followers of Jesus believed that such barriers had, in principle, been swept away. They were a new creation, a new humanity. They were reunited with each other, with the marvelous world of creation, which also had been renewed, and with God.

They knew that they would have to work to sustain this renewal, just as they would have to work to practice their new freedom. All Jesus had done was show them how to be freed and renewed and give them hope that their efforts would not be in vain; that "all" was, however, everything that was needed. It was everything.

They saw that it was possible, despite human weakness, to sustain an intimate relationship with God that would transform all their other relationships and in turn be transformed by the illumination revealed in renewed human intimacies with one another.

The barriers between humans and God had been swept away. As a later metaphor would put it, the gates of heaven were open again.

There was nothing wrong with that metaphor—the gates of a castle opened when peace is restored to the land. But in the hands of allegorizers and the literalists it too became a monster: God, the great IRS accountant in the sky, waiting for a bucket of the blood of Jesus before he swung open the creaking gates.

Again a systematic and artificial thought structure had been elaborated in which a metaphor was twisted out of its own internal configuration and reduced to a logical absurdity.

It may be that these twin thought systems, redemption and renewal purchased from a double-entry bookkeeper God, did not disturb men and women who lived in other ages. In our own, however, they are both profoundly offensive—which has not prevented teachers and preachers pushing them home and then shrugging their shoulders with the cop-out response "It's a mystery," when their people recoil in horror.

Perceive, if you will, that those who would turn the metaphors into contractual and juridical arrangements have, in fact, perverted the original meaning. Both metaphors originally expressed extravagant joy at the revela-

all God talk is metaphorical

tion in Jesus of the generous love of God. When the allegorizers and the theologians and the teachers and the preachers were through with their perversions of the metaphors, God appears vicious and cruel and brutal and monstrous.

Nice going, guys.

Now is the time to make a crucial point: all God talk is metaphorical, poetic, analogous—theology included. The theologian is using poetic language just as much as anyone else who talks about God. His poetry tries to be cool, restrained, analytic, systematic—as language should be when it becomes the tool for rational reflection. But no one should think that the restraint of the most philosophical theology means that it says "God is . . ." and does not mean "God is like . . ."

VIP

The good theologians are conscious that they are using poetry. When their analytical reflections lead them to absurdity, they know that somehow they have missed the point of the poetry. The second-rate theologians, however, think that because their sentences sound prosaic they are speaking the same language as science and that no matter how absurd the rational conclusions they draw from the metaphors of the Bible may be, they nonetheless have to be true because the thought process that led to them is so rational.

(In fact, science doesn't work that way either. It relies on metaphor as much as theology does.)

Any time you hear an account of our salvation by Jesus that seems odd, hold it up against your memories of Father Shea's poem. If the story being told you does not conform to the story of the dancing storyteller of God putting to rout fate and sin and death, if it is not a story you can whisper to your babes as they fall asleep at night, then it's not about Jesus, our Savior.

So what does it mean to say that Jesus was our Savior?

It means at a bare minimum and also at the poetic maximum that by his life, death, and resurrection Jesus exorcised sin and fate and death—not completely, not totally, but in principle and definitively.

By his life and death Jesus taught us how to live and die. By his resurrection he promised that the lunatic God who is his Father will validate our lives and deaths just as he validated the life and death of Jesus. Jesus saved us by promising us victory and by showing us how to share anticipation in that victory.

Jesus saved us by showing us how to live generously and gracefully and how to die confidently and bravely and by guaranteeing that we would no more live and die in vain than he did.

The Catholic theological tradition has always insisted that the salvation won by Jesus had to be "real," it had to really and truly transform the human condition. It would not be sufficient for the transformation to be "moral"; salvation could not mean that the world was a better place because Jesus had lived a good life, told marvelous stories, and died unjustly and bravely. Such "exemplary" salvation (salvation by good example)—it was rightly insisted— was not quite good enough. There had to be a "real" (or sometimes a "meta-physical") change in the human condition. Is not my minimum/maximum account of Jesus as our Savior nothing more than "exemplary" salvation?

RC tradition

I don't think so, and neither do the Catholic theologians with whom I have consulted on this delicate but important point.

Jesus' sacrifice of himself for others and the Father's validation (acceptance) of the sacrifice through the resurrection of Jesus actually do change the existential nature of the human condition, precisely because they drastically transform the possibility of human interpretation of life and death. We now understand from the study of human language that language is the way we respond to reality and the way we define it and therefore create it. A change in the way we give meaning to life and death actually transforms these two central realities as they are experienced in the human condition. The world we create with our language, our images, our metaphors is radically different now than it was before Jesus came to tell us how much God loves us. We know how ultimately love is stronger than hatred and life is stronger than death. That very knowledge, made certain by faith, transforms the world.

The world is changed by our pictures of it and by our responses to those pictures. The great transformation begun by Jesus is still in process. Sometimes the process seems terribly slow and erratic, but it continues. The Omega Point of Father Teilhard de Chardin (the goal of all creation) is still a long way off. But because of Jesus we are closer than we once were.

Jesus then transformed the human condition by showing us how to live and how to die and promising us that death was not the end. *

---

*When I read Rabbi Neusner's many works and note that he says that Christianity is a religion of salvation and Judaism a religion of sanctification I become uneasy, because I suspect that he and I do not mean the same thing by the word *salvation* (and possibly not by the word *sanctification* either). In my sense of the word it means the discovery of the possibility of transformation, of sanctification, of metanoia (profound change), in Saint Paul's word. Jesus surprised us with a whole new set of possibilities. That surprise—and the real and powerful change in the human condition caused by the surprise— may have been radically necessary for the renewal of humankind, but it creates only the possibility that as individuals and peoples we can become the new humanity. Salvation is an essential beginning, a fundamental reorientation, and a disturbing challenge. Sanctification is still up to us (with God's help, as in all other things human). As I understand it, the old faith/works controversy between Protestants and Catholics has now been pretty well straightened out by ecumenical dialogue. However, in the response of the Council of Trent to the early controversy on the subject, the distinction between salvation and sanctification emerged. In the Catholic world view, then and now, both are needed.

Jesus lived generously and gracefully. He died bravely and confidently. He lived for others and he died for others. So must we all live and die.

He told stories that brought hope and joy. He allied himself with sinners seeking mercy and with the religious illiterate (the "poor") who were rejected by the religious establishment. He freed people from the excessive burdens of dry legalism. He healed the sick and the neurotic. He gave sight to the blind, hearing to the deaf, mobility to the lame, even life to the apparent dead. He restored faith and confidence to those who had lost both. He refused to back down in the face of corrupt authority. He denounced injustice, hypocrisy, and oppression. He knew full well that both his stories and his actions made his eventual death almost inevitable. He kept on telling the stories and working his signs.

He was not a wimp. Generosity and grace did not mean that he let phonies and fakers and hypocrites push him around. He did not back away from arguments. He did not tolerate foolishness or meanness. He rebuked stubborn incomprehension. When it became clear that those in power wanted to do him and his followers in, he went on the run, ducking around the corners of Palestine so that he could continue to teach his closest followers.

Like the rest of us, he did not want to die. Indeed he was, like the rest of us, afraid to die. But when he knew that death, and, indeed, a horrible death, was inevitable, he faced it with courage and self-possession. He attempted to make it more bearable for his mother and his friends who remained by his refusal to complain or to feel sorry for himself.

He lived the way we would all like in our better moments to live—only he lived that way all the time. He died the way we all want to die—only he died that way with total confidence that his death was not the end.

As individual actions, the events in the life and death of Jesus may not have been remarkable. It is the total, the combination, the aggregate that made him remarkable, so remarkable that, as I shall say in the next chapter, his followers, especially after they encountered him not dead but still alive, concluded that there was something more than human in him. They understood as they reflected on his words and his deeds, on what he did and what he said, on the stories he told and the generosity of his life, that even as he had said, he had a unique and special relationship with God.

So at the end of the day on the fourteenth of Nisan, the body was put in the tomb and the stone was rolled across the entrance. A traveler in Jerusalem that day who might have heard about the death of the Galilean rabbi would have said, quite reasonably, that it was the last of him. He would soon be forgotten.

He would not have been more wrong. Even today we still lean over the beds of our children as they sleep at night and tell the story of the undying dancing man. *

---

*I must add a word about the image of Jesus as a political revolutionary, so dearly beloved by the so-called Liberation theologians. First of all, it is nearly blasphemous to identify Jesus, who bitterly denounced violence, with the cause of violence. There may be times when we must fight and times when we must revolt, but at these times let us do what has to be done in the name of justice or survival and not in the name of Jesus. Jesus was not a Zealot and quite explicitly rejected the Zealot cause. He may have been executed as a political revolutionary, but that was part of the injustice, since a political revolutionary was the last thing he was. He denounced injustice and attacked the political religious establishments, radical enough behavior. But he certainly did not preach that arms should be taken against either.

There are different varieties of Liberation theology. Some of the liberationists are not Marxists and do not support violent revolution. They merely call for radical change in the social systems of their countries in the name of elementary justice. Surely no one can disagree with such calls, though one may wonder how sophisticated some of their plans for remaking society really are.

But other Liberation theologians are Marxists and believe in and support in the name of Jesus violent, Marxist revolution.

Jesus was not a gun-toting Marxist revolutionary. To depict him as one does violence to history, theology, and right reason.

These theologians are guilty of idolatry, of identification of a highly contingent political and social ideology with the message of God. They are intolerably self-righteous because they justify their idolatry in the name of the poor with whose cause they have identified. But there is no reason to believe that the poor want them to act as their representatives. Indeed, for all their posing and posturing, the Liberation theologians are middle-class academics who live comfortable lives on academic tenure and travel the world on expense accounts preaching revolution to other bourgeoisie academics like themselves. They could not revolt their way out of wet paper bags even if their lives depended on it. Nor could they lead a pack of starving vampires to a blood bank. Indeed, if there was ever a real Marxist revolution in their countries they would quickly be put up against a wall and shot, on the perfectly reasonable grounds that they were parasites living off the people.

Finally, they are ignorant about Marxism. They believe as unassailably true that Marxism and only Marxism will improve the lot of the poor. In fact, the lesson of history is that Leninist dictatorships do not, in fact, improve the lot of the poor but merely replace an old and inefficient ruling class with a new and equally inefficient but much more oppressive ruling class.

The iron law of revolutions (excepting the American and perhaps the Polish) is always that a revolution increases the power of whatever ruling class may emerge.

After the revolution there is more oppression rather than less.

25

GREELEY

Jesus—Who He Was

We must start with the basic data:

The followers of Jesus had felt themselves to be sick and in need of healing; Jesus healed them. They felt themselves chained and in need of liberation; Jesus freed them. They felt themselves scattered and in need of reunion; Jesus reunited them. They felt themselves weary and despondent; Jesus renewed them.

Who was he, they then asked themselves. Who was this man who had the power and the will to heal us, who had the strength to free us and the love to do so? Who was this generous, graceful storyteller who lived and died bravely in the service of others and in the process healed us and renewed us and created in us this marvelous, surprising exuberance?

Given the kind of salvation we have experienced, who must he have been to have saved us so?

They concluded with a paradox that has shaped the Christian history: he was a man just like us in all things but sin, yet he was also something more than human. To have done what he did, to have transformed us and the world around us the way he did, he must have had a special union with God. God must have been present in him in a unique way, utterly distinct from God's presence in the rest of us.

There can be no question that this was the experience of the followers of Jesus. Nor can there be any debate that the paradox with which they tried to articulate their experience has challenged Christians ever since.

A paradox is a very special kind of metaphor, one that gets special attention by posing as a contradiction.

Any reflection on the paradox of Jesus that misses or underemphasizes one of its two components (divinity and humanity, to use the words of later theology) must be rejected, as must any reflection that carries us too far away from the enthusiasm and wonder, the mystery and the fascination, the hope and the confidence that filled the first Christians.

Because we are reflective creatures we must attempt to untangle the paradox, to find some reasonable articulation of what occurs within the blinding light of the Jesus experience. But in the process of seeking such rational explanations we must neither make the explanation an end in itself nor forget the primary datum of the early Christian experience of paradox, which is, after all, the object of our reflections—and not the Greek philosophical terms in which the paradox would later be expressed.

We must strive mightily in our reflections not to forget the joy and hope that Father Shea captures again for us in his story of the dancing, undying man.

Although there are a number of different Christologies in the Christian Scriptures, Jesus himself was monumentally uninterested in questions about who he was. He had better things to do than debate about whether he was a prophet or a messiah or Elias returned from the dead. He had stories to tell, work to do, a mission to fulfill. What difference did it make who he was? Could not his vision of God stand on its own? Was not the message itself a sufficient credential? And if it wasn't, what kind of credential would be acceptable?

As a Protestant scholar once remarked, after Easter the proclaimer became the proclaimed. The messenger became the message. The storyteller became the story. I've always suspected that Jesus might not be altogether pleased with this development. He did not want questions about his precise credentials and nature to interfere with the stories he was telling, the picture of God to which he was bearing witness. For much of Christian history that is precisely what has happened. Folks are so busy debating about who Jesus was and is that they seem to have very little time to listen to his stories or to ponder his message.

A phenomenon that may not be altogether undeliberate: the challenge of what he said can be ducked effectively if you divert your energies to the question of who he is.

I put the question of who he was in third place both because I think it can be answered only after one has reflected on what he said and what he did and because I think that's where Jesus himself would want it to be placed.

Why don't you simply say, I am asked when I worry about this situation, that he is God or the Son of God or the Messiah?

I worry about it because none of those are particularly good answers in the present situation.

We are all sons and daughters of God in some sense. If Jesus is the Son of God in a special way, then it remains to be specified in what special way. So the title only begs the question.

It can of course be accurately said that he is God, but only if you understand the doctrine of communication of idioms that evolved at and after the Council of Chalcedon in the fifth century. At this council the Trinitarian and Christological debates which tore at the church of the early centuries were resolved with the decision that Jesus was a divine person with a divine and human nature. That doctrine was an adequate response to the controversies of the time and preserved the essential tension between the experience of Jesus among the early Christians—someone human like us and yet someone radically different from the rest of us.

But it is a teaching that can be fully understood only if one is familiar with the debates that went before it, debates that seem remarkably arcane to most people today. Moreover, the two Greek words we translate as *nature* and *person* did not mean then quite what they mean today. Someone has remarked that among men and women of our day, *person* today means something rather like what *nature* meant in the fifth century and *nature* today means something like what *person* did then.

I think myself that this is an exaggeration, but it is certainly true that the Chalcedonian formulation, as adequate as it was in its time and as true and as much a matter of faith as it is today, is hardly an effective pedagogical theorem for our time.

According to that doctrine, you can predicate of the person whatever would be true of either nature. Thus you can accurately say that God died, because you mean that the human nature of the person who was God died. You can say that Jesus is God because, even though we experienced directly his human nature, that human nature belonged to a person who is God. In the same way Mary is the mother of God because she is the mother of the human nature of the person who is God.

While such a terminology is perfectly orthodox and indeed preserves and protects the orthodox tradition, it is not of much use today to those ordinary Christians who do not happen to have training in the Greek philosophical debates of the first half of the first millennium of the Common Era—which is to say practically everyone.

All right, call him Messiah then. After all, that's what Christ means, isn't it? Jesus Messiah?

But *messiah* is a word that has been used in many different senses and is likely to create more confusion than clarity. The late George McRae, S.J., in a book edited by Rabbi Neusner, reported that there were many different meanings attached to the word in the Judaism of the time of Jesus. Moreover, the word also has several different meanings in the Christian Scriptures (when it is something more than a proper noun—the last name of Jesus), and none of these meanings overlap the range of meanings available to Jews at the time. Thus then and now *messiah* means different things to

Jews and Gentiles. On both sides most people are not aware that they are talking about different understandings of the word, talking, in fact, past one another.

Scripture scholars say that it is virtually certain that Jesus never used the term of himself. It is surely valid to apply it to him the way the early Christians did as they struggled to articulate their experience of Jesus. But one must understand that the word when used of Jesus has taken on a new meaning that it did not have in Israel.

When a Jew demands of a Christian, "You expect me to believe that Jesus was the Messiah, don't you?" the proper answer is, "Not the way we ordinarily use the term."

When a Christian says to a Jew, "Why don't you accept Jesus as Messiah?" the correct answer is, "He may be in the way you define the term, but not in the way we ordinarily use it."

Does one have to note that in the heated controversies of the past two thousand years such precision and restraint have been rare?

The Chalcedonian formula has the merit that it contains within itself the paradoxical assertion that Jesus was both God and human, a position that has not always been easy to maintain in the course of Christian history. One aberration has been to deny the divinity of Jesus. He was either merely a man like us or some lesser spirit, but not God. Such heresies as Nestorianism and Arianism embraced in one way or another this position, as do more recent doctrines such as those professed in *Jesus Christ Superstar* and *Godspell* and by much of liberal Protestantism: Jesus was merely a man, a remarkable man, it is true, but still a man and in no way really different from the rest of us.

The trouble with that position, one with which the modern secular mentality is very comfortable indeed, is that it does not correspond to the reaction of the early Christians who were convinced on the basis of their experience of Jesus that he was something more than just an ordinary human, that he had a special relationship with God, and that in him God intervened in human history in a unique and special fashion.

The "great and good man theory" is intellectually satisfying—and not too disturbing religiously if you like your religion without paradox and surprise. It fails only when one begins to take the data of Bible and tradition seriously.

The other aberration has, perhaps surprisingly to us moderns, been far more popular. It simply denies or minimizes the humanity of Jesus. To the Gnostics and their successors in the second and third centuries, the Docetists, Jesus was not human at all but only appeared to be human. (The Latin *docere* means "to appear.") He was a god who acted as though he was human but in fact was simply going through the motions of an actor on a stage.

Later the Monophysites (from the Greek, meaning "one nature") flatly denied that Jesus had a human nature at all. He was divine and that was that.

Monophysite and Nestorian churches still survive, the latter in the Middle East, the former in Egypt and Ethiopia. They are historical and political and cultural relics rather than serious heresies. But just as the denial of the divine component in Jesus is the temptation of liberal Protestants, so the virtual denial of the humanity of Jesus is the temptation of conservative church leaders.

A parish I was in twenty years ago was investigated by the Vatican because it was reported to be teaching strange doctrines about Jesus. It turned out that the objectionable words were found in a Sunday Gospel reading in which Jesus was called a man, a translation that had been approved by the Catholic hierarchy. Call Jesus a man—which he was—even with the sanction of the bishops and you'll have obnoxious little bureaucrats running around warning you about the danger of shocking the faithful. When asked whether we should tell the faithful that Jesus was not a man (which would have been heresy), the fussy functionary (now a bishop) said that we must be prudent. He did not specify what that meant.

No obnoxious curialist would have come running to our rectory if it appeared we had slighted the humanity of Jesus. It is prudent, I guess, to violate the paradox so long as you do it in the direction of divinity.

Another heresy that began very early and was indeed based on some tentative attempts at explanation in the Christian Scriptures is Adoptionism: Jesus was a man whom God adopted at the time of his passion and death as a special son. It was an explanation that seemed to finesse many of the problems but overlooked the instinct of the first Christians that the integration of God and man in Jesus was present during his life, too.

The names of these heresies really don't matter, but their existence and their persistence without the formal names into our own time show how difficult it is to arrive at a balance between the two poles of the Christological tension. Even in the books of the Christian Scriptures there were several different tentative Christologies, all of them orthodox enough but all open to later misinterpretation and misunderstanding.

The datum was clear enough—human like us and yet more than human—but the explanations have always been difficult. Paradoxes are always hard to untangle.

I suppose I have read at least a dozen Christology books in the last decade. All of them are brilliant. Some of them I could even understand when I was reading them. None of them remained in my mind for more than a day or two after I closed the book. And none of them were any help at all in preaching or teaching.

Some may have helped their authors obtain tenure, however.

I am not suggesting that attempts at formal Christology should be abandoned. Rather I am contending that any effort to unravel a paradox is bound to be less than satisfactory. We continue to be left with the blinding paradox experienced by the first Christians that in Jesus God and humanity were mixed in a special union.

Much of the debate about the nature of Jesus down through the centuries has missed the critical implication of the Incarnation. The most important point of the enfleshing of God in Jesus is not the divinizing of one human, but the humanizing of God. When God is made flesh, the whole of humanity is sanctified and the whole of creation of which humankind is a part. Humankind is lifted up to God indeed, but this is done so that God may reach down and embrace humankind.

Thus when a foolish Catholic bishop condemned Martin Scorsese's *Last Temptation of Christ* on the grounds that it "has more of this world than of the next," he himself slipped into a theological error: the aim of the Incarnation is not to create a vision of the next world, but to renew and sanctify this world.

What did Jesus himself think about the subject? If the various Christology theories, however helpful some of them may be, are finally inadequate, might we not at least cling to Jesus' own self-consciousness?

Two observations are appropriate:

1. Jesus spoke about God with a confidence and authority that none of the prophets had claimed. He swept away legalisms with a wave of his hand. He proclaimed religious truth in his own name as one who had the right to do so. He told wild stories of God as one who knew God well enough to be able to tell such stories without falling back on any authority but his own.

2. He claimed an affectionate intimacy with God that no one else ever dared claim. The Father in heaven was "Abba"—"Daddy." On the face of it, the use of that term of special and intimate relationship with God would have been blasphemous for an ordinary human. Jesus would have been excused from blasphemy only if, in fact, he was conscious of such a unique familiarity with God.

These two facts from the life of Jesus are the beginning of a legitimate "trajectory" (to use the word favored by theologians) that runs through the response of the early Christians, the emergent Christologies of the books of the Christian Scriptures, and the teachings of the councils of the first half of the first millennium of the Common Era. They are the most elementary data available to us, the same data on which the early Christians reflected when they began to formulate the paradox of "human just like us in all things sin alone excepted" (The Epistle to the Hebrews) and yet somehow more than us, someone radically and uniquely and specially united to God.

The exercise of protecting the integrity of the paradox while we reflect on the meaning of the Christ experience is not merely an academic or intellectual effort.

For if Jesus is not human, then he is not a savior (or a high priest, in the words of the Epistle to the Hebrews) who understands all the trials of being human, and if he is not divine then he does not have the special access to God (special knowledge and love of God) that validates his stories and his death and the powerful healing we experience in him.

For later centuries and millennia the Christian insight that all of creation was saved in Jesus would be of great importance. At the very time that the world religions and especially the Platonism that dominated philosophy in the Roman empire were rejecting creation and human flesh as evil constraints on the human spirit, the early Christians were asserting that because God took on human flesh in Jesus, the world was good, the body was good, the flesh was good.

It was not an insight that survived unchallenged in Christian history. Indeed, for many years, the insight, however honored in theory it might have been, was paid little attention in practice.

Even today, as we shall see in the next chapter, the implication of the Incarnation for our attitudes toward the human body is hardly perceived by all Christians or all church leaders. Saint Augustine, the great Catholic thinker who utterly misunderstood this conclusion from the doctrine of the Incarnation, still exercises great influence: many still think that the body and its longings are somehow dirty or shameful or sinful.

How then do they explain that Jesus had a body, that God, in his eagerness to reach down and embrace us, in some fashion united himself with human flesh just like ours, sin alone excepted?

In truth, they don't really even try to explain it. Rather, they express outrage at the suggestion that Jesus' humanity was really like ours. Ah, yes, they don't bear the name, but the Monophysites are alive and well.

In their implicit denial of the humanity of Jesus they ignore the exuberant joy of the followers of Jesus: we thought the dim light was dusk. It turned out to be dawn.

26

GREELEY

Women and Jesus

In the summer of 1988 outrage exploded around the land over Martin Scorsese's brilliant and breathtaking film *The Last Temptation of Christ*. Scorsese had dared to raise the question of the relationship of Jesus to women and therefore the question of the sexuality of Jesus.

It is a question that has lurked off the record for many years. For a long time, under the influence of the pessimism of Saint Augustine and the body-rejecting spirituality of Plato, Christians were afraid to ask it, even afraid to think it. In the era after Sigmund Freud, men and women were willing to think it and discuss it in whispers, but hardly to mention it openly.

The Last Temptation thrust the question into the public domain and revealed how much fear of and distaste for the human body and its functions continues to lurk just beneath the surface of Christian faith in the Incarnation.

The issue of the eroticism of Jesus can no longer be swept under the carpet. It is a test of what we mean by the humanity of Jesus.

The real question, John Shea has remarked to me, is not about the sexuality of Jesus but about our own sexuality. We ask the question about Jesus so that we might understand better our own sexual nature. The Scripture tells us nothing about the sexual experience of Jesus, so we have to fall back on theological analysis. In the process we work with our own conception of the nature of human nature and especially of sexual human nature. We either project onto Jesus our own sexual problems and hang-ups or learn from him what mature human sexuality is about.

First of all, one must insist that the "last temptation" is no temptation at all.

The fundamentalists (Catholic and Protestant) who were offended by the scenes in Scorsese's film where Jesus experiences uncertainty and fear (temptations) and the attraction of a woman (an appeal against the choice he had made) were in fact, for all their righteousness, victims of Docetism—the teaching that Jesus was not really human at all but only appeared to be human.

Those who would exclude the poignancy and joy of erotic desire from the life of Jesus wish to deny him full humanity to protect him from what they take to be evil. They are possessed by the curious notion (as Bruce Marshal once put it) that God made an artistic and ethical mistake in ordering the dynamics of the procreation and nurturing of human young. That is yet another heresy: Manichaeism. Curiously enough, the opponents of Martin Scorsese shared this heresy with Nikos Kazantzakis, who wrote the novel on which the film was based.

In the humid world of Nikos Kazantzakis where spirit constantly wrestles with flesh, marriage may well be the ultimate threat to the flaming spark of spirit seeking self-transcendence. But in the world of the Christian heritage marriage is not a temptation but a sacrament: human passion in a hint and a revelation of God's passion for us.

Might Jesus have imagined lovemaking, and parenthood with a woman? The Christian must say that of course he might, but that such a fantasy would be neither sin nor, strictly speaking, a temptation.

As with Zorba and Saint Francis, Kazantzakis used Christ as an inkblot onto which he projected his own philosophy and his religious search. By his own admission, his book is not a biography but a "confession of every man who struggles." Kazantzakis's philosophy was a mix of Henri Bergson's "elan vital" and Friedrich Nietzsche's "overman" ("superman") with a strong dash of Sigmund Freud thrown in for good measure.

Zorba, Saint Francis, Jesus—like Kazantzakis himself—were all depicted as struggling to break away from the bonds of flesh and become spirit. Jesus is Zorba the Christ.

Spirit must shed flesh; soul must rid itself of body; the human elan must strive to transcend its own physical constraints and to seek to "flame out" in a glorious burst of transcendence. "The spirit . . . is a carnivorous bird which is incessantly hungry; it eats flesh and, by assimilating it, makes it disappear."

This theme pervaded the novel and the film.

Domesticity—wife, children, hearth and home—is the implacable foe of such transcendence precisely because it mires spirit in the cares and pleasures of the material world. It is the last temptation in the sense of being the ultimate enemy.

If God is enfleshed, somehow, in Jesus, then flesh is not evil and marriage is not a temptation and Kazantzakis misunderstood Jesus completely. The

Christian believes that the real "original sin" is not a conflict between flesh and spirit understood as a conflict between body and soul, but between the generous, self-giving propensities of the human personality and the fearful, self-protecting dimensions of the human character. Jesus taught us not how to overcome the flesh but rather how to give ourselves to and for others.

There are two theories about how Jesus became conscious of his special mission in the world, both of them compatible with the Scriptures. His "messianic consciousness" according to one theory was with him from the very beginning. He knew who he was and what was his destiny from the moment of his birth or from the moment of his first conscious thought or from the moment of his conception. He lived his life as an unswerving walk down the path to Golgotha. This is, I think, the more traditional theory and is certainly what was taught in Catholic schools and seminaries before the Second Vatican Council. We used to see pictures in our religion books of the young boy Jesus playing with a cross.

Ugh.

The second theory, more commonly propounded by theologians today, argues for the slow dawning of "messianic consciousness." Jesus always knew that he was special, but the substance and the direction of his unique relationship to God evolved as he matured. Such a view is more compatible with a fully human maturation process and with the words of Scripture saying he grew in wisdom and age and grace before God and man.

Did he mature sexually then?

He was human, wasn't he?

The Epistle to the Hebrews (chapter 5) is clear and forthright about the humanity of Jesus: Jesus is a human like us in all things, sin alone excepted. There are only two possible reasons why Jesus would be devoid of male hormones and hence immune to the erotic appeal of women: either he was not human or the chemistry between men and women is sinful. But Jesus is human and the desire that leaps between man and woman is not evil. Therefore, Jesus was as capable as any human male of experiencing the desirability of women and doubtless often did.

In his maturation Jesus experienced the dawning of sexual consciousness, with all its mystery and delight, just as much as any other young man would, sin alone excepted.

What was that experience like?

We do not know and we cannot imagine. But we do know the result. His relationships with women, as depicted in the Bible, were so special, so different from those of the ordinary men of his time and of other religious leaders (even to this day) that Temple University theologian Leonard

Swidler says in his book about women in the Bible that the behavior of Jesus toward women by itself was enough to suggest Incarnation. Jesus related to women as human equals and treated them with respect and affection, with gentleness and wit, with honesty and concern for their dignity. Jesus genuinely liked women and they liked him. His erotic reactions to them would differ from those of other men only in that there would be no hint of exploitation, manipulation, or violation. He was a model of sexual maturity in his relationships with women.

There is not a single incident in the Gospels where Jesus puts down a woman or treats a woman with contempt or speaks slightingly of a woman or blames a woman or speaks harshly to a woman. Nor is there a single episode in which one can say Jesus treated a woman as anything less than a full equal. This is behavior that would stand out even in our own time, to say nothing of a time when women were usually no better than slaves.

Compare Jesus with the fourteenth-century friars who said that women were traps designed by the devil or swamps to drag down men's souls or painted tombs filled with rottenness. Compare him with a seminary rector of our own time who said that every woman was a womb waiting to be fecundated. Compare him with our seminary spiritual director who warned us to stay away from the ballet during vacations for fear that the bodies of the ballerinas would cause us dirty thoughts.

The same director assured us that Jesus was human but felt no "sexual movements." By which I presume he meant that Jesus could turn off his hormone system by a simple act of the will.

Humans like us in all things save sin? And, it would seem, hormones.

Could Jesus, so effective in dealing with women, also desire them? Desire, for example, Mary, the adolescent sister of Lazarus who sat by his feet and looked up at him in mute adoration?

Let us speculate a little about the nature of Jesus' relationship with Mary and Martha and Lazarus. The three are obviously young, middle teens in all probability, because they are not married. They also seem to be orphans because there is no hint of parents. That Martha and Mary are entertaining Jesus indicates that they are responsible for the house and the meals. Lazarus, their brother, is perhaps technically the head of the family but probably still too young (thirteen or fourteen?) to be able to arbitrate the squabbles between his sisters.

Jesus must stand in a foster father/big brother relationship with them. He loves them; they love him. He enjoys being with them; they delight in having him as a guest.

And Mary has a crush on him. Like many other adolescent women, she adores an older man, thinks doubtless that she has fallen in love with him, and acts, from her sister's view, like a bit of a "geek" when Jesus is in the house.

Is this a sexual longing in Mary, the sister of Lazarus? It is as much sexual as is any such adolescent crush. Later commentators would suggest that she was really adoring a man who she thought was the Son of God. But that is reading into the Scripture later theological concerns. All Scripture tells us is that she loved Jesus.

Moreover, Jesus' gentle rebuke to Martha must mean that he accepted that love and was pleased by it.

(We are told this, by the way, in passing. The Evangelist is concerned with the contrast between the two women's behavior and is not interested in drawing conclusions about the deeper meaning of the triad.)

What happens to an adult male when he is the object of such adoration from an attractive young woman?

He is flattered by it, embarrassed a little perhaps, but also delighted by her unspoiled and defenseless affection. How else can you possibly react?

Chase her away? Tell her to stop adoring you? Warn her of the danger of such naive worship? Decide never to come back to the house because she was an "occasion of sin"?

That's what seminary spiritual directors of forty years ago would have said. It is not, however, what Jesus did. No way.

Rather, he encouraged her affection and stayed at her house during the week in Jerusalem just before he died.

In the light of her simple and uncomplicated love he probably felt peace and serenity after the bitter debates and the difficult journeys of his ordinary life. The house in Bethany was an island of tranquillity in his existence.

Surely he realized that her love was shallow, like that of every girl child overnight turned woman. But he did not patronize her or make fun of her or flee from her. Obviously, he did not take advantage of her innocence. He accepted her love for what it was and returned that love in the way a mature man respectfully and firmly responds to adolescent worship.

Might Jesus have imagined kissing and caressing her, taking off her clothes and fondling her breasts, and finally taking her with firm and gentle love to his bed? If such feelings are sinful, then obviously Jesus did not have them.

But are feelings of desire sinful? Or do they become sinful only when they degrade the person desired in deed or in fantasy? Do you degrade a woman merely by being possessed by tender and delicious images of her?

The proper question is, rather, how Jesus could have desired her if he had a male human nature.

If Jesus did not experience the vivid and powerful appeal of youthful beauty, then the claim of the Epistle to the Hebrews that he was acquainted with all things human (except sin) would be untrue.

Male human nature has been designed to desire women. While desire may lead to evil deeds, it is not evil in itself. The human species is designed by God (working through the evolutionary process) so that the sexes desire one another with imperious delight. That desire becomes lust only when it degrades, physically or mentally, the one desired, when it turns her (him) into an object to be used, exploited, or degraded without respect and reverence for his (her) dignity and worth as a person. Lust is debasing the desired person, either in reality or fantasy, into a thing.

The longing Jesus might have felt for that lovely young woman would have been marked by affection, reverence, respectful amusement, tenderness, delicate concern for her innocent naïveté, and above all regard for the different missions in their lives. When the desire of male human nature are refined by such mature constraints, however, they do not make a woman any less appealing.

Did Jesus love this admirable young woman? Who can deny that? Was there a strong erotic component in his love? If he was human, how could there not be? Did he think of her often when he was not in Bethany? Was he enchanted when he saw her smile and heard her laugh after a long trip through the mountains to Bethany? Might the thought that his death, for all humankind indeed, was especially for her have sustained him through his agony?

If you want to deny those possibilities, you must be prepared to argue that they are sinful or that Jesus wasn't human.

Might he have been in love with Mary, the sister of Lazarus?

If being in love is an emotion in which all restraint and all concern about the rest of life are brushed aside, then Jesus would not have fallen in love. If, on the other hand, it is a reaction of bliss—controlled and focused bliss—when you are with someone you love or away from that person but thinking of her/him, then who is prepared to say that such a response is evil? Is it not one of the great joys of being human?

If desire is sin, then every man in Chicago who walks down Michigan Avenue on a summer day is fated by his hormones to sin many times even before he gets to Oak Street Beach. But there is no fate at all that constrains him to degrade even in his head any of the lovely sights he encounters.

Ironically, Pope John Paul got into trouble with the press of the world when, in the context of a long discussion of the difference between desire and lust, he said that it was wrong for husbands to lust after their wives, to degrade their wives into things to be used, either in their imagination or in their lovemaking: a stand with which feminists would agree enthusiastically if they had read it context.

Jesus desired women, as every man with human nature desires women, but he never lusted after them. They were always delightful persons, never dehumanized objects to be used. In our own lives we (men and women both) wander back and forth across the dividing line, but there is nonetheless a basic orientation in our attitudes toward each other, either lust or desire.

You can desire a woman (your spouse or even another woman) for decades without ever becoming fundamentally lustful, either in thought or in deed.

The Son of God desire a woman? God himself is frequently depicted in the Bible as desiring every woman and every man, too, with a passion that makes the sexual desire seem weak.

If we read through Saint Luke's Gospel and permit ourselves to consider the relationships between Jesus and women in that Gospel (or consider the story of the woman by Jacob's well in Saint John's Gospel), is his tenderness and poise with them, his respect and affection, more impressive because we believe that he felt no desire for them? Or is it more impressive because we see how sexual desire has been focused into mature esteem and sophisticated enjoyment?

Women must have been overwhelmed by Jesus' charm. Why not? What other reaction to him was possible? There was no erotic component to their reaction to him? Surely no one can believe that. He was not the kind of man who was erotically attractive? Give me a break!

Might Jesus have married the sister of Lazarus, as Kazantzakis depicts him doing after the death of Magdalen—Mary and her sister Martha, too, in a bigamy that was tolerated by Mosaic law?

One must reply that Jesus did not marry her or anyone else, but that does not mean he could not have done so.

Jesus chose to be celibate—an unusual choice for a Jew of his time—presumably to facilitate his mission. But that was a free choice and not the result of an extrinsic rule imposed by someone else as a condition for the mission—like the celibacy rule for Roman Catholic clergy today. Could he have chosen otherwise and still carried on his mission?*

---

*Can we be sure that Jesus was not in fact married? A few commentators argue that he probably was married, basing their argument on the virtually universal obligation among Jews of his time to marry and bring forth children. The vast majority of commentators, however, reply that we hear nothing in the

God did not say to Jesus, "You can be my special son, but you have to promise not to marry."

The Catholic theologians with whom I've consulted say that Jesus could have freely chosen marriage and family and still carried out his mission. The notion of Jesus procreating children will only seem repulsive to those who find procreation evil.

As a theologian said to me, the Son of God was meant to confront all the aspects of being human. To remove from his life the possibility of marriage and fatherhood would be to exclude that dimension of human experience. Such an exclusion would falsify the fifth chapter of the Epistle to the Hebrews in which it is said that Jesus experienced all that we experience, sin alone excepted.

Jesus was an extraordinary man—charming, elusive, fascinating, mysterious, tender, powerful, magnetic, compassionate, sophisticated, and incredibly patient. Moreover, he was a mesmerizing storyteller. He overwhelmed men and women alike with the strength and depth and beauty and mystery of his character. Mary, the sister of Lazarus, had it right: how could you help loving a man like him?

Scripture about a wife or children and we surely would if such existed—especially since the ideal of celibacy had yet to emerge by the time the Gospels weer being written. Moreover, Jesus was different from other Jews of his time, strikingly different. What would have been unacceptable in others, on the face of the evidence was not deemed unacceptable in him. John the Baptist was not married either, and no one thought that strange.

What about the possibility that Jesus had married as an adolescent, as almost all young men of his time did, and that his wife and children had died—a not uncommon event in that time of short life expectancies? Might that have been a turning point in the development of his "messianic conscious-ness," his sense of mission? Obviously we know nothing about whether that happened or not. A Catholic theologian answered my question with a shrug of his shoulders and the comment, "So what if it did happen? How would that have detracted from what he said and what he did? Isn't it a totally irrelevant issue?"

I guess it is. Unless you happen to believe that marriage defiles a person.

I hasten to add that some popular books claiming to be accounts of a secret organization made up of Jesus' descendants have no basis in scholarly research but are absurd nonsense and should be treated as such.

27

NEUSNER

Jesus

And behold, one came up to him saying, "Teacher, what good deed must I do to have eternal life?" And he said to him, "Why do you ask me about what is good? One there is who is good. If you would enter life, keep the commandments." He said to him, "Which?" And Jesus said, "You shall not kill, you shall not commit adultery, you shall not steal, you shall not bear false witness. Honor your father and your mother, and you shall love your neighbor as yourself." The young man said to him, "All these I have observed, what do I still lack?" Jesus said to him, "If you would be perfect, go, sell all you possess and give to the poor, and you will have treasure in heaven; and come, follow me." When the young man heard this, he went away sorrowful, for he had great possessions.

Avot 2:1: Rabbi [Judah, the patriarch] says, "What is the straight path which a person should choose for himself? Whatever is an ornament to the one who follows it, and an ornament in the view of others. Be meticulous in a small religious duty as in a large one, for you do not know what sort of reward is coming for any of the various religious duties. And reckon with the loss [required] in carrying out religious duty against the reward for doing it; and the reward for committing a transgression against the loss for doing it. And keep your eye on three things, so you will not come into the clutches of transgression. Know what is above you. An eye which sees, and an ear which hears, and all your actions are written down in a book."

Avot 2:8 A. Rabban Yohanan b. Zakkai received [it] from Hillel and Shammai.

B. He would say, "If you have learned much Torah, do not puff yourself up on that account, for it was for that purpose that you were created."

Avot 2:9 A. He said to [his disciples], "Go and see what is the straight path to which someone should stick."

B. R. Eleizer says, "A generous spirit."

C. R. Joshua says, "A good friend."

D. R. Yose says, "A good neighbor."

E. R. Simeon says, "Foresight."

F. R. Eleazar says, "Good will."

G. He said to them, "I prefer the opinion of R. Eleazar b. Arakh, because in what he says is included everything you say."

H. He said to them, "Go out and see what is the bad road, which someone should avoid."

I. R. Eleizer says, "Envy."

J. R. Joshua says, "A bad friend."

K. R. Yose says, "A bad neighbor."

L. R. Simeon says, "Defaulting on a loan—."

M. R. Eleazar says, "Bad will."

N. He said to them, "I prefer the opinion of R. Eleazar b. Arakh, because in what he says is included everything you say."

Christians want to know only one thing about Judaism and one thing about the Jews. What does Judaism think about Christ? And why don't the Jews believe in Christ? In asking these questions, they frame a fundamental issue, one that draws us together in the pages of this book. It is, What is Judaism to Christianity? And what is Christianity to Judaism? Here we see how the encounter with Jesus bears the weight of that question, and when we meet Paul we find yet another way in which the question weighs down dialogue. The reason Christianity cares what Judaism thinks of Jesus is obvious. Jesus lived and died as a Jew, and so did all his immediate disciples. The initial foundations of the church were laid in synagogues throughout the Roman empire. So Christianity begins in the heart of Judaism. But then most Jews did not adopt the faith of a very few in their midst, and, by definition, that simple fact has endured through the ages. So Christians ask, "Why not?"

But the question produces answers that carry us far beyond the limits of the initial inquiry. For the answer is not, "Why not? Well, because . . ." That is to say, it is rare for the Judaic answer to speak of Jesus, as in, "Why do you reject Jesus?" "Because he ate with sinners and tax collectors." I do not think that conversation ever took place. Since the Jews live as a tiny minority in the Christian world, their answers tend to be circumspect, courteous, and politic. Thus Jesus comes out (depending on the Jewish respondent) as "a great man," "a great prophet," "a Reform rabbi," "a stupendous ethical figure," and on and on—but it is always Jesus, never Christ. And that is the nub of the matter. Then the Christian side to the dialogue has gotten a polite evasion: he's okay, but deal us out of the church that people made up in his name.

But that is precisely the problem confronting the church. It worships not Jesus the man but Christ the Son of God. And Christ God Incarnate is Son of God in a way in which no other human being has been or can be Son (or daughter) of God. Jesus, a great man, is not unique, only special (and anyone who has studied the Gospels recognizes that simple fact). But if Jesus is not Christ, unique as God-man, then Christianity in all of its historical forms celebrates a quite fine fellow but is not a religion that brings God to this world. Indeed, it is a fancy form of humanism. Now—Heaven forfend!—that is not what Jews mean to say. But by being other than

Christians that is precisely what they do say, by their very presence in this world. And, as a matter of fact, that is all they can say. The alternative is to say, "You're right, for lo, these two thousand years we've been wrong. Lead me to the baptismal font." The being of the one negates the being of the other.

And after the dialogue, that fact presents in a fresh and painful way the problem that has weighed down Christian faith from the beginnings on the first Easter: what are we to Judaism, and what is Judaism to us? The stakes for religious confidence then prove considerable. Acknowledging the Scriptures of Judaism (our written Torah) as the Old Testament, recognizing the profoundly Jewish world in which Rabbi Jesus was born, taught, lived, died, was buried, and (after all) also was raised from the dead, the pain of rejection then renews itself day by day in rejection even now: the prophet still is without honor in his own village, except by the standards of the village: man, not God.

Three positions outline the possibilities. One position is that Christianity comes out of Judaism and owes much to Judaism. But it is better than the Judaism from which it emerged. So Christianity forms a continuum with its Israelite past. The second is that Christianity has no roots in Judaism whatsoever. Christianity not only began at Easter, but also constituted an essentially new thing, without roots of any kind in the Judaic past. The third is that Christianity is (a) Judaism.

The first position is popular these days. Many now argue that Christianity improved upon Judaism. Jesus was a reforming rabbi. The second view denies Christians any links with the Hebrew Scriptures, with ancient Israel, with Abraham, Sinai, prophecy. Christianity begins in the first century, deriving no nourishment from the roots deep within the life of ancient Israel and its Scriptures (in my language, the Torah). In order to argue that Christianity is new and unprecedented, these folk maintain that there is a radical discontinuity between Christianity and Judaism. The most extreme statement of that position would define a Bible consisting of only the New Testament, but not the Old.

The third position, predominant until the recent past, is that Christianity took over and rewrote the whole of the past of Judaism, therefore making its own what others—we Jews—claim for ourselves and setting itself out as a Judaism and the only right and true one: now Christianity. Abraham believed before he knew the full form of the faith; Sinai points to Christ; the prophets prophesized his coming; the history of humanity forms a continuum, from Adam at the start to the last Adam, who is Christ.

Each of these positions defines the relationship between Christianity and

Judaism in its own way. It follows that all of them yield for the pattern of the social relationships of the great majority, and the tiny minority marks each particular one to itself. A Christianity that improves upon, while continuing, Judaism will deem Judaism an inferior religion, a fossil, desiccated, lacking all reason for being. Jews continuing in their faith beyond the advent of Christ then are incorrigible and stubborn, ignorant and triumphant in their unbelief. This Christianity takes the form of a triumphant daughter, lording it over a misguided mother. A Christianity that builds upon fallow ground, not on the tilled earth of Israel, the Jewish people, bears no special bonds to Judaism, which worships yet another false god. That Christianity is wholly estranged from Judaism but, by reason of the Gospels' narratives, violently hostile to it. That Christianity in defining its relationship with Judaism then denies a special tie of a godly nature but works out a distinctive exchange of a demonic character. A Christianity that discovers in the entire heritage of Israel its heritage, that reads itself into all that happened from Adam to today, recognizes—and can disagree with—another reading of that same past. Whether sister and brother, whether cousins, first or second or third, that Christianity understands itself as part of the family and, as a matter of fact, the part that bears the blessing promised to the line of Abraham.

Why the issue matters is not difficult to explain. If Christianity emerges out of Judaism, then there are common commitments and goals. But then Christianity explains itself by setting forth the ways in which it has improved upon its past in Judaism, and that leads to the view that Christianity is superior and alive, Judaism is inferior and deceased. And there is a constant need to denigrate and deny to Judaism all salvific promise. If Christianity bears no relationship to a Jewish past, then Christians bear no ties to Jews today. But, of course, Christianity emerges from a hostile Judaism. Lacking any ties, that Christianity exacts from generation to generation its vengeance for long ago. And how are we supposed to work together in a shared world? But a Christianity that is neither reforming Judaism nor a religion without a past faces Israel, the Jewish people, with confidence but also with respect. Not an utterly fresh and unprecedented religion, but a Judaism, like other Judaisms, Christianity affirms itself. For it has taken over and rewrittten the whole of the heritage—the Torah—of ancient Israel.

That is the position that I take. But it competes with the two other views. The position that Christianity has no Jewish roots comes to expression among anti-Semites who are Christians and who wish to deny all things Jewish, including (in the time of the Nazis) the Jewish origins of Jesus. In a more popular form, the un-Jewish Christianity comes to expression when represented from the Christian pulpit in the contrast between Judaism of the vengeful God and Christianity of the merciful God, in the obliteration in Christian discourse of the Old Testament origins of the ethical and moral teachings of Jesus, and in a variety of parallel ways.

It is these days more a habit of mind and of speech than of doctrine. The position that sees Christianity as essentially a continuation of Judaism but an improvement on Judaism is commonplace and popular. It is taken to be a favor to Judaism to acknowledge the Jewishness of Jesus; people are supposed to be glad to be reassured that "we are all Semites" and that the shared beginnings, in ancient Israel, assure the minority faith a position of honor and respect. And yet—and yet, quite how much honor derives from serving as Brand X to the new, improved product? And how much respect do you get knowing that your younger sister did things right when you did them wrong: "when we were gone astray . . ."?

So let's go back and see whether Jesus isn't really a rabbi but a nicer, smarter, better rabbi than any other rabbi or really not a rabbi at all. That is a small way of asking a large question. For the issue works itself out in what we have to say about Jesus and Judaism, and that is as it should be. For Christ is Christianity, and Christianity has made of him whatever it has required; that was and is his service to the church founded in his name. Through the ages what people had to say about Jesus turns out to bear their message to their own time and place.

So what about Jesus as a reforming rabbi? Well, Jesus is called "Rabbi," a title of respect meaning "my lord." It is not a title particular to Judaism but used to honor sages in general. But since *rabbi* stands for *sage*, it is common to allege that Jesus was a rabbi, thus teaching Judaism. I think that statement is true, if we just add "a kind of": Jesus was a kind of rabbi, teaching a kind of Judaism. But he certainly was very different from other kinds of rabbis, teaching another kind of Judaism. So we cannot identify Jesus as a rabbi like rabbis in general. Everything in the Gospels as I understand them argues precisely the opposite. If he was a rabbi, he was unique among rabbis.

Take, for example, the very specific case of whether Jesus with his disciples is comparable to a rabbi with his sages known to us from the writings of sages. I'll show that Jesus certainly is like a rabbi, but he is also not like any rabbi known to us in his time or for a long time afterward. What does Jesus have in common with Rabbi Judah the Patriarch (ca. 140–210) or with Yohanan ben Zakkai (ca. 1–80)? A lot—and nothing.

These typical rabbis gathered disciples and taught them Torah. So, too, did Jesus. So one absolutely fundamental trait of a rabbi is that he was a teaching sage, not a teacher only, but a teacher of wisdom, of a doctrine.

These typical sages, moreover, taught not this and that, but fundamental principles that affect all of one's conduct everywhere. Judah asks, "What is the straight path which a person should choose?" Yohanan asks, "What is the straight path, to which someone should stick?" The question is the same, and I don't see it as much different from, "Rabbi, what good deed must I do to have eternal life?"

And what about the answers? Rabbi Jesus answers with the most practical of the Ten Commandments as well as Leviticus 19:18: "You will love your neighbor as yourself." The Talmud of Babylonia many centuries later alleges that Hillel, a rabbi of about the same time as Jesus, and Aqiba, a rabbi at the end of the first century, did too. Hillel said, "What is hateful to yourself, do not do to your neighbor. All the rest is commentary. Now go, learn." Hillel's was a message of surpassing love. So in Pirqe Avot Hillel says, "Be disciples of Aaron, loving peace and pursuing peace, loving people and drawing them near to the Torah." So too, "If I am not for myself, who is for me? And when I am for myself, what am I? And if not now, when?"

To Aqiba are assigned sayings of God's surpassing love:

Precious is the human being, who was created in the image [of God]. It was an act of still greater love that it was made known to him that he was created in the image [of God], as it is said, "For in the image of God he made man" (Gen. 9:6). So, too, he is given the following: "Everything is foreseen, and free choice is given. In goodness the world is judged. And all is in accord with the abundance of deed[s]."

If contemporaries of Jesus had seen him with his disciples, would they have thought him unusual? Not very likely. We see Yohanan ben Zakkai with his, asking them to bring to him answers to life-forming questions. Would Jesus have found alien the replies concerning a generous spirit, friendship, a good neighbor, foresight, and especially goodwill? No, I think any student of the Gospels will agree that Jesus could have approved all of these answers. And scholarship for a century has shown the rich and extensive points in common between Jesus and other rabbis of his age. For one obvious example, to Jesus is given this saying: "Therefore do not be anxious about tomorrow, for tomorrow will be anxious for itself. Let the day's own trouble be sufficient for the day." And to Eliezer ben Hyrcanus is assigned the same saying. That the Golden Rule was a commonplace among sages is well known; sages from the land of Israel to China recognized the same self-evident truth. But when we move from ethics to deeper matters of human existence, would Jesus have agreed (to take one example) with the conception that in goodwill is encompassed all virtue, and in ill will all vice?

No, I think not. Why not? Because Jesus had a different message, one so different that people in his time had considerable difficulty grasping it. The commandments are not enough? Sages understood that. They condemned hypocrisy and ostentatious piety. "Go, sell all you possess and give it to the poor and you will have treasure in heaven"? For parallels to that statement I search the pages of the oral Torah in vain. And it is only the beginning of the matter.

Let's take Jesus' more profound message to his disciples, represented by the following:

> "If the world hates you, you know that it has hated me before it hated you. If you were of the world, the world would love its own; but because you are not of the world, but I chose you out of this world, therefore the world hates you. Remember the word that I said to you, 'A servant is not greater than his master.' If they persecuted me, they will persecute you; if they kept my word, they will keep yours also. . . .
>
> "And if any one will not receive you or listen to your words, shake off the dust from your feet as you leave that house or town.
>
> "So have no fear of them; for nothing is covered that will not be revealed, or hidden that will not be known. What I tell you in the dark utter in the light, and what you hear whispered proclaim upon the housetops."

And then again, take Jesus' claim, running through all four Gospels, of standing in a special and unique relationship with God, so that his disciples related to God through him in that same way:

> "He who receives you receives me, and he who receives me receives him who sent me."

That is a very remarkable statement. What makes it different from anything we can find assigned to a rabbi in the writings of the oral Torah is that Torah does not figure. Rabbis know that in studying the Torah they hear God's word and learn God's will. They know that when three study the Torah together—or even two, even one—God is present in the form of the Shechinah, the presence. She is with the master and disciples. But that other she, the Torah, is the medium and the mediator between God and humanity. The "me" of "he who receives me" for the Torah can be, and always is, only one thing: the Torah itself.

So these sayings assigned to Jesus by the church, the attitudes expressed in them, which characterize the accounts of all four Evangelists, shed a very different light on matters. They give us a rabbi who is telling his disciples things to which in all of the oral Torah we find no counterpart. For there is more than a message. Here we find a mission. Those who receive Jesus' disciples receive him and therefore the One who sent him. And that is a claim that sages in the oral Torah make for everyone who studies Torah, but not for one particular master—never. So here, in the simplest and best-known passages of the Gospels, we find that same claim of absolute uniqueness that would be made after Easter as well.

Jesus is like a rabbi, but he simply is not a rabbi. For he said and did things that other rabbis did not say and do, indeed, could not have said and done. For the fundamental and nonnegotiable claim of Christianity rests on the uniqueness of Jesus Christ. And, as a matter of fact, viewed in a this-worldy way by appeal to the sources of the time, that claim, challenged time and again, is always validated: like but not alike. And that means not alike. He invariably emerges as something else again. In the context of the Judaism we know in the union of the written and the oral Torahs, Jesus is simply incomprehensible. In that setting he is wholly other. That must mean, then, the same for Christianity. It is simply different from the Judaism portrayed by its own writings and by the other writings of the age that have formed Judaism as we know it, that is to say the oral Torah. So, as a matter of fact, Christianity is not talking about a rabbi at all and the fact that Jesus fits well into the life of the Torah of his day bears little consequence for Christianity.

And that brings us back to our own day: why do people today debate whether long ago Jesus was really just another rabbi, was a reforming rabbi, or was no rabbi at all? The issue concerns the relationship between Christianity and Judaism, and what makes the issue not chronic but acute is the catastrophe of the Judeocide in Europe that people call the Holocaust. From the Nazi period onward, much of Christianity, in order to affirm its love of God and hatred of the anti-Christ, Hitler, and his Nazis, has formulated its relationship with Judaism in language and symbols meant to identify with the Jewish people, God's first love. To signal his opposition to anti-Semitism, Pope Pius XI in 1937 said, "Spiritually, we are all Semites," and in the aftermath of the Holocaust successive popes have claimed for Roman Catholic Christianity a rightful share in the spiritual patrimony of Abraham. The epoch-making position of Vatican II marked only a stage forward in the process of conciliation and reconciliation that has marked the Roman Catholic framing of its relationship with both the Jewish people and Judaism. And the important Protestant communions have accomplished no less.

But there are costs. In their eagerness to redefine their relationship with Judaism, Christians have set aside the inherited claim that Christianity was autonomous, unique, a revision of not only the future but also the entire past of humanity and especially of Israel. Instead, Jesus the Jew, Jesus the rabbi, came to the fore, and Jesus the Savior, without precedent and without parallel, in the dialogue spoke with a hushed voice, if at all. But when did Christianity suffice with the claim that it was part of ancient Israel or that it had not adopted and remade but merely adapted for its own use the Torah of ancient Israel? The answer is, from the beginnings rarely and from the third century never, until our own times.

The earliest Christians were not Gentiles who became Jews; they were Jews who thought that what we call Christianity was Judaism. More to the point, while critical of much that he saw, the Jesus of the Gospels to whom Christianity appealed did not merely reform and improve. Nor did Christianity emerge so as to constitute a reform movement within Israel. It was not a religious sect that came along to right wrongs, correct errors, end old abuses, and otherwise improve upon the givens of the ancient faith. Whatever the standing of the old Israel, the new Israel was seen to be truly Israel, a point to which we will return when we talk about Paul.

And that meant Christianity would not be represented as merely a reform movement, playing the role, in the drama of the history of Christianity, of the Protestant Reformation to Judaism's Roman Catholic church. Christianity was born on the first Easter, with the resurrection of Jesus Christ, as the church saw matters. And that event was unique, definitive, and universally significant for all humanity.

But in representing Christianity as a reform movement within an antecedent and ongoing Judaism, this received self-understanding of the church was set aside. And, I am inclined to think, our century has witnessed a fundamental theological error. It was an error committed with good intention and in goodwill. But it has been a considerable mistake. Judaism did not in the end benefit, and Christianity was injured by the conception of Jesus as a reforming rabbi, and of Christianity as an improvement on Judaism in continuity with Judaism. The theological error is to represent Christianity as a natural, this-worldly reform, a continuation of Judaism in the terms of Judaism. The New Testament would then be read in light of the Old, rather than the Old in light of the New.

That explains much that has happened in the study of the Gospels in the past century. We now are supposed to go to the Judaic writings of the age or of the age thereafter to discover the context in which Christianity was born. In search of facts and explanations of details, that is the right way to do things. In search of answers to questions of meaning and truth, it is monumentally irrelevant. For Christianity then is understood to be represented by the Bible or the New Testament in particular: a problem of reading writing, not of sifting through the heritage of tradition that the church conveyed. The theological error of seeing Christianity as continuous and this-worldy, rather than as a divine intervention into history and as supernatural, affected not only the Christian understanding of Christianity. It also carried in its wake a theory of who is Israel, Israel after the flesh, that contradicted the position of the church before our time. For, curiously, the received tradition had better things to say about Israel after the flesh, that is to say us Jews, and about our religion than did the philo-Semitic approach meant to overcome the anti-Semitism that the Gospels and Christian preachings have fostered in the past.

The church, in the tradition of the apostle Paul in Romans, affirmed the salvation of Israel through the heritage of Abraham and Sarah. But now, that prior "Judaism" that had produced Christianity was given an autonomous standing, on the one side, and also assigned negative traits, on the other. What happened was that Christianity became necessary in merely this-worldy terms to reform Judaism and that reformed Judaism defined the theological verities for Christianity. It was a Christian theology of Judaism. But it set forth an "if-only" theology of Judaism.

By that I mean it was a theory of Judaism that held that if only Judaism were done rightly, it would have been (and would be) all right with God. So the faults of "the Jews" or of "Judaism" were contrasted with the virtues of Jesus and of Christianity. Judaism then required reformation: Judaism now is a relic. Judaism bore deep flaws, ethical flaws. The upshot was that the principal value of Jesus was not as Christ risen from the dead but as a teacher of ethics, as though the Sermon on the Mount contained much that would have surprised informed hearers on one's duty to the other or on the social responsibility of the society. What is surprising about the Sermon on the Mount is not the ethics but the manner of presenting the ethics, by one with an authority that did not rest on mere discipleship and that is precisely what the Evangelists said at the time and afterward. But now Christians, for their part, found themselves in a subordinate position in the salvific story of humanity, becoming not the true Israel by faith in Christ Jesus (as Paul would want us to maintain) but merely Israel by default—that is, by default of the old Israel.

And that observation draws us back to the point at which I began, namely, the affirmation of the church as "Semitic," the declaration, in the very teeth of Nazism, that "spiritually, we are all Semites," the insistence upon the Judaic heritage of the church and of Christianity. Given the tragedy of Christianity in the civilization of Christian Europe, perverted by Nazism and corrupted by communism, given the natural humanity that accorded to suffering Israel, Israel after the flesh, for the first time finding an honorable place within the faith, we must admire the intent. Everyone meant well and today means well. But the result is an un-Christian reading of the New Testament and, as a matter of fact, a misunderstanding, from the viewpoint of the history of religion, of the New Testament and the whole of the Bible as well.

If Christianity understands itself as autonomous, unique, then Christianity cannot be a mere reformation. And not only so, but remember this: we Jews maintain that the Torah of our rabbi Moses, encompassing both the written Torah and the oral Torah, bears no relationship whatsoever to any other revelation that God may have had in mind. We furthermore hold that what God wants of all humanity rests in the commandments to the children of Noah. So what kind of compliment is it to say we were so bad that Christianity came along to correct our errors? We are no relic; ours is not the unreformed sediment, nor are we the stubborn and incorrigible heirs of a mere denial. We bear the living faith, the Torah, of the one true God, creator of Heaven and earth, who gave us the Torah and who implanted within us eternal life: so is the faith of Israel, God's first love. But in the context of this tragic century we too have found reasons to affirm the picture of the first century as an age of reform, of Christianity as profoundly interrelated with Judaism.

What about the starting point, the context of the first century? Christianity claimed to reread the whole of the Israelite past and present, to be a variety of Judaism and, in fact, the only right Judaism. Judaism as we now know it does no less. For through the oral Torah Judaism rereads the whole of the Israelite past, and it forms in its own view the only right Judaism. And, speaking descriptively not theologically, of course both are right. For at the time there was no one normative, orthodox Judaism, and the dominant Judaism was not identical with what we today know as Orthodox Judaism. For as a matter of mere description, based on all of the writings Jews regarded as holy, we can identify one Judaism in the first centuries B.C. and A.D. only if we can treat as a single cogent statement everything all Jews wrote. That requires us to harmonize the Essene writings of the Dead Sea, Philo, the Mishnah, and the variety of scriptures collected in our century as the Apocrypha and Pseudepigraph of the Old Testament, not to mention the Gospels! That is to say, viewed as statements of Judaisms—that is, of religious systems—the writings attest to diverse Judaisms.

In that context, the formative writings of what we call Christianity form statements of systems, and whether we call them Judaisms or Christianities really does not affect how we shall read them—*in that context*. For reading a text in its context and as a statement of a larger matrix of meaning requires us to accord to each system, to each Judaism, that autonomy, that unique-ness, that absoluteness, that every Judaism has claimed for itself and, it goes without saying, that all Christianities likewise have demanded.

Each document is to be read in its own terms, as a statement *of* a Judaism or, at least, *to* and so in behalf of a Judaism. Each theological and legal fact is to be interpreted, to begin with, in relationship to the other theological and legal facts among which it found its original location. The inherited descriptions of the Judaism of the dual Torah (or merely "Judaism") have treated as uniform the whole corpus of writing called the oral Torah. They have further treated Christianity as unitary and harmonious; so it may have become, but in the first century I think both the founder of this place and his protagonists, Peter and Paul, would have found that description surprising.

When we define religion in the way that I have, we have a different task from the one of harmonization. It is the task of describing the Judaisms and the Christianities of the age, allowing each its proper context and according to each its correct autonomy. What of the relationship between (a) Judaism and (b) Christianity? There we have to appeal to Judaic writings where they bear facts that illuminate Christian ones, but we must not then reduce Christian writings to the status of dependence and accord to them a merely recapitulative task: reform, for instance.

The upshot is simple. Among the religious systems of the people, Israel, in the land of Israel, one of which we call Christianity, another of which we call Judaism—and both names are utterly post facto—we find distinct social groups, different people talking about different things to different people. Each had its way of life and world view and definition of itself as "Israel," and all appealed to the Torah. But everyone read the Torah in the way that his or her Judaism insisted it was to be read.

28

GREELEY
Saint Peter

The day after Pope John Paul II had been elected, rumors swept Rome that he had been married as a young man. His wife, the story said, had died during the war, before the young Karol Wojtyla entered the seminary.

The ineffable Cardinal John Krol of Philadelphia rose at the English-language press conference and denounced this rumor as a vile communist plot to discredit the pope. A Roman cynic, more cynical than whom no one is, whispered in my ear, "It would be nice for a change to have a pope that you could be confident was capable of marriage."

I must make a terrible confession: that night on an American TV network I raised the question whether it was also a communist plot to spread the rumor that Peter the Fisherman, in Catholic theory the remote predecessor of Pope John Paul II, had been married.

How, it was demanded of me, did I know that Peter was married?

Because the Bible says he had a mother-in-law. You can't have a mother-in-law without having a wife.

Cardinal Krol, I'm told, was not amused.

I didn't add that it was reasonable to assume that all the Apostles were married men because it was expected that everyone marry in the Judaism of that time. Jesus, who did not marry, was the rare exception.

It was suggested to us in the seminary that Peter's wife had already died. No one addressed themselves to the question of the wives of the others, because there was no proof that they had wives. But the impression was given that Jesus had imposed a demand for ecclesiastical celibacy on his followers a full millennium before the church made it a requirement.

The reaction to Peter's marriage both in the Vatican in October 1978 and in the seminary thirty years earlier is illustrative of the historical doublethink that Catholic teachers and preachers have tried to impose on their people—often in the name of not shocking them.

It is similar to that of a onetime liberal theologian who turned conservative and was made a cardinal (and died in a house of ill repute). After he made cardinal, he claimed in a marvelous anachronism that the College of Cardinals was of divine origin, actually instituted by Jesus himself.

He offered no proof. Apparently, he thought that if you were a cardinal you didn't need proof.

It's been a long way since Peter the Fisherman said to the lame man at the gate of the temple, "Gold and silver I do not have, but what I have I give. Arise and walk!"

A long way and much of it down.

We have to return to the Scriptures to reestablish contact with the experience of the risen Jesus that shaped the stories of salvation that the early Christians told, so we must go back to them and read of Peter the Fisherman if we are to understand what is essential in the church and what is historical accident and accretion.

The first pope was a loudmouthed braggart, a coward, and a traitor. Some popes have been better since then. But all of them have been just as subject to human faults and failings as Peter the Fisherman—even if the Vatican tries to treat each pope as without imperfection as long as he is still alive.

The church is composed of human beings. Whoever pretends that is not so lies.

Peter had, on the record, admirable qualities, too. He was warm, enthusiastic, openhearted, and guileless, the kind of man who is a wonderful companion but not a friend you can count on when the lights go out in the room.

He fit the pattern of the kind of person for whom Jesus seemed to have a special liking—the generous, extroverted, effervescent, impetuous type. Jesus was partial to people like Zaccheus (the short publican who climbed a tree in order to see him), James and John, the fiery "sons of thunder," Mary Magdalen, and his own mother. Jesus loved everyone, but he seems to have had extra-fond feelings for outgoing people who did not calculate their enthusiasms.

Peter certainly fit that model. His quick tongue and energy made him a natural leader. Unfortunately, beneath his enthusiasms he was a coward. Later, in the power of the Easter experience he would find the strength and courage to hold his cowardice in check. But he was still a leader inclined to vacillate and hesitate, as the debate over admission of the Gentiles into the new community demonstrated. Peter was a good man, one who would finally die for Jesus, but he was not the ideal leader and certainly not a man without faults.

Why did Jesus make Peter leader of his community?

Probably because he liked him and because among the circle of his followers Peter was the best to be had.

Did Jesus therefore intend to found a "church"?

The answer to the question is both "no" and "yes."

If one means did Jesus imagine the complete organizational structure of the Catholic church as it exists today with the Code of Canon Law, the Roman Curia, the College of Cardinals, the elaborate and forbidding Vatican protocol, the near worship given to the pope, the system of papal nuncios, the appointment of bishops by the Vatican, the answer is that of course those elements of the church were not built into the intention of Jesus. He did not intend to set up a completely new institution, distinct from the institution of Judaism, if only because Judaism as an institution did not yet exist either.

If one means did Jesus realize that his closest followers would form themselves into a community that would continue his work and did he give those followers instructions about how their community should act and did he promise them his assistance, then the answer is that yes, Jesus did form a church.

We must remember that in the disorganized pluralism of Second Temple Judaism the question of formal institutions did not arise. To expect Jesus to have organized such an institution is to impose on him a set of concerns that did not exist in his time and that his contemporaries would have been unable to understand.

There was a "trajectory"—that is, a legitimate path—between what Jesus did and the rough and ready organization that we see revealed in Paul's epistles and a trajectory between that church and subsequent developments. There is then a sense in which the church as we know it was founded by Jesus. There is continuity between his band of followers and the present ecclesiastical structure. But most of what constitutes that structure cannot claim to have been in the mind of Jesus when he gathered his friends and disciples around him.

To claim that almost everything in the Catholic church today (including, as did the disorderly-house cardinal, the College of Cardinals) is of divine origin is to fly in the face of history. The claim can be made only by someone who is culpably ignorant of history.

Take two examples: the election of the pope and the appointment of bishops.

For half a millennium at least the pope was nominated by the parish priests of Rome (a fiction that is still maintained by appointing the cardinals as technical pastors of Roman parishes). After they selected a candidate, they brought him out on the balcony of Saint Peter's. If the crowds cheered for him and thus confirmed his election, he was crowned. If the crowds booed, the cardinals returned to try again.

Similarly, all bishops were elected by the priests and people of their cities; any other form of election was considered by the early popes to be gravely sinful. *"Qui praesidet super omnes, ab omnibus eligatur,"* said Pope Saint Leo I. "He who presides over all should be chosen by all."

I agree with Saint Leo. The current form of papal appointment (begun to defend the people against the local rulers who had usurped selection rights from the people) virtually guarantees bishops who are mediocre, incompetent, time-serving functionaries.

There are very few customs in the Catholic church that could not be jettisoned tomorrow without changing its essential nature in the slightest. I am not suggesting that everything in the current Vatican system should be abandoned; I am merely saying that much could be abandoned without affecting the primary functions and responsibilities of the community of the followers of Jesus in the slightest. In fact, a drastic reform (not the game of musical chairs that currently passes as reform) would be an enormous benefit to the church. The Vatican organization is the classic example of the Iron Law of Oligarchy: it is a means become an end in itself. The end for which it exists is often barely noticed as the health and wealth of the institution becomes the principal concern and the preaching of the Gospel and the service of the members of the church are forgotten.

What did Jesus expect of the community that would continue his work? What did he expect of Saint Peter and his followers?

1. He expected his church to be human—that is, made up of human beings and hence subject to all the weaknesses and temptations that affect all human organizations.

Many young ex-Catholics say they will return to the church only when the church improves itself, when it rids itself of all the cowardice and oppression and ignorance and stupidity in which it is mired, when it becomes again the church Jesus founded. The answer to them is, Yes, the church must always be reformed, but when they find a perfect church they should join it at once—and realize that the instant they join it their perfect church will have become imperfect.

The mistake these young perfectionists make is to think that the church as Jesus founded it was made up of men and women who were somehow better than the current leadership and membership. A quick reading of the Christian Scriptures should change that view.

The other side of the coin is the pretense of church leaders that the leadership is not only perfect but sacred, that somehow the human limitations of the band of the followers of Jesus were transcended somewhere in the course of history and now we have a church that is governed by men who are near-saints and rarely make mistakes.

If I say that the average American bishop is an incompetent, dishonest, ambitious, timid fool, I am being rather less critical of this typical bishop than the Christian Scripture is of the bishop's remote predecessors. (I may also be giving a more favorable description of the current hierarchy than the facts warrant.) When was the rule passed that said that candor about church leaders was no longer permitted and that with the episcopal ring came the right to immunity from criticism?

I suppose it was passed when the church found a way to select a better quality of leadership than Jesus did!

Or deceived itself into thinking it had found better leaders.

Some of the third-rate theologians who work for the Roman Curia are now arguing that the rules about the rights and freedoms of individual members that apply to other organizations do not apply to the church because Jesus founded the church. Since it is of "divine origin," the church is not held to respect the ordinary "laws" of institutional structure.

One of those "laws" is called in Catholic social theory the Principle of Subsidiarity. It is the pragmatic rule that nothing should be done by a higher and larger organization that can be done just as well by a lower and smaller one. Pope John said that principle applies to the church as well as to all other organizations made up of human beings. The curial theological hacks reject that idea and say that because of its "divine origin" the church is not held by the Principle of Subsidiarity, which, however, continues to apply to all other human organizations.

Such a claim is utter nonsense. If Peter had been an archangel instead of a human being, it might be arguable that Jesus intended to exempt the community of his followers from the ordinary safeguards of any human community. The curial theologians are claiming that while Jesus was fully human and subject to all the limitations to which human nature is subject, the church he founded is more than human and immune from the limitations that affect all human organizations.

The Principle of Subsidiarity is intended to prevent the misuse of centralized power, which has isolated itself from problems among the ordinary members and smaller communities within the organization. The curial theologians contend, in effect, that the church doesn't need this safeguard because the central authority is not subject to such a failing.

Only a total disregard for the facts of history can make possible such impudent folly.

The church is at least as human as Peter the Fisherman, which is to say very human indeed, totally human, its founder's virtue and commitment to it alone excepted. The inconsistency between origin and behavior and the hypocrisy that results are perhaps most noticeable in the Catholic church, which makes such lofty claims for itself and is so patently and pathetically human in its ordinary behavior. But none of the Christian churches are immune from inconsistency and hypocrisy. Indeed, some of the other leaders, admitting that they are sinners (something a Catholic bishop would be most reluctant to do unless he claimed the admission as an act of virtue), are even worse in their simpering phoniness. If I select my own church for comment, the reasons are ecumenical. We should each criticize our own before we criticize others.

2. Jesus also insisted that those who held authority and power in his church were to exercise it as a service, just as he washed the feet of his apostles at the Last Supper. The notion that priests and bishops and pope are servants who meekly wash the feet of their followers is hilarious in the church today. They lord it over their followers just as Jesus warned them not to. Peter the Fisherman would be furious if he saw the way power and authority are currently abused in the Catholic church (and in the other Christian churches, too). It was not the way the Master acted and not the way Peter dared to act, conscious as he was that the Master was near.

It is often suggested that bishops should move out of their mansions, abandon their chauffeur-driven cars, put aside their fancy titles and elaborate vestments, and live "just like everyone else." I don't much mind where men live or what they wear or even what they are called. In my own archdiocese the last cardinal was always called "Your Eminence" (in violation of the practice of the universal church, which has replaced that with "Mr. Cardinal"). The current cardinal is called "Joe." Yet power is as centralized as it always was and there is no more trust than there used to be.

I think it would be helpful if bishops heard confessions, said masses on Sunday in a parish, and moderated teen club dances. But I don't think such modifications of behavior will affect the abuse of power by church leadership in the absence of radical reform. Anyone who says that power is exercised as humble service in the Catholic church today (or any other church) probably needs a long period of time in a psychiatric institution.

One cannot expect perfection in any human institution. When Jesus organized his community of human members he made a decision that guaranteed that within that community in years and centuries to come, the all too human men and women who obtained power to serve the community would misuse that power to lord it over the community and to work out their often twisted emotional needs. I am not shocked or scandalized and my faith is certainly not troubled by the arrogant incompetence and the terrible abuse of power currently to be observed in the Catholic church.

I'm merely angry; that's all. Moreover, I think my anger is a thoroughly appropriate reaction. Does not Paul boast proudly of how he resisted Peter to his face?

If you loved the church, I hear it often said, you wouldn't criticize it. Or you would leave it and leave it alone.

But if you love the church you do criticize it. In a community made up of humans, only criticism causes change. Those who in the name of love (but actually in the service of either fear or their own ambitions) refuse to be critical, refuse to speak the truth, are in fact traitors.

As for leaving the church because one is dissatisfied with the way the leadership acts, does one move out of a city because one is critical of city government? Does one reject the United States because one disapproves of the current administration? Does one move out of a neighborhood because one is critical of the way the neighbors' kids behave? Does one leave a spouse because the spouse is less than perfect?

The injunction to stop criticizing or leave assumes that the church is not an institution composed of human members and human leaders, not made up of men like Peter the Fisherman.

When Paul disagreed with Peter, he neither remained silent nor withdrew from the community. Rather he stayed and argued—which is what one does in human organizations when there is disagreement and criticism. Paul thus provided the model for all subsequent disputes in the church—as did the Fisherman by his moderate and temperate reply.

3. The community of the followers of Jesus, in his obvious intent, was to be the group where the Good News was preached and the Bread was broken. The excitement stirred up by his stories and the experience of salvation encountered by the early Christians in the life, death, and resurrection was to be reproduced and represented down through the ages in the teaching and the community meal of his followers. That is why the church exists—to continue the Jesus experience in time and space. And that's what the church does, not only in its best moments but even in its worst moments. It is precisely in the local parishes of the world where the word is preached (often badly) and the Eucharist celebrated (often without elegance or grace)

that the strength and power of the religious heritage are activated again. Peter and the Apostles, the pope and the bishops (or whatever they call the leaders in your church) exist to make possible and to facilitate the local celebration. The task of the institution is to hold the community together. Without the institution the community would soon disintegrate. Without the community the institution would have no reason to exist.

In the Catholic heritage, the institution is not merely a necessary evil. Despite all its human flaws, the institution is a positive good precisely because it makes possible the preaching of the word and the celebration of the Eucharist in all the local manifestations of the community throughout the world and at all times. The community and the institution taken together to form the church are a sacrament of Christ, a revelation, and a continuation of his presence through time and space. This continuation may in some times and places be more effective than in others, because the church is made up of human beings who are more transparently good in some times and places than in others. It is never perfect, since its members and leaders are always less than perfect. Nonetheless, it is the way to Jesus still at work among us, healing and freeing, dancing away fate and sin and death.

And doing so, be it carefully noted, through the work of frail and flawed human beings like Peter the Fisherman.

4. Jesus promised the community of his followers that he would be with them always. The data about their conviction of this promise are unassailable. The Lord was always with them, they were convinced, always near. The promise did not mean that they would cease to be limited human beings, did not make them immune from all mistakes, all miscalculations, all forms of ignorance and stupidity. It meant that, come what may, he would be with them always, fending off the ultimate disaster. The gates of Hell would never triumph.

The last two characteristics of the community of the followers of Jesus are the ones that make it so attractive, despite the human flaws of its leaders and members: taken together they mean that through the church Jesus is still with us.

I emphasized the humanity of the church at the beginning because it is so obviously proclaimed in the Bible and because so many of the critics and the defenders seem to want to deny it that humanity, either to denounce it for the absence of a perfection it does not have or to claim for it a perfection it cannot have.

It often may not be much of a church, but it is the only one we have.

Catholicism, I will argue in subsequent chapters, is an extraordinarily attractive religious heritage. That is why most Catholics remain in it despite the ignorance and incompetence and idiocy of so many of our leaders today (and, again, I may present too favorable a portrait of them). They know that their faith is not based on the virtue of the leadership—even when some of their leaders are good and brave men, as Peter the Fisherman eventually became in the power of the risen Jesus. They know rather that the faith is in Jesus, who still reveals himself to us in and through the church, in and through, not archangels, but human beings like Peter the Fisherman.

29

GREELEY

Saint Paul and the Gentiles

Saint Paul, I think, gets too many bum raps.

Many people, educated in the conventional wisdom of thirty years ago, assert that Jesus did not start the Christian church but Paul did.

Many, particularly women, would persuade us that Saint Paul was a chauvinist. Or antisex.

Still others are convinced that Paul was a rigid, sectarian fanatic.

All three positions, according to contemporary scholars, are dead wrong.

Paul has been unfairly stereotyped by those who have a grudge against Christianity.

That the Jesus movement would ever depart from the cultural matrix of Judaism was unthinkable to Paul. It was, in fact, unthinkable to everyone until the decade after Paul's death and the fall of the Temple in Jerusalem.

Paul's theory of Christianity was one of radical egalitarianism.

Paul was not a rigid sectarian, not after his encounter with Jesus at any rate, but a liberal in the controversies that raged within the Pharisees, of which Paul was surely one.

Paul was an enthusiast, a man of enormous energy and drive. He was also a man of his own time, and in some of the "household codes" he adopted as advice for the communities he had started he simply repeated the conventional wisdom of his time about the role of women (though, as we shall see, his own practice was sharply at odds with that conventional wisdom). He was a sharp debater and an all-night speaker, but his basic world view, on the one hand profoundly Jewish, was also utterly universalistic. If one wants to blame Paul at all for major historical change, he was the first one to try to apply the universalism of Isaiah in practice. That universalism, channeled to Paul through his Jesus experience, meant that YHWH was not only the God of everyone, but now the God for everyone.

As Father Roland Murphy, O. Carm., a good friend of both the rabbi and myself, points out with a neat touch of (Chicago) Irish wit, if it were not for Saint Paul's expansion of prophetic universalism to include the Gentiles, I would not be part of the tradition of Israel and hence the rabbi and I would be unable to read the Bible together!

Paul (or Saul; Jews in the Greek world usually had two names that sounded almost the same) was surely the best educated of the first followers of Jesus. He had been raised and educated in the city of Tarsus, the capital of Cilicia, a center of culture at the eastern end of the Roman empire. He had at least some training in Greek rhetoric and had been a student of the great rabbi Gamaliel in Jerusalem. Paul's background and environment made the other apostles look like uncultivated peasants.

He was a Jew and proud of it, a Pharisee and proud of it, a master of Aramaic as well as Greek and proud of it, and probably an official rabbi and proud of it. *

Paul was a liberal rabbi, as would be expected from a disciple of Gamaliel on the side of the liberal wing of the Pharisees in the debate about Gentile converts, a debate that preoccupied them before it became a concern of the Jesus movement.†

If one does not begin a reading of Saint Paul with the perspective that he was a cultivated liberal, one will simply not understand him.

It is also important to understand the Jewish factor in the Roman empire. There were more Jews outside Palestine than in it. In every city of any importance on the rim of the Mediterranean world there was a Jewish community and a synagogue. Moreover, Judaism was a much more missionary religion then than it is now. One estimate is that as many as one-sixth of the population of the Roman empire were either Jews or proselytes. For many of the inhabitants of the empire the worship of YHWH was more noble and enlightened than the increasingly gross official pagan religion, although they did not find the dietary laws or the circumcision requirement to their taste.

Hence most pagans who were attracted to Judaism elected to stay in the proselyte limbo. Should the full rigor of the law be demanded of them? The Pharisees argued just as the early Christians would later argue. Paul's position in favor of liberalism on this problem was not a revolutionary Christian innovation but a logical conclusion from a position that many rabbis already held.

---

*He had to have been a rabbi, some argue, because he had official credentials. If he were a rabbi, then he would have to have been at least forty years old and married. Thus his reference to the widowed might well apply to himself.

†I will use the name Jesus movement in the present chapter because separation from the matrix of Jewish religious pluralism was not an issue in the time of Paul. In his view one could be both Christian and Jewish, a position I believe still is true. All Christians are Jews whether they know it or not and whether Jews know it or not. Christianity is a Jewish religion just as the rabbi's Judaism is a Jewish religion.

The synagogues around the Mediterranean were a network along which many Jewish missionaries traveled both to preach their own brand of Judaism and to try to proselytize among the pagans. The diaspora Jews were generally more affluent and more literate than their counterparts in Palestine (many of them, like Paul, even citizens of Rome, something else of which he was proud), but they felt religiously inferior because they lived so far from Jerusalem and because they did not always live up to Jewish laws as strictly as did those in the homeland. They were, therefore, eager to entertain and listen to the wandering rabbis and Pharisees who turned up on their doorsteps with news from Jerusalem and the latest word on the most important Jewish controversies.

Thus Paul was not exceptional (not at first) either in his missionary journeys or in his liberal position on religious issues. Moreover, there was an approved network along which he could plan his missionary journeys. We call him the Apostle to the Gentiles because he was more likely to preach to Gentiles (many of them almost certainly proselytes) than the others were. But Peter had already made the decision to admit Gentiles into the Jesus movement when he welcomed the centurion Cornelius (certainly a proselyte). Paul always visited the synagogue first and never seemed to think that he was rejecting his Jewish background. Only after the fall of the Temple and the formalization of Judaism in the early Talmudic synthesis did the men and women in the Jesus movement begin to think of themselves as anything but Jews.

The synagogue Jews often ran Paul out of town, but just as often they invited him back. Many of them joined his communities with no thought that they were leaving Judaism behind.

Such flexibility was easy enough in the world of Paul's time, although it would be much more difficult to be that flexible by the end of the first century of the Common Era. For Christians to be expelled from the synagogue was an appalling experience. Few of them left on their own initiative.*

To understand the Christian condition of the first century one must always remember that there was at least as much pluralism among Christians as among Jews and for the same reason—the distances to be traveled, the lack of central authority, and sincere differences over policy and practice. It is a serious mistake to read back into that time a unity that was achieved only centuries later (in both of the Jews' religions).

---

*The writings attributed to Saint John are intended in part to console his community in the trauma of their expulsion. Some scholars think that the community of John had been expelled not only from the synagogue, but also from the Christian community in their city.

In a town like Antioch, for example, there might have been as many as twenty communities, twenty different homes to which various Christians came to hear the word and break the bread (often on Sunday morning or even Sunday evening, after having attended the synagogue on Friday night). Some of these household communities might be "in communion" with one another, and others might not speak to one another. The wandering teacher, the itinerant Christian Pharisee,* could stir up these eager people to heights of religious enthusiasm, sometimes enriching enthusiasm and sometimes (as we know from Paul's letters to his churches) divisive fervor.

So Paul may have been an exception to the rule in that he was a Christian Pharisee missionary (though there were others, including some of his friends and former friends), but there was already a "job description" of itinerant Jewish teacher into which he fit very nicely. The substance of his teaching was very different from that of the other itinerants, but his audiences and later his congregations knew what he was because they had seen many others like him.

There were many complaints against him, as there always are against brilliant, industrious, and determined men. But the knock on him in his own time was not that he was too strict but that he was too liberal.

After his Jesus encounter, Paul seemed to understand that YHWH was for everyone. More vigorously than anyone else of his time, he concluded that everyone could be a lover of YHWH and that, while they became Jews in some sense when they elected to join the Jesus movement, they were not held to the full rigors of the Jewish law.

---

*Paul was by his own admission a Pharisee; it was not a claim of which he was ashamed. The Pharisees also get something of a bum rap in the Christian Scriptures. When the Gospels were written (much later than Paul's epistles) some Pharisaic factions were already trying to edge the Jesus movement out of Judaism. But the Pharisees, like everything else religious in that time, came in various sizes and shapes. There were certain positions on which they all agreed—personal responsibility to God, the obligation to love everyone (at least every Jew), zealous respect for the Law (about whose obligations they argued fiercely among themselves), and belief in the Resurrection—a term the first Christians appropriated from them to describe their Jesus experience on Easter morning.

Jesus certainly shared some of their positions, especially over against the Sadducees (the priestly class), who denied the resurrection of the body and considered only the first five books of Scripture canonical. Jesus was surely influenced by them—as well as by the Essenes (those fervent folk who lived in the monastery above the Dead Sea). But Jesus was Jesus and nothing else. Might he actually have belonged to either group? It is not unlikely that he listened to the rabbinic debates in Jerusalem before his public life began. He may well have visited an Essene monastery now and again. But Jesus was his own man (and his Father's), and he would not have lasted long in either community, precisely because he would not and could not tolerate the excessive legalism of most of those in both movements, the kind of furious legalism that drove Paul to Damascus and to his date with Jesus on the road.

Paul does not, as the turn-of-the-century scholar Adolph Harnack argued, represent the beginnings of the church. Rather, he represents the definitive thrust out of the Jewish community to embrace everyone. Paul was the first one to take literally and apply in practice the universalism preached by the later prophets, developed in principle during the Second Temple era, and an inevitable consequence of experiencing the God about whom Jesus preached.

Paul was the first Jewish universalist.

And therefore the first Catholic.

He also began to see that God was everywhere and that in some fashion even the pagans knew in their hearts the Good News.

Thus on the Acropolis in Athens Paul told the citizens of that sophisticated city that the niche for the unknown God was, in fact, reserved for the God he was preaching. It was a ploy that Catholics would use many, many times in the centuries to come. They would see in the pagan deities of a land in which they were preaching anticipations of God and appropriate the customs and symbols and even the gods and goddesses and "baptize" them— convert them into Christian customs and symbols and saints. Thus in Ireland the harvest feast of Lugnasa would become Mary's Day in harvest time, Lug himself would become a model for Jesus, the fertility symbol of the male and female combined would become the Celtic cross representing Jesus and Mary, the goddess Brigid would become a Christian Saint Brigid, but with the same responsibilities for poetry and spring and new life, and the Brigid cross made of reeds, a sun symbol, would become a sign of Christ, the light of the world.

Everything good, true, and beautiful was, in principle, Catholic.

Paul did not push adaptation, as we call it, that far, but he was the first one to express the instinct that in the power of the Jesus experience the whole of creation was transformed and that everything had been redeemed, including the material world. The Christians, still thinking of themselves as Jews, were thrust out to the rest of the world, too. If God had embraced humankind in and through Jesus, then he had embraced all humans and had responded to the longings that had always lurked in the human soul.

At a time when the other world religions were moving away from the material world and the human body, the Jesus movement was embracing both, because God had already done so in and through Jesus.

Catholicism would often waver from its best insights. What was done in Ireland was only barely done in the Slavic countries and not done at all in India and Japan (the idiots were already in control in the Roman Curia) and is today being done nervously and over curial opposition in Africa.

Suspicion about the body and the world of which it was a part would be reinstated in Catholicism by Saint Augustine and persist even to our own time. The universalism of Saint Paul would not be accepted even by those who, like Saint Augustine and his later disciples, claimed Paul as their own.

But the universalism was there just the same and in its best moments Catholicism understood what Paul meant by his most important words, written down in the Epistle to the Galatians even before the Gospels were composed.

> All are baptized in Christ, you have all clothed yourselves in Christ, and there are no more distinctions between Jew and Greek, slave and free, male and female, but all of you are one in Christ Jesus.

Many scholars feel that this proclamation was a reflection on a daily rabbinic prayer that Paul has deliberately changed to conform to the Jesus experience:

> Praised be God that he has not created me a Gentile! Praised be God that he has not created me a woman! Praised be God that he has not created me a slave.

Paul would return to this theme many times in his writings—in Romans 10:12, Corinthians 12:13, and Colossians 3:11. In the last the list is longer:

> Here there cannot be [male and female,]* Greek and Jew, circumcised and uncircumcised, barbarian, Scythian, slave, free person, but Christ is all and in all.

These are stirring words, exciting proclamations of equality that are far from being realized even in our time and must have seemed almost as mad as the parables of Jesus in that time. To ignore the radical egalitarianism of Saint Paul or to pay no attention to it when reading (out of context) his "household codes" is irresponsible and dishonest.

Paul, proud of his Jewish and Pharisee background, preached Jesus to the Gentiles because the Jesus he had experienced and God revealed in Jesus did not accept such distinctions. Paul did not reject his Jewish roots; rather, he extended the love of the God of the Jews to the whole world. In the process he tore away all the distinctions that set humans against one another.

The household codes, such as the one in the fifth chapter of the Epistle to

---

*"Male and female" is bracketed because it is found only in some texts of the epistle. It may have been added by editors conscious of the parallel passages. Or it may have been cut by editors who did not approve of Paul's sexual egalitarianism.

the Ephesians,* must be read in the context of such radical egalitarianism. They are "lists" of advice that teachers gave to their followers in that time and not new religious revelations (an Ann Landers column rather than a Sunday sermon). But Paul adjusts them to fit his universalist religious vision. The theme of the Epistle to the Ephesians is that Christians must relate to one another as God relates to us, that they must give themselves to one another as Jesus gave himself to us. The husband, the father, the master must give himself in loving service to the wife, the child, and the slave as Jesus sacrificed himself for all humans.

As for the husband and the wife, their love, Paul asserts, is a mirror of the love between Jesus and his people, restating the image from the Jewish Scripture now not in story but in explicit theological statement. At a time when the great philosophers were saying that marriage and sexual love imprisoned the human spirit, Paul was insisting, good Jew that he was, that married love revealed God's love. As a Jewish universalist, he had to dissent from the conventional wisdom of the Gentile universalist.

Whatever household customs might survive, they had to be exercised in that profoundly egalitarian context. Paul was no more a social revolutionary than Jesus was. The social order that existed would continue to exist for a time; it would be subverted eventually when the Christian ethos of service for others transfigured it completely.

If that metamorphosis has yet to occur the reason is, as G. K. Chesterton would remark, not that Christianity has been tried and found wanting, but that it has been found hard and not tried.

Paul wrote his letters on the run—dictating them, usually on a journey, in response to specific problems in specific communities. Moreover, his Greek, while vigorous and impassioned, is not always clear. If one gives every passage in all the epistles equal weight and examines each passage out of context, then one can twist Saint Paul's teaching to mean almost anything one wants it to mean.

But such rigid fundamentalism, especially when it is practiced by those who no longer believe or who wish to ridicule or to make a case against Christianity, is intellectually dishonest bigotry. It makes Paul into an inkblot that reveals more about the prejudices of the one who reads him that way than it does about Paul.

To ignore Paul as a radical universalist and egalitarian is to misunderstand

---

*The frequently made assertion that Paul's remark that it was better to marry than to burn proves his contempt for sex is intellectually dishonest. The word *burn* means "to be consumed with passion," and the point of Paul's observation is that marriage assuages human passion.

him completely. And not to see him as a profoundly Jewish universalist and egalitarian is to misconstrue him irresponsibly. Finally, to interpret him as contemning the human body (especially when he used it as a metaphor for Christ and the church) is to misread totally his doctrine that all creation has been transformed in the Jesus experience.

His encounter with Jesus on the road to Damascus changed Paul's life. Because the converted Paul introduced a radically new egalitarian and universalist vision, the event on the Damascus road also changed human history. Those who twist Paul to mean the very opposite of what he said may feel satisfied with themselves when they have completed such distortions, but they don't know what they're talking about.

30

NEUSNER
Paul

"For not all who are descended from Israel belong to Israel, and not all are children of Abraham because they are his descendants; but 'through Isaac shall your descendants be named' [Gen. 21:12] means that it is not the children of the flesh who are the children of God but the children of the promise are reckoned as descendants."

Romans 9:6–8

"If the dough offered as first fruits is holy, so is the whole lump; and if the root is holy, so are the branches. But if some of the branches were broken off, and you, a wild olive shoot, were grafted in their place to share the richness of the olive tree, do not boast over the branches. If you do boast, remember it is not you that support the root, but the root that supports you. You will say, 'Branches were broken off so that I might be grafted on.' That is true. They were broken off because of their unbelief, but you stand fast only through faith. . . ."

Romans 11:16–20

The apostle Paul would do well in today's Israeli parliament, the Knesset, because he understood the full weight and meaning of the word *Israel,* whether state of . . . , land of . . . , people of . . . , or God of . . . And because of that fact, Paul will have put forth ferocious arguments in the angry debate, perennially at the head of the political agenda, concerning who is a Jew, which is to say who is Israel. That issue comes to the fore whenever the Israelis have to organize a new Knesset, because the Orthodox-religious-political parties insist that the state take a position on that issue of the faith. They want to delegitimize all Judaisms but their own, and they want the state to do it for them. Why would Paul have understood? Because his problem was the same: to define who is a Jew and to do so in such a way that his definition would prevail.

He had a special task, and that proves remarkably congruent to the contemporary debate. Today the issue is joined in terms of not who is a Jew but who can become a Jew and how that is to be done. In Israeli politics, spilling over the entire diaspora, conversion defines the arena for debate: how does one become a Jew, which is to say, join that "Israel" of which Scripture speaks? And that is precisely the issue that confronted Paul: how do Gentiles become Jews? But even that fact does not capture the full coherence of the ways in which the issue is framed in the first and in the twentieth centuries. For in Judaism of our own time, conversion involves circumcision and baptism (immersion), and this must be done, so the Orthodox-political parties maintain, only under the auspices of an Orthodox rabbi. And in Paul's time the question of circumcision loomed.

That explains why Paul faces a familiar problem in Judaism. It is to define the true faith by answering the question of who can become a Jew and how this is accomplished. That forms the crux of the matter in contemporary religious debate as much as in the first century. The reason is simple. There are, and then there were, many Judaisms, many views of what God's revelation to Moses at Sinai meant and means now. Paul wanted his Judaism to be the only Judaism. No wonder when I read the letters of Paul my eye comes to rest on the letter to the Romans, with its profound and thoughtful reflections on what it means to be Israel.

Paul joins two issues here, the one of becoming Israel and the other of what God wants of Israel. And the two cannot be separated, either in his letter or in the logic of the issue. "You stand fast through faith." By this Paul means that deeds such as circumcision of infant males and of male converts are not required to join in Israel. Paul's Israel is made up of those whom God has identified for God's own. So the issue of keeping the Torah's commandments is part of the "who is a Jew" debate in Paul's terms. Other Judaisms took the view that a person becomes Israel by doing what God wants. That means it is not a matter only of birth, but deed. The two matters— conversion and principles of the faith—are not to be separated. And I think Paul would have had to face them even had he not turned to the Gentiles and converted many of them to become Israel through faith in the saving grace of Jesus Christ. He would have confronted the issue as soon as a single Jew in his community produced a male child. Circumcise? Then the Torah's requirements apply even now, after Christ is risen from the dead. Don't circumcise? Then how are we Israel any more? Paul scarcely stood alone in raising the question. Peter in Jerusalem faced it also, and it took a revelation from God to get him to eat unclean things. But that was it: circumcision, the first rite of passage for the male child into the community of Israel, for Peter was never in doubt.

How Paul solves the problem is through a powerful metaphor. He compares Israel to an olive tree. A branch breaks off. That is the Israelite who does not believe in Christ. A branch is grafted on. That is the Gentile who does. The roots sustain; the branch becomes part of the tree. We can explain the unbelief of the unbeliever and also the salvation of the convert:

fully Israel, now nourished by the same root as had always sustained the holy people. So Israel is compared to an olive tree, standing for Israel encompassing Gentiles who believe but also Jews by birth who do not believe, Israel standing for the elect and those saved by faith and therefore by grace. These are complex and somewhat disjoined metaphors, but they form a coherent and simple picture when we see them not in detail but as part of the larger whole of Paul's entire system. For the issue of Israel for Paul forms a detail of a system centered upon a case in favor of salvation through Christ and faith in him alone, even without keeping the rules of the Torah.

As a thinker in an age of new beginnings Paul in the first century compares Paul to Ezra 450 years earlier. Each faced questions without any real precedent. Returning from Babylonia to the land of Israel as a Persian agent, Ezra had to rethink the whole meaning of being Israel. Is Israel only the Jews in Palestine, that is, Israel in the land of Israel? No, Ezra knew, there were Jews in many other lands. But Israel in the land was special, because it is through the relationship to the land that Israel lived out the promises of God to Abraham, Isaac, and Jacob. So Ezra in compiling the Torah portrayed the land as a gift, not as a given, and Israel in the land as Israel after the promise to the patriarchs and matriarchs, beginning with Abraham and Sarah. That encompassing comparison for Ezra meant that we, here and now, in Jerusalem after the destruction and in process of renewal, are the very people of whom the Torah (remember, just now being compiled) speaks. So Ezra thinks through a comparison: we are like them because we are in the land that is promised to us, we receive the gift, the Torah speaks of us in particular, and the promises to the founding generations are kept to us. For Ezra the Torah is immediate and present: it explains who his "we" really are.

Paul is living in another age of new beginnings, and he reflects very deeply on who is this group that, in his mind, is now the Israel to whom the promises were made, through whom the promises are kept. And in doing so he formed the model of thinking about what it means to be Israel, which later on meant the church or the mystical body of Christ. Paul was the first, but not the last, to appeal to metaphor to explain what had no precedent in perceived society. That is to say, because he could not point to anything to which the Christian church was to be compared, he had to invent a new thing altogether. In his case, it is a new conception of Israel: we are now not another sect but a new Israel altogether; Israel sui generis.

Christian social thinkers in late antiquity understood themselves to be something essentially new, not merely a new group but a new *kind* of group altogether. As soon as Christians coalesced into groups, they asked themselves what sort of groups they formed. They, in fact, maintained several positions. First, they held that they were a people, enjoying the status of the Jewish people. By claiming, as Paul does, to form Israel, the Christians could identify themselves with the received political and historical self-consciousness. So they were part of Israel—that is, a species of the genus, Israel—a different part from the old, to be sure—and continued the Israel of ancient times, not a new group but a very old one. That is the force of the passage in Romans that stands at the head of this chapter. Others further defined themselves as not only a new people but as a new type of group, recognizing no taxonomic counterpart in the existing spectrum of human societies, peoples, or nations.

The claims of the Christians indeed varied according to circumstance, as the great historian of Christianity Adolph Harnack summarizes matters in a passage of stunning acuity:

> Was the cry raised, "You are renegade Jews"—the answer came, "We are the community of the Messiah, and therefore the true Israelites." If people said, "You are simply Jews," the reply was, "We are a new creation and a new people." If again they were taxed with their recent origin and told that they were but of yesterday, they retorted, "We only seem to be the younger People; from the beginning we have been latent; we have always existed, previous to any other people; we are the original people of God." If they were told, "You do not deserve to live" the answer ran, "We would die to live, for we are citizens of the world to come, and sure that we shall rise again."[*]

The Christians found themselves, therefore, laying claim to a variety of identities as a social group, and not all of their identities proved mutually compatible. To be part of Israel after all is not the same thing as to be a wholly new people. To be citizens of Rome is not the same thing as to be denizens of the world to come. To be a third people, a no-people that has become a people, a people that has been called out of the people—all of these choices faced the new group. These reflections on the classification of the new group—superior to the old, sui generis, and whatever the occasion of polemic requires the group to be—fill the early Christian writings. In general, there were three choices: Greeks or Gentiles, Jews, or Christians as the new people.

And this brings us back to Paul. Paul faced the need, in general, to

---

[*]Adolph Harnack, *The Mission aand Expansion of Christianity in the First Three Centuries,* trans. James Moffatt (London, 1908), 241, 244.

explain the difference, as to salvific condition, between those who believed and those who did not believe in Christ. But it focused, specifically, upon the matter of Israel, and how those who believed in Christ but did not derive from Israel (that is, were Gentiles, born of a mother who was not a Jew) related to both those who believed and also derived from Israel and those who did not believe but derived from Israel. Do the first-named have to keep the Torah? Are the nonbelieving Jews subject to justification? What transformed the matter from a chronic into an acute question—the matter of salvation through keeping the Torah—encompassed, also, the matter of who is Israel.

In this same context Paul's Letter to the Romans presents a consistent picture. In chapters 9 through 11 he presents his reflections on what and who is (an) Israel. Having specified that the family of Abraham will inherit the world not through the law but through the righteousness of faith (Rom. 4:13), Paul confronts Israel as family and redefines the matter in a way coherent with his larger program. Then the children of Abraham will be those who "believe in him that raised from the dead Jesus our Lord, who was put to death for our trespasses and raised for our justification" (Rom. 4:24–25). For us the critical issue is whether or not Paul sees these children of Abraham as Israel.

The answer is in his address to

> . . . my kinsmen by race. They are Israelites, and to them belong the sonship, the glory, the covenants, the giving of the law, the worship, and the promises; to them belong the patriarchs, and of their race, according to the flesh, is the Christ. God who is over all be blessed for ever.
>
> Romans 9:3–4

Israel then is the holy people, the people of God. But Paul proceeds to invoke a fresh metaphor, Israel as olive tree, and so to reframe the doctrine of Israel in a radical way:

> Not all who are descended from Israel belong to Israel, and not all are children of Abraham because they are his descendants . . . it is not the children of the flesh who are the children of God, but the children of the promise are reckoned as descendants.

Here we have an explicit definition of Israel, now not after the flesh but after the promise. Israel, then, is no longer a family in the concrete sense in which, in earlier material, we have seen the notion. "Israel after the flesh" who pursued righteousness, which is based on law, did not succeed in fulfilling that law because they did not pursue it through faith (Rom. 9:31), "and gentiles who did not pursue righteousness have attained it, that is, righteousness through faith" (Rom. 9:30).

Now there is an Israel after the flesh but *also* "a remnant chosen by grace . . . the elect obtained it . . . " (Rom. 11:5–6), with the consequence that the fleshly Israel remains, but Gentiles ("a wild olive shoot") have been grafted "to share the richness of the olive tree" (Rom. 11:17). Do these constitute Israel? Yes and no. They share in the promise. They are Israel according to the earlier definition of the children of Abraham. There remains an Israel after the flesh, which has its place as well. And that place remains with God: "As regards election they are beloved for the sake of their forefathers. For the gifts and the call of God are irrevocable" (Rom. 11:28–29).

I cannot imagine making sense of the remarkably complex metaphor introduced by Paul—the metaphor of the olive tree—without understanding the problem of thought that confronted him and that he solved through, among other details, his thinking on Israel. The notion of entering Israel through belief but not behavior ("works") in one detail expresses the main point of Paul's system, which concerns not who is Israel but what faith in Christ means.

We see the importance of being Israel. For without Israel, Paul would have had no system. He found that he had to focus attention on the definition of the social entity Israel. This was not because he was a Jew himself or because he went out to speak to Gentiles. It was because he wanted to draw people together into a community and he had to explain precisely what that community was. For that purpose, Gentiles had to work out their relationship with a Jew. That Jew, Jesus, is moreover represented as the fulfillment of promises to Jews by the God of the Jews. How avoid the question of Israel when the faith of which Paul spoke was, after all, in the God who had given the Torah to Israel? The starting point of faith for Paul, located in the Torah that he preached, left him no choice. Once God is the God who is known through the Torah, then the social entity is going to have to be Israel, however that be defined.

Christians from Paul's time onward, through the Gospels, written a generation later, and up to the formation of the Bible as the Old Testament along with the New, have followed Paul's example. They have claimed to find a place for themselves within Israel or to be now "the true Israel." Some have then contradicted Paul's insistence that Israel after the flesh remains the olive tree and dismissed the living Jewish people as a relic or a fossil and the living faith of Judaism as a no-faith. Others, particularly since the Holocaust, have formed a powerful claim that through Jesus Christ the

Gentiles have come to Sinai and so found a place for themselves within that Israel that God has loved from Abraham and Sarah onward.

So Christianity is the olive branch, grafted onto the tree. In consequence, Christianity is not new but very old: right from the beginning. Christianity begins with the first man; Christianity now fully and *for the first time in history* grasps the whole and complete meaning of the Scriptures of ancient Israel. Christianity did not begin with Jesus whom the church called Christ, but with humanity, in the first man, reaching its fulfillment in Jesus Christ, risen from the dead. That position left open the question of the place, in God's plan, for the Israel "after the flesh" that all of the Evangelists and Paul identified as the bearers of the grape cluster and the original children of Abraham, Isaac, and Jacob.

But that position left no doubt as to the autonomy of Christianity, its uniqueness, its absoluteness. Christianity did not suffice with the claim that it was part of ancient Israel or that it had adopted the Torah of ancient Israel. The earliest Christians were not Gentiles who became Jews; they were Jews who thought that their Christianity was Judaism. Can I agree with their position? No and yes. Theirs was a Judaism. But there was no Judaism by which all definitions were to be measured. Paul's deep thought made possible the formation of (a) Judaism, which is to say a religious system that rests upon the foundations of the Torah, as Christianity does in affirming the Torah as the Old Testament. But in Paul's time, just as in our own, there was no single Judaism. There were various groups of Jews reading the Torah, each in its own way, and Paul's small group was one of them.

Why do I find impossible the definition of one sole, orthodox Judaism in the first centuries b.c. and a.d.? It is because in that time many different kinds of readings of the same Torah flourished. We cannot form of all of them a single coherent statement. For to do so we should have to harmonize the Essene writings of the Dead Sea, Philo, the Mishnah, and the variety of Scriptures collected in our century as the Apocrypha and Pseudepigraph of the Old Testament, not to mention the Gospels! Only if we pick and choose, today, by our own convictions, the authentic from the inauthentic can we claim that then, two thousand years ago, there was one orthodoxy, that is, an Orthodox Judaism. But if we do not wish to project our own beliefs to an earlier time, we have to admit the simple fact that, in the time of Paul, that olive tree was full of grafted-on branches and produced a wild variety of olives. And the variety of Christianities we observe in the writings of Paul himself, rich as they are in controversies with everyone round about within the church.

The Judaisms and the Christianities of the age—each has its proper context and enjoyed integrity and autonomy. What does that mean for our own lives together here and now? As bearers, all of us, of the heritage of Israel and the fundament of truth of Sinai, we have therefore to affirm that God works in mysterious ways. We Jews can live with that mystery. That is why I dwell on the seven commandments of Noah, to which all humanity everywhere is subject. They provide Judaism's theory of the other. God asks that much, and if you do it, you are what God wants you to be, no less but also no more. Why so much is asked of us and so much less of others? That is the mystery of eternal Israel. We not only live with that mystery; we are that mystery.

In that context, we now look back at the first century from a new perspective. We understand that Christianity is Christianity not because it improved upon Judaism, because it was a Judaism, because Christians are "spiritual Semites," or (to complete the catalog) because Christianity drew upon Judaism or concurred in things that Judaism taught. Christianity is Christianity because it forms an autonomous, absolute, unique, and free-standing religious system within the framework of the Scriptures and religious world of Israel.

It suffices, therefore, to say that the earliest Christians were Jews and saw their religion as normative and authoritative: Judaism. That affirmation of self then solves the problem that troubles Christians when they (wrongly) see themselves as newcomers to the world of religion: why Judaism as a whole remains a religion that believes other things, or, as Christians commonly ask, "Why did (and do) the Jews not 'accept Christ'?" or "Why, after the resurrection of Jesus Christ, is there Judaism at all?"

Christians want to know *why not*. My answer to that question is simple: Judaism and Christianity are completely different religions, not different versions of one religion (that of the Old Testament, or, the written Torah, as Jews call it). The two faiths stand for different people talking about different things to different people. And that explains why not: Judaism answers its questions in its way, and it does not find itself required to answer Christianity's (or Islam's or Buddhism's) questions in the way that these are phrased. Judaism sees Christianity as aggressive in its perpetual nagging of others to accept salvation through Jesus Christ. The asking of the question—*why not?* rather than *why so?*—reflects the long-term difficulty that the one group has had in making sense of the other. And my explanation of the difference between Christianity and Judaism rests on that simple fact.

If we go back to the beginnings of Christianity in the early centuries of the Christian Era, we see this picture very clearly. Each addressed its own agenda, spoke to its own issues, and employed language distinctive to its adherents. Neither exhibited understanding of what was important to the other. Recognizing that fundamental inner-directedness may enable us to interpret the issues and the language used in framing them. For if each party perceived the other through a thick veil of incomprehension, the heat and abuse that characterized much of their writing about one another testifies to a truth different from that which conventional interpretations have yielded. If the enemy is within, if I see only the mote in the other's eye, it matters little whether there is a beam in my own.

But if we see the first century from the perspective of the twenty-first, that is not how matters are at all. Now we can affirm what has taken twenty centuries for us to understand, which is that we all really do believe in one God, who is the same God for each of us, and whom alone we serve in reverence. And that shared life in God and for God defines the relationship of Judaisms and Christianities, then as it does now. But now, through the suffering of us Jews, eternal Israel, and through the response to our suffering of you Christians, we can see that truth, as before we did not and could not perceive it. So our awful century has left some good for the age that is coming.

31

GREELEY

Mary, Jesus' Mother and Ours

Mary, the mother of Jesus, defines the Catholic religious sensibility. She represents all that Catholics find attractive in their heritage and all that many Protestants find repellent. Despite the attempts of some naive Catholic ecumenicists to deemphasize Mary, Catholicism without Mary would no longer be Catholicism.

Mary illustrates the universalism experienced in the risen Jesus and articulated by Saint Paul, radically applied to the new creation, a creation that is now seen as a metaphor for God.

Grace is now everywhere.

Mary represents quintessential Catholicism as a religion of incarnational universalism—a religion that simultaneously asserts the value of that in humankind which transcends time and place and the value of that which is rooted in time and place.

Mary stands for the mother love of God.

> The Christ-child lay on Mary's lap,
> His hair was like a light
> (O weary, weary were the world,
> But here is all aright.)
> The Christ-child lay on Mary's breast
> His hair was like a star
> (O stern and cunning are the kings,
> But here the true hearts are.)
> The Christ-child lay on Mary's heart
> His hair was like a fire.
> (O weary, weary is the world,
> But here the world's desire.)
> The Christ-child stood at Mary's knee
> His hair was like a crown
> And all the flowers looked up at Him
> And all the stars looked down.

The core of the devotion to the Mother of Jesus is that the relationship between the child and his mother depicted in the crib scene and in Chesterton's carol is a metaphor for the relationship between God and us. God loves us as a mother loves her newborn babe.

It is not a new metaphor surely; Israel knew it long before the birth of Jesus. It is, however, a remarkably durable metaphor. As long as there is a religion that suggests that mother love is a metaphor for God's love, that religion, no matter how idiotic its leadership, will have an enormous appeal to ordinary human beings.

As a woman friend of mine (who is not at all sure she wants women ordained) said, "Anyone who has ever had a mother or been a mother *knows* that the way we love a child is the way God loves us."

If you want to fight Catholic devotion to Mary, don't begin with the superstitious practices you might have seen in some church of recent immigrants. Start with Notre Dame de Paris. Any religious heritage deserves to be judged by its best moments, not its worst.

If you're offended by Mariolatry don't begin with "Mother Beloved" sung at high school proms; begin with the origins, meaning, and purpose of the devotion. Then ask yourself if you're sure the world would be a better place without her.

Or consider it this way: if you're a feminist and want a womanly deity, Mary's the only one currently available in the marketplace.

Catholics have been unduly defensive about Mary. When they say that we make her into a goddess, we should, instead of denying it, affirm that indeed Mary's role is the same as that of the goddesses in the pagan religions: she reflects the mother love of God.

You *worship* Mary, Protestants often say, and we hasten to say that we don't. We should reply that what we worship is the womanliness of God.

God, we should insist, is androgynous. In God those characteristics we honor separately in men and women (and as personality adjuncts when they are to be found in the opposite sex, such as tenderness in men) are combined. But we must imagine God and we must use human metaphors to tell the stories of our experience of God's love. God, as theologian Rosemary Ruether has said, is both male and female, neither male nor female.

Jesus disclosed to Catholics the love of God as father, the manly love of God. Mary disclosed the love of God as mother, the womanly love of God. They may have a different relationship to God (there is no Incarnation in Mary*), but the sociological function of the symbolism is the same.

In order to fend off at the beginning radical feminist complaints (and thus be done with them for the rest of this chapter) I note that both sacraments of God's love are notably androgynous—Jesus displayed remarkable tenderness and Mary remarkable strength. Indeed, the latter in her role at the wedding feast at Cana might even be said to have been pushy.[†]

We know rather little about Mary directly from Scripture—the infancy narratives, the Cana story in Saint John, the dialogue (also in Saint John) on Golgotha. In the few scenes we have she appears as an impressive woman. Moreover, since sons reflect their mothers, we know much about Mary through her son. But the early Christians knew enough about her (as we do, too) to be able to imagine (make metaphors) about who she was and what she did.

Already in Saint John's Gospel she has become a metaphor for the church. Just as Mary gave birth to Jesus, the church brings him alive for the world.

But to understand the Mary metaphor we must look not so much to the passages in the Bible directly about her, but to the wonder, surprise, renewal, and rebirth that the early Christians experienced in and through Jesus. Everyone and everything had been rejuvenated by Jesus: human nature, the human race, the human condition, and the whole of creation of which humanity was a part. In the chapter on Saint Paul we saw how the implications of God embracing humankind in the Incarnation exploded into Pauline universalism—and Paul thus became the first Catholic. The flip side of the coin of universalism was sacramentality: the whole of creation is a metaphor for God.

The idea that the cosmos is a metaphor was not original to the Jesus movement and to the church into which the movement later evolved. Israel knew it, too, as I suggested in earlier chapters (so about this I'm sure that the rabbi and I can't disagree). But in the volcanic optimism of the Jesus experience his followers were willing to push that idea much further than the prophets were willing to push it. The prophets were, quite properly from

---

*The Brazilian theologian Leonardo Boff suggests that there is a personal (hypostatic) union between Mary and the Holy Spirit, somewhat like the union between the Second Person of the Trinity and Jesus. It's a wild notion, though in some ways not unattractive. Interestingly enough Boff found himself in trouble with the Vatican not because of this suggestion but because in his Liberation theology he had subjected the Curia to a Marxist analysis. It shows what's important these days.

†As I have observed to the rabbi, a basis for dialogue between Jews and Irish Catholics is that both groups are fond of strong women. It's a good thing that we are, because we don't get much choice in the matter.

their perspective, reluctant to attempt any association with the pagan nature religions. YHWH was not a fertility god (not by the time of the
prophets, whatever he might have been in pre-Sinai popular religion), but
the Lord of creation, independent of all creation.

The early Christians knew no such restraint or fear. Their experience of
Jesus was too powerful ever to be tainted by pagan errors. Therefore, they
felt perfectly free to expropriate any and all pagan symbolisms and practices
that seemed to fit their purposes.

Their universalism enabled them to search everywhere for reflections of
God. Their optimism enabled them to "baptize" whatever reflections they
found. Hence they became sacramentalists: they used baptized pagan metaphors to describe their experience of God.

It is perhaps too simple to say that Mary the Mother of Jesus became a
baptized mother goddess. The early Christians did not simply pour water
over the head of the lovely Egyptian goddess Nut and say that now her name
was Mariam. Rather, they assigned to the Mother of Jesus functions analogous to those played by the mother goddesses like Nut.

Consider this description of the Queen of Heaven:

> The apparition of a woman began to rise from the middle of the sea with so
> lovely a face that the gods themselves would have fallen down in adoration of
> it. First the head, then the whole shining body gradually emerged and stood
> before me poised on the surface of the waves.
>
> Her long hair fell in tapering ringlets on her lovely neck and was crowned
> with an intricate chaplet in which was woven every kind of flower. Just above
> her brow shone a round disc like a mirror, like the bright face of the moon,
> which told me who she was. . . . Her many-colored robe was of finest linen,
> part was glistening white, part crocus-yellow, part glowing red and along the
> entire hem a woven border of flowers and fruit clung swaying in the breeze.
> But what caught and held my eye more than anything else was the deep black
> luster of her mantle. She wore it slung across her body from the right hip to
> the left shoulder, where it was caught in a knot resembling the boss of a
> shield; but part of it hung in innumerable folds, the tasselled fringe quivering.
> It was embroidered with glittering stars on the hem and everywhere else and
> in the middle beamed a full and fiery moon.
>
> Apuleius, *The Golden Ass**

In title and appearance the Queen of Heaven sounds like Mary the
Mother of Jesus as honored by Catholic Christians. But in fact she is a pagan
goddess:

---

*Robert Graves, *The Greek Myths* (London: Penguin, 1960).

I am Nature, the universal Mother, mistress of all the elements, primordial child of time, sovereign of all things spiritual, queen of the dead, queen also of the immortals, the single manifestation of all gods and goddesses that are. . . . Though I am worshipped in many aspects, known by countless names, and propitiated with all manner of different rites, yet the whole round earth venerates me.

Not quite the Mother of Jesus, not by a long shot. The substance of the metaphor again is more important than the metaphor. But not completely different either. The images were out there. The Christians did not simply copy Apuleius. Rather, they rearranged the images to tell a story that was different but not completely different.

In Ireland Lugnasa was a harvest festival, an uproarious celebration of the fertility of the fields and the flocks, an enormous sigh of relief that once again the powers of the universe had provided enough food for wintertime. In Christian Ireland it became the Feast of the Assumption or Lady Day in Harvest, an expression of gratitude to God who feeds us just as a mother does. Already Mary was representing the mother love of God.

Our Lady of Guadalupe is clearly a pagan fertility goddess (Mexicans will tell you that she's pregnant) transformed (quite possibly transformed even before she came to Mexico from Spain) into the Mother of Jesus. Is she sufficiently transformed to be Christian? Some scholars (not Mexican, I hardly need add) claim that she has not moved through the gray area that is the boundary between pagan folk religion and orthodox Christianity. I think, however, that their argument is historical. From the sociological perspective Guadalupe does indeed represent the mother love of God for all poor Mexicans.

The trouble with the sacramentality of incarnational universalism—the trouble with Catholicism—is that it is easily susceptible to pagan influences and can become a folk religion that is more pagan than Christian. The Hebrew prophets were well advised to worry about that possibility. A sacramental religious sensibility demands of those possessed by it that they always be wary of folk religion and superstition.

The trouble with the opposite approach is that it tends to remove God from the world and make it a bleak and dour place. If you believe that everything is sacrament, that grace is everywhere, paganism always lurks. If you believe that the only sacrament is Jesus and him crucified, you have made the world grim indeed and must be wary of despair.

Christianity needs both emphases. But if you wish to understand Catholicism, you must realize that it alone of the religious traditions of YHWH has chosen sacramental optimism and with a vengeance: Mary and the angels and the saints and the shrines and the statues and the stained-glass windows and the incense and all the other practices that Protestants abhor and about which Jews tend to feel nervous (although they are more likely than Protestants or Muslims to have sacramental imaginations—how could they not?).

God for Catholics lurks everywhere. S/he is not a radically absent God but a disturbingly present God—YHWH still pushing his way into the human condition, like Mary pushed herself into the crisis at the wedding feast at Cana.

The gamble to absorb the world and everything in it that seemed good, true, and beautiful was a great risk. Sufficient evidence is not in yet to say whether the gamble was a success. The world continues to be sacred, as it was in pagan times, but now because God (and not just spirits) lurks everywhere. Such a view is an extremely attractive approach to life and makes the world a warmer and more appealing place. I think it is the reason the Catholic tradition has such a hold on its people, despite the foolishness that they have been often taught and doddering incompetents (again I may be too generous) who exercise authority in the church. Once a Catholic, always a Catholic precisely because once Catholic imagery has flowed into your imagination, it will always remain, in part because it is too beautiful and too much fun to give up.

Much of the Catholic religious sensibility is passed on around the Christmas crib.* The little kid is fascinated: angels and animals, shepherd kids and wise men (with token integration), a mommy and daddy and a baby—how wonderful!

"Who is the baby?" the kid demands.

"That's Jesus," her mommy tells her confidently.

"Well, who's Jesus?"

Not altogether sure of the communication of idioms, the mother still replies, "Jesus is God."

"Oh," says the child.

God as a baby? Well, why not? Everyone has to be a baby once. Mommy said so.

"Well, who's the lady holding the baby?"

---

*Just as a lot of the Jewish religious sensibility is transmitted at the Seder. If I were Jewish I might be a little worried that Catholics are celebrating the Seder now too. Let Catholics see an attractive metaphor, and the first thing you know they'll appropriate it for their own.

The mass, of course, is also a Seder, a reenactment of one that happened in an upper room in Jerusalem in the year 30 c.e.

"That's Mary."

"I see. . . . Who's Mary?"

The mother hesitates, uneasy with the communication of idioms but still confident in her own faith. "Well, Mary is God's mommy."

That's fine with the little girl. Everyone who is anyone has a mommy. So why not God, too?

Later she may learn in theology class that in the experience of the Incarnation Christians came to believe the reproductive process is a sacrament of God's life-giving power.

It is only a small psychological step, however, and one perhaps already made for the little girl to say, "God loves me like a mommy."

Gerard Manley Hopkins asked why May is Mary's month.

> Well but there was more than this
> Spring's universal bliss
> Much, how much to say
> To offering Mary May.
>
> When drops-of-blood-and-foam dapple
> Bloom lights the orchard-apple
> And thicket and thorp are merry
> With silver-surfed cherry
>
> And azuring-over greybell makes
> Wood banks and brakes wash wet like lakes
> And magic cockoo call
> Caps, clear, and clinches all—
>
> This ecstasy all through mothering earth
> Tells Mary her mirth till Christ's birth
> To remember and exultation
> In God who was her salvation.

Now you may not buy any of this, and that is surely your privilege. In fact, you may find it horribly repellent. But don't dismiss it as silly and ignorant superstition practiced by men and women who religiously are still peasants.

The imagery is the result of a well-thought-out view of the world and a gamble that nature religions and world religion can be combined. Moreover, it is based ultimately on an experience of renewal of the world in salvation by Jesus and on metaphors that abound in the Hebrew Scripture. If you want to fight with Catholicism about a symbol that Henry Adams said was the most important in Western history, argue about the premises on which this symbolism is based and not on what the nuns told you or your Catholic friends or the proliferation of votive candles in Italian American churches.

> Simple as when I asked her aid before;
> Humble as when I prayed for grace in vain
> Seven hundred years ago, weak, weary, sore
> In heart and hope, I ask your help again
>
> You who remember all, remember me;
> An English scholar of a Norman name
> I was a thousand who then crossed sea
> To wrangle in the Paris schools for fame
>
> When your Byzantine portal was still young
> I prayed there with my master Abelard
> When Ave Maris Stella was first sung
> I helped to sing it here with St. Bernard.
>
> When Blanche set up your gorgeous Rose of France
> I stood among the servants of the queen
> And when St. Louis made his penitence
> I followed barefoot where the King had been.
>
> For centuries I brought you all my cares
> And vexed you with the murmurs of a child
> You heard the tedious burden of my prayers
> You could not grant them, but at least you smiled. *

The Mary metaphor is based on the experience of sexual differentiation that is part of the human condition. Men experience women and women experience themselves as powerful, tender, life-giving, nurturing, inspiring, wise. Is that not, we ask, the way God is, too? A man enchanted in every way possible by a woman wonders if perhaps that's a hint of divine enchantment. A woman, experiencing her life-giving, life-nurturing, life-enhancing, man-attracting power, also wonders, May this not be the way God feels?

Catholicism accepts such experiences as sacramental and encodes them in the metaphor, the story of Mary the Mother of Jesus.

You may choose to ignore sexual differentiation as sacrament. Then you have no problem. But if you consider it to be a hint of God's power as well as a blessing from God, then you will have to find a story that conveys that experience better than the Mary story does and resonates more powerfully with men and women than the Mary story does.

---

*Henry Adams, "Hymn to the Virgin of Chartres."

Lots of luck.

About a quarter of the letters of complaint I receive about my fiction (and they are, I hasten to add, outnumbered by favorable letters in a ratio of at least ten to one) object to my narrator, Monsignor Blackie Ryan, refer-ring to God as "She."

Filled with the righteousness that only the religiously constipated can muster, such complainers tell me that they never heard of that before.

I don't doubt the truth of their assertion, but because they have not heard it does not mean that it is not part of the Catholic heritage, if a theme that is usually played in a minor key. From Jesus, who compared himself to a nursing mother, to Pope John Paul I, this image has been repeated frequently.

The medieval theologians and mystics believed that all human relation-ships were metaphors, that they all told us something about the nature of our relationship with God. God was a father, a mother, a lover, a friend, a knight, a brother, a sister. Especially a mother—we must drink the milk of truth from the breasts of God, our loving mother.

Moreover, even today, about a third of the population (higher for Catho-lics, lower for Protestants) imagine God as equally mother and father or more mother than father. There is no correlation with age or sex for this image, so it is apparently always out there, even if it has historically been ignored by teachers and theologians.

In a study of young people we found that, despite the neglect of Mary by the parish clergy in recent years, the image is still the most powerful in the religious imagination of young adult Catholics and very appealing to young Protestants, too.

There may be no more May processions, but Mary is alive and well and it would appear on the level of imagination an ecumenical asset instead of a liability.

Moreover, the assertion of some feminists that the Mary image has been too blighted by its association with an inferior role for women is not sustained by the data. Among young people there is no link at all between Mary and chauvinism. On the contrary, for men a strong image of Mary correlates with more frequent prayer, more liberal social attitudes and concerns, and better sexual fulfillment in marriage for both the husband and his wife.

I am furious that this rich and ancient and powerful and most Catholic of metaphors has been disregarded in the name of shallow ecumenism by a badly educated clergy who can only remember the saccharine devotions they were taught in Catholic schools and in the seminary.

What can you do with people who are convinced that nothing much worthwhile happened before 1965, who have never read Hopkins or Adams, who never sang the *Ave Maris Stella*, and who think that Notre Dame de Paris ought to be sold and the money given to the poor (quite unaware that the state and not the church owns the cathedral)?

Nothing, I suppose.

The image of Mary the Mother of Jesus representing the mother love of God and the experience of sexual differentiation as sacramental will survive them. So will the gamble of incarnational universalism on which it is based. Only when humankind tires of the picture of a mother and child hinting at what God is like will the *Dei Mater Alma* fade from human consciousness.

Which is to say never.

> The blue mantle hangs useless from the peg
> Dusk and darkness dim the window
> Stale air presses heavy on the land
> Summertime—and yet we are cold.
>
> No passion in the empty house
> No laughter in the shabby garden
> No rapture in the frigid heart.
>
> Long gone she who used to wear the sky—
> Bright Brigid, sweet Astarte, gentle Nut;
> Long gone, too, betwitching teenage peasant
> Who bore the world anew
>
> Who tamed the Norman fury
> Who warmed the Saxon soul
> Who kept alive the Polish hope
> And calmed the crackling Celt.
>
> Worthless the mantle and brown her garden
> For whom the world once sang
> "Dei Mater Alma."
>
> The generous belly, the breast soft and warm
> The merry eye, and the tender hand
> All long, long gone.
>
> Now the icy ideologue, the ivory ikon
> The sickly cult, the papal text
> The dry debate, the dismal "no."

Where gone, Madonna, and how long?
Alive? Well, in what galaxy?
And ourselves orphans, chilled and alone,
Among the rotting roses.

The wind shifts
The mantle lifts
White fingers on blue cloth
Flashing brown eyes in the sudden sunlight,
A smile explodes against the gloom
Laetare, Alleluia!

32

NEUSNER
Mary—Can She Be Jewish Too?

. . . and going into the house they saw the child with Mary his mother, and they fell down and worshipped him . . .

An angel of the Lord appeared to Joseph in a dream and said, "Rise, take the child and his mother and flee to Egypt" . . . and he rose and took the child and his mother by night and departed to Egypt . . .

Then Herod, when he saw that he had been tricked by the wise men, was in a furious rage, and he sent and killed all the male children in Bethlehem and in all that region who were two years old or under . . . Then was fulfilled what was spoken by the prophet, Jeremiah:

> "A voice was heard in Ramah,
> wailing and loud lamentation,
> Rachel weeping for her children;
> she refused to be consoled,
> because they are no more."

When Herod died, behold, an angel of the Lord appeared in a dream to Joseph in Egypt, saying, "Rise, take the child and his mother and go to the land of Israel, for those who sought the child's life are dead."

And he rose and took the child and his mother and went to the land of Israel.
Matthew 2:11, 13–14, 16–21

Jews have trouble enough dealing with Jesus, not in the Christian reading life and teachings, with which we can identify, but in the claim that, in a unique way, he is God's only begotten son. What, then, are we to make of Mary? Mary, after all, is called Mother of God and revered and loved by Roman Catholics; she is bearer of profound religious sentiments indeed. But if we cannot grasp how any one man is more God's son than any other, then how can we make sense of how any one woman is more God's mother than any other? That is why, in the serious exchange of belief and conviction that, in our own time, Roman Catholics and Jews undertake, we bypass Mary in silence. We pretend Catholics are Protestants, for whom Mary is not a critical figure, and we deny by our silence the Roman Catholic reverence for Mary, worship through Mary of the God we share with them.

And the truth is, when my work on this book with Father Andrew Greeley was aborning, I took for granted that I could not write a chapter on

Mary. Jesus, of course, and Paul, indeed yes: I could understand something about them and the things that concerned them. But of Mary what is there to say?

But in my own studies I have found a figure in the Judaic reading of the Bible that stands in Judaism for some of the things that, in Roman Catholic Christianity, Mary represents. So the capacity of Roman Catholic Christians to revere Mary, the power of Mary to arouse in Catholic hearts and souls a greater love for God than they would otherwise feel, the response to Mary and the power of Mary seem not so alien as they did before.

For what Mary stands for is a woman who bears a special relationship to God, a relationship so compelling that God will respond to Mary in a way in which God will not respond to any other person. So when I ask myself, Do we have, in the Judaic reading of Scripture, a figure that can show me how a woman may accomplish with God what no man can do, do we have in Judaism a counterpart to Mary, a live and lovely woman to whom God listens, whose prayers carry weight more than any man's, the answer is self-evident.

And, curiously, the Judaic Mary plays a critical role in the very passage in which Mary and Jesus figure as principals. The story of the birth of Jesus to the Virgin Mary draws attention to the one figure in the Hebrew Scriptures that provides a counterpart, and, not only so, but the very way in which Mary's ancient Israelite counterpart enters the tale is exactly the way in which, in the ancient sages' reading of Scripture, Rachel plays her part. Mary in the Gospel of Matthew flees with Joseph and the infant Jesus into exile. As she goes into exile, so the first Gospel indicates, there is weeping for the slaughter of the infant children and the one who weeps is Rachel.

Now to the Judaic reader the story of exile, slaughter, and mourning involving Rachel is strikingly familiar. For we find in the rabbinic reading of the Book of Lamentations in the work Lamentations Rabbah a closely parallel account. Indeed, the intervention of Rachel in the story at hand runs so close to the Roman Catholic conception of the Virgin's power to intervene and intercede that, understanding and feeling the anguish of Rachel, I can reach out, also, to the Roman Catholic capacity to invoke the power of Mary, virgin and saint, in her special relationship to God.

Lest these statements seem extravagant, let me forthwith lay out the representation of Rachel and her special power before God. What is important to me in this presentation is not merely that Rachel weeps for Israel going into exile the way Rachel weeps, in the First Gospel, for the slaughter of the innocents as Joseph, Mary, and Jesus go into exile. That parallel is interesting and illuminating, but not to the point. What I find striking is the parallel between Rachel's unique relationship to God and Mary's unique relationship to God. For that is something we Jews are not accustomed to noting, and yet here it is.

R. Samuel bar Nahmani said, "[When God contemplated destroying the Temple and sending the Israelites in exile to Babylon,] Abraham forthwith commenced speaking before the Holy One, blessed be he, saying to him, 'Lord of the world, when I was a hundred years old, you gave me a son. And when he had already reached the age of volition, a boy thirty-seven years of age, you told me, "offer him up as a burnt-offering before me"!

" 'And I turned mean to him and had no mercy for him, but I myself tied him up. Are you not going to remember this and have mercy on my children?'

"Isaac forthwith commenced speaking before the Holy One, blessed be he, saying to him, 'Lord of the world, when father said to me, "God will see to the lamb for the offering for himself, my son" (Gen. 22:8), I did not object to what you had said, but I was bound willingly, with all my heart, on the altar, and spread forth my neck under the knife. Are you not going to remember this and have mercy on my children!'

"Jacob forthwith commenced speaking before the Holy One, blessed be he, saying to him, 'Lord of the world, did I not remain in the house of Laban for twenty years? And when I went forth from his house, the wicked Esau met me and wanted to kill my children, and I gave myself over to death in their behalf. Now my children are handed over to their enemies like sheep for slaughter, after I raised them like fledglings of chickens. I bore on their account the anguish of raising children, for through most of my life I was pained greatly on their account. And now are you not going to remember this and have mercy on my children!'

"Moses forthwith commenced speaking before the Holy One, blessed be he, saying to him, 'Lord of the world, was I not a faithful shepherd for the Israelites for forty years? I ran before them in the desert like a horse. And when the time came for them to enter the land, you issued a decree against me in the wilderness that there my bones would fall. And now that they have gone into exile, you have sent to me to mourn and weep for them.'

"Then Moses said to Jeremiah, 'Go before me, so I may go and bring them in and see who will lay a hand on them.'

"Said to him Jeremiah, 'It isn't even possible to go along the road, because of the corpses.'

"He said to him, 'Nonetheless.'

"Forthwith Moses went along, with Jeremiah leading the way, until they came to the waters of Babylon.

"They saw Moses and said to one another, 'Here comes the son of Amram from his grave to redeem us from the hand of our oppressors.'

"An echo went forth and said, 'It is a decree from before me.'

"Then said Moses to them, 'My children, to bring you back is not possible, for the decree has already been issued. But the Omnipresent will bring you back quickly.' Then he left them.

"Then they raised up their voices in weeping until the sound rose on high: 'By the rivers of Babylon there we sat down, yes, we wept' (Ps. 137:1).

"When Moses got back to the fathers of the world, they said to him, 'What have the enemies done to our children?'

"He said to them, 'Some of them he killed, the hands of some of them he bound behind their back, some of them he put in iron chains, some of them he stripped naked, some of them died on the way, and their corpses were left for the vultures of heaven and the hyenas of the earth, some of them were left for the sun, starving and thirsting.'

"Then they began to weep and sing dirges: 'Woe for what has happened to our children! How have you become orphans without a father! How have you had to sleep in the hot sun during the summer without clothes and covers! How have you had to walk over rocks and stones without shoes and sandals! How were you burdened with heavy bundles of sand! How were your hands bound behind your backs! How were you left unable even to swallow the spit in your mouths!

"Moses then said, 'Cursed are you, O sun! Why did you not grow dark when the enemy went into the house of the sanctuary?'

"The sun answered him, 'By your life, Moses, faithful shepherd! They would not let me nor did they leave me alone, but beat me with sixty whips of fire, saying, "Go, pour out your light." '

"Moses then said, 'Woe for your brilliance, O temple, how has it become darkened? Woe that its time has come to be destroyed, for the building to be reduced to ruins, for the school children to be killed, for their parents to go into captivity and exile and the sword!'

"Moses then said, 'O you who have taken the captives! I impose an oath on you by your lives! If you kill, do not kill with a cruel form of death, do not exterminate them utterly, do not kill a son before his father, a daughter before her mother, for the time will come for the Lord of heaven to exact a full reckoning from you!'

"The wicked Chaldeans did not do things this way, but they brought a son before his mother and said to the father, 'Go, kill him!' The mother wept, her tears flowing over him, and the father hung his head.

"And further Moses said before him, 'Lord of the world! You have written in your Torah, "Whether it is a cow or a ewe, you shall not kill it and its young both in one day" (Lev. 22:28).

" 'But have they not killed any number of children along with their mothers, and yet you remain silent!'

"Then Rachel, our mother, leapt to the fray and said to the Holy One, blessed be he, 'Lord of the world! It is perfectly self-evident to you that your servant, Jacob, loved me with a mighty love, and worked for me for father for seven years, but when those seven years were fulfilled, and the time came for my wedding to my husband, father planned to substitute my sister for me in the marriage to my husband.

" 'Now that matter was very hard for me, for I knew the deceit, and I told my husband and gave him a sign by which he would know the difference between me and my sister, so that my father would not be able to trade me off. But then I regretted it and I bore my passion, and I had mercy for my sister, that she should not be shamed. So in the evening for my husband they substituted my sister for me, and I gave my sister all the signs that I had given to my husband, so that he would think that she was Rachel.

" 'And not only so, but I crawled under the bed on which he was lying with my sister, while she remained silent, and I made all the replies so that he would not discern the voice of my sister.

" 'I paid my sister only kindness, and I was not jealous of her, and I did not allow her to be shamed, and I am a mere mortal, dust and ashes. Now I had no envy of my rival, and I did not place her at risk for shame and humiliation.

" 'But you are the King, living and enduring and merciful. How come then you are jealous of idolatry, which is nothing, and so have sent my children into exile, allowed them to be killed by the sword, permitted the enemy to do whatever they wanted to them?!'

"Forthwith the mercy of the Holy One, blessed be he, welled up, and he said, 'For Rachel I am going to bring the Israelites back to their land.'

"That is in line with this verse of Scripture: 'Thus said the Lord: A cry is heard in Ramah, wailing, bitter weeping, Rachel weeping for her children. She refuses to be comforted for her children, who are gone. Thus said the Lord, Restrain your voice from weeping, your eyes from shedding tears; for there is a reward for your labor, declares the Lord; they shall return from the enemy's land, and there is hope for your future, declares the Lord: your children shall return to their country' (Jer. 31:15–17)."

What I find striking in this story is how very much Rachel is like Mary (or Mary like Rachel)—that is, the one who succeeds when all other intervention fails. Abraham, Isaac, and Jacob and Moses—the four most important figures in the firmament of Judaism—all make appeals that God forgive the Israelites, who had sinned, and not take them into exile and destroy their holy city and temple. Nothing much happens. The holy men are told by an implacable God, "It is a decree from before me." All the people can hope for is that, in due course, when the sin is expiated by suffering, God will be reconciled with them and restore them to the land.

Moses has to report this back to "the fathers of the world," Abraham, Isaac, and Jacob. The dirge then rises, curses of nature's witnesses to Israel's catastrophe. And this yields the climax: "And yet you remain silent," namely, God. Rachel speaks in the same manner as the fathers of the world, Abraham, Isaac, and Jacob. But she speaks of not sacrifice but love, invoking her power of expressing love for her sister through self-restraint and self-sacrifice. This address of Rachel's introduces into the argument with God what the men had not invoked, which is the relationships within the family. Rachel's message to God is to relate to Israel with the love that comes from within the family, the holy family. Let God love Israel as much as Rachel had loved Leah. Should Rachel not have been jealous? She should have been. Did she not have the right to demand justice for herself? She did. Yet look at Rachel.

And, Rachel's message goes on to God, "If I could do it, so can you. Why this excess of jealousy for idolatry, which is nothing, that 'you have sent my children into exile?' "

And God responds not to Abraham, Isaac, Jacob, Moses, or Jeremiah, but to Rachel: "For Rachel I am going to bring the Israelites back to their land." And he did. So too as Joseph, Mary, and Jesus go into exile, Rachel weeps, and the result is the same: the family will come home and does come home.

That's why I can find in Mary a Christian, a Roman Catholic Rachel, whose prayers count when the prayers of great men, fathers of the world, fall to the ground. God listens to the mother, God responds to her plea, because—so Hosea has it, among so many of the prophets—God's love for us finds its analogy and counterpart in the love of the husband for the wife and the wife for the husband and the mother for the children, above all, that love. No wonder when Rachel weeps, God listens. How hard, then, can it be for me to find in Mary that sympathetic, special friend that Roman Catholics have known for two thousand years! Not so hard at all.

Is this just a scholastic point about parallels? I hope not. My point is just the opposite. My problem with Mary, the heart of Roman Catholic Christianity, is how to find a way of understanding, with empathy, what Roman Catholics say and, more to the point, how they feel, about Mary. If the Roman Catholic faith centers, as it does, upon a figure that is wholly other, with whom I cannot identify, for whom, in my own experience, I can find no counterpart, then in the end I can never make sense of my friend Father Greeley and the things he cherishes. But if I can say, Yes, in your world, your path leads you to the feet of Mary, and coming out of my world I can follow that quest and that yearning of yours, then there can be sympathy, perhaps even empathy.

The importance of Rachel for me, in this context, is that in her I can find that counterpart and model of the woman who has God's ear. Then Father

Greeley's faith is no longer wholly other. It is not my own, never was, never can be. But it is a faith I can grasp, try to understand, learn to perceive with respect as a road to God, to the same God who gave me the Torah at Sinai and to whom I said at Sinai, as Israel, to the holy people: "We shall do and we shall obey." That God, who demands obedience, hears the voice of Rachel, so why not Mary?

33

NEUSNER

Is God Male or Female?

How does Scripture propose to settle the question of God's gender? Israel achieves its authentic relationship to God when Israel is feminine to God's masculine role; its proper virtue when it conforms to those traits of emotion and attitude that the system assigns to women. In chapter 7 I raised that question, but in the years since then, I have learned more about the subject. The main point that I have found out is simple: the Torah in fact portrays God as androgynous. Because our traits correspond to God's, God too turns out to share in and value the gender traits of both sexes.

Why does the issue matter? The reason is that, even now, presentations of the Scriptures as well as of the liturgy of Judaism and Christianity struggle with the gender language appropriate for use in referring to God. Oxford University Press, for example, has tried to make the Bible "gender-inclusive," by speaking of the father-mother and by avoiding "he" and "him" when speaking of God. So too, the United Church of Christ, the Methodists, and the Presbyterians have struggled with the problem. It is natural to turn back to the Torah—the written Torah as mediated by the oral Torah—in this dialogue of ours. When a rabbi and a priest read Scripture together, they will want to share the challenges of contemporary sensibility as well. For the issue of language contains within itself very profound questions about God's gender and relationship to gender.

The Torah as our sages present its teaching holds that God wants holy Israel now to embody traits defined as feminine. Specifically, holy Israel plays the role of woman to the nations' ravishing man, so that, in the world that is coming, Israel may find itself transformed into man—but man still with woman's virtues. That is why any account of the feminine in the Torah must represent its account of God as profoundly androgynous in its fundamental structure and system. The unity of the Torah comes to expression in its portrayal of the profound complementarity and mutual dependency of the two sexes, each prior in its realm and exemplary in its virtue. The unity of the two parts of the Torah in a profound sense finds its corporal counterpart in the unity of man and woman.

Not only so, but the androgyny was made to stand, in the life of human relationships between the sexes, for the condition of Israel among the nations: feminine Israel, masculine nations—for now. That remarkable sense for the proportion, balance, and deep harmony of the feminine and the masculine, realized in the here and now of normative behavior and belief, action and attitude alike, accounts for the success of Judaism through the ages in governing that specific "Israel" that it aspired to define. The Judaism of the dual Torah is neither masculine nor feminine, but something else: (1) a perfect union of the two, (2) according to the masculine priority in setting the forms, the feminine the status of the exemplary in determining the substance in all matters that count.

Let me spell out some of the sources that portray a serially feminine, then masculine, Israel, and a God that values the virtues of both genders but the feminine ones more. How, specifically, does Israel's androgyny come to expression? It turns out to be serial: now feminine, in the end of days, masculine. The relationship of Israel to God is the same as the relationship of a wife to the husband, and this is explicit in the following:

Song of Songs Rabbah to Song 7:10
7:10   I am my beloved's, and his desire is for me.

XCIX:i.1.   A.   "I am my beloved's, and his desire is for me:"

B.   There are three yearnings:

C.   The yearning of Israel is only for their Father who is in heaven, as it is said, "I am my beloved's, and his desire is for me."

D.   The yearning of a woman is only for her husband: "And your desire shall be for your husband" (Gen. 3:16).

E.   The yearning of the Evil Impulse is only for Cain and his ilk: "To you is its desire" (Gen. 4:7).

F.   R. Joshua in the name of R. Aha: "The yearning of rain is only for the earth: 'You have remembered the earth and made her desired, greatly enriching her' (Ps. 65:10).

G.   "If you have merit, the rains will enrich it, but if not, they will tithe it [the words for enrich and tithe differ by a single letter], for it will produce for you one part for ten of seed."

Here, therefore, we find that gender relationships are explicitly characterized, and, with them, the traits associated with the genders as well.

The passage permits us to identify the traits the sages associate with feminine Israel and masculine God, respectively. These traits of submission, loyalty, and perfect devotion do not exhaust the feminine virtues. But they take priority, because they set forth the correct attitude that feminine Israel must take in regard to the masculine nations, not only in relation to the masculine God.

Song of Songs Rabbah to Song 2:7, 3:5, 5:8, 8:4

Song 2:7: "I adjure you, O daughters of Jerusalem"

Song 3:5, "I adjure you, O daughters of Jerusalem, by the gazelles or the hinds of the field"

Song 5:8, "I adjure you, O daughters of Jerusalem, if you find my beloved, that you tell him I am sick with love"

Song 8:4, "I adjure you, O daughters of Jerusalem, that you not stir up nor awaken love until it please"

XXIV:ii.   1.   A.   R. Yosé b. R. Hanina said, "The two oaths [Song 2:7: 'I adjure you, O daughters of Jerusalem,' and Song 3:5, 'I adjure you, O daughters of Jerusalem, by the gazelles or the hinds of the field'] apply, one to Israel, the other to the nations of the world.

B.   "The oath is imposed upon Israel that they not rebel against the yoke of the kingdoms.

C.   "And the oath is imposed upon the kingdoms that they not make the yoke too hard for Israel.

D.   "For if they make the yoke too hard on Israel, they will force the end to come before its appointed time."

4.   A.   R. Helbo says, "There are four oaths that are mentioned here [Song 2:7, 'I adjure you, O daughters of Jerusalem,' Song 3:5, 'I adjure you, O daughters of Jerusalem, by the gazelles or the hinds of the field,' Song 5:8, 'I adjure you, O daughters of Jerusalem, if you find my beloved, that you tell him I am sick with love,' Song 8:4, 'I adjure you, O daughters of Jerusalem, that you not stir up nor awaken love until it please'], specifically,

B.   "he imposed an oath on Israel not to rebel against the kingdoms and not to force the end [before its time], not to reveal its mysteries to the nations of the world, and not to go up from the exile [Simon:] by force.

C.   "For if so [that they go up from the exile by force], then why should the royal messiah come to gather together the exiles of Israel?"

The point is unmistakable and critical. Israel is subject to an oath to wait patiently for God's redemption, not to rebel against the nations on its own; that is the concrete social politics meant to derive from the analogy of Israel's relationship to God to the wife's relationship to the husband: perfect submission, and also perfect trust. Rebellion against the nations stands for arrogance on Israel's part, an act of lack of trust and therefore lack of faithfulness. Implicit in this representation of the right relationship, of course, is the promise that feminine Israel will evoke from the masculine

God the response of commitment and intervention: <u>God will intervene to</u> <u>save Israel, when Israel makes herself into the perfect wife of God.</u>

The upshot is, Israel must fulfill the vocation of a woman, turn itself into a woman, serve God as a wife serves a husband. The question then follows: is it possible that the Torah asks men to turn themselves into women? And the answer is, that demand is stated in so many words. Here we find a full statement of the feminization of the masculine. The two brothers, Moses and Aaron, are compared to Israel's breasts, a reversal of gender classifications that can hardly be more extreme or dramatic:

Song of Songs Rabbah to Song 4:5

4:5 Your two breasts are like two fawns, twins of a gazelle, that feed among the lilies.

XLIX:i.   1.   A.   "Your two breasts are like two fawns:"

B.   this refers to Moses and Aaron.

C.   Just as a woman's breasts are her glory and her ornament,

D.   so Moses and Aaron are the glory and the ornament of Israel.

E.   Just as a woman's breasts are her charm, so Moses and Aaron are the charm of Israel.

F.   Just as a woman's breasts are her honor and her praise, so Moses and Aaron are the honor and praise of Israel.

G.   Just as a woman's breasts are full of milk, so Moses and Aaron are full of Torah.

H.   Just as whatever a woman eats the infant eats and sucks, so all the Torah that our lord, Moses, learned he taught to Aaron: "And Moses told Aaron all the words of the Lord" (Ex. 4:28).

I.   And rabbis say, "He actually revealed the Ineffable Name of God to him."

J.   Just as one breast is not larger than the other, so Moses and Aaron were the same: "These are Moses and Aaron" (Ex. 6:27), "These are Aaron and Moses" (Ex. 6:26), so that in knowledge of the Torah Moses was not greater than Aaron, and Aaron was not greater than Moses.

6.   A.   Happy are these two brothers, who were created only for the glory of Israel.

B.   That is what Samuel said, "It is the Lord that made Moses and Aaron and brought your fathers up" (1 Sam. 12:6).

7.   A.   Thus "Your two breasts are like two fawns:"

B.   this refers to Moses and Aaron.

So too, principal documents of the Torah, and the actors within the uniquely male bastion, the house of study, are set forth through the same process of metaphorical feminization, all being women:

2.   A.   R. Isaac interpreted the verse to speak of components of the Torah: " 'There are sixty queens:' this refers to the sixty tractates of laws [in the Mishnah].

B.   " 'and eighty concubines:' this refers to the lections of the book of Leviticus.

C.   " 'and maidens without number:' there is no end to the Supplements.

D.   " 'My dove, my perfect one, is only one:' They differ from one an-other, even though all of them derive support for their conflicting views from a single proof-text, a single law, a single argument by analogy, a single argu-ment a fortiori."

3.   A.   R. Yudan b. R. Ilai interpreted the verse to speak of the tree of life and the garden of Eden:

B.   " 'There are sixty queens:' this refers to the sixty fellowships of righ-teous persons who are in session in the Garden of Eden under the tree of life, engaged in study of the Torah."

5.   A.   [Continuing 3.B:] " 'and eighty concubines:' this refers to the eighty fellowships of mediocre students who are in session and study the Torah beyond the tree of life.

B.   " 'and maidens without number:' there is no limit to the number of disciples.

C.   "Might one suppose that they dispute with one another? Scripture says, 'My dove, my perfect one, is only one:' all of them derive support for their unanimous opinion from a single proof-text, a single law, a single argu-ment by analogy, a single argument a fortiori."

6.   A.   Rabbis interpret the verse to speak of those who escaped from Egypt:

B.   " 'There are sixty queens:' this refers to the sixty myriads aged twenty and above who went forth from Egypt.

C.   " 'and eighty concubines:' this refers to the eighty myriads from the age of twenty and lower among the Israelites who went forth from Egypt.

D.   " 'and maidens without number:' there was no limit nor number to the proselytes."

It is not surprising, therefore, that, having reviewed the main components of the faith, the framer should revert at the end to feminine Israel:

10.   A.   Another explanation: "My dove, my perfect one, is only one:" this speaks of the community of Israel, "And who is like your people, like Israel, a nation that is singular in the earth" (2 Sam. 7:23).

B.   "the darling of her mother:" "Attend to me, O my people, and give ear to me, O my nation" (Is. 51:4), with the word for "my nation" spelled to be read "my mother."

C.   "flawless to her that bore her:" R. Jacob translated in the presence of R. Isaac, "Beside her, there is no child belonging to the one who bore her."

D. "The maidens saw her and called her happy:" "And all the nations shall call you happy" (Mal. 3:12).

E. "the queens and concubines also, and they praised her:" "And kings shall be your foster-fathers" (Is. 59:23).

So the three points of application of our base-verse to the feminine gender of the faith's principal parts are, first, Israel vis-à-vis the nations of the world, then the genealogy of the family of Abraham, Isaac, Jacob, then Torah, and finally, Israel. I cannot imagine a more satisfying repertoire of meanings identified with the social components of the system, nor a clearer message than the one that is given: in the here and now, Israel is feminine, in the age to come, it will be masculine. But femininity and its virtues—submission, loyalty, trust—are to be cherished, because these represent the media of Israel's future salvation—and, not at all incidentally, its return to whole masculinity.

The androgyny of Israel and, in context, also of God, yields a doctrine of virtue that unites the traits of both genders. Specifically, the Torah is presented by our sages as teaching that the Israelite was to exhibit the moral virtues of subservience, patience, endurance, and hope. These would translate into the emotional traits of humility and forbearance. And they would yield to social virtues of passivity and conciliation. The hero was one who overcame impulses, and the truly virtuous person, the one who reconciled others by giving way before the opinions of others. All of these acts of self-abnegation and self-denial, accommodation rather than rebellion, required to begin with the right attitudes, sentiments, emotions, and impulses, and the single most dominant motif of the rabbinic writings, start to finish, is its stress on the right attitude's leading to the right action, the correct intentionality's producing the besought decision, above all, accommodating in one's heart to what could not be changed by one's action. And that meant, the world as it was. Sages prepared Israel for the long centuries of subordination and alienation by inculcating attitudes that best suited people who could govern little more than how they felt about things.

The feminine traits, according to Song of Songs Rabbah, are patience, submission, deep trusting; conciliation and accommodation; Israel is represented as feminine, therefore accepting and enduring. What, in concrete terms, does it mean for androgynous Israel to feel the feelings of a woman—and how do we know which emotion is feminine, which masculine? Israel is to cultivate the virtues of submission, accommodation, reconciliation, and self-sacrifice—the virtues we have now seen are classified as feminine ones. But, later on, in time to come, having realized the reward for these virtues,

Israel will resume the masculine virtues—again, in accord with the classification just now set forth—of aggression and domination.

An epitome of the oral Torah's sages' treatment of emotions yields a simple result. Early, middle, and late, a single doctrine and program dictated what people had to say on how Israel should tame its heart. And it is not difficult to see why. In this world, Israel was a vanquished nation, possessed of a broken spirit. Sages' Judaism for a defeated people prepared the nation for a long future. The vanquished people, the brokenhearted nation that had lost its city and its temple, had, moreover, produced another nation from its midst to take over its Scripture and much else. That defeated people, in its intellectuals, as represented in the rabbinic sources, found refuge in a mode of thought that trained vision to see things otherwise than as the eyes perceived them. And that general way of seeing things accounts also for the specific matter of the feminization of Israel: Israel now was to endure as a woman, so that, in the age to come, it would resume its masculine position among the nations: dominant and determinative. Among the diverse ways by which the weak and subordinated accommodate to their circumstance, the one of iron-willed pretense in life is most likely to yield the mode of thought at hand: things never are, because they cannot be, what they seem. The uniform tradition on emotions persisted intact because the social realities of Israel's life proved permanent, until, in our own time, they changed. The upshot was that rabbinic Judaism's Israel was instructed on how to tame its heart and govern its wild emotions, to accept with resignation, to endure with patience, above all, to value the attitudes and emotions that made acceptance and reconciliation matters of honor and dignity, and, therefore, also made endurance plausible.

What have feminine virtues to do with God's traits? The reason that emotions form so critical a focus of concern in Judaism is that God and the human being share traits of attitude and emotion. They want the same thing, respond in the same way to the same events, share not only ownership of the Land but also viewpoint on the value of its produce. For example, in the law of tithing, the produce becomes liable to tithing—that is, giving to God's surrogate God's share of the crop of the Holy Land—when the farmer deems the crop to be desirable. Why is that so? When the farmer wants the crop, so too does God. When the householder takes the view that the crop is worthwhile, God responds to the attitude of the farmer by forming the same opinion. The theological anthropology that brings God and the householder into the same continuum prepares the way for understanding what makes the entire Mishnaic system work.

Israel must be like God: as God is humble, long-suffering, and patient, so

Israel must be humble and avoid arrogance. That counsel leaves no doubt that the doctrine of emotions, feminine in classification by the documents' own characterization, encompasses man as much as woman, God as much as Israel. The upshot is clear: Israel must be like God, and the way in which it must imitate God finds definition in virtue. And the definition of virtue comes to feminine Israel from its relationship with God. In the definition of a religious system, whole and entire, it would be difficult to identify a more complete, a more closed circle; androgynous Judaism encompasses God, the Torah, and Israel, all together and all at once.

How are the masculine and feminine reconciled and made one? Through the feminization of Israel in virtue, attitude, and emotion, Israel will attain that unearned grace (the Hebrew word is *zekhut*) to which God will respond by the sending of the Messiah. Keeping the commandments as a mark of submission, loyalty, humility before God is the rabbinic system of salvation. These are explicitly labeled feminine virtues. So Israel does not "save itself." Israel never controls its own destiny, either on earth or in heaven. The only choice is whether to cast one's fate into the hands of cruel, deceitful men, or to trust in the living God of mercy and love. The stress that Israel's arrogance alienates God, Israel's humility and submission win God's favor, cannot surprise us; this is the very point of the doctrine of emotions that defines rabbinic Judaism's ethics.

Emotions classified by the sages as masculine ones—arrogance, impatience—produce disaster; feminine ones, redemption. This is spelled out in so many words. The failed Messiah of the second century, Bar Kokhba, above all, exemplifies arrogance against God. He lost the war because of that arrogance. His emotions, attitudes, sentiments, and feelings form the model of how the virtuous Israelite is not to conceive of matters. In particular, he ignored the authority of sages:

Yerushalmi Taanit 4:5

[XJ] Said R. Yohanan, "Upon orders of Caesar Hadrian, they killed eight hundred thousand in Betar."

[K] Said R. Yohanan, "There were eighty thousand pairs of trumpeters surrounding Betar. Each one was in charge of a number of troops. Ben Kozeba was there and he had two hundred thousand troops who, as a sign of loyalty, had cut off their little fingers.

[L] "Sages sent word to him, 'How long are you going to turn Israel into a maimed people?'

[M] "He said to them, 'How otherwise is it possible to test them?'

[N] "They replied to him, 'Whoever cannot uproot a cedar of Lebanon while riding on his horse will not be inscribed on your military rolls.'

[O]   "So there were two hundred thousand who qualified in one way, and another two hundred thousand who qualified in another way."

[P]   When he would go forth to battle, he would say, "Lord of the world! Do not help and do not hinder us! 'Hast thou not rejected us, O God? Thou dost not go forth, O God, with our armies' " [Ps. 60:10].

Bar Kokhba treats heaven with arrogance, asking God merely to keep out of the way. Israel had to choose between wars, either the war fought by Bar Kokhba or the "war for Torah."

What then is called for? These are the feminine virtues it is to exhibit: negotiation, conciliation, not dominance, not assertiveness. The paradox must be crystal clear: Israel acts to redeem itself through the opposite of self-determination, namely, by subjugating itself to God. Israel's power lies in its negation of power. Its destiny lies in giving up all pretense at deciding its own destiny. So weakness is the ultimate strength, forbearance the final act of self-assertion, passive resignation the sure step toward liberation. Israel's freedom is engraved on the tablets of the commandments of God: to be free is freely to obey—or disobey. That is not the meaning associated with these words in the minds of others who, like the sages of the rabbinical canon, declared their view of what Israel must do to secure the coming of the Messiah. The passage, praising Israel for its humility, completes the circle begun with the description of Bar Kokhba as arrogant and boastful. Gentile kings are boastful; Israelite kings are humble.

Reconciliation with a circumstance of weakness bears within itself enormous strength; power lies in turning the enemy into a friend; power lies in overcoming one's own natural impulses. But then, the entire history of humanity will respond to Israel's will, to what happens in Israel's heart and soul. With the Temple in ruins, repentance can take place only within the heart and mind. Self-abnegation, forbearance, and the other feminine virtues turn out to define the condition for the redemption of Israel. Israel can free itself of control by other nations only by humbly agreeing to accept God's rule. The nations—Rome, in the present instance—rest on one side of the balance, while God rests on the other. Israel must then choose between them. There is no such thing for Israel as freedom from both God and the nations, total autonomy and independence. There is only a choice of masters, a ruler on earth or a ruler in heaven.

This Judaic system explicitly held that humility and forbearance were feminine virtues and at the same time articulately declared its social entity, its "Israel," to be feminine in relationship to God. And that Israel dominated among the Jews, so that from late antiquity to our own day, the feminine virtues were normative; even in the academies, or especially there, robustness gave way to refinement, Gentile masculinity to Israelite masculinity. So let us not at the end lose sight of the remarkable power of this religion of humility, for, after all, it is a religion that endures not in long-ago books of a faraway time and place, but in the lives of nearly everybody who today practices a Judaism. It is a religion of mind and heart, but also family and community, one that asks entire devotion to God, not only the parts of life God can command, the life of the people together in community, but especially the secret places of existence not subject to God's will but only one's own.

Men must feel like women, women must act like (true, authentic, Israelite) men. But they can act like men, because the authentic Israelite man exhibits virtues that, for women, come quite naturally. What was asked of the women was no more than the men themselves accepted at the hand of the nations. What was demanded of the men was no more than the relationship that their wives endured with them, which was identical to what Israel affirmed with God. The circle then is closed: God is to Israel as the nations are to Israel as man is to woman—for now. But, of course, as we have seen, that is only now; then matters will right themselves. By its femininity now, Israel will regain its masculinity. To turn survival into endurance, pariah status into an exercise in godly living, the sages' affective program served full well. Israel's hero saw power in submission, wealth in the gift to be grateful, wisdom in the confession of ignorance. Like the cross, ultimate degradation was made to stand for ultimate power. Like Jesus on the cross, so Israel in exile served God through suffering. True, the cross would represent a scandal to the nations and foolishness to (some) Jews. But Israel's own version of the doctrine at hand endured and defined the nation's singular and astonishing resilience. For Israel did endure and endures today.

34

GREELEY

The Womanliness of God

"Make him stop saying that!" Bryant Gumbel, my one-time altar boy, commanded the rabbi.

"I won't!" the rabbi responded firmly. "I agree with him."

Gumbel threw up his hands in despair. Here were two very proper clerics—the rabbi more proper than the priest—both insisting that God could be imagined as womanly.

"See!" I said, unable as always to resist the temptation of the last word.

It was a great session taped for the *Today* show, one of the best and most lively of such TV programs in which I have ever participated—a proper rabbi (well, not too proper), a priest-seanachie, and a New Orleans black Catholic who by his own admission didn't quite make it to Mass every Sunday but who was shocked that a priest would speak of God as she.

You missed that trialogue? So did everyone else. It never appeared on the air. The rabbi and I have always suspected that it was but one example of many we encountered when the first edition of this book appeared (and was enthusiastically reviewed by the *New York Times*, which made it official) that there were some people on both sides who were not at all pleased with the relaxed conversation that the book represented, not theologians or official leaders, but members of both religions who didn't quite understand what we were talking about but were uneasy that we were talking about it. (And I certainly don't include my former acolyte among them.*)

All God talk is metaphorical, even the most abstract of theological terminology.† The best we can do when we try to talk about (and image) God is to use metaphors—God is like a father, like a vine, like a lover, like a king. When we use such metaphors we realize that God is also unlike the opposite role in the human relationship we have implied. Juliet is like the

---

*Though I could name names if I had to.

†I think the rabbi and I share with David Tracy that the most basic name of God is Love. Even if God is called that in just so many words for the first time by St. John, she is described as love often in the TNK, as the previous chapter makes clear.

sun, but she isn't the sun and the sun isn't Juliet either. She is not as durable or as bright as the sun, but she does bring light and warmth, however temporary, to Romeo. God is like a human lover, but also very unlike a human lover too. Nonetheless, the image of God as a human lover suffers, as do all metaphors of God, from defect and not from excess. God is more loving and more passionate than the most loving and passionate of human lovers.

So the story implied in the image of a human relationship we may use to give God a name merely says that our relationship with God is somewhat like a human relationship of which we have experience but is also very different. Implied is always the suggestion that whatever a king or a father or a mother or a lover possesses that is like God is much more powerful and loving in the Reality we are trying, however poorly, to approximate. Those who attempt to tame the power of metaphor miss the point.

Juliet is much better than the sun.

Some metaphors are better hints of what God is like than others. But there is no reason why a male metaphor is better than a female metaphor. God is both male and female and neither male nor female, and hence it is legitimate to picture her in either fashion and especially as the rabbi does, with marvelously creative storytelling skill, in the previous chapter as changing back and forth from one to another as the relationship between God and human changes, grows, and develops.

Pope John Paul I, who said in one of his audience talks during his brief and glorious September that we must think of God as our father but even more as our mother, would surely have agreed.

In this metaphor of the changing patterns of behavior between man and woman in their relationship and especially in their intimacy, the rabbi finds the meaning "in front of the text" and of St. Paul's syntactical struggles over marriage as the "Great Sacrament"—the great hint of what God is like. As man and woman alternate being both tender and strong with one another, each reveals to the other the womanliness and the manliness of God. In their (quasi)androgynous relationship, they reveal the androgyny of God in whom both the perfections of woman and the perfections of man are seamlessly combined.

How else could it have been said that God created them in his own image and likeness, male and female he created them? To be in God's image means that woman and man are equal metaphors for God and that there are manly and womanly dimensions of God in both man and woman.

Explained that way it sounds a little complicated, as do all (foolish?) attempts to explain a story. But the story of how a mix of gender differentiation and overlapping characteristics image God better than does a one-gender image of God (as the rabbi tells it) hardly needs an explanation.

Most of the letters I get about my novels are positive. But the most hateful of the negative letters (accounting for perhaps one out of four of the hate letters) rail against my references to God as "she." Poor Blackie Ryan, my priest-detective, is accused of terrible things—all the way from heresy to being "politically correct" for his careful balance in referring to God as both "she" and "he."

Such folk are so rigid that conversation with them is impossible. I have found that Sunday congregations delight in the "balanced" use of the terminology as soon as it is explained to them in the terms I have used in this chapter.

The rabbi has done me one better by suggesting that God is not only Love, not only Love between man and woman, but also a Love Story. God *is* a Romance. God *is* a Love Story—and one with a Happy Ending.

After an intricate, complex, and sometimes almost indecipherable plot.

So to restrict the metaphors for God to one gender is to miss not only half the story, but a lot more than half.

The previous chapter ought to demolish forever the hoary falsehood that the TNK is patriarchal. Doubtless some of the customs described and some of the behavior recounted are appallingly oppressive of women, but there is a deeper story of God and God's love which the rabbi has teased out of the meaning in front of the text that says just the opposite—to say nothing of the frequent references to God as mother to Israel, laboring to give birth, bending over to nurse, especially in Deuteronomy. Those who see the TNK is totally patriarchal have not read it very closely.

I was particularly impressed with the playful commentary of the Song of Songs Rabbah that the rabbi cites, playful commentary on an extremely playful work.

The Song is a problem. How did it get into the Scriptures in the first place? It is obviously secular and erotic love poetry (according to Roland Murphy, probably written by a woman). Like all erotic love, the love story in the Song is a potential sacrament of God's love. It has been allegorized so often and in such dense detail that it often seems drained of the raw eroticism that some would think has no place in the Bible. Moreover, it has been bowdlerized in translation so that its erotic edge is often lost. There is a reference to an organ of the woman's body that is surrounded with wheat and lilies. Commentaries refer to these as symbols of fertility and then translate the name of the organ as "navel"!

When I am challenged by the prurient and the prudish (usually the same person) about the allegedly "steamy" passages in my novels, I invariably cite the Song of Songs as being "steamier." They usually look at me blankly, innocent of comprehension. They've never heard of the Song, much less read it. How and why have we covered up the recurrent erotic imagery in the TNK and the Christian Scriptures?

The passage from the Rabbah that the rabbi quotes is allegory, but unlike much of the allegorizing of the Song it does not destroy the erotic nature of the passage but enhances it because it celebrates a woman's breasts as her glory and her ornament, her charm and her honor and her praise. One would be wary of reading that quote in a Christian church (and perhaps in a Jewish synagogue) during a weekly service. There would surely be gasps of horror from the congregants.

It would be difficult for a man to hear the passage and not imagine a beautiful and vulnerable naked woman. Perhaps it would also be difficult for a woman to read it and not picture herself naked and vulnerable and adored by a man. One cannot believe that the commentator who wrote that passage was unaware of these reactions. He makes his allegorical point, but he also introduces an erotic charge into his allegory which adds a meaning "in front of the text" that humans in his time and in ours can hardly miss.

A naked woman a metaphor for God? As perhaps the most beautiful of all creations, how could she not be a hint of God's beauty?*

To shift the metaphor (though perhaps not) one can also imagine that the woman lover in the Song is Lady Wisdom, an aspect of the deity which calls and attracts through the beauty of creation, the God who charms instead of the God who makes rules. Moreover, in the Rabbi's analysis such metaphoric vulnerable charm is not the monopoly of only one gender.

God as vulnerable charm? If that is one of the pictures that lurks in the womanly image of God, is it not utterly false to both the Jewish and the Christian traditions?

Only to those who have not read the TNK or the Christian Scriptures carefully. Or to those who have permitted an overlay of Greek philosophy to obscure completely the stories in both Scriptures.

Human charm is perhaps the most powerful metaphor we have of God's charm, the one that tells us more than does any other metaphor what God is like. Religious leaders are reluctant to depict God as the one who calls, attracts, even seduces. They much prefer a God who pushes, who orders,

---

*An observation that excludes all exploitation and all pornography.

who makes rules. Such a God is easier to deal with because not quite so scary or unpredictable.

Yet once you introduce the image of the womanliness of God, it is impossible to ignore any longer God's charm. Perhaps that is why there is so much resistance to the image among the pious and the prudish and the prurient.

35

NEUSNER

What Judaism Can Teach Christianity about Reading Scripture

The rabbi has tried to offer through his priest one lesson to faithful Christians. It is that the Bible of Judaism—that is, Scriptures as read and interpreted by the rabbis who flourished in the early centuries of the Common Era—can make a contribution to Christian faith. Specifically, these rabbis show us how to read Scripture so that Scripture forms a commentary on everyday life as much as everyday life brings with it fresh understanding of Scripture. When we follow the sages' efforts to give concrete meaning to that belief, we find for the faithful Jew and Christian today a vivid way to read Scripture as God's message for the here and the now. I have given significant examples, for my priest, of ways in which the Bible of Judaism may help us all to worship, serve, and love God through the study of the Torah, God's word to Israel and the world. Let me state in a single paragraph what I think is to be learned from our sages.

It is this simple but profound conviction: that there is a constant interplay, an ongoing interchange, between everyday affairs and the word of God in the Torah that is Scripture. What we see reminds us of what Scripture says, and what Scripture says informs our understanding of the things we see and do in everyday life. That is what, in my view, the critical verse of Scripture, "In all thy ways, know Him," means. And the deep structure of human existence, framed by Scripture and formed out of God's will as spelled out in the Torah, forms the foundation of our everyday life. Here and now, in the life of the hour, we can and do know God. So everyday life forms a commentary on revealed Scripture, on the Torah, and Scripture, the Torah, provides a commentary on everyday life. Life flows in both directions.

Now let me spell this out. Judaism brings Scripture into the world and the world into Scripture. The rabbi means to shape his understanding of the world out of the resources of God's revelation of the beginnings of humanity and, especially, of God's people, Israel. That example serves Jews and Christians today, struggling as they do to hold together (for Jews) the Torah and the demands of modern life and (for Christians) the Word and the world. The great sages, honored with the title of rabbi, transformed the Torah into a plan and design for the world, the everyday as an instance of the eternal. When we see how they did it and reflect upon the profound results for faith they achieved, we learn an important lesson.

It is how we may turn what we are into what we may become, following the example of Israel's sages, who find in Scripture the message for their age and the model of what they might attain. They read Scripture as God's picture of creation and humanity. They read the life of the streets and marketplaces, the home and the hearth, the nations and the world, as an ongoing commentary on Scripture and the potentialities (not all of them good) of creation. So, as I said, life—truth—flows in both directions. Reading Genesis as we do, against the background of our world, we encounter the story of the beginnings of humanity in a new way. It is now an account not of a distant past, but of a living and abiding present. For "our sages of blessed memory," as we Jews call these masters of the Torah, teach us to turn Scripture into a paradigm of truth even for our own time.

Searching for those beginnings with the model of our sages in mind will not fulfill that quest—no one brings us to the end—but it will uncover paths we might otherwise not find. It is that way of reading the map that is the Bible that I have wanted to offer my priest and friend. The reason is that I believe the ancient rabbis of Judaism teach important lessons to believing people today. These lessons are of two kinds, the how and the what, how to read Scripture, what to find there. Specifically, the ancient rabbis show us how to read Scripture in a way that we can follow. They show us ways of responding to Scripture that we may not have imagined. They also teach us dimensions of scriptural meaning that we may not otherwise grasp. We Jews and Christians, revering Scripture as the written part of God's one whole Torah (for our part) or as the Old Testament (for the Christian part), do well to seek in our encounter with the teachings of the living God the wisdom, imagination, and insight of the ages. Ours is a task no prior generation, back to the beginnings, has had to take up.

In an age of militant secularism and hostility to the biblical origins of the civilization of the West—and of the world—we come together to sustain the faith of one another. In my book I want to contribute some modest measure of my own faith, Judaism, as that faith may add to the faith of our Christian neighbors, for all of us now dwell together in the new catacomb, the darkness of disdain for our common faith in one God, creator of heaven and earth, judge of all humankind. This is a message of shared religious faith. I draw as a rabbi on treasures I mean to share with Christians. I come with humility to the faith of others. I hope to give, as others have in our day given of their faith, their grace, to us Jews. But I seek as a rabbi to derive wisdom and strength from the faith of my priest, my Christian teacher. That is why I have appreciated his novels, in which, through fiction, he has not only portrayed but also conveyed religious conviction. His love for God, his understanding of God—these have taught me meanings for loving and understanding God.

I as a rabbi have not meant merely to teach lessons on how ancient rabbis used to read Scripture but on how from their example we may derive a more profound understanding of ourselves through Scripture, Genesis in particular. At stake here is not what was going on long ago, but what will happen in the twenty-first century. For to us Jews the Hebrew Scriptures, the written Torah, form the record of God's picture of humanity. We encounter the written Torah not (in anthropological terms) as humanity's projection of itself onto eternity, but (in theological ones) as God's picture of humanity in time. So in Scripture we take up choices explored by Judaism, learning from them through their example the freedom to bring our world to Scripture and to reshape our world in the encounter with Scripture. That kind of freedom I think Christians will find liberating and honest.

Then what kind of dialogue is possible between a rabbi and a priest? Clearly, it must be a new kind. Let me spell out why it cannot be the familiar dialogue at all.

First, as I argued just now, there can never be a dialogue between the religions, Judaism and Christianity. That cannot take place, even while faithful Christians and believing and practicing Jews have much to teach one another.

Second, there is no point in having a dialogue of essentially secular, scholarly exchange. That I think is not only complete but bankrupt, because it has little to offer any longer. Through debate on the original or correct or authoritative meaning of Scripture from the first century to the present, Judaism and Christianity have framed the issues that have separated them. Historians appealed to the original meaning, theologians to the correct one, in their apologetics. In the nineteenth century, when historical scholarship made its impact upon biblical studies, Judaic and Christian scholars continued to raise as the critical issue the proper meaning of the historical and philologically informed exegesis of a verse of Israelite Scripture.

That framing of issues served to create a great apologetic for Judaism, but also to close off all possibilities of mutual illumination. For Judaism then appealed to "the plain meaning of Scripture," which excluded the Christological reading of the Hebrew Scriptures and therefore dismissed as null the classification "Old Testament." And Christianity, commanding the world as it did, affirmed as self-evident the received faith.

We may say, therefore, that the history of Judaism and of Christianity may be defined as the exegesis of the biblical exegesis that each presented to its own faithful—and, naturally, in disputation and confrontation, to the other as well. A theological claim of apologetics in both Judaism and Christianity, therefore a bitterly debated issue, is which party truly carries forward the revelation of Sinai, the Torah of Israel in ancient times. The claim of Judaism appeals for proof that it is Judaism that states, in the here and now, the true intent and meaning of Scripture, to the midrash documents we have surveyed.

The kind of dialogue to which I think we may look forward is a dialogue about what I have called midrash, that is to say the reading of Scripture in light of our lives and our lives in light of Scripture. You, dear Father Greeley, have much to teach me about how Scripture illuminates your life, and therefore my life, which intersects with yours in this shared world of ours. And I hope that I can offer you lessons of the same kind: life under the aspect of the eternity captured in the timely words of the written part of the Torah.

Does that mean you have to sit humbly for the instruction of a rabbi about the meaning of the written part of the Torah, which you know as the Old Testament? Nothing could be further from my mind. The great apologists for Judaism in the nineteenth and twentieth centuries have faced the Christian and Gentile world, both hostile and friendly, with the claim that we know what Scripture really means, which is to say means in its own historical setting—we do; you don't. That view rests upon the notion that what Judaism says in theology and law simply restates the fundamental, revealed truths of Scripture.

Accordingly, if people wish to come to Sinai, then the road that is straight and true passes through Judaism. The law and theology of Judaism derive from "the book," the Bible. And that is true, but not in the sense in which people make the statement. For "the Bible," meaning "the Old Testament and the New Testament," is a Protestant category, accepted neither by Roman Catholic Christianity, with its appeal to Scripture and also tradition preserved by the Holy Church, nor by Judaism, with its appeal to the Torah in two media, oral and written.

The kind of midrash I have offered to you, Father Greeley, leads me to a different perspective from the polemical one of the nineteenth and earlier twentieth centuries. In my judgment, Judaism in the oral Torah states the profound theological and legal doctrines of the written Torah precisely as accurately and definitively as the New Testament imparts its full and complete meaning upon the Old Testament—no less, no more.

You and I do not appeal to history to validate the faith. Neither one of us thinks that if we can show, for example, through midrash, that the original sense of a verse of Scripture pointed to precisely the conclusion reached by the Judaic or Christian exegete-theologian or exegete-legist, then Judaism or Christianity, in that detail, correctly states the original, historical, therefore valid sense of Scripture, the verse of Scripture at hand. Since midrash works its enchantment for Matthew as much as for the authorship of Genesis Rabbah, we may affirm that, just as midrash links the two Torahs into one, so midrash links the two Testaments into one.

On that basis, Christianity and Judaism may take up a fruitful dialogue on the foundation of both Scripture and midrash. The encounter in Scripture between contemporary Judaism and Christianity finds renewal in the recognition of the power of midrash. That dialogue finds purpose and vitality in the possibilities of renewing the labor of midrash—but now in common, in humility before the (by both parties) shared revelation of the one God who made us all and whom, in our flesh, we wish to imitate. For it is through our shared reverence for and reading of the Torah (oral and written) and the Bible (New and Old Testaments) that God can tell us what it means to be "in our image, after our likeness."

Let me spell out in a few words precisely what I should want, as a rabbi, to teach Christianity about the written Torah which is the Old Testament to them. It is contained in this mode of addressing Scripture that we call midrash. If in these pages I have succeeded in teaching anything at all, it is the midrashic mode of reading Scripture taught to me by the sages of Judaism.

Midrash shows us how the Judaic sages have taught me as a rabbi to mediate between God's word and my own world, equally and reciprocally invoking the one as a metaphor for the other. The sages learned from Scripture about what is meant for humanity to be "in our image, after our likeness," and they learned in the difficult world in which they lived how life in God's image of humanity, as Scripture set forth that image, was to be not only endured but lived in full holiness. It was to be the godly life on earth (in the language of Judaism), God incarnate (in the language of Christianity), life as the imitation of God (in language shared by both). In concrete terms, in the midrash, many passages of which I shall offer as my picture of how a rabbi reads the Bible, we Jews see not "the Old Testament" or "the Hebrew Bible" but the one whole Torah, oral and written, that is Judaism. And in the model of Matthew (and not Matthew alone) Christians receive Scripture as a principal component of the Gospel of Jesus Christ. These twin affirmations unite us. In that dual Torah, but also in that Gospel of the incarnate God, Scripture, read in the prism of midrash, forms a commentary on everyday life—as much as everyday life brings with it fresh understanding of Scripture.

That theological conviction, moreover, frames a theology of culture, one that constantly refers to Scripture in the interpretation of everyday life and to everyday life in the interpretation of Scripture. Such a theology of culture invokes both the eternal and continuing truths of Scripture and also the ephemeral but urgent considerations of the here and the now. Midrash then forms that bridge, defines that metaphor, holds in the balance those two words of the here and now and the always. It reads the one in the light of the other, imparting one meaning to both, drawing each toward the plane of the other. Midrash reads the everyday as the metaphor against which the eternal is to be read and the eternal as the metaphor against which the everyday is to be reenacted. In this fact I find a theological method pertinent to tomorrow's theologies of both Judaism and Christianity. Let me state matters with heavy emphasis.

There is a constant interplay, an ongoing interchange, between everyday affairs and the word of God in the Torah—Scripture. What we see reminds us of what Scripture says—and what Scripture says informs our understanding of the things we see and do in everyday life. That is what, in my view, the critical verse of Scripture, "In all thy ways, know Him," means. And the deep structure of human existence, framed by Scripture and formed out of God's will as spelled out in the Torah, forms the foundation of our everyday life. Here and now, in the life of the hour, we can and do know God. So everyday life forms a commentary on revealed Scripture—on the Torah— and Scripture, the Torah, provides a commentary on everyday life. Life flows in both directions.

Seen theologically, therefore, midrash thus holds together two competing truths, first, the authority of Scripture, second, that equally ineluctable freedom of interpretation implicit in the conviction that Scripture speaks now, not only then. Joining the two, each in balance and proper proportion, midrash as the process of mediation between the word of God in Scripture and the world in which we live and serve realizes the continuity, in the here and now, of the original revealed Torah-Testament. Forming a profoundly conservative and constructive power in the cultural, and also the political, life of Israel, the Jewish people, midrash legitimates innovation in the name of the received revelation, while preserving the vitality and ongoing pertinence of revelation in the present age. Eternity in time comes to realization in the processes of midrash, which, through literary means, define a sacred society, a consecrated culture.

The world reveals not chaos but order, and God's will—the order of the world—works itself out not once but again and again. That is the meaning of God's order for the world. If sages could find out how things got going, they might also find meaning in today and method in where they were heading. That is why they looked to a reliable account of the past and searched out the meaning of their own days. They form a model for our midrash, too. To give one concrete example: bringing to the stories of Genesis that conviction that the book of Genesis told not only the story of yesterday but also the tale of tomorrow, the sages transformed a picture of the past into a prophecy for a near tomorrow. And we can do no less.

The sages therefore present us with a model—therefore also a theological program for culture—of how through close reading of Scripture and of one's own world, too, people mediated between the received and the givens of their own time. In the written Torah they hoped to find, and they did find, the story of the day at hand, which, they anticipated, would indeed form the counterpart and conclusion to the story of beginnings. From creation to conclusion, from the beginnings of salvation in the patriarchs and matriarchs to the ending of salvation and its fulfillment in their own day: this is what our sages sought to discover. We read Scripture in light of our own concerns—but then listen carefully to the teachings of the Torah about contexts like our context and circumstances like those we face.

The sages of Judaism exercise a freedom of interpretation, by insisting that God speaks through the Torah to Israel everywhere and continually. But when in the writings we shall survey they brought to the written Torah the deepest anguish of the age, they allowed that component of the Torah to speak to them in the here and now. The bridge they built brought traffic in both directions, from today to Sinai, from Sinai to the present moment. That is what I mean when I represent midrash as mediator. The principal mode of thinking in midrash translates the metaphor into a policy of culture, for it requires us to look deeply at something, for in the depths we find something else, as each thing stands for another and all things possess a potentiality of meaning never close to the surface, always in the depths of God's revealed will in the Torah. And that account of the continuity of culture under the aspect of midrash leads us to the limits of this world, whose borders mark the bottom boundary at the threshold of the other.

36

NEUSNER

Thinking About "the Other" in Religion—It Is Necessary, but Is It Possible?

Now we come to the nub of the matter. Religions can teach one another. These pages have shown that fact. But can they communicate with one another? That is another question, and it defines the single most important problem facing religion for the next hundred years, as for the last, as an intellectual one: how to think through difference, how to account, within one's own faith and framework, for the outsider, indeed, for many outsiders.

The power of religion is shown by its power to disrupt civilization, as in Ireland, the Middle East, and parts of Africa, Asia, and North America. But that power also reminds us of its pathos, which is the incapacity of religions to form for themselves a useful theory of the other. That, not secularization, defines the critical task facing religions: their excess of success in persuading the believers so that believers not only love one another, they hate everybody else.

The commonplace theory of religious systems concerning the other or the outsider, consigning to incomprehensibility the different and the other, finds ample illustration here. What do you do with the outsider? Find the other crazy (as did Ayatollah Khomeini and Jim Jones of Jonestown), declare the other the work of the devil (as the ayatollah did with us), or declare the other subject to such metaphors as unclean, impure, dangerous, to be exterminated, as the Germans—Christians, ex-Christians alike—did with the Jews. These will no longer serve, if they ever did. Religions will have to learn how to think about the other, not merely to tolerate the other as an unavoidable inconvenience or an evil that cannot be eliminated. For reasons I shall explain, religions face the task of thinking, within their own theological framework and religious system, about the place, within the structure, of the other outside of it. And that is something no religion has ever accomplished up to this time.

Religions have spent their best intellectual energies in thinking about themselves, not about the outsider. Why should this be so? The reason is that religions form accounts of a social world, the one formed by the pious; they set forth a world view, define a way of life that realizes that world view, and identify the social entity that constitutes the world explained by the world view and embodied in the way of life: world without end. The this-worldly power of religion derives from its capacity to hold people together and make them see themselves as not a given but a gift: special, distinctive, chosen, saved—whatever. But the very remarkable capacity of religions to define all that is important about a person, a family, a group also incapacitates religions in a world in which, it is clear, difference must be accommodated. For in explaining the social world within, religions also build walls against the social world without, and in consequence religions impose upon the other, the outsider, a definition and a standing that scarcely serve the social order and the public interest.

For theories of "the other" that afford at best toleration, at worst humiliation and subordination, may have served in an age of an ordered society, but they do not fit a time in which social change forms the sole constant. It is one thing to design a hierarchical society defined by religion when one religion is on top, all others subordinated, as was the case in the Islamic nation(s) from the seventh century and as was the case in Christian Europe until the rise of the nation-state. A hierarchy based upon religion, with Islam at the apex, Christianity and Judaism tolerated but on the whole well-treated minorities, served so long as all parties accepted their place. So too, Christian European society before the Reformation had its dual theory of religious difference within the social order: the Christian state, headed by the pope, Christ's deputy; and the monarch, the secular Christian counterpart. In such an order, Judaism found its place as testimony, Islam was kept at bay across the Pyrenees or Mediterranean and then forced back into the Near East itself, and paganism would be eliminated. But with the shaking of the foundations, in the Reformation, for instance, the social order trembled, Christianity in the West became two, then many, and the hierarchical structure tottered. Then what of the other? Jews were driven to the east, the more tolerant, pioneering territories of Poland, Lithuania, White Russia, the Ukraine, Islam would then be ignored, and Christians would spend centuries killing other Christians—some theory of the other! Some theory of the social order!

The solution of the seventeenth century was simple: the head of state defines the governing church. That served where it served. The solution of the eighteenth century was still more simple: tolerate everything, because all religions are equally ridiculous. But no religion accepted either theory of religious difference, and it was with no theory of the other of religious difference formed within religious conviction and loyalty that the West entered its great ages of consolidation and expansion and fruition, then dissolution and civil strife, in the nineteenth and twentieth centuries. The civil war of Western, then world, civilization proved no age for thinking about the social order, and the pressing problem of religious accommodation of religious difference hardly gained attention. The reason is that, from 1914 to nearly the present day, it was by no means clear that humanity would survive the civil war fought at such cost and for so long. With a million killed in one battle in 1915, with twenty million Soviet citizens killed in World War II after a prior ten million Soviet citizens were killed by their own government in the decade preceding the war, with six million Jews murdered in factories built to manufacture death—with humanity at war with itself, religions could hardly be expected to reconsider long-neglected and scarcely urgent questions.

Yet, it is obvious, religious theories of religious difference—that is, a theory formed within the framework of a religious world view, way of life, and social entity about those beyond that framework—do impose upon us an urgent task now. Part of the reason is the simple fact that we have survived the twentieth century. In 1945 no one knew we would and many doubted it. But the atomic peace is holding, and the threat of armed conflict on a global scale diminishes.

That adventitious fact by itself would hardly precipitate deep thought within religion on the requirements of the social order: how to get along with the outsider. But a more important fact does. It is that, as I said before, the two-hundred-year campaign against religion on the part of forces of secularization has simply failed. Faith in God, worship of God, life with God—these testimonies to the vitality of religions and therefore also of religion are measurable: people go to church or synagogue, they observe this rite and that requirement, they make their pilgrimages, and by these quite objective measures of the fact of human action, the vast majority of most of the nations of the world are made up of religious believers of one kind or another. All claims that secularization is the established and one-way process and the demise of religion forms the wave of the future have defied the facts of religious power and (alas) worldly glory. Not only is religion strong in its own realm; religious affiliations and commitments define loyalties and concerns in the larger social world of politics and culture. Anyone who doubts it had better try to explain without religion the intense opposition to abortion manifested by from one-third to nearly half (depending on the framing of the issue) of the voting population of this country—like it or not. In the formation of social groups, for instance, where we live, how we choose our friends, and whom we marry, religion remains a critical indicator.

And that brings us back to the century rushing toward us, an age of parlous peace, a time in which, for the first time in human history, we have the opportunity of a period of sustained peace—but only if . . . We can have peace on earth only if we find sources of goodwill for one another, for in the end, moved by hatred, we may well bring down upon ourselves the roof of the temple that is over us all. Hatred of the other, after all, forms a powerful motive to disregard love of self, and anyone who doubts that fact had better reconsider the history of Germany from July 1944 through May 1945. At that time, when everyone knew the German cause was finished, hatred of the other sufficed to sustain a suicidal war that ended with the absolute ruin of all Germany; more people died in the last nine months of World War II than in the first five years. And all that kept Germany going on the path to its own complete destruction was hatred: drag them all down with us. So much for the power of hatred. There is, then, no guarantee, despite the *pax atomica* that protects us now, of a long-term peace. There is good reason to tremble when we consider how hatred, brewed within religious theories of the other as the devil, for example, leads nations to act contrary to all rational interest.

So there really is a considerable and urgent task before religions today, the task of addressing a question long thought settled by the various religious systems that now flourish. It is the question of the other. And the question is to be framed in terms that only religions can confront, that is to say, the theological theory of the other. The theological question of the other has been framed in these terms: how, as a believing person, can I make sense of the outsider? And for a long time that had to make do. But now we have to reframe the question: how, as a believing person, can I make sense of the outsider with not mere tolerance of difference but esteem for a faith not my own?

To expand the question, how can I form a theory of the other in such a way that within my own belief I can respect the other and accord to the outsider legitimacy within the structure of my own faith?

I say very simply that no Western religious tradition has ever answered those questions. None have tried. The hierarchical theory of religions has served by which, as I said, Islam at the apex made room for Christianity and Judaism and eliminated everything else; or Christianity at the apex (always in theory, sometimes in practice) found a cave, a cleft in the rock, for Judaism, kept Islam out of sight, and eliminated everything else. Judaism for its part expressed its hierarchical counterpart by assigning to undifferentiated humanity (Islam and Christianity never singled out for special handling) a set of requirements for a minimal definition of a humane and just social order, with holy Israel, God's first love, responsible for everything else. Of you God wants civility, of us holiness: a hierarchy with one peak and a vast flat plain, no mountain of ascent in between.

When we take note of how religions in the past and present have thought about the other, we may perceive the full weight of the task that is now incumbent upon us. For, looking backward, all our models tell us what not to do, but we have scarcely a single model to emulate. The reason is that religions thinking about the other do so solely in terms of themselves. We then discern the unprecedented character of the next phase in theological reflection: a Christian theology of the other in terms of the other for faithful Christians, a Judaic theology of the other in terms of the other for believing Jews. That effort at treating as legitimate and authentic a religion other than our own and with it and on its account, treating as worthy of respect because of their religion religious people different from ourselves, we have never seen on this earth before, though in the past quarter-century the beginnings of the work have been attempted, so far as I know solely by Roman Catholic and mainstream Protestant theologians. The question is, Is this possible for Judaism on Christianity and for Christianity on Judaism?

Ours is an intellectual task, for if we cannot in a rational and rigorous way think religiously about the other, then the good works of politics and the ordering of society will not be done. And the dimensions of our task are formidable. For we have seen what does not serve. Tolerance works only in a climate of indifference; when you care, so it seems, you also hate. Toleration works where law prevails, but the limits of the law are set by sovereign power, and the range of difference on the other side of the border stretches to the last horizon. So are we able, in wit and imagination, mind and intellect, to form a theory of the other coherent with the entire structure of the world that our religious world view, way of life, and account of the "us" that is the social entity comprise? The issue of coherence is critical, and that matter of cogency with the whole religious system explains why theological propositions are at stake. Tolerance is a mere social necessity but, we all recognize, simply not a theological virtue. Anyone who doubts should recall the ridicule that met the position: "It does not matter what you believe, as long as you're a good person," not to mention, "It does not matter what you believe, as long as you believe something."

But beyond tolerance and before theology—that is where we now stand. The history of religion is teaching us about the failures of the past, so closing off paths that lead nowhere. Can religious systems make sense of what lies beyond the system? In my judgment the answer must be affirmative, because the question comes with urgency.

Where to begin? I think it is with the recognition of the simple fact that the world really is different beyond its difference from us. By that I mean religious systems differentiate within but homogenize the world beyond. They find it possible to conduct a detailed exegesis of their own social order, forming their own hierarchy within, but when it comes to the world beyond the limits of the system, everything is represented as pretty much the same. And that is a component of the systemic coping with difference: we are differentiated because we matter; the outside is undifferentiated because there difference is trivial. But Catholics hate Protestants, and the hatred has nothing to do with us Jews, and Protestants have contempt for Catholics, leaving us out as well. And we nurture our spite, too. So difference is not only within the system, and that means systems must think about more differences than until now they have tended to encompass.

When religious systems address the differences among outsiders, they will quite naturally reframe the question of difference in yet another way. They will not only understand that Christians are all Christians only to Jews or Muslims, but to Christians, Christians are profoundly divided. They will also understand that difference applies within: the participants of a system participate in many systems. Pluralism is existential, not only social; all of us live in many systems, working our way through many worlds, mostly serial worlds, but sometimes synchronous ones. I am not quite sure how any of us holds together the worlds of work and home, vocation and avocation, or the considerable range of loyalties that divide our hearts. But most of us do. Then, in this context, we are not only systemically Judaic or Christian or Buddhist. We are systemically defined within other frameworks as well. Those of us who are intellectuals live within one framework, with its way of life and world view and social entity; those of us who are politicians live within another, with its way of life, world view, and political class; those of us who are athletes live by yet another schedule and do other things; and so it goes, and that is to speak only of the intersecting systems of the common life. What shall we then say of home and family and its confusion? In all, the happy chaos of our lives belies the neat and orderly hierarchy that religious systems impute to the social world. Whether or not in times past people lived so neatly ordered I cannot say, but today they do not. Religion matters not only because it integrates, it matters because it is one of the sole media of integration left to us. But for all of its power to define who we are and what we want to be and to what "us" we belong, religion too forms only one circle, concentric perhaps, with more of the circles of our lives than others, but coexistent with the lives of only a few specialists. For the rest, religious difference is just another difference. Now that is something for theology to think about. And when theology addresses difference within, then quite naturally a theory of difference beyond will take shape. But it is, after all, asking much of a theology of Judaism to think about difference within the social world of Judaism. Recognizing that fact—and it is, after all, a fact—contradicts the integrating task that the religious system performs and that theology is meant to explain. This is a time for intellectuals to do their work courageously.

37

NEUSNER

Can Christianity and Judaism Conduct Dialogue? Yes, Says the Rabbi—Six Years Later

So Greeley was right and I was wrong—nothing new about that. We argue all the time, as good friends should, and on this issue as on others, he scored. Anyhow, that does not surprise me; I've always considered Greeley, if not a terribly productive scholar, a luminary, always with something important and compelling to say. And here, I've always been right.

Previously, I said I thought religious people could communicate, since the capacity to convey feeling and thought to another person marks us as human. But I did not think religious systems can communicate. That is because a religious system—an account of a social entity singled out by God, the worldview of that social entity, the way of life of that social entity—closes in around itself. It succeeds in differentiating within, but it sees the outside world as undifferentiated. That means a religious system enjoys its greatest success at the very point at which it fails, explaining to the faithful who they are and what they mean, unable to tell them why others are different but also bear meaning. That is what I meant when I said religious systems talk about different things to different people.

But what if religious systems should talk about the same topics to different people and turn out to say the same things about those topics? Then each has the capacity to share with and nourish the other. And, it follows, an authentically religious dialogue, an exchange in which each shares with the other what it has learned about God, may commence. It is the possibility of dialogue about what matters in religion, which is to say, life with God, that I called into question. But in experience and in reflection in the chapter of life that unfolded just as this book reached its conclusion I have learned concrete answers to that question.

Experience comes first. When I wrote my chapters for the first edition of this book I lived among nominal Christians in an essentially secular community, in a university in which religion was studied in the biological manner, like a frog under dissection. My colleagues in Religious Studies at Brown University made a living at the study of a subject that engaged them in theory, but at least some of them did not greatly respect those who studied the subject out of conviction and commitment. There were, then, no Christians with whom to engage in religious exchange about religious truth—what have you learned about God, what have I learned, that we may share. In 1990 I had the good fortune to move South—or rather, to a place in the South where southern and midwestern America have come together.

Among my colleagues, black and white (at Brown they were all white) and Baptist and Catholic and Methodist, are people who not only pray but believe in the power of prayer, for whom God is not a philosophical problem but a living presence. In Rhode Island I knew no mainstream Catholics, only an occasional dissenter, whereas here, the Catholic Bishop of St. Petersburg (since elevated to serve as Archbishop of Miami) and I formed a comfortable friendship. My students at Brown, with rare exceptions, studied about religion as a chapter in someone else's culture, a way of understanding the world out there. Here my students study about religion as they would study about their friends' and neighbors' lives—and their own, as a means of self-understanding. There I knew no Muslims; here my classroom in Talmud is enlightened by their intense interest in how to realize the commandments of holiness in the political structure of the social order. Above all, there I knew no Bible-believing Christians, and here in St. Petersburg, Florida, we live in the center of a deeply Christian world, with churches on every other street corner.

Not only so, but, in the New York–New England circle, I found the practice of Judaism treated as irrelevant and slightly peculiar. One experience suffices to show why I concluded that Judeo-Christian dialogue cannot take place in any serious way, that is, beyond the exchange of pleasantries or shared political positions. When Mircea Eliade organized the editorial board for the *Encyclopedia of Religion*, to be published by Macmillan, I was asked to serve as the editor for Judaism. I agreed. Then I received the call to the first meeting. It was to take place in New York City, on Passover. When I explained that I could not attend such meetings on Passover or on the Sabbath ("Six days shall you labor and do all your work"), I was dropped in favor of a Reform rabbi, who would have no problems with the schedule dictated by these scholars of religion.* This experience strengthened my impression that, in the end, Christianity is not really a religion at all, only a rather prejudiced social attitude.

---

*Eliade's own earlier years as a Romanian Fascist had left him with no deep respect for Judaism.

But I was soon to learn that Christianity, as much as Judaism, is a vital and complex, living set of religious systems, with much to teach about matters of substance. The school was the Protestant South, both black and white, on the one side, and a quite unusual Roman Catholic community based in Rome, on the other.

In the encounter with living Christianity, Protestant and Catholic and Orthodox, black and white, as well as in an incipient engagement with practicing Muslims, I found more than the exchange of neutral facts—we eat this, not that, and we don't care what you eat; you study the Bible and we study the Torah. What I have encountered is the sharing of deeply held religious realities, not to convert or even persuade the other, but to give full expression of oneself and one's deepest convictions out of devotion to the other. When eating (a vegetarian meal) at the bishop's table, we would begin with his blessing of the food, and then I would break the bread; he received it as if the Host. I brought him rabbinic writings, and he gave me the Pope's book. My intent was not to show him the truth of Scripture read as part of the Torah, and his was not to dazzle me by the Pope's brilliance into accepting his faith. Mine was to share another way of scriptural encounter, and his was to accord access to spiritual truth as his Pilgrim People had encountered truth.

Not only at home, but overseas, I found myself engaged in a religious dialogue that I had declared beyond the capacity of religious systems to sustain. Like everything interesting, it came about by accident. In February 1989, I went on a lecture trip to some Italian universities. In Rome I met Bishop Pietro Rosanno, the head of the Gregorianum, a Vatican university where I lectured. He approached me to attend in Warsaw on September 1, 1989, a memorial meeting to commemorate the German attack on Poland of September 1, 1939. I asked, "Why me?"

He answered, "Because of the present controversy at Auschwitz about the Carmelite convent, no Jewish organization in the world will send a representative to this commemoration."

I: "But I don't represent anyone but myself, never have, never will."

He: "We want you."

I: "Then I'll come. Surely some Jew should stand there, that day, to remember, to bear witness. If no one better, then I will stand there."

The Catholics in Warsaw, in September 1989, conducted the commemoration with dignity and respect. That did not make the encounter with Poland those days less searing. I cannot report uniformly friendly crowds as I walked around wearing my skullcap. Nor did the press show a comprehending face. I was besieged by reporters, asking me about the controversy at

Auschwitz, and my addresses—Judaic, theological, and uncompromising, but not about the politics of the moment—attracted interest only for what I did not say. The organizers of the meeting, the Community of St. Egidius, an organization of Catholic laypeople devoted to the cause of peace, which, in subsequent years, would mediate peace agreements in Mozambique and in Algeria, won my confidence by their manifest goodwill, expressed out of religious conviction; they earned my respect by their dignity. When after I saw the chaotic and tense situation created by the media and insisted that they assign a press officer to walk with me whenever I left my hotel room, to deal with potentially explosive situations, I won theirs. I got no headlines, but valued friends, in Warsaw.

And in Warsaw was born a shared enterprise, in which, over time, I would anoint myself as "the Rabbi of the Community of St. Egidius." Over later years I attended their international meetings of prayer for peace. At these meetings, the faithful of Judaism met for our prayers—it would be the afternoon prayer, Minhah, joined with certain appropriate Psalms and other readings of Scripture—just as did the various Christian communions, Muslims, Buddhists, and practitioners of other religions. Some years later I made a lecture tour of Italian universities, speaking on Judeo-Christian relationships for meetings organized by the Community. It was in these encounters over the years that I found myself talking not as a rabbi to outsiders, but as part of a human community, rich in diversity, united in quest of the service of God. In the shared piety, in the faces of the Community's young people patiently listening to their rabbi's broken Italian, trying to convey a lesson of the Torah spoken out of faith, not merely academic curiosity, I encountered the reality of a shared religious faith and found in it a sustaining moment.

I shared these experiences with Father Greeley. Indeed, I told him, since I was doing a favor for his boss (the Pope), that he owed me something in return. It was, specifically, to be a new novel (I had read all the ones then in print), to read on my overseas travels. So, year after year, I gave him notice, and he soldiered on, providing me with the required novel, on time, without complaint. I would then hand the newest Greeley on to my friends in the Vatican; it was my only venture into evangelism, and it has turned out not entirely without good result, though I am not inclined to predict he will be elected the next pope, or even the one after that (may he live to 120 years!).

Greeley is right that we share much: a common God, common stories, common metaphors. We are joint heirs of the revelation of ancient Israel, the revelation of Moses and the prophets, through which God is made manifest to us both. But experience has taught me we may serve also each to correct the other, to improve the other. Let me make this specific. The beam in the eye of Christianity is, of course, its imperialism, the Christian caricature of Israel, the religious community, as a mere ethnic group. The beam in my own eye, not so difficult to discern, is Judaic isolationism, not so much self-righteousness as standoffishness, which holds that God has given us six hundred thirteen commandments, but to everybody else, only seven. There is, after all, a certain pride in Amos's saying, "Only you have I known . . . therefore will I visit . . . ," and in our certainty that the dreadful things that have happened to us bear meaning, expressing a clear divine intent; other people just have disasters. God's love for the land, God's infinite concern for everything we do, the message of Leviticus 26 and Deuteronomy 32—these do spill over, perhaps quite naturally, into a certain isolationism: God cares what I eat for breakfast, but God cares only that you organize a just social order. God cares for me more than God cares for you. Perhaps that conclusion need not follow from the doctrine of "the seven commandments assigned to the children of Noah," meaning, everybody but us, but still, when I weigh 613 against 7, we do come out ahead.

Christianity really did bring the written Torah to the whole world. Christianity really did form the ideal of an entire civilization framed around the principles of the Torah, for instance, the Ten Commandments. Much that Jesus said comes to him from the Torah, and still more would have pleased sages of his and later times, had they learned some of the fine things he said. [*] Christian imperialism carries to an extreme the remarkable accomplishment of Christianity: along with imperial Islam, bringing knowledge of the Lord God, creator of heaven and earth, to the whole earth. We bear witness to the costs of that accomplishment, reminding the other to remember.

For our part, the prophet of the Gentiles came to curse, as so many have done, but stayed to bless:

> For from the top of the mountains I see him, from the hills I behold him;
> lo, a people dwelling alone, and not reckoned among the nations!
>
> Numbers 23:9

We have more than suffered and survived, we have risen from the dead, we have endured. Coming out of the death camps built to murder them, the survivors, along with Jewry throughout the world, had the option to take, each one, his or her own way outward and away. After such horrors, who would want to be a Jew, or who would want ever again to raise a child to be a

---

[*] I expand on this point in my *A Rabbi Talks with Jesus: An Intermillennial, Interfaith Exchange* (New York: Doubleday, 1993).

Jew? But that is not what happened. Most of Israel, the Jewish people, joined with the tiny community then in the land of Israel to form, three years beyond Auschwitz, the State of Israel; and most of Israel, the Jewish people, determined to renew the life of Israel, not only the state in politics and the people in the ethnic mosaic of the West, but also, for more than a few, that holy Israel whom God first loved. But in rising from the grave, we too exact a price, first of all of ourselves: at what cost? at all costs? These are the questions of a Christianity that does not want to see us repeat the mistakes of Christianity.

I have a question to which Christianity may help find answers. The Torah tells us that we are like God, and, speaking to Israel, requires us to be a kingdom of priests and a holy people. How humanity may be like God, how a people, nation, or community may become "a holy people"—these form questions addressed to the outer limits of imagination. Christianity, Judaism, along with Islam—these three know God through a revelation that, at its end, claims to form connections to the beginning: Torah, Christ, Qu'ran. All three are testimonies, each in the eye of its beholder, to what God is like, therefore to what God wants of us, to what the holy people is supposed to be like, therefore to what God wants us to do together. For the issue is not one of politics or sociology, it is a fundamental question of what it means to love God, in particular, the God who is made known in the Torah, the Bible, and the Qu'ran, for all three of us claim that we are speaking of one and the same god, the One God.

Do the Torah, Christ, and Qu'ran speak to the same humanity? All three speak of living life under God, one God, the only God, the same God for us all. All three give testimony to a good that is sovereign and good. All three share fundamental assumptions, such as, in the words of Walter Moberly:

> the dignity of human life, the centrality of love, trust, obedience, mercy, forgiveness; the living of the life of faith in community; prayer as the essential medium between God and humanity. *

Christians, Jews, Muslims respond, as deep calls to deep: we can respond to the poetry of the other, the yearning for God conveyed by the other, the love of God that nourishes the other. Should we lose all this, in the name of theological affirmation with a merely down-home consequence? Having dismissed a discredited relativism but never opened the way to ecumenism,

---

*Personal letter, August 8, 1991.

we undertake a small thing indeed: to find in the stories we tell ourselves the face and form of the other portrayed in the story that the other tells too. Toward a Judeo-Christian dialogue of quest, each for a tale to tell the authentic humanity of the other, events of this awful century have brought us. It is time. And there is no other way.

38

GREELEY

This Time the Rabbi Is Right!

It is not good for my humility to hear the rabbi say that I was right all along. Nonetheless I welcome his agreement, which I think is nothing more than the result of recognizing what he always held implicitly and was able to perceive more clearly once he was able to escape the narrowness of the Ivy League. Yes, of course we have the same stories, the same God, the same images, the same celebrations.

To answer the question he asks at the end of the last chapter: Yes, the Torah, Jesus, and the Qu'ran speak to the same humanity. Yes, we must respond to the poetry and the stories of one another and not get hung up on differences in "down-home" affirmations. Yes, we must search for the tales that tell the authentic humanity of the other. Yes, it is time. Yes, there is no other way.

To answer all these questions positively is not, as the rabbi properly states, to say that all three traditions are the same, only that they are similar. It is not to dismiss theological differences (Christians are hardly likely to abandon the Trinity). It is rather to assert, on the basis that religion is story before it is anything else and after it is everything else, that without denying the differences we nonetheless bracket them for a time so we can listen to one another's stories and in so doing recognize a face that is much more like our own than it is different from our own.

If we Christians can bracket for a moment the affirmations of the early councils about the Trinity and rather tell the Trinity as a story of a God in whom there is so much knowledge and so much love that it overflows into two other persons, might Jews catch a hint of the face of the Holy One (her name be praised!) and Allah who is One?

But to engage in this dialogue about stories of God, we must first

1. Learn to restrain our own enthusiastic fanatics who permit themselves to see only a face so different from our own that we must hate it and destroy it.

2. Learn to control our own legalists who believe that stories are derived from rules instead of vice versa.

3. Strive to understand one another's culture so that we know the context of the stories the others tell—which is what, by his own testimony, enabled the rabbi to understand the Baptists in Florida, something of which I suspect most of his former Ivy League colleagues are incapable. *

4. Urge patience upon our theologians who want to reduce a story to nonfiction as soon as they can—without bothering to listen to the story first.

5. Persuade our leaders that stories must come first if we want to see the human face of one another—and the human face of God, whom we must imagine in some fashion as having a human face, whether, as the rabbi has argued elsewhere, that face is seen in the stories of Jesus or the stories of the Talmud. If we see the human face of God in one another, we are already halfway home. Only halfway indeed, but that's better than being frozen still at the starting post.

These are not easy tasks. However, the leaders and the rule makers and the theologians all have important roles to play in religious heritages, as do the enthusiasts. We—the rabbi and I and those who agree with us—do not want to eliminate them. We merely want to say to them, "All right, already," which I take it means "Gimme a break," or "Slow down a bit."

As I said in the first edition of this book, I feel that many of the differences in emphasis that seem to separate the rabbi and me come from our different academic disciplines and methodologies rather than from our different religions. The rabbi studies texts (as well he should) as a textual critic. I study images and stories as a sociologist of the religious imagination. We converge because the rabbi discovers stories in the texts and I learn about the meaning of the texts from the stories the rabbi tells me that are in the texts. I write novels that the rabbi likes—and we both like the ineffable Blackie Ryan—and I admire the stories he tells like the one in a previous chapter about the womanliness of God, God as a married lover who is both tender and strong, and each at the proper moment.†

---

*As someone who learned late in life that the best Sunday homily is a story that parallels and illumines the story in the Gospel of the day, I confess a deep admiration for Nassir-al-din. I also confess that sometimes I change him to a mildly eccentric West of Ireland canon who is somewhat comprehensible in my culture. Same story though—such as the one in which the canon searches for the key not in the parish house basement where he lost it but in the fairgrounds where all the people of the village are.

†Sometimes I wonder what the conservative Catholic leaders with whom the rabbi associates think about his stories about me. Surely they conflict with what these leaders know as a matter of absolute certainty to be true about me. And when he praises my novels, they must be certain that the rabbi is talking about someone else!

So after five years we find that we progress in our dialogue, perhaps more than we would have believed possible when we began.

My view at the beginning of the conversation—from the perspective of my own academic training and discipline and perhaps too from the perspective of my role as a seanachie—is that there was a "soup"* of images, stories, rituals, festivals, and experiences in the Second Temple era, a soup we might call for want of a better name "Israel." This soup was cultural, not denominational. Israel was not an organized religion like its daughters today. We must bracket our ordinary meaning of religion to understand Israel. While there were temple clergy and rabbinical scribes, there was no institutionalized social structure of the sort that came into being towards the end of the first century of the Common Era and that we tend to picture as an essential part of a religion today. Such a social structure was both unnecessary and impossible until then. The situation before that time was fluid, problematic, incredibly pluralistic—perhaps like the religious culture of pre-Christian druid Ireland.

Out of this soup there developed four religions in something approaching the modern sense of the word—Greek Christianity, Jewish Christianity, the Judaism of the dual Torah, and indirectly Islam. Jewish Christianity is the most interesting of the four for three reasons:

1. We know so very little about it because it disappeared halfway (more or less) through the first millennium and left little trace behind.
2. It played an important part (how important we cannot estimate precisely now) in the shaping of Islam.
3. It might have been a bridge between the Christianity of the world of Greece and Rome and the Judaism of the dual Torah.

What would Christianity look like if it had not been shaped by the Trinitarian and Christological disputes of the first five centuries?† Suppose that Jewish Christianity had survived and in, let us say, 650 of the Common Era reestablished contact with the West. How would these two forms of Christianity, shaped by different experiences, have explained themselves to each other?

This conversation, in Lady Wisdom's wisdom, did not occur. Since those were not particularly tolerant times, perhaps it is just as well. Maybe it is

---

*In a sense analogous to the post–big bang soup of which the cosmologists speak or the raw mix of chemicals out of which the biologists say life came. How clever of Lady Wisdom, by the way, to create such fascinating soups!

†To ask this question is not to question the importance of these disputes or the necessity of the councils which resolved them. It is merely to wonder how a Christianity untroubled by the subtle questions of Greek philosophy might have developed in a world where that philosophy was unknown.

only in our own era that such conversations become possible—and not always and everywhere even today.

It is beyond my professional competence to say whether we can recreate the culture and the stories and the imagery of Jewish Christianity in, let us say, the third century of the Common Era. I would hope that we can and that the scholars who are trained to resolve such questions proceed with all deliberate speed.

The result of our origins in this common religious soup is that we all share similar images, stories, rituals, and festivals (as well as having developed some of our own). We have more in common with one another than any of us do with Hinduism or Buddhism or the religion of the Parsees* and certainly more than with the various forms of nature religion which still flourish around the world.

The problem is complicated by the fact that the Islamic stories have been filtered through a dialogue partner that has ceased to exist.

Nonetheless, we share in some fashion such primordial images as Prophet, (Davidic) King, Paschal Lamb, Unleavened Bread, Moses, Adam, Messiah, Spouse, Father, Vineyard. But we attached different meanings to these narrative images.

How different?

That's why we have to listen to the stories: to find out at the pretheological level how different.

The rabbi contributed a very important essay to a very important book which examined the different meanings of the word "Messiah" in the Second Temple era. The conclusion the team of scholars came to was that the early followers of Jesus used the term in a sense that was different from the sense in which the word was used by Jews of the same era. That finding is very important indeed because it will bring an end to the foolish and fruitless debate between Jews and Christians about whether Jesus was the Messiah. The answer is evident: he was in a Christian sense of the word. He was not in any (rabbinic) Jewish sense of the word.

However, if the debate is over, the dialogue ought to begin. The meaning of the term in the Jewish and Christian usages is not univocal. But it is not totally equivocal either. The term, sopped up if you will from the primal soup, has an analogous meaning in the two traditions. It does not mean the same thing in both traditions—that now is clear. But it does not mean completely different things either. Now that we are clear about the differ-

---

*Perhaps more in common with them than with any of the others.

ences, can we not begin to listen to the two stories of an anointed one who-is-to-come so that we may see what they have in common? Can we begin to see in the stories of the two anointed ones who are different but not completely different the face of the same God who does not repent the promise made to humanity? Can we suspend the debate about whether Jesus is the Messiah to ask whether and in what sense we might find in similarities between our two stories some evidence of a messianic component in his life and work with which we can both live? A component which reveals the implacably faithful love of God about which we all agree?*

To ask that question is not to answer it or even to suggest that we might have an answer next year or the year after. Or ever. It is rather to suggest that such a line of questioning is an important one to follow. Scholarship and sensitivity to storytelling can pursue this line of questioning only if both skills are free to do their work without any demands for immediate answers or any undue interference from the lawyers and the leaders and the theologians—whose importance neither the scholars nor the storytellers are about to deny.

There are tricky aspects of such conversation. The dual Torah as we now have it makes it quite clear that there are to be no graven images in Jewish houses of worship. And, sure enough, there are none today. The synagogue is as unlike a Catholic church—with its myriad of angels and saints—as a house of worship could possibly be. Yet, as the rabbi tells me, many of the synagogues that the archaeologists have discovered from the Second Temple era displayed abundant imagery. What's going on?

We don't know. But we do begin to realize that easy and quick generalizations based on reading the more proximate past into the more ancient one can be deceptive and dangerous. The stories are different, no mistake about that. But they may not always be as different as they at first seem.

To repeat, the goal of such conversations is not to find that the stories—like the story of the Messiah—mean exactly the same thing. Patently they do not. Rather the goal is to find out in which ways they are similar and thus discover the human face and the divine face too which lurk behind the stories.

It is important that such conversations, which have hardly begun, push ahead and at once. It is time.

There is no other way.

---

*As much as I admire the rabbi's clever creation of a dialogue with his fellow rabbi, the Jesus of St. Matthew, and as much as I think it is an important contribution to the conversation, I must confess that I don't think it goes far enough. Who do You think You are? the rabbi demands of Jesus. A very good question. How does the rabbi think Jesus (who clearly did not like any kind of labels) would have answered that question?

General Index

Index to Biblical and Talmudic References

FATHER ANDREW M. GREELEY is perhaps the most widely recognized priest in the United States. A scholar, journalist, and best-selling novelist, he is the author of one hundred fifty books. He is professor of social science at the University of Chicago and professor of sociology at the University of Arizona.

RABBI JACOB NEUSNER is the most prolific scholar of his generation in the field of Jewish studies. The author or editor of more than five hundred books, he is Distinguished Research Professor of Religious Studies at the University of South Florida and visiting professor of religion at Bard College.